Plutarch: *On the Face which Appears in the Orb of the Moon*

# Brill's Plutarch Studies

# Brill's Plutarch Text Editions

*Editors*

Lautaro Roig Lanzillotta (*University of Groningen*)
Delfim F. Leão (*University of Coimbra*)

*Editorial Board*

Lucia Athanassaki
Mark Beck
Ewen L. Bowie
Timothy Duff
Rainer Hirsch-Luipold
Judith Mossman
Anastasios G. Nikolaidis
Christopher Pelling
Aurelio Pérez Jiménez
Luc van der Stockt
Frances B. Titchener
Paola Volpe Cacciatore

VOLUME 7

The titles published in this series are listed at *brill.com/bps*

# Plutarch: *On the Face Which Appears in the Orb of the Moon*

*Introduction, Edition, English Translation, and Commentary to the Critical Edition*

*By*

Luisa Lesage Gárriga

BRILL

LEIDEN | BOSTON

Library of Congress Cataloging-in-Publication Data

Names: Plutarch, author. | Plutarch. De facie quae in orbe lunae apparet. |
   Plutarch. De facie quae in orbe lunae apparet. English.
Title: Plutarch: De facie quae in orbe lunae apparet : introduction, edition, English
   translation, and critical commentary / by Luisa Lesage Gárriga.
Other titles: De facie quae in orbe lunae apparet
Description: Leiden ; Boston : Brill, [2021] | Series: Brill's Plutarch studies. Brill's
   Plutarch text editions, 2666-0199 ; volume 7 | Includes bibliographical
   references and index. | In Greek with English translation on opposite
   pagination.
Identifiers: LCCN 2021002170 (print) | LCCN 2021002171 (ebook) |
   ISBN 9789004458079 (hardback ; acid-free paper) | ISBN 9789004458086
   (ebook)
Subjects: LCSH: Astronomy, Ancient–Early works to 1800. | Plutarch. De facie quae
   in orbe lunae apparet.
Classification: LCC PA4368 .D33 2021 (print) | LCC PA4368 (ebook) |
   DDC 532.3–dc23
LC record available at https://lccn.loc.gov/2021002170
LC ebook record available at https://lccn.loc.gov/2021002171

Typeface for the Latin, Greek, and Cyrillic scripts: "Brill". See and download: brill.com/brill-typeface.

ISSN 2666-0199
ISBN 978-90-04-45807-9 (hardback)
ISBN 978-90-04-45808-6 (e-book)

Copyright 2021 by Luisa Lesage Gárriga. Published by Koninklijke Brill NV, Leiden, The Netherlands.
Koninklijke Brill NV incorporates the imprints Brill, Brill Nijhoff, Brill Hotei, Brill Schöningh, Brill Fink, Brill
mentis, Vandenhoeck & Ruprecht, Böhlau Verlag and V&R Unipress.
Koninklijke Brill NV reserves the right to protect this publication against unauthorized use. Requests for
re-use and/or translations must be addressed to Koninklijke Brill NV via brill.com or copyright.com.

This book is printed on acid-free paper and produced in a sustainable manner.

# Contents

**Abbreviations**  VII

**Introduction**  1
1   History of the Text  1
    1.1  *Manuscripts*  1
    1.2  *Printed Editions*  6
2   The Text  11
    2.1  *The Lost Beginning*  11
    2.2  *Composition of the Text*  11
    2.3  *Date and Location of the Dramatic Action*  12
3   Characters  12

**Editorial Criteria**  25
1   Agreements and Discrepancies between E and B  25
2   The Critical Apparatus  26

***Sigla***  27
1   *Conspectus Codicum*  27
2   *Editores Citati*  27
3   *Commentatores Critici Citati*  28
4   Other *sigla*  30

**Edition & English Translation**  32

**Commentary to the Critical Edition**  112

**Appendix 1: Discrepancies between the Manuscripts**  209
**Appendix 2: Emmendations by the Manuscripts**  213
**Bibliography**  219
**Index Nominum et Locorum**  229

# Abbreviations

## Journals

| | |
|---|---|
| AJPh | *American Journal of Philology*. Baltimore: Johns Hopkins University Press. |
| ANRW | *Aufstieg und Niedergang der römischen Welt: Geschichte und Kultur Roms im Spiegel der neueren Forschung*. Berlin: De Gruyter. |
| ASNP | *Annali della Scuola Normale Superiore di Pisa, Classe di Lettere e Filosofia*. Pisa: Pisa University Press. |
| Byzantina | *Byzantina: Annual Review of the Centre for Byzantine Research*. Thessaloniki: Aristotle University Press. |
| CFC(G) | *Cuadernos de Filología Clásica. Estudios Griegos e Indoeuropeos*. Madrid: Complutense University Press. |
| CIMAGL | *Cahiers de l'Institut du Moyen-Âge Grec et Latin*. Copenhague, Paludan. |
| CPh | *Classical Philology: a Journal Devoted to Research in Classical Antiquity*. Chicago: Chicago University Press. |
| CQ | *Classical Quarterly*. Oxford: Oxford University Press. |
| CR | *Classical Review*. Oxford: Oxford University Press. |
| ExClass | *Exemplaria Classica: Journal of Classical Philology*. Huelva: Huelva University Press. |
| Fortunatae | *Fortunatae: Revista Canaria de Filología, Cultura y Humanidades Clásicas*. La Laguna: La Laguna University Press. |
| GIF | *Giornale Italiano di Filologia*. Roma: Herder. |
| GRBS | *Greek, Roman and Byzantine Studies*. Durham: Duke University, Department of Classics. |
| Hermathena | *Hermathena: a Trinity College Dublin Review*. Dublin: Trinity College Press. |
| Hermes | *Hermes: Zeitschrift für klassische Philologie*. Stuttgart: Steiner. |
| Histos | *Histos: The New Electronic Journal of Ancient Historiography*. Durham: Durham University Press. |
| Humanitas | *Humanitas: Revista do Instituto de Estudos Clássicos*. Coimbra: Coimbra University Press. |
| ICS | *Illinois Classical Studies*. Urbana: Illinois University Press. |
| Information Historique | *L'Information Historique: Revue Illustrée paraissant tous les deux mois pendant la période scolaire*. Paris: J.B. Baillière. |
| JRS | *The Journal of Roman Studies*. London: Society for the Promotion of Roman Studies. |
| Mnemosyne | *Mnemosyne: Bibliotheca Classica Batava*. Leiden: Brill. |

| | |
|---|---|
| *Pallas* | *Pallas: Revue d'Études Antiques.* Toulouse: Presses Universitaires du Mirail. |
| *Ploutarchos* | *Ploutarchos: Journal of the International Plutarch Society.* Logan: Utah State University Press. |
| *QUCC* | *Quaderni Urbinati di Cultura Classica.* Pisa: Serra. |
| *RET* | *Revue des Études Tardo-antiques.* Université de Montpellier: Textes pour l'Histoire de l'Antiquité Tardive. |
| *Revue du Seizième Siècle* | *Revue du Seizième Siècle. Société des études rabelaisiennes.* Paris: Champion. |
| *RhM* | *Rheinisches Museum für Philologie.* Frankfurt am Main: Sauerländer. |
| *RHT* | *Revue d'Histoire des Textes.* Turnhout: Brepols. |
| *SCO* | *Studi Classici e Orientali.* Pisa: Istituti Editoriali e Poligrafici Internazionali. |
| *Segno e testo* | *Segno e testo: International Journal of Manuscripts and Text Transmission.* Cassino: Cassino University Press. |
| *SMU* | *Studi Medievali e Umanistici.* Roma: Viella. |

## Series and Collections

| | |
|---|---|
| Bailly | Bailly, A., *Dictionnaire Grec-Français* (Paris: Librairie Hachette, $^{16}$1950 [1895]). |
| DGE | Rodríguez Adrados, F., *Diccionario Griego-Español* (Madrid: CSIC, 1980). |
| DK | Diels, H., & Kranz, W., *Die Fragmente der Vorsokratiker. Griechisch und Deutsch* (Hildesheim: Weidmann, $^{17}$1974 [1903]). |
| LSJ | Liddell, H.G., Scott, R., & Jones, H.S., *A Greek-English Lexicon* (Oxford: Clarendon Press, $^{9}$1996 [1843]). |
| Page | Page, D.L., *Poetae Melici Graeci* (Oxford: Clarendon Press, 1962). |
| RE | Von Pauly, A.F., Wissowa, G., Kroll, W., et al., *Real-Encyclopädie der classischen Altertumswissenschaft.* |
| SVF | Von Arnim, H., *Stoicorum Veterum Fragmenta* (Stuttgart: Teubner, $^{2}$1964 [1903]). |
| TGF | Snell, B., Kannicht, R., & Radt, S.L., *Tragicorum Graecorum Fragmenta* (Göttingen: Vandenhoeck & Ruprecht, 1971–2004). |
| TLG | *Thesaurus Linguae Graecae* (Irvine: University of California, 1972). |

## Other

| | |
|---|---|
| BNF | Bibliothèque Nationale de France. |
| CNRS | Centre National de la Recherche Scientifique. |

# ABBREVIATIONS

CSIC     Consejo Superior de Investigaciones Científicas.
IRHT     Institut de Recherche et d'Histoire des Textes.
PUF     Presses Universitaires de France.

# Introduction

*On the Face which Appears in the Orb of the Moon*—Περὶ τοῦ ἐμφαινομένου προσώπου τῷ κύκλῳ τῆς σελήνης in its Greek version and *De facie quae in orbe lunae apparet* in Latin (*De facie* from now on)—is one of the treatises included in Plutarch's *Moralia*. Its content deals exclusively with the moon, covering nearly every topic concerning its nature and function. No single aspect has been neglected, all of the following questions are treated in this work: the features of its surface; its movements, size, and distances to other astral bodies; the phaenomena of phases, eclipses, and reflection of light; and its function both in the universe and in human life.

The fascinating topic of the treatise has attracted the attention of a wide range of scholars throughout history: philologists from Nicolas Leonicus to Harold Cherniss revised and corrected its text; astronomers as Johann Kepler or mathematicians as Lucio Russo commented on the theories included in the treatise; historians of religions and of philosophy as Franz Cumont and Pier Luigi Donini placed it in the wider cultural context of its time.

## 1 History of the Text

### 1.1 *Manuscripts*

Only two manuscripts transmit *De facie*: *Parisinus graecus* 1672 and *Parisinus graecus* 1675, the mss. known as E and B respectively.[1]

These two manuscripts' position within the Plutarchan *stemma* results from Maximus Planudes' project to edit Plutarch's work.[2] The project was initiated with the copy of the manuscript currently known as *Ambrosianus gr.* 859 (α), in which ten copyists participated, among them Planudes himself. After its revision, a second copy of this manuscript was made, known nowadays as *Parisinus gr.* 1671 (A). This work was finished during the summer of 1296, and Planudes revised and corrected it himself. It contains everything Planudes could gather during his life, namely the *Lives* and treatises 1–69 of *Moralia*.[3]

---

[1] The IRHT has also provided these manuscripts with a unique identifying number called 'dictyon:' 51296 for E, and 51299 for B.

[2] Byzantine monk (1260–1330) famous for his labor both as a copyist and a collector of ancient works.

[3] This can be inferred from the note ταῦτα πάντα εὑρέθησαν, written at the end of *Marcianus gr.* 481 in his own handwriting, together with a list of *Lives* and 69 treatises of *Moralia*—i.e., exactly the content of A.

After Planudes' death, his disciples continued his initiative. They first composed *Vaticanus gr.* 139 (γ), a manuscript that contains, together with the works included in A, also the treatise *Quaestiones convivales* (*Quaest. conv.*). Subsequently, with aid of a testimony now lost,[4] they produced the manuscript known as *Parisinus gr.* 1672 (E), containing the *Lives*, the version of *Moralia* included in γ, and eight other treatises (No. 70–77 in this manuscript).[5] This represents every single work of Plutarch that has reached us.[6] The other manuscript also containing our treatise, *Parisinus gr.* 1675 (B), is a copy of E, although likely also through at least one intermediary step.[7] This manuscript contains 36 treatises of *Moralia*, among which No. 70–76.[8]

The following stemma has been constructed for the lines specific to manuscripts E and B that were detailed above:

---

[4] While R. Flacelière, "La tradition manuscrite des traités 70–77 de Plutarque," *REG* 65 (1952) 354, suggested the existence of one manuscript, which he called δ, M. Manfredini, "La tradizione manoscritta dei *Moralia* 70–77 di Plutarco," *ASNP* 6 (1976) 461, proposed the existence of at least two different manuscripts. The eight treatises are: 70. *Amatorius*, 71. *De facie*, 72. *De Pythiae*, 73. *Adversus Colotem*, 74. *De communibus notitiis*, 75. *De genio Socratis*, 76. *De malignitate Herodoti*, 77. *De animae procreatione*.

[5] It contains all the *Lives* we know of and all 78 extant treatises from *Moralia* (69 treatises gathered by Planudes, together with treatises 70–77 of an unknown source, and *Quaest. conv.*, treatise 78). This system of numeration, derived from the order of treatises in Planudes' edition—with the later addition of nine new treatises—is conventionally used to refer to medieval manuscripts, for it is closer to their classification than the modern numeration.

[6] Due to its genesis, E is sometimes referred to as *Corpus Planudeum* (Manfredini, "La tradizione manoscritta," 453). Other scholars, among which F.C. Babbitt, *Plutarch's Moralia*, vol. 1 (Cambridge-Massachusetts: Loeb Classical Library, 1927) XIX, considered that the *Corpus Planudeum* should be manuscript A, given that it contains the works which Planudes could gather in his life.

[7] G.R. Manton, "The Manuscript Tradition of Plutarch *Moralia* 70–7," *CQ* vol. 43, 3–4 (1949) 104, denominated this intermediate manuscript η. Of course, there are many other manuscripts that contain parts of Plutarch's writings, but none of them preserves *De facie*, which is the reason why they are not treated in this book.

[8] A lost manuscript, later used to make the first printed edition, appears to have been composed in the same fashion as B. On this manuscript, see below, and footnote 23.

# INTRODUCTION

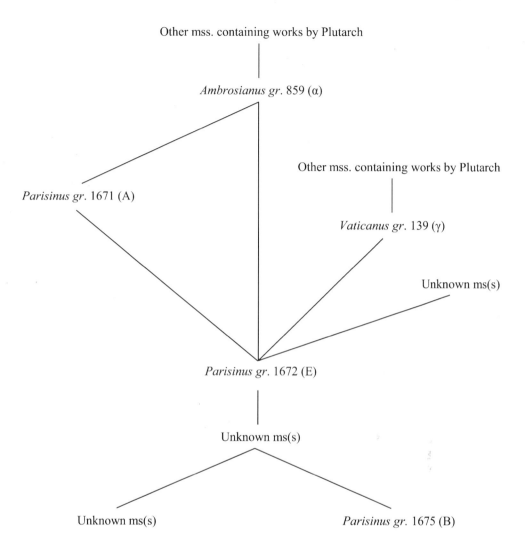

Manuscript *Ambrosianus gr.* 859 (α) was composed from to Planudes' initiative. After its completion, Planudes checked it (α²). *Parisinus gr.* 1671 (A) is a copy of the former, also revised by Planudes (A²). Manuscript *Vaticanus gr.* 139 (γ) was copied after Planudes' death—with the addition of *Quaest. conv.* Manuscript *Parisinus gr.* 1672 (E) was composed with eight other treatises (70–77) through the testimony of manuscripts now lost. Manuscript *Parisinus gr.* 1675 (B), which is the only other ms. beside E that also contains treatises 70–76, was copied from E through the testimony of manuscripts now unknown. Another copy parallel to B, today also unknown, may have served for the elaboration of the first printed edition.

*Parisinus gr.* 1672 is currently held in the *Bibliothèque Nationale de France* (BNF from now on) in Paris.[9] Recent analysis has dated the manuscript to *circa* the beginning of the second half of the 14th century.[10] It was acquired in Constantinople for the library of the king of France, Louis XIV, in 1688.[11]

*Parisinus gr.* 1672 is a large format manuscript (435×330 mm.) made with high quality parchment and a binding consisting of thick wood covered by red leather. The binding is secured by a metallic band with no title, and the only decoration is a golden garland in the center. The manuscript contains 962 *folia* with the text disposed in two wide margins columns—each of which contains an average of 40 lines. Its script is composed with elegant lower-case letters, supplemented by the infrequent use of sophisticated, red-ink capital letters.[12]

Scholars have distinguished up to four hands in the manuscript.[13] Two of them have been identified as Manuel Tzykandyles (treatise 77) and George Galesiotes (treatise 78). The other two remain anonymous copyists: while the first one copied *Lives* and treatises 1–57 of *Moralia*, the second one is responsible for treatises 58–76, thus including *De facie*. Some studies point to the possibility of identifying the latter copyist with the so-called Anonymous G.[14]

*De facie* occupies *folia* 809v to 819v under the title περὶ τοῦ ἐμφαινομένου προσώπου τῷ κύκλῳ τῆς σελήνης—with the drawing of a moon replacing the last word due to the lack of space.

*Parisinus gr.* 1675 is also housed at the BNF in Paris. The manuscript has been dated to *circa* 1430 on the basis of its gold filigrees.[15] It was purchased by Guil-

---

9   See H. Omont, *Inventaire sommaire des manuscrits grecs de la Bibliothèque Nationale* 2 (Paris: Alphonse Picard, 1888) 120–121.

10  For more information on this issue, see M. Manfredini, "Un famoso codice di Plutarco: il *Paris. gr.* 1672," *SCO* 39 (1989) 130; N. Wilson, "Some Notable Manuscripts Misattributed or Imaginary I. Maximus Planudes and a Famous Codex of Plutarch," *GRBS* 16 (1975) 95–97; and J. Irigoin, "Histoire du texte des 'Œuvres Morales' de Plutarque," in *Plutarque. Œuvres Morales*, vol. 1 (Paris: Belles Lettres, 1987) CCLXXIV. Previous studies dated this manuscript soon after 1302: see for instance Manton, "The Manuscript Tradition," 97.

11  This date is given by R. Caballero, "La tradición manuscrita del *De exilio* de Plutarco," *ASNP* 5 (2000) 164. Manfredini, "La tradizione manoscritta," 475 n. 93, however, stated that it reached Paris at an earlier date, namely in 1668.

12  See Manfredini, "Un famoso codice," 127–131, for further details on this manuscript.

13  See Caballero, "La tradición manuscrita," 163–164. To these a fifth *amanuensis* should be added, commissioned with the πίναξ or bibliographic catalogue and with Appianus' *excerpta*, which occupy the last pages of the manuscript (cf. Manfredini, "La tradizione manoscritta," 354 n. 5).

14  See I. Pérez Martín, "El estilo 'Hodegos' y su proyección en las escrituras constantinopolitanas," *Segno e testo* 6 (2008) 389–458.

15  See H. Omont, *Inventaire sommaire des manuscrits grecs*, 122–123; and Irigoin, "Histoire du texte," CCLXXV n. 3, for further details.

laume Pellicier from Antonio Eparco and arrived to the city in 1540.[16] It had previously belonged to the latter's father, who might have lent it to Aldus Manutius and Demetrius Ducas for the composition of the first printed edition.

Manuscript *Parisinus gr.* 1675 is a high quality paper codex of a size significantly smaller than *Parisinus gr.* 1672 (275×195mm.). The binding is composed of red leather decorated with floral motives on a hard cover; the title ΠΛΟΥΤΑΡΧΟΥ ΠΑΡΑΛΛΗΛΑ is on top, and the royal coat of arms is in the center. It contains 526 *folia* with 30 lines of text per page and relatively tight margins. Its script is composed of fine, lower-case letters with a capital letter at the beginning of each treatise.[17]

*De facie* occupies *folia* 403v to 419v with the same title that appears on *Parisinus gr.* 1672.

At the end of the 18th century, Daniel Wyttenbach noted the dependence of *Parisinus gr.* 1675 (B from now on) with respect to *Parisinus gr.* 1672 (E from now on) in the preface to his edition of *Moralia*.[18] However, Max Treu, in a study published almost a century after that of Wyttenbach, suggested that B was independent from E.[19] Strikingly enough, his conclusions were accepted until the mid-20th century.[20]

Notwithstanding this extended opinion, the numerous lacunae, mistakes, and omissions shared by both manuscripts reveal an evident relation of dependence. This point has been stated by more recent studies.[21] My own analysis of *De facie*'s text seems to confirm the conclusions reached by these studies. B shows some *lectiones deteriores* with respect to E, and, concerning the few

---

16  Guillaume Pellicier was a French diplomat sent to Venice by the king of France, François I, in order to acquire manuscripts for the recently created *Biliothèque de Fontainebleau*. Antonio Eparco was born in Corfu in 1491 and became a renowned collector of Greek manuscripts after moving to Venice.

17  See also the description included in H. Omont, *Catalogue des manuscrits grecs de Fontainebleau sous François $I^{er}$ et Henri II* (Paris: Imprimerie Nationale, 1889) 144.

18  D. Wyttenbach, *Plutarchi Chaeronensis Moralia*, vol. 1 (Oxford: Typogr. Clarendoniano, 1795) LXXIII.

19  M. Treu, *Zur Geschichte der Überlieferung von Plutarchs Moralia*, vol. 2 (Oława: Dr. v. A. Bial, 1881) VI.

20  G.N. Bernardakis, *Plutarchi Chaeronensis Moralia recognovit Gregorius N. Bernardakis*, vol. 1 (Leipzig: Teubner, 1888) XV–XVI; P. Raingeard, *Le peri toy prosopoy de Plutarque* (Paris: Belles Lettres, 1934) XIII; and R. Flacelière, *Plutarque. Sur les oracles de la Pythie. Texte et traduction* (Paris: Belles Lettres, 1937) 84–85.

21  The first being that of Manton, "The Manuscript Tradition," 97–104; followed by Flacelière, "La tradition manuscrite," especially 353, after changing his previous opinion on the matter.

*lectiones potiores* that it presents, scholarly discussion has not yet reached consensus as to whether they are due to tradition or conjecture.[22] In any case, although a relationship between both is quite certain, it seems improbable that B descends directly from E. Perhaps a lost manuscript copied from E served as an intermediary for the copy of B.[23]

## 1.2  Printed Editions

The *editio princeps* of Plutarch's work, known as the Aldine edition, was edited by the Greek Demetrius Ducas for Aldus Manutius' press in Venice, and was published in March, 1509.[24] It maintains the order of treatises of the Planudean project, and *De facie* occupies pages 931 to 953. When readings in the two manuscripts are not identical, the *editio princeps* tends to follow B, instead of E, which is the main reason why some assume that Ducas based his edition of *De facie* on B.[25] Notwithstanding the high number of correspondences between B and the Aldine edition, two facts suggest that the latter was not based on this manuscript: 1) when compared to B, Ducas' edition also shows important omissions; and 2) B does not show any of the personal marks left by Ducas in the manuscripts he used for the edition of other treatises—for instance in *Ambros. gr.* 881 (J).

Lionel Pearson suggested that together with B perhaps another manuscript could have been copied from the alleged intermediary manuscript between E and B.[26] This would have been similar to B but included some differences as well. Pearson assigned to that hypothetical manuscript the name 'αλδ,' and further suggested that it was the manuscript used by Ducas to prepare his edition of *De facie*.[27]

---

22  See Manton, "The Manuscript Tradition," 99–103; and Flacelière, "La tradition manuscrite," 360–362 on this issue. For the agreements and discrepancies between E and B regarding the text of *De facie*, see "Editorial Criteria," and Appendix 1.

23  See above, footnote 8, and the *stemma* in p. 3.

24  D. Ducas (ed.), *Plutarchi Opuscula LXXXXII, index Moralium omnium & eorum quae in ipsis tractantur* (Venice: Aldus Manuzius, 1509).

25  Manton, "The Manuscript Tradition," 104 n. 1. Manfredini, "La tradizione manoscritta," 463 n. 57, found up to 600 occurrences in which the Aldine edition coincides with a reading included in B but not in E, against 36 cases in which it follows a reading of E instead.

26  L. Pearson, "Notes on the Text of Plutarch *De malignitate Herodoti*," *AJPh* 80 (1959) 257–259.

27  Raingeard, *Le peri toy prosopoy*, XV, already proposed the hypothesis that both the Aldine and the *Basiliensis* editions might have been composed on the basis of a lost manuscript that does not correspond with either E or B.

A second printed edition, traditionally referred to as *Basiliensis*, was published by Frobenius and Episcopius in 1542 in Basel.[28] Its text is based on that of the Aldine edition with which it shares omissions and mistakes when compared to the manuscripts. It also provides some readings of its own; perhaps not as many as one would expect from the cover's statement: *multis mendarum milibus expurgata*. The text of *De facie* occupies pages 778 to 797.

In 1572, Henri Estienne (Stephanus) published in Geneva a new edition of *Moralia* that has been ever since the canonical version for the order of Plutarch's works.[29] It follows the order of the Aldine edition until treatise No. 18, and from there on it presents its own order—*De facie*, for example, occupies position No. 63. Also, besides its own pagination (*De facie* appears in pages 1692–1742), this edition adds the pagination of the Aldine edition on the margins.

Stephanus incorporated many personal corrections, as well as some taken from other scholars, such as Vulcobius, Leonicus, Giannotti or Turnebus.[30] He also considerably improved the punctuation of the text, making its comprehension easier without the need of substantial retouches.

Two years later in Basel, Wilhelm Holtzman (known as "Xylander") presented a new edition (*De facie* occupies pages 601–616), which includes abundant indexes. Xylander's corrections are almost identical to the ones included in the commentary to his translation that was published four years earlier (1570).[31]

In the preface to his edition, Xylander stated that he encountered no aid whatsoever in the manuscripts.[32] I would venture that the manuscripts he was referring to are not the two manuscripts that have transmitted *De facie*, but other manuscripts nowadays lost. This is due to the fact that he maintained errors appearing in the Aldine and the *Basiliensis* editions which do not come from E and B. Also in the preface, written in 1572, he complained about the

---

28  J. Frobenius & N. Episcopius (eds.), *Plutarchi Chaeronei Moralia Opuscula, multis mendarum milibus expurgata* (Basel: Frobenium & Episcopium, 1542).

29  H. Stephanus, *Plutarchi Chaeronensis quae extant opera, cum Latina interpretatione*. vol. 2 (Geneva: apud Henr. Stephanum, 1572).

30  For an updated study on the work of this humanists, see L. Lesage Gárriga, "Aldinas Anotadas: una puesta al día de la contribución de los humanistas a través del estudio de *De facie*," *CFC(G)* 28 (2018) 243–265.

31  G. Xylander, *Plutarchi Chaeronensis philosophorum et historicorum principis varia scripta, quae Moralia vulgo dicuntur, vere autem Bibliotheca et Penus omnis doctrinae appellari possunt* (Basel: per Eusebium Episcopium, 1574); and *Plutarchi Ethicorum sive Moralium*, vol. 3 (Basel: Thomas Guarinus, ²1619 [1570]).

32  Xylander, *Plutarchi Chaeronensis*, [no pagination].

recently published edition of Stephanus and accused him of stealing part of his research. It is possible that he was bothered by the fact that Stephanus' edition came out before he was able to finish his own.

The last edition of Plutarch's complete works made in the 16th century was published in Frankfurt in 1599 and reprinted twice (Frankfurt, 1620 and Paris, 1624).[33]

The editors of this edition (*Andreæ Wecheli heredes*) presented the Greek text and a Latin translation in two columns per page, paralleling one another. While the Greek text proceeds from Stephanus' edition, from 1572, the translations are retrieved from those of Cruserius and Xylander—for *Lives* and *Moralia*, respectively—published in 1573 and 1570. There is, therefore, no correspondence between the Greek text and the translations.[34]

Ever since D. Wyttenbach used the text from this edition to prepare his own in the 18th century, the pagination of this edition has become the referent to quote Plutarch's works.[35] Each page is divided in paragraphs of ten lines, and each line is assigned a letter (A to F).[36]

A century and a half would pass before the publication of a new edition of *Moralia*. Johann Jacob Reiske prepared the text in several volumes, although his death in 1774 made this edition posthumous (Leipzig, 1774–1782—*Moralia* from 1777 onwards). *De facie* appeared in vol. 9 in 1778 (pages 640 to 726).[37]

Interestingly enough, in the preface he mocks a young scholar who was also interested in editing *Moralia*, doubting his skills as editor.[38] This young man

---

33  Wecheli's Heirs (eds.), *Plutarchi Chaeronensis Omnium quae exstant operum tomus secundus, continens Moralia, Gulielmo Xylandro interprete*, vol. 2 (Franckfurt: Andreæ Wecheli heredes, 1599).

34  The editors also provided the prefaces written by the translators for their own works, thus provoking the curious situation of an edition combining the work of Stephanus and Xylander that includes the preface of the latter criticizing Stephanus' edition. In any case, both of them were dead before the publication of this edition: Xylander died in 1576 and Stephanus in 1598.

35  Although there is general consensus about this matter, we do find some discordant voices: Babbitt, *Plutarch's Moralia*, vol. 1, XXIV; and H. Cherniss, "Notes on Plutarch's *De facie quae in orbe lunae*," *CPh* 46, 3 (1951) 137, state that the pagination is the same of Xylander's edition of 1574—however, *De facie* occupies pages 601 to 616, which proves this statement wrong.

36  However, the edition has errata in its pagination: while *De facie* should appear in pages 920 to 945 (and so is cited), the page in which it begins actually has the number 910, followed by 931, 932, 933, after which the right order is recovered (from 924 to the end of the treatise). The reprinting solved this issue.

37  J.J. Reiske, *Plutarchi Chaeronensis quae supersunt omnia opera*, vol. 9 (Leipzig: Impensis Gotth. Theoph. Georgi., 1778).

38  J.J. Reiske, *Plutarchi Chaeronensis quae supersunt omnia opera*, vol. 1 (Leipzig: Impensis Gotth. Theoph. Georgi., 1774) XXXI.

was Wyttenbach, whose edition would be published between 1795 and 1830 in Oxford and would eventually become a point of reference in the field. In Wyttenbach's edition, *De facie* appeared in vol. 4, in 1797 (pages 721–828).[39] Together with the edition, he was preparing a thorough commentary. Unfortunately, the commentary ends abruptly at 392D, mirroring the abrupt death of Wyttenbach.

Wyttenbach compared many manuscripts. In fact, he provides a list of about 30 manuscripts transmitting Plutarch's work to which he assigns a letter as reference. Hence, our contemporary lettering of E and B for *Parisinus gr.* 1672 and *Parisinus gr.* 1675. And as mentioned above, he is also responsible for the current citation of Plutarch's works: he appointed a number and a letter to refer to passages, following the pagination of 1599's edition, and also assigned a number (represented by a Greek letter) to the different parts within a treatise, which are now used as chapter references.

Almost simultaneously, Johann George Hutten worked on his edition of *Moralia*. Although the publication of the whole series started and finished before that of Wyttenbach (Tübingen, 1791–1804), Hutten's *De facie* was published in 1801 (vol. 13, pages 27 to 98) after Wyttenbach's *De facie*.[40] Despite the fact that Hutten also criticized Wyttenbach's abilities—he, in fact, quotes Reiske's criticism—he seems to depend on him in great measure, which makes his work far less important than that of Wyttenbach.[41]

Next came the appearance of the so-called "Great Collections." Publishing houses created projects involving several scholars to publish *Lives* and *Moralia*. The first was Collection Didot (Paris, 1839–1841), published in two volumes with Latin translation. Johann Friedrich Dübner was editor in charge, and scholarly literature is divided about the value of his work.[42] In the case of *De facie* (vol. 2, 1841, pages 1126–1157), he closely followed Wyttenbach, integrating in the text what his predecessor mentioned as possible reading in the apparatus.[43] However, on a number of occasions Dübner does suggest noteworthy conjectures.

Bibliotheca Teubneriana (Teubner) was the next editorial house to publish *Moralia*, for which it offers two different editions. Rudolf Hercher led the first publishing team, but only completed the first volume before his death. Gregory Bernardakis was appointed his successor and published the rest of the volumes

---

39  See footnote 18, above.
40  J.G. Hutten, *Plutarchi Chaeronensis quae supersunt omnia*, vol. 13 (Tübingen: Impensis Joannis Georgii Cottae, 1801).
41  Hutten, *Plutarchi Chaeronensis quae supersunt omnia*, vol. 1, VIII–IX.
42  See for example Babbitt, *Plutarch's Moralia*, vol. 1, XXV, who stated that his conjectures are indistinguishable from the manuscripts' readings.
43  J.F. Dübner, *Plutarchi Scripta Moralia*, vol. 2 (Paris: Firmin Didot, 1877).

between 1888 and 1896. *De facie* appeared in 1893 (vol. 5, pages 402–472).[44] Given this scholar's tendency to suggest conjectures rather than to properly collate the manuscripts, this edition is generally considered unsatisfactory.

Teubner initiated a vast re-edition of *Moralia* at the beginning of the 20th century. Max Pohlenz, William Roger Paton and Johann Wegehaupt were editors-in-chief and chose to appoint fantastic philologists for the edition of individual treatises, which resulted in a carefully edited text. Pohlenz himself was in charge of *De facie*, which was published in 1955 (vol. 5, fasc. 3, pages 31–89)—and re-edited in 1960 with minor modifications by Hans Drexler.[45] Pohlenz's textual choices are to a certain extent based on previous scholarship, accepting, perhaps too often, modifications to the text transmitted by the manuscripts in order to facilitate the reading.

Frank Cole Babbit assumed the responsibility of Loeb Classical Library's edition of *Moralia*. This project became one of the most valuable editions thanks to the cooperation of great philologists. Harold Cherniss was in charge of *De facie*, published in 1957 (vol. 12, pages 34–222).[46] He provided a clear text and his work is among the most complete editions of this treatise.[47] It should be noted that the proximity in time between the editions of Pohlenz and Cherniss made it impossible for these scholars to consult each other's text; a fact that Cherniss lamented in his introduction.[48]

From 1963 onwards Belles Lettres (Collection Budé) has been publishing its own collection of *Moralia*, but *De facie* has not appeared yet. However, this editorial house published the text of *De facie* prepared by Pierre Raingeard as his doctoral dissertation in 1934.[49] He chose the text of the manuscripts over corrections and conjectures by previous scholars.

Finally, in 1988 the publishing house M. D'Auria launched *Corpus Plutarchi Moralium* under the supervision of Paolo Cosenza, Italo Gallo, and Luigi Torraca. Each treatise is published with an Italian translation and commentary. Pier Luigi Donini completed *De facie* in 2011 (vol. 48, pages 124–245), although he depended on Pohlenz and Cherniss.[50]

---

44  G.N. Bernardakis, *Plutarchi Chaeronensis Moralia recognovit Gregorius N. Bernardakis*, vol. 5 (Leipzig: Teubner, 1893).

45  C. Hubert & M. Pohlenz (eds.), *Plutarchus. Moralia*, vol. 5, fasc. 3 (Leipzig: Teubner, ²1960 [1955]).

46  H. Cherniss & W.C. Helmbold (eds.), *Plutarch's Moralia*, vol. 12 (Cambridge-Massachusetts: Loeb Classical Library, 1957).

47  Cherniss, "Concerning the Face," 29.

48  Cherniss, "Concerning the Face," 33.

49  P. Raingeard, *Le peri toy prosopoy de Plutarque* (Paris: Belles Lettres, 1934).

50  P.L. Donini, *Plutarco. Il volto della luna* (Naples: M. D'Auria, 2011) 107–108.

## 2 The Text

### 2.1 *The Lost Beginning*

There is general agreement that the beginning of the treatise is mutilated: the opening *ex abrupto* and the lack of any sort of introduction evince that at least a short part must have been lost during textual transmission.[51]

Notwithstanding this, there is no consensus regarding the content of the lost portion. Cherniss suggested that Sulla arrives right at the moment in which the company is about to recapitulate an earlier conversation, and promises to tell a story afterwards if he is allowed to listen.[52] Hubert Jr. Martin, more cautiously, suggested that "enough background information" must have been provided, although it cannot be known which details exactly were included.[53]

### 2.2 *Composition of the Text*

For the date of composition, the treatise provides no internal evidence. The identification of some of the characters as historical, however, enable us to search in other writings for evidence in order to advance a probable date of composition.[54] The information provided by two sources is determinant: on the one hand, we have the dinner in Plutarch's *Quaest. conv.* 8, organized in Rome around 98 CE, which included Sulla, Lucius, and Theon as guests; on the other hand, according to Ptolemy's *Almagest*, Menelaus was in Rome in 98 for astronomical observations.[55] This allows for the assumption that the meeting of these four people, together with Plutarch and perhaps his brother Lamprias, could have taken place that same year, in Rome. Two of the three remaining characters seem to be literary creations and provide no additional information—only Apollonides, if historical, would remain un-situated. This sets a *terminus post quem*: it is plausible to think that Plutarch wrote the treatise not long after the meeting. Consequently, against hypotheses regarding earlier dates, my contention is that the composition of *De facie* should be roughly dated to the turn of the 1st century into the 2nd century.

---

51  For a general view on this issue, see H.Jr. Martin, "Plutarch's *De facie*: the Recapitulations and the Lost Beginning," *GRBS* 15 (1974) 73–88.
52  Cherniss, "Concerning the Face," 14.
53  Martin, "Plutarch's *De facie*: the Recapitulations and the Lost Beginning," 74.
54  See below, "Characters."
55  A detailed analysis of these sources is provided in L. Lesage Gárriga, *Plutarch's Moon: A New Approach to* De facie quae in orbe lunae apparet, in preparation.

## 2.3 Date and Location of the Dramatic Action

The evidence to date and locate the dramatic action is scant, and only two passages provide some hints. While the second passage (937D) simply mentions the participants' decision to stop their promenade and sit, and does not help to narrow down the place of the action, the first passage (931DE) describes a total solar eclipse that supposedly occurred not long before the meeting of the interlocutors of the dialogue. Some of the suggested eclipses are those of April of 59, March of 71, January of 75, December of 83, and June of 113.[56] While the identification of the eclipse helps us set the date of the dramatic action, it does not, however, provide any evidence to determine the location. Against the traditional claim that the location of the eclipse and that of the meeting had to be one and the same, there is no internal evidence in the text which supports this view. It is more reasonable to assume that Plutarch recalls a total solar eclipse that some characters might have seen and others could have heard of. In order to narrow down the location, resorting to sources other than *De facie* is necessary. On the basis of *Quaest. conv.* 8 and of Ptolemy's testimony (above), the most reasonable conclusion is that the meeting took place in Rome, where many of the characters seem to have been around 98 CE.

## 3 Characters

A total of eight characters appear in the dialogue, even though not all of them participate equally. The first speaker in the manuscript, as we have it, is Sulla.[57] After briefly alluding to "his myth," he immediately declares his interest in a lecture about the moon to which he did not attend.[58]

After Lamprias completes his account of that lecture, he asks Sulla to tell a story that he had promised as a requisite to participate as listener.[59] At this point, the reader finds out that Sulla's presence is, as a matter of fact, the literary device that enables the development of the whole treatise: both the recapitulation and the narration of the myth depend on his participation. However, the

---

56  In Lesage Gárriga, *Plutarch's Moon*, in preparation, based on a recent re-evaluation of astronomical observations from the past, I provide a new analysis of the Greek text and conclude which of these eclipses is more plausible to have been the one described by Plutarch.

57  920B, Ὁ μὲν οὖν Σύλλας ταῦτα εἶπε· "τῷ γὰρ ἐμῷ μύθῳ προσήκει κἀκεῖθέν ἐστιν."

58  920B, ἀλλὰ εἰ δεῖ τι πρὸς τὰς ἀνὰ χεῖρα ταύτας καὶ διὰ στόματος πᾶσι δόξας περὶ τοῦ προσώπου τῆς σελήνης προσανακρούσασθαι, πρῶτον ἡδέως ἄν μοι δοκῶ πυθέσθαι.

59  937CD, Ὥρα δὲ καὶ Σύλλαν παρακαλεῖν, μᾶλλον δὲ ἀπαιτεῖν τὴν διήγησιν, οἷον ἐπὶ ῥητοῖς ἀκροατὴν γεγενημένον.

intervention of another character, Theon, will delay Sulla's myth once again until 940F, moment in which Sulla finally intervenes, closing the treatise with his myth.[60]

During Sulla's intervention, we discover that he is Carthaginian (942C).[61] According to Raingeard, the references to the musicality of the spheres in 944AB and to Persephone "counter-earth" in 944C, both of Pythagorean tone, denote his adherence to this philosophical school.[62] However, the fact that the content of Sulla's myth derives from another person, the Stranger, as he warns the audience (941A, "Well, I am only the narrator"), should prevent us from associating its content with Sulla.[63]

The Sulla of *De facie* appears to be the same character as the Sulla presented in *Romulus* 15: a Carthaginian and a man of culture and grace.[64] The description fits the personality of our Sulla, who, albeit presenting himself as a layman, appears to have quite extensive knowledge of optics when he discusses the problem of the half-moon in 929E–930A.[65]

Additionally, Sulla also appears in other treatises such as *De cohibenda ira*, where he discusses with Fundanus the matter of the control of anger; *Quaest. conv.* 8.7–8, where he organizes a welcome dinner for Plutarch and where Pythagorean topics are discussed; and most probably *Quaest. conv.* 2.3 and 3.3.[66]

---

60  940F, ὁ Σύλλας ὑπολαβὼν "ἐπίσχες" εἶπεν "ὦ Λαμπρία, καὶ παραβαλοῦ τὸ θυρίον τοῦ λόγου, μὴ λάθῃς τὸν μῦθον, ὥσπερ εἰς γῆν ἐξοκείλας, καὶ συγχέῃς τὸ δρᾶμα τοὐμὸν ἑτέραν ἔχον σκηνὴν καὶ διάθεσιν," and 945E, Ὑμῖν δέ, ὦ Λαμπρία, χρῆσθαι τῷ λόγῳ πάρεστιν ᾗ βούλεσθε.
61  942C, Πλεῖστον γὰρ ἐν Καρχηδόνι χρόνον διέτριψεν, ἅτε δὴ παρ' ἡμῖν […].
62  Raingeard, *Le peri toy prosopoy*, IX. 944AB, οὐκέτι γὰρ ἐξακούουσιν ἐν τῇ σκιᾷ γενόμεναι τῆς περὶ τὸν οὐρανὸν ἁρμονίας, and 944C, τὰ δ' ἐνταῦθα Φερσεφόνης [οὐκ ἀντίχθονος].
63  941A, Ἐγὼ μὲν οὖν ὑποκριτής εἰμι. Based on Sulla's resourceful intervention in two scenes devoted to Pythagorean issues in *Quaest. conv.* 8 could argue in favor of Raingeard's view.
64  *Rom.* 15, Σέξτιος δὲ Σύλλας ὁ Καρχηδόνιος, οὔτε μουσῶν οὔτε χαρίτων ἐπιδεὴς ἀνήρ.
65  929E–930A, "Πάνυ μὲν οὖν" ὁ Σύλλας εἶπεν "ἔχει γάρ τινα λόγον τὸ πάσης ἐν ἴσαις γωνίαις γινομένης ἀνακλάσεως, ὅταν ἡ σελήνη διχοτομοῦσα μεσουρανῇ, μὴ φέρεσθαι τὸ φῶς ἐπὶ γῆς ἀπ' αὐτῆς, ἀλλὰ ὀλισθαίνειν ἐπέκεινα τῆς γῆς· ὁ γὰρ ἥλιος ἐπὶ τοῦ ὁρίζοντος ὢν ἅπτεται τῇ ἀκτῖνι τῆς σελήνης· ‖ διὸ καὶ κλασθεῖσα πρὸς ἴσα ἐπὶ θάτερον ἐκπεσεῖται πέρας καὶ οὐκ ἀφήσει δεῦρο τὴν αὐγήν, ἢ διαστροφὴ μεγάλη καὶ παράλλαξις ἔσται τῆς γωνίας, ὅπερ ἀδύνατόν ἐστιν."
66  F.H. Sandbach, "The Date of the Eclipse in Plutarch's *De facie*," *CQ* 23 (1929) 16 n. 2; and Cherniss, "Concerning the Face," 3, however, do not believe that the character named Sulla in these scenes is the same Sulla as in *De facie*. As far as the first case is concerned (*Quaest. conv.* 2.3), their rejection is based on the fact that Plutarch calls Sulla "the comrade" (καὶ Σύλλας μὲν ὁ ἑταῖρος). However, in *De facie* both Lamprias and Lucius use the same term (ὁ ἑταῖρος) to refer to the comrade who conducted the earlier lecture. As is generally accepted, this comrade is no other than Plutarch himself (see below, "Absent

The main interlocutor of the dialogue fulfills Sulla's wish to hear the different opinions about the moon. It is not until 937C that the reader can identify this character as Lamprias, Plutarch's brother.[67] While it is true that keeping his name hidden could very well be a literary device—an anonymous narrator whose identity as Plutarch's own brother is revealed halfway through the treatise—it might also be that Lamprias' name was mentioned in the lost beginning.

Be that as it may, his name is explicitly mentioned three times in the treatise and all three cases are structurally important, since they mark the closure of a narrative block.[68] In 937D, Theon addresses him after the end of the discussion ("ἐγώ τοι, ὦ Λαμπρία" εἶπεν ...). In 940F Lamprias is interrupted by Sulla, who begs him to stop his speech, in order to allow him to finally narrate the myth (ὁ Σύλλας ὑπολαβών, "ἐπίσχες" εἶπεν "ὦ Λαμπρία ..."). And, in 945E, at the very end of the treatise, as Sulla finishes his myth, he addresses Lamprias one last time (Ὑμῖν δέ, ὦ Λαμπρία, χρῆσθαι τῷ λόγῳ πάρεστιν ᾗ βούλεσθε).

Besides being the moderator, Lamprias voices ideas associated to Platonism, which may *grosso modo* be those of Plutarch himself.[69] His position is percep-

---

characters"). It is interesting to note that the only other character beside Lamprias and Lucius to use that denomination is precisely Sulla in 929E (ἡμῶν τὸν ἑταῖρον). Therefore, if Sulla calls Plutarch "our comrade," it is perfectly plausible that Plutarch does the same in *Quaest. conv.* when referring to Sulla. In the second passage (*Quaest. conv.* 3.3) I am also inclined to think that we are dealing with one and the same Sulla, although it cannot be ascertained. Plutarch talks about a banquet offered by Florus at his home for his friends, including a Sulla (ἦν δὲ τῶν συνήθων τὸ δεῖπνον. ἔφη τοίνυν ὁ Σύλλας ...). Given that the participants are Florus' friends, Sandbach and Cherniss assume that Sulla cannot be the friend of Plutarch. Admittedly, it might very well be the case, but there are reasons to believe that it could also be the same person, friend of both Plutarch and Florus, but mentioned only within the general group of Florus' friends. In fact, an explanation such as "with friends of Florus and our common friend Sulla" or "with friends of Florus and my friend Sulla" would have encumbered the introductory presentation of the scene. B. Puech, "Prosopographie des amis de Plutarque," *ANRW* II, 33, 6 (1992) 4879, reached this conclusion, affirming that Sulla the Carthaginian is one of the assistants in Socius Senecius' and Florus Mestrius' banquets (2.3 and 3.3). Sulla must also have been present in the subsequent scene (3.4)—even if not intervening in it—given that it is the continuation of the same banquet and begins with the words Ὁ μὲν οὖν Σύλλας ταῦτ᾽ εἶπεν.

67  J. Kepler, *Ioh. Keppleri Mathematici olim Imperatorii Somnium, seu opus posthumum de astronomia lunari. Divulgatum a M. Ludovico Kepplero filio, Medicinae Candidato* (Frankfurt: Impressum partim Sagani Silesiorum, 1634) 98, in his list of characters, strangely included Plutarch as a character who speaks in the first person, defending his own ideas, and Lamprias as a mathematician.

68  Pérez Jiménez "Gestos, palabras y actitudes," 66.

69  Nevertheless, both Lamprias and Lucius sometimes distance themselves from the position they defend—i.e., the earthy nature of the moon—and talk about the defenders of

tible from the very beginning (921D) when he confronts the hypothesis of the earthy and heavy nature of the moon with that of the ethereal and luminous star.[70]

Throughout the treatise, Lamprias is a man that enjoys provoking his interlocutors, especially Pharnaces, who represents the rival philosophical school *par excellence*, the Stoa:[71] in 921F Lamprias qualifies the Stoic theory as absurd.[72] Furthermore, he does not mince his words when referring to the comments of other characters, such as that of Apollonides in 935E.[73] His straightforward attitude softens when it concerns Lucius, however. In several cases Lamprias proves to be attentive and caring towards Lucius: in 923E and 928D he provides him with time to prepare a refutation; and in 931D he congratulates his colleague for the nice argumentation he just developed.[74]

Plutarch's brother appears in several other treatises. The theory that he died young was previously used to prove that the treatises in which he appears are from Plutarch's youth.[75] This view is nowadays dismissed, since his archonship in Delphi in 115 is attested in an inscription.[76] In any case, the life or death of the real Lamprias does not necessarily imply a connection with the literary device created by Plutarch in his works.

In *De defectu* he plays the prominent role of narrator, as in *De facie*. In *De E apud Delphos* (485D) and several scenes of *Quaest. conv.* (1.8; 2.2; 8.6 and 9.14) he is presented explicitly as Plutarch's brother. In *Quaest. conv.* some traits of his personality are described: he is said to be quite intelligent, as well as witty and fond of teasing people.[77]

---

that same position in 3rd person plural. See, for instance, 922D, ἅπερ οἱ γεώδη ποιοῦντες ἀπολείπουσιν, 923A, Ἡμεῖς μὲν οὖν οὐδὲν αὐτοὶ παρ' αὐτῶν λέγομεν, οἱ δὲ γῆν ὑποτιθέμενοι τὴν σελήνην ..., and 924E, Εἰ δέ τι τυγχάνει σῶμα τῇ γῇ μὴ προσνενεμημένον ἀπ' ἀρχῆς μηδὲ ἀπεσπασμένον, ἀλλά που καθ' αὑτὸ σύστασιν ἔσχεν ἰδίαν καὶ φύσιν, ὡς φαῖεν ἂν ἐκεῖνοι τὴν σελήνην.

70  921D, Οὐκ ἐθελήσει δέ, οἶμαι, τὴν σελήνην ἐμβριθὲς ὑποθέσθαι σῶμα καὶ στερεὸν ὑμῖν ὁ Κλέαρχος, ἀλλὰ ἄστρον αἰθέριον καὶ φωσφόρον, ὥς φατε.

71  Raingeard, *Le peri toy prosopoy*, X, differently, stated that Lamprias is the figure of conciliation and measure.

72  921F, "χρηστῶς γε" εἶπον "ὦ Λεύκιε, τὴν ἀτοπίαν εὐφήμοις περιαμπέχεις ὀνόμασιν."

73  See below, "Apollonides," and footnote 83, for the specific passage.

74  923E, Πρὸς τοῦτο ἐγὼ τῷ Λευκίῳ χρόνον ἐγγενέσθαι βουλόμενος ἀναμιμνησκομένῳ, and 928D, Λεχθέντων δὲ τούτων, κἀμοῦ τῷ Λευκίῳ τὸν λόγον παραδιδόντος ἐπὶ τὰς ἀποδείξεις βαδίζοντος τοῦ δόγματος; and 931D, "εὖ γε" ἔφην "ὅτι καλῷ λόγῳ καλὴν ἀναλογίαν προσέθηκας."

75  A theory mentioned by Prickard, *Plutarch on The Face*, 15, following Gréard.

76  Cherniss, "Concerning the Face," 5. See G. Dittenberger, *Sylloge Inscriptionum Graecarum* (Leipzig: Hirzelium, 1917) 2. 868c, n. 6, 581.

77  *Quaest. conv.* 1.8: Λαμπρίας δ' ὁ ἀδελφὸς τὴν Ἱερωνύμου δόξαν οὐκ ἀνεγνωκὼς μέν, αὐτὸς δὲ δι' εὐφυΐαν ἐμπεσὼν εἶπεν ὅτι τοῖς προσπίπτουσιν ἀπὸ τῶν ὁρατῶν εἴδεσιν πρὸς τὴν ὄψιν ὁρῶμεν, and 8.6: Ὑβριστὴς δ' ὢν καὶ φιλόγελως φύσει ὁ ἀδελφὸς ἡμῶν Λαμπρίας.

A third character, Apollonides, intervenes in 920F in order to ask what Clearchus' position was.[78] Lamprias answers that Apollonides more than any other person should know it since it is related to geometry, a discipline in which he is said to be versed.[79] A little later he is presented as having knowledge in the fields of both optics and astronomy.[80]

From his many interventions, Apollonides does not appear as the kindest or the brightest of the participants. He interrupts speakers a few times, and on one occasion he jumps in together with Pharnaces.[81] In this latter case, his objection regarding the term "shadow" provokes a harsh remark on the part of Lamprias, who plainly accuses him of being more interested in semantic details than in serious discussion.[82] In this line, it is interesting to note that his knowledge or intelligence is questioned more than once: he is unaware of a theory closely related to his field of expertise—as seen above in 920—; and in 935CE his proclamation that the moon's craters and elevations must be gigantic given

---

78  Prickard, *Plutarch on The Face*, 6; followed by Cherniss, "Concerning the Face," 5; and Mota, *Plutarco*, 9, suggested that his name could be an allusion to the astronomer Apollonius of Perga, and he should be understood as "adept of Apollonius." According to this opinion, consequently, this character is a literary fiction and not a historical person. Differently, in my view, the quantity of interventions and his well-defined personality could provide support for the hypothesis that Apollonides truly existed—while his interventions are rather short, he has the highest number after Lamprias and Lucius: five. To provide just one example, Lamprias in 935F comments that he knows that neither of them has been in Lemnos, as if he knew details about Apollonides' life. Raingeard, *Le peri toy prosopoy*, IX, believed he was a Pythagorean, together with Sulla and Lucius, on the grounds that the text presents him as "un savant," a term Raingeard interpreted as opposed to the *akousmatikoi*. J. Delattre, "À propos du contenu astronomique des parties dialoguées du *De facie* de Plutarque," in A. Lernould (ed.), *Plutarque. Le visage qui apparaît dans le disque de la lune* (Villeneuve d'Ascq: Presses Universitaires du Septentrion, 2013) 103, however, defended that Apollonides represents the Stoa, together with Pharnaces, perhaps because at a given point they share an objection to Lucius' speech (933F). Based on the information provided in *De facie*, he cannot be described as belonging to any of the major philosophical schools.

79  920F, Ὑπολαβόντος δὲ τοῦ Ἀπολλωνίδου τὸν λόγον καὶ τίς ἦν ἡ δόξα τοῦ Κλεάρχου διαπυθομένου, "παντὶ μᾶλλον" ἔφην "ἀγνοεῖν ἢ σοὶ προσῆκόν ἐστι λόγον ὥσπερ ἀφ' ἑστίας τῆς γεωμετρίας ὁρμώμενον."

80  921C, Ἐκεῖνο μὲν γὰρ ἐρωτᾶν ἀσφαλέστερόν ἐστιν, ἢ ἀποφαίνεσθαι σοῦ παρόντος, εἰ τῆς οἰκουμένης εὖρος ἴσοις καὶ μήκος, ἐνδέχεται πᾶσαν ὡσαύτως ἀπὸ τῆς σελήνης ὄψιν ἀνακλωμένην ἐπιθιγγάνειν τῆς θαλάσσης, and 925A, Ἀλλ' ἥλιον μὲν ἀπλέτους μυριάδας ἀπέχειν τῆς ἄνω περιφορᾶς φατε εἶπον "ὦ φίλε Ἀπολλωνίδη."

81  920F, Ὑπολαβόντος δὲ τοῦ Ἀπολλωνίδου τὸν λόγον καὶ τίς ἦν ἡ δόξα τοῦ Κλεάρχου διαπυθομένου, 935CD, Ὑπολαβὼν δὲ ὁ Ἀπολλωνίδης, "εἶτα, ὦ πρὸς αὑτῆς" ἔφη "τῆς σελήνης, δυνατὸν εἶναι δοκεῖ ὑμῖν ...," and 933F, Εἰπόντος δὲ τοῦτο τοῦ Λευκίου, συνεξέδραμον ἅμα πως τῷ ⟨λέγειν⟩ ὅ τε Φαρνάκης καὶ ὁ Ἀπολλωνίδης.

82  934A, Ἐγὼ δέ, "τοῦτο μὲν" ἔφην "πρὸς τοὔνομα μᾶλλον ἐριστικῶς ἢ πρὸς τὸ πρᾶγμα φυσικῶς καὶ μαθηματικῶς ἐνισταμένου."

the size of the shadows casted is quickly ridiculed by Lamprias.[83] This sarcastic and well-argued answer makes Apollonides' last intervention more modest and relaxed than the previous ones: in 936CD he kindly suggests a problem that seems to be shared by him and Lamprias and asks his colleague what solution could be found.[84]

A certain Apollonides appears in *Quaest. conv.* 3.4. Since he is labelled as ὁ δὲ τακτικὸς Ἀπολλωνίδης, there are no strong proofs to claim he is the same character as in *De facie*.[85] The theory of one and the same Apollonides also receives some (circumstantial) support from the fact that the scene in which he appears (3.4) also includes Sulla.

The next character taking part in the conversation is Lucius (921E).[86] He has the highest degree of participation after Lamprias, with whom he recapitulates the previous lecture. His opinions seem to present him as a Pythagorean but given the many points in common between Pythagoreans and Platonists, he tends to agree with Lamprias.

We have already seen that Lucius enjoys continuous support from Lamprias, as if he were his *protégé*; he also seems to share the witty and ironic personality traits of Plutarch's brother. In 921EF, he asks Lamprias not to forget to mention the Stoic theory, taking the chance to condescend and mock this school.[87] In 922F, he answers Pharnaces with a laugh and an affectionate expression clearly used sarcastically, and, in 923C, he mocks Pharnaces' fear that the moon could

---

83   935E, "εὖ γε" ἔφην "ὅτι τοιαύτην ἐξεύρηκας ἀπόδειξιν, ὦ Ἀπολλωνίδη, δι' ἧς κἀμὲ καὶ σαυτὸν ἀποδείξεις τῶν Ἀλωαδῶν ἐκείνων εἶναι μείζονας."

84   936CD, "Τί οὖν" ἔφη "πρὸς αὐτοὺς λεκτέον;" ὁ Ἀπολλωνίδης. "Κοινὰ γὰρ ἔοικε καὶ πρὸς ἡμᾶς εἶναι τὰ τῆς ἀνακλάσεως."

85   Sandbach, "The Date of the Eclipse," 16; and Cherniss, "Concerning the Face," 5, did not believe him to be the same character. K. Ziegler, *Plutarco* (trans. by M.R. Zancan Rinaldini) (Brescia: Paideia, 1965 1965 [*RE* 21, l 1951]) 46; and both Puech, "Prosopographie," 4836; and Pérez Jiménez, "Gestos, palabras y actitudes," 72, in his wake, affirmed that he is indeed the same person and maintained that the reference to "experts in tactic" in *De facie* 927B refers to him. In my view, the reference is used in the broad context of the need of a superior intelligence to order the world. While the passage mentions tacticians, gardeners, and masons, those who attributed the mention of "tacticians" to Apollonides disregard the fact that there is no direct involvement of Apollonides either before or after this passage; additionally, the examples of gardeners and masons cannot be placed in connection with any of the remaining participants of *De facie*.

86   See footnote 87, below.

87   921EF, "ἀλλὰ μὴ δόξωμεν" ἔφη "κομιδῇ προπηλακίζειν τὸν Φαρνάκην, οὕτω τὴν Στωικὴν δόξαν ἀπροσαύδητον ὑπερβαίνοντες, εἰπὲ δή τι πρὸς τὸν ἄνδρα, παντὸς ἀέρος μῖγμα καὶ μαλακοῦ πυρὸς ὑποτιθέμενον τὴν σελήνην· εἶτα οἷον ἐν γαλήνῃ φρίκης ὑποτρεχούσης φάσκοντα τοῦ ἀέρος διαμελαίνοντος ἔμφασιν γίνεσθαι μορφοειδῆ."

fall onto people.⁸⁸ Furthermore, from Lucius' interventions it can be inferred that he is confident in his knowledge and the ideas he defends, and that he knows how to expound them, wining the general approval of the participants.⁸⁹ Also, he proves to be reasonable, asks for help when needed, and is thankful afterwards.⁹⁰

It is almost certain that the Lucius from *De facie* is the same as one of the guests in Sulla's welcome dinner (*Quaest. conv.* 8.7–8), wherein a character called Lucius, a disciple of Moderatus the Pythagorean, appears.⁹¹

Pharnaces intervenes after Lucius' first intervention, in 922E, although a reference was made to him before, in 921E. In his first intervention, he attacks the Academy and its methods.⁹² He clearly represents Stoicism and advocates the moon's semi-igneous nature, which makes him the target of most of the criticisms in *De facie*. Besides being the target of heavy criticism he also has to endure Lamprias' and Lucius' *friendly* expressions, which are used ironically and with the intention to soften their following statements.⁹³ However, he rarely reacts against the offenses and only speaks three times in the course of the discussion, one of them in indirect speech. Due to his scarce participation he has often been considered a fictional character.⁹⁴ His purpose in the narration might have been simply a placeholder for all criticisms directed against Stoicism.

---

88  922F, Καὶ ὁ Λεύκιος γελάσας "μόνον" εἶπεν "ὦ τάν, μὴ κρίσιν ἡμῖν ἀσεβείας ἐπαγγείλῃς," and 923C, οἰκτείρει δὲ τοὺς ὑποκειμένους τῇ μεταφορᾷ τῆς σελήνης Αἰθίοπας ἢ Ταπροβηνούς, μὴ βάρος αὐτοῖς ἐμπέσῃ τοσοῦτον.

89  See, for instance, 931D: Ἐπεὶ δὲ πάντες ἐπῄνεσαν τὸν Λεύκιον.

90  932D, "Ἀλλὰ δὴ τί" ἔφη "μετὰ τοῦτο τῶν τεκμηρίων ἐλέχθη;" and, after Lamprias' assistance, "Ὀρθῶς" εἶπεν "ὑπέμνησας." Prickard, *Plutarch on The Face*, 6, noted that Kepler curiously did not appreciate the character much. According to Kepler, Lucius speaks in a pretentious and patronizing tone.

91  *Quaest. Conv.* 8.7, καταγγείλας δεῖπνον ἄλλους τε τῶν ἑταίρων παρέλαβεν οὐ πολλοὺς καὶ Μοδεράτου τινὰ τοῦ Πυθαγορικοῦ μαθητήν, ὄνομα Λεύκιον.

92  922E, Καὶ ὁ Φαρνάκης ἔτι μου λέγοντος "τοῦτο ἐκεῖνο πάλιν" εἶπεν "ἐφ' ἡμᾶς ἀφῖκται τὸ περίακτον ἐκ τῆς Ἀκαδημείας, ἐν τῷ πρὸς ἑτέρους λέγειν διατρίβοντας, ἑκάστοτε μὴ παρέχειν ἔλεγχον ὧν αὐτοὶ λέγουσιν, ἀλλ' ἀπολογουμένοις δεῖ χρῆσθαι μὴ κατηγοροῦσιν ἂν ἐντυγχάνωσιν."

93  922F, "μόνον" εἶπεν "ὦ τάν, μὴ κρίσιν ἡμῖν ἀσεβείας ἐπαγγείλῃς," 923A, οἱ δὲ γῆν ὑποτιθέμενοι τὴν σελήνην, ὦ βέλτιστε, τί μᾶλλον ὑμῶν ἄνω τὰ κάτω ποιοῦσι, τὴν γῆν ἱδρυόντων ἐνταῦθα μετέωρον ἐν τῷ ἀέρι, πολλῷ τινι μείζονα τῆς σελήνης οὖσαν, 934C, Ἀλλ' οὐκ ἔστιν, ὦ φίλε Φαρνάκη, πολλάς, τὰς ἐκλειπούσας χρόας ἀμείβειν, and 939F, Δέδοικα δὲ ἡσυχάζοντα Φαρνάκην αὖθις ἐρεθίζειν καὶ κινεῖν.

94  In this line, Cherniss, "Concerning the Face," 6, believed that Pharnaces' name was selected due to its Asian sound. Puech, "Prosopographie," 4868, however, warned scholars not to assume that he is a literary creation, since many other characters in his same situation proved to be historical after all. However, his scarce interventions and his rather basic characterization seems to work against Puech.

Next is Theon, who intervenes in indirect speech in 923F to answer Lamprias' question about a quotation of a tragedian.[95] He is said to be from Thebes (Egypt), and he is presented as an expert in literature, as can be seen in 931E and 940A, which mention his ability to quote numerous poets.[96] He also seems to have some astronomical knowledge, as becomes apparent from his admiration of Aristarchus and from the explanation of eclipses he provides in 932DE— a simple description, true, which seems to corroborate his secondary role in the discussion about the moon.[97] To him we owe the second deferral of Sulla's myth. When Lamprias decides, in 937C, that every topic discussed in the previous lecture has been covered and that it is time to hear Sulla's narration, Theon intervenes raising the question regarding the habitability of the moon.[98] This is the beginning of a section that enables a smooth transition from the dialogue to Sulla's monologue.[99]

While it is sure that this Theon is not the same as Plutarch's great friend, present in numerous passages of *Quaest. conv.*, there are two cases (*Quaest. conv.* 1.9 and 8.8) in which the description of one character as Θέων ὁ γραμματικός allows for the conclusion that both are the same person. This might also be the case with the Theon participating in *De Pythiae*, given that in both this treatise and the above mentioned *Quaest. conv.* 8.7–8, he appears together with Plutarch's friend, Philinos.[100]

---

95  923F, Ἀποκριναμένου δὲ τοῦ Θέωνος ὅτι Σοφοκλῆς.
96  939C, when Lamprias replies to Theon's doubts about the habitability of the moon, ὥσπερ ἄνω περὶ Θήβας παρ' ὑμῖν [...] καὶ παρ' ὑμῖν ἐν Αἰγύπτῳ. 931E, Εἰ δὲ μή, Θέων ἡμῖν οὗτος τὸν Μίμνερμον ἐπάξει καὶ τὸν Κυδίαν καὶ τὸν Ἀρχίλοχον, and 940A, διὸ πρὸς σὲ τρέψομαι μᾶλλον, ὦ φίλε Θέων· λέγεις γὰρ ἡμῖν ἐξηγούμενος ταυτὶ τὰ Ἀλκμᾶνος.
97  938D, Ἀλλὰ σὺ τὸν Ἀρίσταρχον ἀγαπῶν ἀεὶ καὶ θαυμάζων, οὐκ ἀκούεις Κράτητος ἀναγινώσκοντος, and 932DE, ἐγὼ δὲ καὶ πειθοῦς τινος δέομαι ταύτῃ μόνον ἀκηκοὼς ὡς ἐπὶ μίαν [μὲν] εὐθεῖαν τῶν τριῶν σωμάτων γινομένων, γῆς καὶ ἡλίου καὶ σελήνης, αἱ ἐκλείψεις συντυγχάνουσιν· ἡ γὰρ γῆ τῆς σελήνης ἢ πάλιν ἡ σελήνη τῆς γῆς ἀφαιρεῖται τὸν ἥλιον. Ἐκλείπει γὰρ οὗτος μὲν σελήνης, σελήνη δὲ γῆς ἐν μέσῳ τῶν τριῶν ἱσταμένης· ὧν γίνεται, τὸ μὲν ἐν συνόδῳ, τὸ δὲ ἐν διχομηνίᾳ.
98  937C, "ἐγώ τοι, ὦ Λαμπρία," εἶπεν "ἐπιθυμῶ μὲν οὐδενὸς ἧττον ὑμῶν ἀκοῦσαι τὰ λεχθησόμενα· πρότερον δὲ ἂν ἡδέως ἀκούσαιμι περὶ τῶν οἰκεῖν λεγομένων ἐπὶ τῆς σελήνης, οὐκ εἰ κατοικοῦσί τινες, ἀλλ' εἰ δυνατὸν ἐκεῖ κατοικεῖν."
99  Prickard, *Plutarch on The Face*, 6, stressed the pleasant tone of Theon's interventions in comparison to those of the other participants and suggested that his role is to temper the tone of the discussion. Probably based on the fact that different passages associate him to different sciences, Raingeard, *Le peri toy prosopoy*, IX, proposed that Theon is an eclectic, but he offers no further support to this statement. Puech, "Prosopographie," 4886, in turn, believed that Theon's name is so common that any effort to identify him is in vain; Delattre, "À propos du contenu astronomique," 106–115, however, disagreed, defending that he is in fact Theon of Smyrna—a writer of Middle Platonic tendency of the 2nd century CE. The text, in my view, does not provide strong enough evidence to establish such a connection.
100 On the historicity of Philinos, see Puech, "Prosopographie," 4869.

In 920E, Lamprias addresses Aristotle, but he will not speak until 928DE. Then, Aristotle laughs at the criticisms directed against the Stoics, because he feels unaffected by them.¹⁰¹ His intervention, however, expresses his frustration for the central role attributed to Stoicism, in an attempt to claim attention for the Peripatos.

Little is known about this character, due to both his discreet presence in *De facie* and to the fact that he appears nowhere else in Plutarch's oeuvre. Most probably, this character is fictional and Plutarch used him as a symbol for the Aristotelian school.¹⁰² He is associated to Aristotelianism from the very beginning, and he will continuously defend the position of this school regarding the moon, in particular regarding its ethereal nature and the circular movement of the astral bodies.¹⁰³

Another character present at the meeting is Menelaus. He never speaks and is therefore sometimes omitted by scholars in their lists of characters.¹⁰⁴ He is referred to in 930A, where Lucius qualifies him as an astronomer (τὸν μαθηματικόν), before proceeding to discredit a theory pertaining to this field.¹⁰⁵

He might very well be Menelaus of Alexandria, whose work has been preserved only through an Arabic translation.¹⁰⁶ Ptolemy mentions him by the epithet ὁ γεωμέτρης and states that he visited Rome to make astronomical observations during the first year of Trajan's reign in 98 CE.¹⁰⁷ If this is indeed

---

101  928DE, Ἀριστοτέλης μειδιάσας, "μαρτύρομαι" εἶπεν "ὅτι τὴν πᾶσαν ἀντιλογίαν πεποίησαι πρὸς τοὺς αὐτὴν μὲν ἡμίπυρον εἶναι τὴν σελήνην ὑποτιθεμένους, κοινῇ δὲ τῶν σωμάτων, τὰ μὲν ἄνω, τὰ δὲ κάτω ῥέπειν ἐξ ἑαυτῶν φάσκοντας· [...] οὐδὲ ἀπὸ τύχης ἦλθεν ἐπὶ μνήμην ὑμῖν, ὥστε ἐμέ τε πραγμάτων ἀπηλλάχθαι."

102  So think Prickard, *Plutarch on The Face*, 6; and Cherniss, "Concerning the Face," 6. Such seems also to be the case with the character named Epicurus, who represents the Epicureans in *De sera*. According to Puech, "Prosopographie," 4837, in case he is not a literary creation, Aristotle might not be his real name, but a name of his own choice to present himself as an adept of that specific philosophical school.

103  920F, ⟨Τοῦτο δὲ⟩ καὶ πρὸς Κλέαρχον, ὦ Ἀριστότελες, οὐκ ἀπιθάνως ἐδόκει λέγεσθαι τὸν ὑμέτερον· ὑμέτερος γὰρ ἀνὴρ Ἀριστοτέλους τοῦ παλαιοῦ γεγονὼς συνήθης· εἰ καὶ πολλὰ τοῦ Περιπάτου παρέτρεψεν, and 928E, εἰ δ' ἔστι τις ὁ λέγων κύκλῳ τε κινεῖσθαι κατὰ φύσιν τὰ ἄστρα καὶ πολὺ παρηλλαγμένης οὐσίας εἶναι τῶν τεττάρων, οὐδὲ ἀπὸ τύχης ἦλθεν ἐπὶ μνήμην ὑμῖν.

104  For instance, Raingerad, *Le peri toy prosopoy*, IX, merely mentioned Menelaus in an example involving Lucius; and V. Ramón Palerm, "Sobre la cara visible de la luna," in V. Ramón Palerm & J. Bergua Cavero (eds.), *Plutarco, Obras Morales y Costumbres*, vol. 9 (Madrid: Gredos, 2001) 123.

105  930A, Καὶ πρός γε Μενέλαον ἀποβλέψας ἐν τῷ διαλέγεσθαι τὸν μαθηματικόν, "αἰσχύνομαι μὲν" ἔφη "σοῦ παρόντος, ὦ φίλε Μενέλαε, θέσιν ἀναιρεῖν μαθηματικήν."

106  Sandbach, "The Date of the Eclipse," 16; Cherniss, "Concerning the Face," 7; and Puech, "Prosopographie," 4859.

107  Ptolemy, *Almagest* 7.3: Μενέλαος δὲ ὁ γεωμέτρης ἐν Ῥώμῃ φησὶ τετηρῆσθαι τῷ ᾱ ἔτος Τραϊανοῦ.

the case, the plural pronoun used in 939C (παρ' ὑμῖν ἐν Αἰγύπτῳ) should be taken as a second reference to Menelaus, which classes him together with Theon as a native from Egypt.

Two other characters, although absent from the meeting do have a relevant role in the development of the narration. One of them is the omnipresent figure of ὁ ἑταῖρος, the comrade that conducted the lecture that Lamprias and Lucius are summarizing. He is cited three times. On the first occasion he is referred to by Lamprias (921F, οὐχ οὕτω δὲ ὁ ἑταῖρος ἡμῶν); in the second by Lucius (929B, Ὁ μὲν οὖν ἑταῖρος ἐν τῇ διατριβῇ); and finally by Sulla (929E, ἡμῶν τὸν ἑταῖρον). He is also indirectly present throughout the discussion in the references made by Lamprias and Lucius when referring to the previous lecture.[108]

It is plausible to think that ὁ ἑταῖρος is no other than Plutarch;[109] and that a real encounter between some of the characters and the author took place, on an occasion in which he lectured on the subject matter of the moon, and that the treatise, as we have it, is the result of adapting that lecture into a work of literary fiction after having organized the ideas and topics discussed.

The second absent character is ὁ ξένος, the Stranger, whom Sulla met in Carthage and who is the source of the narration Sulla shares with the other participants of *De facie*. From the very moment Sulla begins his tale, he presents himself as a simple narrator transmitting the words of this person (941A, Ἐγὼ μὲν οὖν ὑποκριτής εἰμι, [...] τὸν ποιητὴν ἡμῖν εἰ μή τι κωλύει καθ' Ὅμηρον ἀρξάμενον), and only clearly states the identity of the author in 942A (ὡς ἔλεγεν ὁ ξένος).

---

108   921E, πρὸς τὸν Λεύκιον ἔφην ἀποβλέψας "ὃ πρῶτον ἐλέχθη τῶν ἡμετέρων ὑπόμνησον," in 930A, "Ἀλλὰ νὴ Δία" εἶπεν ὁ Λεύκιος "καὶ τοῦτο ἐρρήθη," in 932D, "Ἀλλὰ δὴ τί" ἔφη "μετὰ τοῦτο τῶν τεκμηρίων ἐλέχθη;" in 933C, Παρίημι δὲ ὅσα χωρὶς ἰδίᾳ πρὸς τὰς βάσεις καὶ διαφορήσεις ἐλέχθη, and in 937C, "Ἡμεῖς μὲν οὖν" ἔφην "ὅσα μὴ διαπέφευγε τὴν μνήμην τῶν ἐκεῖ λεχθέντων ἀπηγγέλκαμεν." Cherniss tended to play this character down: he not only corrected the text in places where the comrade is referred to, but also translated passages in an ambiguous way so that they seem to refer to the current speaker (Lamprias, Lucius), instead of to the speaker of the previous lecture. Just to mention a couple of examples, in 921B where the text reads "ἀλλὰ πῇ τὸν ἔλεγχον αὐτῷ προσῆγε;", he corrected the verb in 3rd person into a 2nd person. And in 930E, with "σκευωρεῖσθαι δὲ ἅμα λέγοντι διάγραμμα καὶ ταῦτα πρὸς πολλοὺς οὐκ ἐνῆν," he made Lucius the subject of the participle λέγοντι in his translation, even though the main verb in imperfect (ἐνῆν) points to an indefinite past, not to the conversation taking place at the moment.

109   This is also the position of Prickard, *Plutarch on The Face*, 10; Cherniss, "Concerning the Face," 15. While Martin, "Plutarch's *De facie*," 75, at first preferred to be neutral, he later suggested (88) that the comrade might be present as a complaisant auditor, based on the fact that Plutarch performs this role in *Non posse* 1087C. He was then identifying the comrade with Plutarch. The fact that they speak of this comrade in 3rd person singular makes his presence among the rest of participants rather improbable. Additionally, Pérez Jiménez, "Gestos, palabras y actitudes," 63 only pointed to a Platonist.

He first refers to him in indirect speech, but from 942D onwards he narrates the rest of the story in direct speech ("πολλὰ" εἶπεν "ὦ Σύλλα, περὶ θεῶν οὐ πάντα δὲ καλῶς λέγεται παρ' "Ελλησιν"). He concludes his narration with a last reference to the Stranger in 945D (ἐγὼ μὲν ἤκουσα τοῦ ξένου διεξιόντος [...] ὡς ἔλεγεν αὐτός, ἐξήγγειλαν). The characterization as ξένος, as opposed to βάρβαρος, suggests the high esteem with which the Stranger is considered. He is presented as a man of culture, instructed both in philosophy and in mystery rites, which allows him to convey a type of knowledge not yet acquired by the participants: a knowledge strongly linked to the divine.[110]

Regarding all the characters listed above, whether fictitious or not, none of them—not even Lamprias or Lucius, who defend the theories closest to Plutarch's thought—should be regarded as a spokesperson of the author.[111]

110 942AB, ἀστρολογίας μὲν ἐφ' ὅσον γεωμετρήσαντι πορρωτάτω προελθεῖν δυνατόν ἐστιν, ἐμπειρίαν ἔσχε φιλοσοφίας δὲ τῆς ἄλλης τῷ φυσικῷ χρώμενος, and 942BC, Ἃ μὲν οὖν ἔπαθε καὶ ὅσους ἀνθρώπους διῆλθεν, ἱεροῖς τε γράμμασιν ἐντυγχάνων ἐν τελεταῖς τε πάσαις τελούμενος, οὐ μιᾶς ἡμέρας ἔργον ἐστὶ διελθεῖν. For more details regarding the Stranger, see my analysis in L. Lesage Gárriga, "L'étranger (*De facie*) et Diotyme (*Symp.*): récits de sages absents," in D. Leão & O. Guerrier (eds.), *Figures de sages, figures de philosophes dans l'oeuvre de Plutarque* (Coimbra: Coimbra University Press, 2019) 169–181.

111 As Donini, *Plutarco. Il volto della luna*, 11–12 n. 10, rightly noted, each represents specific purposes or a particular philosophical school, as philosophic-literary creations.

*Edition & English Translation of* **De facie**

∴

# Editorial Criteria

The main position adopted for this new critical edition is to maintain the manuscripts' reading whenever there are no strong reasons to introduce variant readings or conjectures. The choice to maintain the manuscripts' readings does not imply that they transmit Plutarch's text without alterations. My contention is that, unless we have firm proof that a specific reading was not Plutarch's election, there is no strong reason to intervene in the text.

Over the last centuries, interventions in the text have sometimes gone too far and do not always have firm support. On one hand, many times we find interventions with too strong a tendency to regularize the text and produce a perfectly polished construction.[1] What is even worse, conjectures to supply a lacuna often lead to further modifications of the surrounding text, which originally presented no difficulty.

On the other hand, we find interventions with conceptual and philosophical, rather than textual, motivations. In so doing, scholars have sometimes tended to introduce in the text ideas that might support their interpretation of Plutarch's thought. These types of interventions should be avoided at all costs. An example of this is evidenced in 932B, where Kepler corrected the number τεσσαράκοντα ('forty') transmitted by both E and B into τριάκοντα ('thirty'), in order to make the text fit his own calculations.[2]

Against the above mentioned tendencies and following the on-going trend in textual criticism, I avoid the introduction of modifications that are not required by the grammar or by the context.[3] Variant readings, however, are placed in the apparatus for the reader to assess the different possibilities.

## 1 Agreements and Discrepancies between E and B

Neither of the manuscripts mark the subscribed iota. Most of the times this poses no problem, but in a few cases the word might be read as a nominative,

---

[1] I avoid the general tendency to regularize Plutarch's language and style, which means that in cases of crasis, elisions, and hiatus, I simply reproduce the manuscripts' reading. In the particular case of hiatus, I do not think they should be avoided on the grounds of Plutarch's own opinion on the matter, since in *Bellone an pace* 350E he criticizes Isocrates' fear to allow even just one hiatus.
[2] Kepler, *Ioh. Keppleri Mathematici*, 136.
[3] M.L. West, *Textual Criticism and Editorial Technique Applicable to Greek and Latin Texts* (Stuttgart: Teubner, 1973).

which has given rise to different interpretations of particular passages. The relevant cases have been treated in the Commentary to the Edition.[4]

In general, E and B also agree in the transmission of lacunae. These are always marked in the body of text, but in several occasions the sentence preceding or following the lacuna is complete both from a semantic and a syntactic point of view. An illustrative and approximate length has been provided in the apparatus, even if, as Robert Flacelière noted, it does not guarantee that the lost section matched the length transmitted by the manuscripts.[5] In fact, most of the times E and B do not agree on the lengths they provide.

Despite the many collations undertaken over the years by different scholars, there are still divergences between the manuscripts that have not yet been noticed by previous scholarship.[6] Every discrepancy between the manuscripts has been recorded in the critical apparatus, with the exception of differences between οὕτως—οὕτω. In these cases, B provides the correct form either before a vowel or a consonant, and, therefore, the manuscript is followed.

## 2   The Critical Apparatus

The critical apparatus is minimalist whenever possible. EB are only mentioned when not accepted, otherwise their reading is marked with the symbol ]. For instance: ὑμῖν] ἡμῖν Ch.; but ἐρησόμεθα RJ94: χρησόμεθα EB. From the corrections proposed by other scholars, but not accepted in the present edition, only the most relevant are recorded in the apparatus. Finally, I have tried, to the best of my ability, to restore the 16th century handwritten corrections to their original conjecturers.

---

4  See, for example, the headings to 921D, with τοιαύτῃ; and 933A, with ταύτῃ and ὑποφερομένῃ.
5  R. Flacelière, *Plutarque. Dialogue sur les oracles de la Pythie* (Paris: PUF, 1962) 25. He stressed that in *De Pythiae* 396B—which happens to be another of the treatises only transmitted by EB—E leaves a blank of seven letters and B one of 10, but with certainty the lost text must have only been of four letters, given that it belongs to a verse of Homer (*Od.* 7.107).
6  For a complete list of all the discrepancies between E and B, see Appendix 1, and for the emendations by the manuscripts, see Appendix 2. More on the types of discrepancies and their relation to the materiality of the support in E. Mioni, *Introduzione alla paleografia greca* (Padua: Liviana, 1973).

# Sigla

1  **Conspectus Codicum**

E  *Parisinus graecus* 1672, BNF (809v–819v)
B  *Parisinus graecus* 1675, BNF (403v–419v)

2  **Editores Citati**

Ald.  *Plutarchi Opuscula* LXXXXII (Venice: Aldus Manuzius, 1509) 930–953.
  – I.22: Forteguerri, S., Apostolic Vatican Library, Rome
  – SR67: Leonicus, N., Veneranda Ambrosiana Library, Milan
  – RJ94: Turnebus, A., BNF, Paris[1]
Basil.  *Plutarchi Chaeronei moralia opuscula, multis mendarum milibus expurgata* (Basel: Frobenium & Episcopium, 1542) 778–797.
  – Amyot: Amyot, J., BNF, Paris[2]
Steph.  Estienne, H., *Plutarchi Chaeronensis quae extant opera* (Geneva: apud Henr. Stephanum, 1572, vol. 2) 923–969.
Xyl.  Xylander, G., *Plutarchi Chaeronensis philosophorum et historicorum principis varia scripta* (Basel: apud Eusebium Episcopium, 1574) 601–616.
Wyt.  Wyttenbach, D., *Plutarchi Chaeronensis Moralia* (Oxford: Typogr. Clarendoniano, 1795, vol. 4) 721–828.
Hutten  Hutten, J.G., *Plutarchi Chaeronensis quae supersunt omnia* (Tübingen: Impensis Joannis Georgii Cottae, 1801, vol. 13) 27–98.
Dübn.  Dübner, F., *Plutarchi scripta Moralia* (Paris: Firmin Didot, 1841, vol. 2) 1126–1157.
Bern.  Bernardakis, G., *Plutarchi Chaeronensis Moralia* (Leipzig: Teubner, 1893, vol. 5) 402–472.
Raing.  Raingeard, P., *Le Περὶ τοῦ προσώπου de Plutarque* (Paris: Belles Lettres, 1934) 2–48.

---

1 Due to the proximity between the time in which Turnebus worked on his Aldine copy and the publication of the *Basiliensis* edition, I present both in the critical apparatus for the numerous corrections they share.
2 While Amyot and Turnebus must have worked in *De facie*'s text around the same time, Amyot acknowledges his debt to others scholars, among which is Turnebus. Therefore, when both provide the same correction or conjecture, I do not include Amyot in the apparatus, even if in some cases both might be independent from one another.

| | |
|---|---|
| Po. | Pohlenz, M., "De facie in orbe lunae," in C. Hubert & M. Pohlenz (eds.), *Plutarchus. Moralia* (Leipzig: Teubner, 1955, vol. 5, fasc. 3) 31–89. |
| Ch. | Cherniss, H., *Plutarch's Moralia* (Cambridge-Massachusetts: Loeb Classical Library, 1957, vol. 12) 34–223.[3] |
| Lern. | Lernould, A., *Plutarque. Le visage qui apparaît dans le disque de la lune* (Villeneuve d'Ascq: Presses Universitaires du Septentrion, 2013) 21–87. |

## 3 *Commentatores Critici Citati*

| | |
|---|---|
| Xyl.[1570] | Xylander, G., *Plutarchi Ethicorum sive Moralium* (Basel: Thomas Guarinus, 1570, vol. 3). |
| Kepler | Kepler, J., *Somnium, seu opus posthumum de astronomia lunari* (De facie quae in orbe lunae apparet) (Frankfurt: Impressum partim Sagani Silesiorum, 1634). |
| Salmas | Saumaise, Cl., [according to Wyt. *et alii*].[4] |
| Ménage | Ménage, G., Laertius, D., *Laertii Diogenis De vitis dogmatis et apophthegmatis eorum qui in philosophia claruerunt;* [...] *cum uberrimis Aegidii Menagii observationibus* (London: Typis Tho. Radcliffe, 1664). |
| Kalt. | Kaltwasser, J.F.S., *Plutarchs Moralische Abhandlungen.* (Frankfurt: Johann Christian Hermann, 1797, vol. 7). |
| Karsten | Karsten, S., *Philosophorum graecorum veterum praesentim qui ante Platonem floruerunt operum reliquiae* (Amsterdam: Johannis Müller, 1838, vol. 2). |
| Bens. | Benseler, G.E., *De hiatu in oratoribus Atticis et historicis Graecis, libri duo* (Freiberg: J.G. Engelhardt, 1841). |
| Meineke | Meineke, A., "Kritische Blätter," *Philologus* 14 (1859). |
| Madv. | Madvig, J.N., *Adversaria critica ad scriptores graecos* (Copenhagen: J.H. Schultz, 1871, vol. 1). |
| Emp. | Emperius, A., *Opuscula philologica et historica* (Göttingen: F.G. Schneidewin, 1874). |
| Bergk | Bergk, Th., *Poetae lyrici graeci* (Leipzig: Teubner, 1882, vol. 3). |

---

3 Pohlenz and Cherniss in some cases offer the same correction or conjecture. Given that they were not able to consult each other's work, in such cases, both are included in the critical apparatus.

4 While I have been able to check all the editions and studies included in the list above, for attributions to Claude Saumaise I rely on Wyttenbach and following editors. This is due to the fact that no one provided the title of the work in which Saumaise supposedly made the corrections to *De facie*.

| | |
|---|---|
| Papabas. | Papabasileios, G.A., *Athena* 10 (1898) [according to Cherniss].[5] |
| Arnim | – Von Arnim, H., *Stoicorum Veterum Fragmenta* (Stuttgart: Teubner, 1903, vol. 2). |
| | – Von Arnim, H., *Plutarch über Dämonen und Mantik* (Amsterdam: Johannes Müller, 1921). |
| Apelt | Apelt, O., "Zu Plutarch und Plato" (Jena: Universitäts-Buchdruckerei G. Neuenhahn, 1905). |
| Herw. | Herwerden, H. van, "Novae curae criticae Moralium Plutarchi (Ed. Bern.)," *Mnemosyne* 37 (1909). |
| Adler | – Adler, M., *Dissertationes philologae Vindobonenses* (Vienna-Leipzig: Bibliopola Acad. Lit. Caes. Vind., 1910). |
| | – Adler, M., "Zwei Beitrage zum Plutarchischen Dialog De facie in orbe lunae" (Nikolsburg: Verlag des K.K. Staats-Gymnasium, 1910). |
| | – Adler, M., "Ein Zitat aus des Megasthenes Ἰνδικά bei Plutarch," *Festschrift Moriz Winternitz* (Leipzig: O. Harrassowitz, 1933). |
| Prickard | Prickard, A.O., *Plutarch on The Face Which Appears on the Orb of the Moon* (Winchester: Warren & Son / London: Simpkin, 1911). |
| Purser | Purser, L.C., "Mr. Prickard's Translation of Plutarch's *De facie*," *Hermathena* 16 (1911). |
| Paton | Paton, W.R., "Review of Prickard, Plutarch on the Face in the Moon (Winchester, 1911)," *CR* 26 (1912). |
| Hart. | Hartman, J.J., *De Plutarcho scriptore et philosopho* (Leiden: Brill, 1916). |
| Kron. | – Kronenberg, A.J., "Ad Plutarchi *Moralia* (Continued)," *Mnemosyne* 52 (1924). |
| | – Kronenberg, A.J., "Ad Plutarchi *Moralia* (Continued)," *Mnemosyne* 10 (1941). |
| Raing. | Raingeard, P., *Le Περὶ τοῦ προσώπου de Plutarque* (Paris: Belles Lettres, 1934). |
| Sandb. | Sandbach, F.H., "Second Meeting," *Proceedings of the Cambridge Philological Society* (1943). |
| Ch. | Cherniss, H., "Notes on Plutarch's *De facie quae in orbe lunae*," *Classical Philology* 46, 3 (1951). |
| Görg. | Görgemanns, H., *Untersuchungen zu Plutarchs Dialog De facie in orbe lunae* (Heidelberg: Heidelberg University Press, 1970). |
| DK | Diels-Kranz, *Die Fragmente der Vorsokratiker* (Hildesheim: Weidmann, $^{17}$1974). |

---

[5] The same problem, noted in footnote 4 of this section, concerns the attributions to Papabasileios. In this case, I have had to rely on Cherniss, given that I have not been able to access the journal cited by this scholar.

| | |
|---|---|
| Lehnus | Lehnus, L., *Plutarco. Il volto della luna* (Milan: Piccola Biblioteca Adelphi, 1991). |
| Schmidt | Nix, L. & Schmidt, W., *Heronis Alexandrini opera quae supersunt omnia* vol. 2. Mechanica et Catoptrica (Berlin: De Gruyter, $^2$2010). |
| Do | Donini, P.L., *Plutarco. Il volto della luna* (Naples: M. D'Auria, 2011). |
| P.J. | – Pérez Jiménez, A., "En el reino de las Moiras: comentario estilístico de Plu., *De facie in orbe lunae* 945C–945D," *Giornale italiano di filologia* 67 (2015). |
| | – Pérez Jiménez, A., "De Titios y Tifones. Anotaciones estilísticas a Plu., *De facie in orbe lunae* 945B," in A. Setaioli (ed.), *Apis Matina. Studi in onore di Carlo Santini* (Trieste: Trieste University Press, 2016). |
| | – Pérez Jiménez, A., "Los habitantes de la Luna (Plut., *De fac.* 944C–945B). Notas críticas sobre las propuestas textuales y traducciones del XVI," in F. Frazier & O. Guerrier (eds.), *Plutarque. Éditions, Traductions, Paratextes* (Coimbra: Coimbra University Press, 2016). |
| | – Pérez Jiménez, A., "Selenographic Description: Critical Annotation to Plutarch, De facie 944C," in J. Opsomer, G. Roskam & F.B. Titchener (eds.), *A Versatile Gentleman. Consistency in Plutarch's Writing* (Leuven: Leuven University Press, 2016). |
| | – Pérez Jiménez, A., "Las regiones fértiles de la tierra: nueva propuesta crítica a Plu., *De facie* 938D," in M. Sanz Morales, R. González Delgado, M. Librán Moreno & J. Ureña Bracero (eds.), *La (inter)textualidad en Plutarco* (Cáceres-Coimbra: Coimbra University Press, 2017). |

## 4  Other *sigla*

| | |
|---|---|
| *s.l.* | *supra lineam*: correction of a manuscript over the line |
| *i.l.* | *infra lineam*: correction of a manuscript under the line |
| *i.t.* | *in textu*: correction of a manuscript in the text itself |
| *vac.* | *vacat*: blank of 2/3 letters |
| *lac.* | *lacuna* |
| *no sign. lac.* | manuscripts do not signal a lacuna |
| *add.* | *addidit*: addition where manuscripts do not signal a lacuna |
| *suppl.* | *supplevit*: proposal for filling a lacuna in the manuscripts |
| *post* | added after |
| *ante* | added before |
| *pro* | instead of |
| *vel* | or |
| *corr.* | *correxit*: corrected |

## SIGLA

| | |
|---|---|
| *coni.* | *coniecit*: conjectured |
| *del.* | *delevit*: deleted |
| *om.* | *omisit*: omitted |
| *secl.* | *seclusit*: secluded |
| *transp.* | *transposuit*: transposed |
| *dupl.* | *duplicavit*: repeated |
| *punct. corr.* | *punctum correxit*: punctuation corrected |
| *iteratio sententiae* | repetition of sentence |
| *sec.* | *secundum*: proposal following that of a previous scholar |
| *in app.* | *in apparatu*: proposal not included in the main text |
| *in comm.* | *in commentario*: proposal not included in the main text |
| *et alii* | proposal accepted by most scholars but not in the present edition |
| *mss.* | manuscripts |
| ⟨ ⟩ | addition in the body of text |
| [ ] | seclusion in the body of text |
| \| | beginning of a new passage according to the traditional pagination |
| ‖ | beginning of a new page according to the traditional pagination |

# Edition & English Translation

920B | 1. … Ὁ μὲν οὖν Σύλλας ταῦτα εἶπε· "τῷ γὰρ ἐμῷ μύθῳ προσήκει κἀκεῖθέν ἐστιν· ἀλλὰ εἰ δεῖ τι πρὸς τὰς ἀνὰ χεῖρα ταύτας καὶ διὰ στόματος πᾶσι δόξας περὶ τοῦ προσώπου τῆς σελήνης προσανακρούσασθαι, πρῶτον ἡδέως ἄν μοι δοκῶ πυθέσθαι." "Τί δὲ οὐκ ἐμέλλομεν" εἶπον "ὑπὸ τῆς ἐν τούτοις ἀπορίας ἐπ' ἐκεῖνα ἀπωσθέντες; Ὡς γὰρ οἱ ἐν νοσήμασι χρονίοις πρὸς τὰ κοινὰ βοηθήματα καὶ τὰς συνήθεις 5 διαίτας ἀπειπόντες ἐπὶ καθαρμοὺς καὶ περίαπτα καὶ ὀνείρους τρέπονται, οὕτως

C ἀναγκαῖον ἐν δυσθεωρήτοις καὶ | ἀπόροις σκέψεσιν, ὅταν οἱ κοινοὶ καὶ ἔνδοξοι καὶ συνήθεις λόγοι μὴ πείθωσι, πειρᾶσθαι τῶν ἀτοπωτέρων καὶ μὴ καταφρονεῖν, ἀλλ' ἐπᾴδειν ἀτεχνῶς ἑαυτοῖς τὰ τῶν παλαιῶν καὶ διὰ πάντων τἀληθὲς ἐξελέγχειν·

2. ὁρᾷς γὰρ εὐθὺς ὡς ἄτοπος ὁ λέγων τὸ φαινόμενον εἶδος ἐν τῇ σελήνῃ πάθος 10 εἶναι τῆς ὄψεως ὑπεικούσης τῇ λαμπρότητι δι' ἀσθένειαν, ὃ ⟨πρόσωπον⟩ καλοῦμεν, οὐ συνορῶν ὅτι πρὸς τὸν ἥλιον ἔδει τοῦτο γίνεσθαι μᾶλλον ὀξὺν ἀπαντῶντα καὶ πλήκτην· ὥς που καὶ Ἐμπεδοκλῆς τὴν ἑκατέρων ἀποδίδωσιν οὐκ ἀηδῶς διαφοράν,

ἥλιος ὀξυβελὴς ἠδὲ ἰλάειρα σελήνη, 15

D τὸ ἐπαγωγὸν αὐτῆς καὶ | ἱλαρὸν καὶ ἄλυπον οὕτω προσαγορεύσας· ἔπειτα λόγον ⟨οὐκ⟩ ἀποδιδοὺς καθ' ὃν αἱ ἀμυδραὶ καὶ ἀσθενεῖς ὄψεις οὐδεμίαν διαφορὰν ἐν τῇ σελήνῃ μορφῆς ἐνορῶσιν, ἀλλὰ λεῖος αὐταῖς ἀντιλάμπει καὶ περίπλεως αὐτῆς ὁ κύκλος. Οἱ δ' ὀξὺ καὶ σφοδρὸν ὁρῶντες ἐξακριβοῦσι μᾶλλον καὶ διαστέλλουσιν ἐκτυπούμενα τὰ εἴδη τοῦ προσώπου καὶ τῆς διαφορᾶς ἅπτονται σαφέστερον· ἔδει 20 γάρ, οἶμαι, τοὐναντίον εἴπερ ἡττωμένου πά⟨θημα⟩ ὄμματος ἐποίει τὴν φαντασίαν, ὅπου τὸ πάσχον ἀσθενέστερον, ⟨σαφέστερον⟩ εἶναι τὸ φαινόμενον. Ἡ δὲ ἀνωμαλία

---

1 Ὁ μὲν οὖν Σύλλας B: Ὀαυνοσυλλας E: ἀκούσωμεν οὖν ὁ Σύλλας Po. *in app.*: ὁ οὖν Σύλλας *conieci* ‖ γάρ] *del.* RJ94: γ' Wyt. (*et poterat item παρ' ἐμοὶ in app.*): τῷ παραμέσῳ *pro* τῷ γὰρ ἐμῷ Madv. 3 προσανακρούσασθαι] προανακρούσασθαι RJ94: προσανεκρούσασθε Wyt. *et alii* 4 τούτοις] ταύταις Wyt. *in app.* ‖ ἐκεῖνα Po.: ἐκείνους EB: ἐκείνας RJ94 4–5 ἀπωσθέντες *punct. corr.* Basil.: ἀπωσθέντες. EB 11 πρόσωπον *supplevi: lac.* 8 lit. EB: ὅπερ *corr. et ἀνάκλασιν suppl.* RJ94: ἀμβλυωπίαν Amyot: ἀμβλυώττειν Xyl.¹⁵⁷⁰: μαραυγεῖν Wyt. *in app.*: μαρμαρυγὰς Raing. *in app.*: μαρμαρυγὴν Po.: μαραυγίαν Ch. 11–12 καλοῦμεν *punct. corr.* Basil.: καλοῦμεν; EB 15 ὀξυβελὴς ἠδὲ ἰλάειρα RJ94 (ἰλάειρα *sic*): ὀξυμελὴς ἠδὲ λάιρα EB: ὀξυμελὴς ἠδὲ λάινα Ald. Basil.: ὀξυβελὴς ἠδὲ λάινα Amyot: ὀξυβελὴς ἠδ' αὖ ἰλάειρα Xyl.¹⁵⁷⁰: ὀξυβελὴς ἠδ' ἰλάειρα Wyt.: ὀξυβελὴς ἠδ' ἠδ' ἰλάειρα Purser 17 οὐκ *add. post* λόγον Emp. 21 πάθημα *supplevi* (*sec.* πάθημά τι Raing. *in app.*): πά *et lac.* 5 lit. EB: τὰ *pro* πά Ald. Basil.: τοῦ *pro* τὰ RJ94: τὰ πάθη Amyot: πάθος Wyt. *in app.* 22 ὅπου B: οπου E ‖ σαφέστερον *add. post* ἀσθενέστερον Hutten (*sec.* Amyot τὸ ἀσθενὲς *vel* ἐναργέστερον *et* σαφέστερον *add. post* ἀσθενέστερον): *no sign. lac.* EB: ἐστιν σαφέστερον *add. post* ἀσθενέστερον Wyt. *in app.*

1. ... So Sulla said the following: "well, it concerns my myth and originate from it, but if there is any need to take a step back on the opinions which are at hand and on everyone's lips regarding the face of the moon, I think that I would like to know about those first." "How could we not do so," I said, "since by the difficulty in these we were pushed towards other opinions? Just as those with chronic diseases who are tired of common remedies and usual diets turn to expiations and amulets and dreams, so in puzzling and difficult explanations, when the common, standard, and familiar arguments are not convincing enough, it is necessary to give a shot to those that are more unconventional and not belittle them but to let ourselves be absolutely enchanted by the ancients and to evidence truth by any means necessary.

    Sulla

    Lamp.

2. Well, you see right away how absurd is the one who says that the figure appearing on the moon, which we call ⟨face⟩, is an affection of vision conceding to brilliance due to weakness, without realizing that this should rather have occurred with respect to the sun, which strikes keen and violent—so too Empedocles presents the difference between them somewhere not unpleasantly:

'The keen-shafted sun and the gentle moon,'

assigning to the moon what is attractive, cheerful, and harmless—; and without providing a reason for which blurry and weak sights see no variation of shape in the moon, but its orb shines for them even and full. Differently, those who possess an acute and strong sight distinguish and discern better the forms of a face being modelled and perceive the variations more clearly; in fact, it should have been, I think, the opposite case, if an ⟨affection⟩ of the weakened eye created the image: the weaker the subject affected, ⟨the more distinct⟩ should be the appearance. And the unevenness too refutes

E καὶ παντάπασιν ἐλέγχει τὸν λόγον· οὐ γὰρ ἐπὶ συνεχοῦς | σκιᾶς καὶ συγκεχυμένης ὄψις, ἀλλὰ οὐ φαύλως ὑπογράφων ὁ Ἁγησιάναξ εἴρηκε·

πᾶσα μὲν ἥδε πέριξ πυρὶ λάμπεται· ἐν δ' ἄρα μέσσῃ
γλαυκότερον κυάνοιο φαείνεται ἠύτε κούρης
ὄμμα καὶ ὑγρὰ μέτωπα· τὰ δὲ ῥέθει ἄντα ἔοικεν· 5

ὄντως γὰρ ὑποδύεται περιιόντα τοῖς λαμπροῖς τὰ σκιερὰ καὶ πιέζει, πάλιν ὑπ' αὐτῶν καὶ ἀποκοπτόμενα, καὶ ὅλως πέπλεκται δι' ἀλλήλων ⟨ὥστε⟩ γραφικὴν τὴν δια⟨τύπωσιν⟩ εἶναι τοῦ σχήματος. ⟨Τοῦτο δὲ⟩ καὶ πρὸς Κλέαρχον, ὦ Ἀριστότελες,
F οὐκ ἀπιθάνως ἐδόκει λέγεσθαι τὸν ὑμέ|τερον· ὑμέτερος γὰρ ἀνὴρ ὁ Ἀριστοτέλους τοῦ παλαιοῦ γεγονὼς συνήθης· εἰ καὶ πολλὰ τοῦ Περιπάτου παρέτρεψεν." 10

3. Ὑπολαβόντος δὲ τοῦ Ἀπολλωνίδου τὸν λόγον καὶ τίς ἦν ἡ δόξα τοῦ Κλεάρχου διαπυθομένου, "παντὶ μᾶλλον" ἔφην "ἀγνοεῖν ἢ σοὶ προσῆκόν ἐστι λόγον ὥσπερ ἀφ' ἑστίας τῆς γεωμετρίας ὁρμώμενον· λέγει γὰρ ἀνὴρ εἰκόνας ἐσοπτρικὰς εἶναι καὶ
921A εἴδωλα τῆς μεγάλης θαλάσσης ἐμφαινόμενα τῇ σελήνῃ τὸ καλούμενον πρό||σωπον. Ἥ τε γὰρ ὄψις ἀνακλωμένη πολλαχόθεν ἅπτεσθαι τῶν οὐ κατ' εὐθυωρίαν ὁρωμέ- 15
νων πέφυκεν· ἥ τε πανσέληνος αὐτὴ πάντων ἐσόπτρων ὁμαλότητι καὶ στιλπνότητι κάλλιστόν ἐστι καὶ καθαρώτατον· ὥσπερ οὖν τὴν ἶ⟨ριν⟩ οἴεσθε ὑμεῖς ἀνακλωμένης ἐπὶ τὸν ἥλιον τῆς ὄψεως ἐνορᾶσθαι τῷ νέφει λαβόντι νοτερὰν ἡσυχῇ λειότητα καὶ ⟨πῆ⟩ξιν, οὕτως ἐκεῖνος ἐνορᾶσθαι τῇ σελήνῃ τὴν ἔξω θάλασσαν οὐκ ἐφ' ἧς ἐστι χώρας, ἀλλ' ὅθεν ἡ κλάσις ἐποίησε τῇ ὄψει τὴν ἐπαφὴν αὐτῆς καὶ τὴν ἀνταύγειαν· 20
B ὥς που πάλιν ὁ Ἁγησιάναξ εἴρηκεν, |

ἢ πόντου μέγα κῦμα καταντία κυμαίνοντος
δείκελον ἰνδάλλοιτο πυριφλεγέθοντος ἐσόπτρου."

---

1 ἐπὶ] ἔστι A.I.43 *et alii*   3 μέσσῃ E: μέσῃ B   5 τὰ δὲ ῥέθει Salmas: τὸ δ' ἐρεύθει EB   6 περιιόντα RJ94: περιόντα EB: πέριξ ἐντὸς Wyt. *in app.*   6–7 καὶ ... ἀποκοπτόμενα] καὶ *del. ante* ἀποκοπτόμενα RJ94: αὐτὰ ἀνακοπτόμενα *pro* ὑπ' αὐτῶν καὶ ἀποκοπτόμενα Wyt. *in app.*: καὶ πιέζεται *add. ante* καὶ πιέζει Bern. *in app.*: ἐκεῖνα καὶ πιέζεται *add. post* πιέζει Adler: καὶ ἀποκόπτοντα *add. post* ἀποκοπτόμενα Purser: πιεζόμενα *add. post* πιέζει Po. Ch.   7 ὥστε suppl. Wyt. *in app.*: *lac.* 5 *lit.* E, 8 *lit.* B: ὥστε εἰκόνα αὐτῶν Amyot: ὡς μονονοῦ Po. *in app.*   8 διατύπωσιν suppl. Kepl.: *lac.* 5 *lit.* E, 8 *lit.* B: διαγραφὴν Amyot ‖ Τοῦτο δὲ suppl. Bern.: *lac.* 7 *lit.* EB: προσώπου Amyot: ὅθεν αὐτὸ τοῦτο Wyt. *in app.*: αὐτὰ δὲ ταῦτα Raing. *in app.*: ταὐτὸ δὲ Po.   9 ἀνὴρ Bern.: ἀνήρ EB: ὁ ἀνὴρ Dübn.   ‖ ὁ Ἀριστοτέλους Raing.: ὁ ἀριστοτέλης EB: Ἀριστοτέλους RJ94: τοῦ Ἀριστοτέλους Kepl.   11 Ἀπολλωνίδου Wyt.: ἀπολλωνιάδου EB   13 ἀνὴρ Dübn.: ἀνήρ EB   15 ὄψις RJ94: ἴτυς EB: ἀκτίς Po.   ‖ κατ εὐθυωρίαν E: κατευθυωρίαν B   17 ἶριν suppl. SR67: ἶ *vac.* 2 *lit.* E: *vac.* 3 *lit.* B   19 πῆξιν suppl. RJ94 (*vel* τῆξιν): *vac.* 2 *lit. et* ξιν EB: σύντηξιν Xyl.¹⁵⁷⁰: σύμπηξιν Bern. *in app.*   20 τῇ ὄψει Wyt. *in app.*: τὴν ὄψιν EB: τῆς ὄψεως RJ94

the argument entirely: as our vision does not fall upon a continuous and blurred shadow, but Agesianax said it not badly when he wrote:

> 'all of it gleams with fire encircled, but within | shines brighter than blue an eye of a maid | and a sensual brow: similar in appearance to a visage.'

Truly, the dark spots submerge beneath the bright ones encompassing them and they constrain, being in turn also cut by the others, and are intermingled completely with one another, ⟨so as to⟩ make the ⟨delineation⟩ of the figure look like a painting. ⟨This⟩ point, Aristotle, seemed also formulated against your Clearchus not unconvincingly—no doubt the man is one of yours, being as he was an acquaintance of the ancient Aristotle; even though he distorted many teachings of the Peripatos."

3. Here Apollonides interfered and asked what the opinion of Clearchus was. "Anybody else," said I, "more than you should be unaware of a theory which is built, so to say, on the hearth of geometry; indeed, the man affirms that the so-called 'face' results from mirrored images and reproductions of the great ocean showing on the moon. So the visual ray reflected from many points reaches by nature objects that are not directly visible; and the full moon itself is, among all mirrors, the finest and purest in uniformity and brilliance. Then, just as you people think that the rainbow is seen by the reflection of the visual ray to the sun in a cloud where the moisture has softly become smooth and condensed, so he thought that the outer ocean is seen in the moon, that is, not in the place where it really is, but where the refraction produces the contact of the ocean with the visual ray and its reflection to us. So did Agesianax say it somewhere again:

Apoll.
Lamp.

> 'Or the great wave of ocean waving opposite | appears to be a reproduction in a mirror of flames.'"

4. Ἡσθεὶς οὖν ὁ Ἀπολλωνίδης, "ὡς ἴδιον" εἶπε "καὶ καινὸν ὅλως τὸ σκευώρημα τῆς δόξης, τόλμαν δέ τινα καὶ μοῦσαν ἔχοντος ἀνδρός· ἀλλὰ πῇ τὸν ἔλεγχον αὐτῷ προσῆγε;" "Πρῶτον μὲν" εἶπον "εἰ μία φύσις τῆς ἔξω θαλάσσης ἐστί, σύρρουν καὶ συνεχὲς ... πέλαγος, ἡ δὲ ἔμφασις οὐ μία τῶν ἐν τῇ σελήνῃ μελασμάτων, ἀλλ' οἷον ἰσθμοὺς ἔχουσα, τοῦ λαμπροῦ διαιροῦντος καὶ διορίζοντος τὸ σκιερόν. Ὅθεν ἑκάστου τόπου χωρισθέντος καὶ πέρας ἴδιον ἔχοντος, αἱ τῶν φωτεινῶν ἐπιβολαὶ τοῖς | σκοτεινοῖς, ὕψους εἰκόνα καὶ βάθος λαμβάνουσαι, τὰς περὶ τὰ ὄμματα καὶ τὰ χείλη εἰκόνας φαινομένας ὁμοιότατα διετύπωσαν· ὥστε ἢ πλείονας ἔξω θαλάσσας ὑποληπτέον, ἰσθμοῖς τισι καὶ ἠπείροις ἀπολαμβανομένας, ὅπερ ἐστὶν ἄτοπον καὶ ψεῦδος, ἢ μιᾶς οὔσης, οὐ πιθανὸν εἰκόνα διεσπασμένην οὕτως ἐμφαίνεσθαι. Ἐκεῖνο μὲν γὰρ ἐρωτᾶν ἀσφαλέστερόν ἐστιν ἢ ἀποφαίνεσθαι σοῦ παρόντος, εἰ τῆς οἰκουμένης εὖρος ἴσοις καὶ μῆκος, ἐνδέχεται πᾶσαν ὡσαύτως ἀπὸ τῆς σελήνης ὄψιν ἀνακλωμένην ἐπιθιγγάνειν τῆς θαλάσσης καὶ τοῖς ἐν αὐτῇ τῇ μεγάλῃ θαλάττῃ πλέουσι, νὴ | Δία, καὶ οἰκοῦσιν, ὥσπερ Βρεττανοῖς, καὶ ταῦτα μηδὲ τῆς γῆς, ὥς φατε, πρὸς τὴν σφαῖραν τῆς σελήνης κέντρου λόγον ἐπεχούσης. Τουτὶ μὲν οὖν" ἔφην "σὸν ἔργον ἐπισκοπεῖν· τὴν δὲ πρὸς τὴν σελήνην [ἢ] τῆς ὄψεως κλάσιν, οὐκέτι σὸν οὐδὲ Ἱππάρχου· καίτοι γε φίλε πρίαμ... ἀλλὰ πολλοῖς οὐκ ἀρέσκει φυσιολογῶν περὶ τῆς ὄψεως ⟨ὡς⟩ αὐτὴν ὁμοπαθῆ κρᾶσιν ἴσχειν καὶ σύμπηξιν εἰκός ἐστι μᾶλλον ἢ πληγάς τινας καὶ ἀποπηδήσεις οἵας ἔπλαττε τῶν ἀτόμων Ἐπίκουρος. Οὐκ ἐθελήσει δέ, οἶμαι, τὴν σελήνην ἐμβριθὲς ὑποθέσθαι σῶμα καὶ στερεὸν ὑμῖν ὁ Κλέαρχος, ἀλλὰ ἄστρον αἰθέριον καὶ φωσφόρον, ὥς φατε, τοιαύτῃ τὴν ὄψιν ἢ θραύειν προσήκει ⟨ἢ⟩ καὶ ἀποστρέφειν, ὥστε οἴχεσθαι τὴν ἀνάκλασιν· εἰ δέ ⟨τι⟩ προσ|αιτεῖταί τις ἡμᾶς, ἐρησόμεθα πῶς μόνον πρόσωπόν ἐστιν ἐν τῇ σελήνῃ τὸ τῆς θαλάσσης ἔσοπτρον,

---

1 Ἡσθεὶς Xyl.¹⁵⁷⁰: πεισθεὶς EB   3 προσῆγε punct. corr. Xyl.: προσῆγε. EB: πρόσαγε RJ94: προσῆγες; Adler ‖ εἰ] ἢ RJ94 et alii   4 lac. 5 lit. EB: del. Ald. Basil.: δηλαδὴ suppl. Bern. in app.: κύκλῳ Po.: ἑαυτῷ Adler: καὶ τὸ supplevi   7 ὕψους SR67: ὕψεις EB ‖ βάθος] βάθους SR67 et alii   12 ἴσοις conieci: ἴσης EB: ἐχούσης SR67: ἴσον ἐχούσης Bern. in app.: τοσαύτης Po.   13 καὶ τοῖς ἐν αὐτῇ τῇ μεγάλῃ] καὶ τῆς ἐν αὐτῇ μεγάλῃ Ald. Basil.: καὶ τοῖς ἐν αὐτῇ μεγάλῃ SR67: καὶ ἐν τῆς αὐτῇ μεγάλῃ Xyl.: ἅμα τοῖς ἐν αὐτῇ τῇ μεγάλῃ Kepl.: ἄλλοις vel ἄλλῃ add. post καὶ τοῖς Bern. in app.   14 νὴ B: νη E ‖ φατε Wyt. in app. (φατὲ sic): ἔφατε EB   15 ἐπεχούσης B et E s.l.: ἐχούσης vac. 3 lit. E   16 ἢ del. RJ94 om. Basil.: καθόλου add. post ἢ Ch.   17 φίλε πρίαμ vac. 3 lit. EB: φίλε πρίαμε suppl. RJ94: φίλε λαμπρία RJ94: φίλε λαμπρία, suppl. et ἀλλὰ del. Xyl.¹⁵⁷⁰: φίλος γ' ἀνήρ, corr. et suppl. Wyt. in app.: φίλε λαμπρία, ὃ μάλα πολλοῖς ἀρέσκει Emp.: φίλε λαμπρία, μέγας ἀνὴρ ἀλλὰ Bern. in app.: ὤφειλε προτιμᾶσθαι Apelt: γ', ἔφη, ὦ Λαμπρία, τοῦδ' ἔστιν Adler: φιλοπράγμων ἀνὴρ Po.: ἐφιλέργει ἀνήρ Ch.   17–18 τῆς ὄψεως ὡς αὐτὴν Po.: τῆς ὄψεως αὐτὴν EB: τῆς ὄψεως αὐτῆς, ἣν Wyt. in app.: τῆς ὄψεως αὐγῇ Dübn.: τῆς ὄψεως αὐγῇ γὰρ ταύτην Bern. in app.: τῆς ὄψεως αὐτῆς, ἣν et τῇ αὐγῇ add. post ὁμοπαθῆ Adler: τῆς ὄψεως ἣν Hart.: τῆς ὄψεως. Αὐτὴν Raing.   20 ὑμῖν] ἡμῖν Ch. (sec. transl. Xyl. Amyot Kepl.)   21 τοιαύτῃ] τοιαύτην Basil.: τοιαύτῃ δὲ Wyt. in app. ‖ ἢ θραύειν Po.: ἢ θραῦσιν EB: [ἢ] θραύειν RJ94: οὐ θραύειν RJ94 ‖ προσήκει] προσήκειν Basil. ‖ ἢ² addidi: καὶ del. Raing.: ἢ pro καὶ Po.   22 τι προσαιτεῖταί τις ἡμᾶς Bern. in app.: προσδεῖταί τις ἡμᾶς EB: παραιτεῖταί τις ἡμᾶς vel προσδεῖταί τι ἡμᾶς Wyt. in app.: προσδεῖταί τις αἰτίας Emp.: προσδεῖταί τι σῆμα Raing.: προσαμυνεῖταί τις ἡμᾶς Po.   23 ἐρησόμεθα RJ94: χρησόμεθα EB

4. Then Apollonides, charmed, said, "how peculiar and wholly novel the scheme of this opinion, that of a man quite gifted in audacity and inspiration; but how did he put forward the refutation against it?" "Firstly," I said, "if the nature of the outer ocean is a single thing, a confluent and continuous ... sea, the appearance of the dark spots on the moon is not unique, but has sort of isthmuses where the bright part delimits and separates the shadowy part. Hence, since each part is separated and has its own limit, the layers of light upon the shadowy, gaining depth and a likeness of elevation, have produced fair likenesses of eyes and lips. Well then, one should conceive of either several outer oceans, divided by some isthmuses and continents, which is ridiculous and false; or, if there is only one ocean, accept that it is not plausible that the image is shown so dispersed. Now, this is safer to ask than to assert in your presence, whether it is possible, if you make equal the width and length of the inhabited world, that every visual ray reflected in similar way from the moon should reach the ocean, also for those who sail in the great ocean itself, by Zeus, and who live in it, as the Britons do; and all of this when the earth, so you say, does not have the relation of center to the orbit of the moon. In any case, this," I said, "is for you to examine; but the refraction of vision concerning the moon is neither for you nor for Hipparchus. Although dear ... but he is not appreciated by many when he theorizes about vision, ⟨thinking that⟩ it is more likely to involve a homogenic blend and fusion than any impacts and rebounds as those that Epicurus imagined of the atoms. Clearchus would not agree to admit that the moon is a heavy and solid body, together with you too, I think, but rather an ethereal and luminiferous star, as you folks say: to such a moon it corresponds that the visual ray either shatters or also diverts; but if someone dismisses our objections, we shall ask how the mirror of the ocean is a face

Apoll.

Lamp.

ἄλλῳ δὲ οὐδενὶ τῶν τοσούτων ἀστέρων ἐνορᾶται· καίτοι τό γε εἰκὸς ἀπαιτεῖ πρὸς ἅπαντας ἢ πρὸς μηθένα τοῦτο πάσχειν τὴν ὄψιν." Ἀλλ ... πρὸς τὸν Λεύκιον ἔφην ἀποβλέψας "ὃ πρῶτον ἐλέχθη τῶν ἡμετέρων ὑπόμνησον."

5. Καὶ ὁ Λεύκιος "ἀλλὰ μὴ δόξωμεν" ἔφη "κομιδῇ προπηλακίζειν τὸν Φαρνάκην, οὕτω τὴν Στωικὴν δόξαν | ἀπροσαύδητον ὑπερβαίνοντες, εἰπὲ δή τι πρὸς τὸν ἄνδρα, παντὸς ἀέρος μῖγμα καὶ μαλακοῦ πυρὸς ὑποτιθέμενον τὴν σελήνην· εἶτα οἷον ἐν γαλήνῃ φρίκης ὑποτρεχούσης φάσκοντα τοῦ ἀέρος διαμελαίνοντος ἔμφασιν γίνεσθαι μορφοειδῆ." "... χρηστῶς γε" εἶπον "ὦ Λεύκιε, τὴν ἀτοπίαν εὐφήμοις περιαμπέχεις ὀνόμασιν· οὐχ οὕτω δὲ ὁ ἑταῖρος ἡμῶν, ἀλλ' ὅπερ ἀληθὲς ἦν ἔλεγεν, ὑποπιέζειν αὐτοὺς τὴν σελήνην σπίλων καὶ μελασμῶν ἀναπιμπλάντας, || ὁμοῦ μὲν Ἄρτεμιν καὶ Ἀθηνᾶν ἀνακαλοῦντας, ὁμοῦ δὲ σύμμιγμα καὶ φύραμα ποιοῦντας ἀέρος ζοφεροῦ καὶ πυρὸς ἀνθρακώδους, οὐκ ἔχουσαν ἔξαψιν οὐδὲ αὐγὴν οἰκείαν, ἀλλὰ δυσκρινές τι σῶμα τυφόμενον ἀεὶ καὶ πυρίκαυστον, ὥσπερ τῶν κεραυνῶν τοὺς ἀλαμπεῖς καὶ ψολόεντας ὑπὸ τῶν ποιητῶν προσαγορευομένους· ὅτι μέντοι πῦρ ἀνθρακῶδες, οἷον οὗτοι τὸ τῆς σελήνης ποιοῦσιν, οὐκ ἔχει διαμονὴν οὐδὲ σύστασιν ὅλως, ἐὰν μὴ στερεᾶς ὕλης καὶ στεγούσης ἅμα καὶ τρεφούσης ἐπιλάβηται. Βέλτιον, οἶμαι, συνορᾶν ἐνίων | φιλοσόφων τοὺς ἐν παιδιᾷ λέγοντας τὸν Ἥφαιστον εἰρῆσθαι χωλόν· ὅτι τὸ πῦρ ξύλου χωρίς, ὥσπερ οἱ χωλοὶ βακτηρίας, οὐ πρόεισιν· εἰ οὖν ἡ σελήνη πῦρ ἐστι, πόθεν αὐτῇ τοσοῦτος ἐγγέγονεν ἀήρ; Ὁ γὰρ ἄνω καὶ κύκλῳ φερόμενος οὑτοσὶ τόπος οὐκ ἀέρος, ἀλλὰ κρείττονος οὐσίας καὶ πάντα λεπτύνειν καὶ συνεξάπτειν φύσιν ἐχούσης ἐστίν· εἰ δὲ γέγονε, πῶς οὐκ οἴχεται μεταβάλλων εἰς ἕτερον εἶδος ὑπὸ τοῦ πυρὸς ἐξαιθερωθείς, ἀλλὰ σῴζεται καὶ συνοικεῖ πυρὶ τοσοῦτον χρόνον, ὥσπερ ἥλοις ἀραρὼς ἀεὶ τοῖς αὐτοῖς μέρεσι καὶ συγγεγομφωμένος; Ἀραιῷ μὲν γὰρ ὄντι καὶ συγκεχυμένῳ μὴ μένειν, ἀλλὰ σφάλλεσθαι | προσήκει· συμπεπηγέναι δὲ οὐ δυνατὸν ἀναμεμιγμένον πυρὶ καὶ μήτε ὑγροῦ μετέχοντα μήτε γῆς, οἷς μόνοις ἀὴρ συμπήγνυσθαι πέφυκεν· ἡ δὲ ῥύμη καὶ τὸν ἐν λίθοις ἀέρα καὶ τὸν ἐν ψυχρῷ μολίβδῳ συνεκκάει, μήτι γε δὴ τὸν ἐν πυρὶ δινουμένῳ μετὰ τάχους τοσούτου· καὶ γὰρ Ἐμπεδοκλεῖ δυσκολαίνουσι πάγον ἀέρος χαλαζώδη ποιοῦντι τὴν σελήνην ὑπὸ τῆς τοῦ πυρὸς σφαίρας περιεχόμενον, αὐτοὶ δὲ τὴν σελήνην σφαῖραν οὖσαν πυρὸς ἀέρα φασὶν ἄλλον ἄλλῃ διεσπασμένον περιέχειν καὶ ταῦτα μήτε ῥήξεις ἔχουσαν ἐν ἑαυτῇ μήτε βάθη καὶ κοιλότητας, | ἅπερ οἱ γεώδη ποιοῦντες

---

2 τοῦτο E: τούτων B ‖ lac. 16 lit. EB: ἀλλὰ suppl. RJ94: ἔγω Amyot: σύ γε Wyt. in app.: ἐάσωμεν ταῦτα, καὶ σὺ Adler ‖ ἔφην Amyot: ἐφ' ὧν EB: εἶπον RJ94: ἐφ' ὃν Kepl.   6 παντὸς] πάντως SR67: παγέντος Po. ‖ μῖγμα Ald. Basil.: μίγμα EB   8 lac. 5 lit. EB: ναὶ σὺ suppl. Amyot: τοῦ προσώπου Wyt. in app.: ταύτῃ Herw.: μάλα vel πάνυ Adler: τοῦ σχήματος Purser: lac. del. Raing.   9 ἡμῶν Ald. Basil.: ὑμῶν EB   10 ὑποπιέζειν] ὑπωπιάζειν RJ94 Basil. ‖ ἀναπιμπλάντας E et B s.l.: ἀναπιπλάντας B   11 σύμμιγμα I.22: σύμμιγα EB   19 ἀὴρ punt. corr. Ald. Basil.: ἀήρ. EB   21 δὲ γέγονε] δὲ ἐγγέγονε RJ94 et alii   23 ἥλοις Ch.: ἧλος EB ‖ ἀεὶ τοῖς αὐτοῖς μέρεσι E: τοῖς αὐτοῖς ἀεὶ μέρεσι B   23–24 συγγεγομφωμένος punct. corr. Wyt.: συγγεγομφωμένος· EB   27 μήτι] μή τοι B s.l. ‖ δινουμένῳ] δινούμενον RJ94 et alii

only in the moon but cannot be seen in any of the numerous stars; however, it is reasonable to require that the visual ray should be affected in this way with regard to all the stars or to none." But ... with a glance at Lucius I said, "recall to me what was stated first among our arguments."

5. And Lucius said: "Let's not give the impression of utterly denigrating Pharnaces, passing over the Stoic opinion like this without addressing it, please say a word to this man who hypothesizes that the moon is a blend of air and soft fire, but then says that what appears to be a figure is the result of the blackening of the air like when in a calm water a shivering runs under the surface." "Very nicely," I said, "Lucius, you cover the absurdity with favorable words. Not so our comrade, but he said, which is in fact true, that they give a black eye to the moon by sullying it with stains and bruises, while simultaneously naming it Artemis and Athena, and making it a mixture and a mass of gloomy air and smouldering fire which neither possesses kindling nor its own light, but is an indiscernible body forever full of smoke and consumed by fire, like among the lightning bolts those which are lightless and called by the poets 'smoking'. Such a smouldering fire, however, the one these men make that of the moon, does not hold at all in endurance or consistency unless it obtains solid matter that is both protective and nourishing. They see this, I think, better than some philosophers, those who jokingly say that Hephaestus is said to be crippled because fire without wood, just like the crippled without a cane, cannot move forward; therefore, if the moon is in fact fire, from where does the air in it come? Because the upper region, which moves in circles, is not made of air, but of a superior substance, whose nature rarefies and irradiates everything; but, if air is there, how does it not disappear being changed into a different form after having been etherealized by fire, but instead survives and coexists with fire for such a long time, as if it had been adjusted and fixed with nails into the same spots forever? By being tenuous and vague, it is appropriate for air not to remain in place but to stagger; and it is not possible for air to have become solidified when it is mingled with fire but partakes neither of moisture nor of earth—the only things with which air can naturally be solidified—; furthermore, speed ignites both the air in stones and that in cold lead, imagine then the air confined in a fire that spins with such great pace. Yet they are displeased with Empedocles, who makes the moon a hail-like rock of air compressed by a sphere of fire, but they themselves say that the moon, even though it is a sphere of fire, contains air dispersed here and there—and all of this having neither clefts nor depths nor cavities in itself, precisely the ones

*Lucius*

*Lamp.*

ἀπολείπουσιν, ἀλλὰ ἐπιπολῆς δηλονότι τῇ κυρτότητι ἐπικείμενον. Τοῦτο δ' ἐστὶ καὶ πρὸς διαμονὴν ἄλογον καὶ πρὸς θέαν ἀδύνατον ἐν ταῖς πανσελήνοις· διορίσασθαι γὰρ οὐκ ἔδει μέλανα καὶ σκιερόν, ἀλλ' ἀμαυροῦσθαι κρυπτόμενον ἢ συνεκλάμπειν ὑπὸ τοῦ ἡλίου καταλαμβανομένης τῆς σελήνης. Καὶ γὰρ παρ' ἡμῖν, ὁ μὲν ἐν βάθεσι καὶ κοιλώμασι τῆς γῆς οὗ μὴ δίεισιν αὐγὴ διαμένει σκιώδης καὶ ἀφώτιστος· ὁ δὲ 5
ἔξωθεν τῇ γῇ περικεχυμένος φέγγος ἴσχει καὶ χρόαν αὐγοειδῆ. Πρὸς πᾶσαν μὲν γὰρ
E ἐστι ποιότητα καὶ δύνα|μιν εὐκέραστος ὑπὸ μανότητος, μάλιστα δὲ φωτός, ἂν ἐπιψαύσῃ μόνον, ὥς φατε, καὶ θίγῃ, διόλου τρεπόμενος ἐκφωτίζεται. Ταὐτὸ οὖν τοῦτο καὶ τοῖς εἰς βάθη τινὰ καὶ φάραγγας συνωθοῦσιν ἐν τῇ σελήνῃ τὸν ἀέρα κἂν καλῷ ἔοικε βοηθεῖν ὑμᾶς τε διεξελέγχει τοὺς ἐξ ἀέρος καὶ πυρὸς οὐκ οἶδα ὅπως μιγνύντας 10
αὐτῆς καὶ συναρμόζοντας τὴν σφαῖραν· οὐ γὰρ οἷόν τε λείπεσθαι σκιὰν ἐπὶ τῆς ἐπιφανείας, ὅταν ὁ ἥλιος ἐπιλάμπῃ τῷ φωτὶ πᾶν ὁπόσον καὶ ἡμεῖς ἀποτεμνόμεθα τῇ ὄψει τῆς σελήνης." 6. Καὶ ὁ Φαρνάκης ἔτι μου λέγοντος "τοῦτο ἐκεῖνο πάλιν" εἶπεν
F "ἐφ' ἡμᾶς ἀφῖκται τὸ περίακτον ἐκ τῆς Ἀκα|δημείας, ἐν τῷ πρὸς ἑτέρους λέγειν διατρίβοντας, ἑκάστοτε μὴ παρέχειν ἔλεγχον ὧν αὐτοὶ λέγουσιν, ἀλλ' ἀπολογου- 15
μένοις δεῖ χρῆσθαι μὴ κατηγοροῦσιν ἂν ἐντυγχάνωσιν· ἐμὲ δ' οὖν οὐκ ἐξάξεσθε τήμερον εἰς τὸ διδόναι λόγον ὧν ἐπικαλεῖτε τοῖς Στωικοῖς πρὶν εὐθύνας λαβεῖν παρ' ὑμῶν ἄνω τὰ κάτω τοῦ κόσμου ποιούντων." Καὶ ὁ Λεύκιος γελάσας "μόνον" εἶπεν
923A "ὦ τάν, μὴ κρίσιν ἡμῖν ἀσεβείας ἐπαγγείλῃς, || ὥσπερ Ἀρίσταρχον ᾤετο δεῖν Κλεάνθης τὸν Σάμιον ἀσεβείας προσκαλεῖσθαι τοὺς Ἕλληνας, ὡς κινοῦντα τοῦ κόσμου 20
τὴν ἑστίαν, ὅτι ⟨τὰ⟩ φαινόμενα σῴζειν ἀνὴρ ἐπειρᾶτο, μένειν τὸν οὐρανὸν ὑποτιθέμενος, ἐξελίττεσθαι δὲ κατὰ λοξοῦ κύκλου τὴν γῆν, ἅμα καὶ περὶ τὸν αὐτῆς ἄξονα δινουμένην. Ἡμεῖς μὲν οὖν οὐδὲν αὐτοὶ παρ' αὑτῶν λέγομεν, οἱ δὲ γῆν ὑποτιθέμενοι τὴν σελήνην, ὦ βέλτιστε, τί μᾶλλον ὑμῶν ἄνω τὰ κάτω ποιοῦσι, τὴν γῆν ἱδρυόντων ἐνταῦθα μετέωρον ἐν τῷ ἀέρι, πολλῷ τινι μείζονα τῆς σελήνης οὖσαν, ὡς ἐν τοῖς 25
B ἐκλειπτικοῖς πάθεσιν οἱ μαθηματικοὶ καὶ ταῖς διὰ τοῦ σκιάσματος παρόδοις τῆς | ἐποχῆς τὸ μέγεθος ἀναμετροῦσιν; Ἥ τε γὰρ σκιὰ τῆς γῆς ἐλάττων ὑπὸ μείζονος τοῦ φωτίζοντος ἀνατείνει καὶ τῆς σκιᾶς αὐτῆς λεπτὸν ὂν τὸ ἄνω καὶ στενόν, οὐδὲ Ὅμηρον, ὥς φασιν, ἔλαθεν, ἀλλὰ τὴν νύκτα θοὴν ὀξύτητι τῆς σκιᾶς προσηγόρευσεν· ὑπὸ τούτου δὲ ὅμως ἁλισκομένη ταῖς ἐκλείψεσιν ἡ σελήνη, τρισὶ μόλις τοῖς αὐτῆς 30

---

2 διορίσασθαι] διωρίσθαι Dübn. *et alii*    3 μέλανα] τὸ μέλαν Wyt. *in app.*: μένοντα *add. post* μέλανα Po. ‖ ἀμαυροῦσθαι E: ἀμαυροῦσθαι B    5 αὐγὴ SR67: αὕτη EB ‖ διαμένει I.22 SR67: διαμελαίνει EB    8 Ταὐτὸ Dübn.: ταυτὸ EB    9 κἂν καλῷ P.J.: κἂν καλῶς EB: παγκάλως Wyt. *in app.*    12 ὁπόσον Steph.: ὁ πόσον EB    14 Ἀκαδημείας Dübn.: Ἀκαδημίας EB    16 δεῖ] δὴ Amyot: ἀεὶ Wyt. *in app. et alii* ‖ ἂν] οἷς *add. ante* ἂν Amyot: τοῖς *add. post* ἂν Wyt. *in app.*: ὧν *add. ante* ἂν Bern. *in app.*    19 Ἀρίσταρχον Ménage: Ἀρίσταρχος EB    19–20 Κλεάνθης Ménage: Κλεάνθη EB    20 σάμιον] ἄσσιον RJ94 ‖ προσκαλεῖσθαι RJ94: προκαλεῖσθαι EB    21 τὰ *add.* RJ94 ‖ ἀνὴρ Dübn.: ἀνὴρ EB    24 ὑμῶν Xyl.: ἡμῶν EB    25 τινι Xyl.: τινὶ EB    27 ἀναμετροῦσιν *punct. corr.* Bern.: ἀναμετροῦσιν. EB ‖ ἐλάττων B: ἐλάττω E    28 ὂν τὸ RJ94: ὄντα EB    29 ὥς φασιν SR67: ὥς φησιν EB    30 αὐτῆς Steph.: αὐτῆς EB

that those who make the moon earthy allow—, and this air evidently rests upon the curvature of its surface. This is both unreasonable concerning the air's permanence and impossible concerning what is observed during full moons: after all, there should not have been a distinction between dark air and shadowy air, but it should become dark when occulted or shine evenly altogether when the moon is caught by the sun. In fact, among us as well, the air within depths and hollows of the earth where the rays of sun cannot penetrate remains shadowy and unlit, and that spreading on the outer surface of the earth possesses light and a bright color. Indeed, it can be easily permeated by every quality and power due to its subtility, above all when it barely grazes light, or as you say, 'touches upon' it, the air, being altogether permutated, is illuminated. Well, this very phenomenon seems to beautifully come in aid of those who propel air on the moon into some depths and ravines and completely refutes you who, I do not even know how, make the sphere of the moon a blend and mixture of air and fire, because there cannot be a shadow that remains on the surface whenever the sun casts its light upon as much of the moon as we delimitate with our vision."

6. Then Pharnaces, while I was still speaking, said: "Here comes once again the distracting ruse of the Academy, when they engage in debate with others every single time they avoid providing the arguments they defend, but must keep the others defending themselves lest they end up accusing the Academy; well, you will not provoke me today into providing an argument in defense of the Stoics against your accusations until I obtain a rectification from you who turn the universe upside down." And Lucius, laughing, told him: "Oh dear, only do not demand a trial against us for impiety, just as Cleanthes thought that the Greeks ought to lay an action for impiety against Aristarchus the Samian on the grounds that he was moving the hearth of the universe, because the man tried to save ⟨the⟩ phenomena by assuming that while the heaven remains still, the earth revolves along the ecliptic as well as simultaneously rotates about its own axis. Surely we express nothing of our own, but those who suppose the moon to be earth, my dearest, in what way do they, any more than you, turn things upside down, when you seat the earth here suspended, even though it is quite bigger than the moon—as mathematicians measure the magnitude of its disappearance during the occurrence of eclipses and its transits through the shadow—? For the shadow of the earth grows smaller as it extends on account that the source of light is bigger, and the fact that the top of the shadow itself is thin and narrow did not escape even Homer, as they say, who called the night 'sharp' due to the sharpness of the shadow; and yet when the moon is caught by this top part during eclipses it escapes in a course of hardly

Pharn.

Lucius

μεγέθεσιν ἀπαλλάττεται. Σκόπει δὴ πόσων ἡ γῆ σεληνῶν ἐστιν, εἰ σκιὰν ἀφίησιν ἢ βραχυτάτη πλάτος τρισέληνον, ἀλλ' ὅμως ὑπὲρ τῆς σελήνης μὴ πέσῃ δεδοίκατε· περὶ δὲ τῆς γῆς ἴσως Αἰσχύλος ἡμᾶς πέπεικεν ὡς ὁ Ἄτλας

C
ἕστηκε κίων οὐρανοῦ τε καὶ χθονός
ὤμοις | ἐρείδων ἄχθος οὐκ εὐάγκαλον· 5

εἰ τῇ μὲν σελήνῃ κοῦφος ἀὴρ ὑποτρέχει καὶ στερεὸν ὄγκον οὐκ ἐχέγγυος ἐνεγκεῖν, τὴν δὲ γῆν κατὰ Πίνδαρον ἀδαμαντοπέδιλοι κίονες περιέχουσι· καὶ διὰ τοῦτο Φαρνάκης αὐτὸς μὲν ἐν ἀδείᾳ τοῦ πεσεῖν τὴν γῆν ἐστιν, οἰκτείρει δὲ τοὺς ὑποκειμένους τῇ μεταφορᾷ τῆς σελήνης Αἰθίοπας ἢ Ταπροβηνούς, μὴ βάρος αὐτοῖς ἐμπέσῃ τοσοῦτον. Καίτοι τῇ μὲν σελήνῃ βοήθεια πρὸς τὸ μὴ πεσεῖν ἡ κίνησις αὐτὴ καὶ τὸ 10 ῥοιζῶδες τῆς περιαγωγῆς, ὥσπερ ὅσα ταῖς σφενδόναις ἐντεθέντα τῆς καταφορᾶς κώλυσιν ἴσχει τὴν κύκλῳ περιδίνησιν· ἄγει γὰρ ἕκαστον ἡ κατὰ φύσιν κίνησις,
D ἂν ὑπ' | ἄλλου μηδενὸς ἀποστρέφηται, διὸ τὴν σελήνην οὐκ ἄγει τὸ βάρος ὑπὸ τῆς περιφορᾶς τὴν ῥοπὴν ἐκκρουόμενον, ἀλλὰ μᾶλλον ἴσως λόγον εἶχε θαυμάζειν μένουσαν αὐτὴν παντάπασιν, ὥσπερ ἡ γῆ, καὶ ἄτρεπτον οὖσαν· νῦν δέ, σελήνη μὲν 15 ἔχει μεγάλην αἰτίαν τοῦ δεῦρο μὴ φέρεσθαι· τὴν δὲ γῆν, ἑτέρας κινήσεως ἄμοιρον οὖσαν, εἰκὸς ἦν μόνῳ τῷ βαρύνοντι κινεῖν, βαρυτέρα δέ ἐστι τῆς σελήνης, οὐχ ὅσῳ μείζων, ἀλλ' ἔτι μᾶλλον ἅτε δὴ διὰ θερμότητα καὶ πύρωσιν ἐλαφρᾶς γεγενημένης. Ὅλως δ' ἔοικεν ἐξ ὧν λέγεις ἡ σελήνη μᾶλλον, εἰ πῦρ ἐστι, γῆς δεῖσθαι καὶ ὕλης
E ἐν ᾗ βέβηκε καὶ | προσπέφυκε καὶ συνέχει καὶ ζωπυρεῖ τὴν δύναμιν· οὐ γὰρ ἔστι 20 πῦρ χωρὶς ὕλης διανοηθῆναι σωζόμενον, γῆν δέ φατε ὑμεῖς ἄνευ βάσεως καὶ ῥίζης διαμένειν;" "Πάνυ μὲν οὖν" εἶπεν ὁ Φαρνάκης "τὸν οἰκεῖον καὶ κατὰ φύσιν τόπον ἔχουσαν, ὥσπερ αὕτη τὸν μέσον, οὗτος γάρ ἐστι περὶ ὃν ἀντερείδει πάντα τὰ βάρη ῥέποντα καὶ φέρεται καὶ συννεύει πανταχόθεν· ἡ δὲ ἄνω χώρα πᾶσα κἄν τι δέξηται γεῶδες ὑπὸ βίας ἀναρριφέν, εὐθὺς ἐκθλίβει δεῦρο, μᾶλλον δὲ ἀφίησιν ᾗ πέφυκεν 25 οἰκείᾳ ῥοπῇ καταφερόμενον."

7. Πρὸς τοῦτο ἐγὼ τῷ Λευκίῳ χρόνον ἐγγενέσθαι βουλόμενος ἀναμιμνησκομένῳ,
F τὸν | Θέωνα καλέσας "τίς" ἔφην "ὦ Θέων εἴρηκε τῶν τραγικῶν, ὡς ἰατροὶ

πικρὰν πικροῖς κλύζουσι φαρμάκοις χολήν;"

---

2 ἢ βραχυτάτη RJ94: ἡ βραχυτάτη EB: ἧς add. ante ἡ βραχυτάτη SR67: τὴν βραχυτάτην pro ἡ βραχυτάτη Wyt. in app.   3 ἡμᾶς] ὑμᾶς Steph. et alii   4 κίων] κίον' RJ94 et alii   6 εἰ] καὶ Wyt. in app.: ἐπεὶ Adler: ἢ Po. Ch.   9 μεταφορᾷ] καταφορᾷ RJ94: περιφορᾷ Ch. ‖ βάρος] βορός B s.l.   11 ῥοιζῶδες E: ῥιζῶδες B   15 ἄτρεπτον οὖσαν· RJ94: ἄτρεπτος ἂν EB: ἄτρεπτον Basil.: ἀτρεμοῦσαν Emp.   17 κινεῖν] μένειν SR67 et alii   23 ὥσπερ] ὅπερ Amyot: ὅσπερ Arnim ‖ αὐτὴ Arnim: αὐτὴ EB: αὐτὸ Ald. Basil.: ἡ γῆ add. ante αὐτὸ Emp.: αὐτῆς Bern.: αὕτη Po. ‖ τὸν μέσον] τὸ μέσον SR67   29 χολήν punct. corr. Ald. Basil.: χολήν. EB

three times its own size. See then of how many moons the earth is made, if it casts a shadow which is, at its narrowest, three-moons large, and yet you still fear that the moon may fall, while, concerning the earth, perhaps Aeschylus convinced us that Atlas 'stood as a column of heaven and earth | holding on his shoulders a burden not easy to hold'. If under the moon runs some delicate air not adequate to support a solid mass, according to Pindar, differently, 'unshakable pillars' enclose the earth; and that is why Pharnaces himself fears not the fall of the earth but pities the Ethiopians or Taprobanians, placed under the moon's transference, least such a weight falls upon them. Notwithstanding this, what prevents the moon from falling is its own motion and the whissing motion of its rotation, comparable with the projectiles placed in slings that prevent the fall by retaining the whirling in a circle: indeed it is natural motion what guides each thing, as long as nothing else deviates it—this is the reason why weight does not guide the moon, being as it is counteracted by the impulse of its circular movement, but there would probably be more reason to wonder if it was perfectly still, like the earth, and motionless. Right now, while the moon has a great reason not to move towards here, it would be plausible that the earth, given that it has no part in other motions, is moved due to its weight alone—in fact it is heavier than the moon, not solely inasmuch as its bigger size, but even more so, precisely because the latter has become lightweight through warmth and blazing heat. All in all, it appears that from the arguments you say, if it is indeed fire, the moon should rather be in need of earth and matter on which to be, where to be durably settled, where to remain, and with which to inflame its power; for one cannot conceive of fire sustained without matter, yet you people say that the earth stands without foundation and root." "Certainly it does," said Pharnaces, "as it occupies the proper and natural place, as is the center for it, for this is the place about which all weights press against in their inclination and towards which they move and converge from everywhere, whereas all the upper space, in the case it would receive something earthy which has been thrown upwards by force, right away rejects it back here or rather sends it back where its particular inclination naturally prompts its descent."

7. At this point, wishing to give some time to Lucius in order to gather his ideas, I called Theon and asked: "Which of the tragic poets, Theon, said that doctors

Lamp.
Theon

'purge the bitter bile with bitter remedies?'"

Ἀποκριναμένου δὲ τοῦ Θέωνος ὅτι Σοφοκλῆς, "καὶ δοτέον" εἶπον "ὑπ' ἀνάγκης ἐκείνοις, φιλοσόφων δὲ οὐκ ἀκουστέον, ἂν τὰ παράδοξα παραδόξοις ἀμύνεσθαι βούλωνται καὶ μαχόμενοι πρὸς τὰ θαυμάσια τῶν δογμάτων ἀτοπώτερα καὶ θαυμασιώτερα πλάττωσιν, ‖ ὥσπερ οὗτοι τὴν ἐπὶ τὸ μέσον φορὰν εἰσάγουσιν· ᾗ τί παράδοξον οὐκ ἔνεστιν; Οὐχὶ τὴν γῆν σφαῖραν εἶναι τηλικαῦτα βάθη καὶ ὕψη καὶ ἀνωμαλίας ἔχουσαν; Οὐκ ἀντίποδας οἰκεῖν, ὥσπερ θρῖπας ἢ γαλεώτας, τραπέντα ἄνω τὰ κάτω, τῇ γῇ προσισχομένους· ἡμᾶς δὲ αὐτοὺς μὴ πρὸς ὀρθὰς βεβηκότας, ἀλλὰ πλαγίους ἐπιμένειν ἀπονεύοντας, ὥσπερ οἱ μεθύοντες; Οὐ μύδρους χιλιοταλάντους διὰ βάθους τῆς γῆς φερομένους, ὅταν ἐξίκωνται πρὸς τὸ μέσον ἵστασθαι μηδενὸς ἀπαντῶντος μηδὲ ὑπερείδοντος, εἰ δὲ ῥύμῃ κάτω φερόμενοι τὸ μέσον ὑπερβάλλοιεν, αὖθις ὀπίσω στρέφεσθαι καὶ ἀνακάμπτειν ἀφ' | αὑτῶν; Οὐ τμήματα δοκῶν ἀποπρισθέντα τῆς γῆς ἑκατέρωθεν μὴ φέρεσθαι κάτω διαπαντός, ἀλλὰ προσπίπτοντα πρὸς τὴν γῆν ἔξωθεν ἴσως διωθεῖσθαι καὶ ἀποκρύπτεσθαι περὶ τὸ μέσον; Οὐ ῥεῦμα λάβρον ὕδατος κάτω φερόμενον εἰ πρὸς τὸ μέσον ἔλθοι σημεῖον, ὅπερ αὐτοὶ λέγουσιν ἀσώματον, ἵστασθαι περικεραννύμενον κύκλῳ περὶ πόλον, ἄπαυστον αἰώραν καὶ ἀκατάπαυστον αἰωρούμενον; Οὐδὲ γὰρ ψευδῶς ἔνια τούτων βιάσαιτο ἄν τις αὐτὸν εἰς τὸ δυνατὸν τῇ ἐπινοίᾳ καταστῆσαι. Τοῦτο γάρ ἐστι τὰ ἄνω κάτω κάνω ⟨κάτω⟩ πάντα τραπέντα πάλιν εἶναι, τῶν ἄχρι τοῦ μέσου κάτω, τῶν δὲ ὑπὸ τὸ μέσον αὖ πάλιν ἄνω γι|νομένων· ὥστε, εἴ τις συμπαθείᾳ τῆς γῆς τὸ μέσον αὐτῆς ἔχων σταίη περὶ τὸν ὀμφαλόν, ἅμα καὶ τὴν κεφαλὴν ἄνω καὶ τοὺς πόδας ἄνω ἔχειν τὸν αὐτόν· κἂν μὲν διασκάπτῃ τὸν ἐπέκεινα τόπον, ἀνακύπτον αὐτοῦ τὸ ⟨κάτω ἄνω⟩ εἶναι καὶ κάτω ἄνωθεν ἕλκεσθαι τὸν ἀνασκαπτόμενον· εἰ δὲ δὴ τούτῳ τις ἀντιβεβηκὼς νοοῖτο, τοὺς ἀμφοτέρων ἅμα πόδας ἄνω γίνεσθαι καὶ λέγεσθαι.

8. Τοιούτων μέντοι καὶ τοσούτων παραδοξολογιῶν οὐ μὰ Δία πεῖραν, ἀλλὰ θαυματοποιοῦ τινος ἀποσκευὴν καὶ πυλαίαν κατανωτισάμενοι καὶ παρέλκοντες, ἑτέ-

---

5 ἔνεστιν punct. corr. RJ94: ἔνεστιν· EB   6 θρῖπας Dübn.: θρίπας EB ‖ τραπέντα] τραπέντας Basil.: τραπέμπαλιν Bern.   7 προσισχομένους· I.22 et punct. corr. Wyt.: προισχομένους· EB   8 μεθύοντες punct. corr. RJ94: μεθύοντες. EB   10 ὑπερείδοντος punct. corr. Basil.: ὑπερείδοντος; EB ‖ φερόμενοι Amyot: φερομένου EB   11 ἀφ αὑτῶν Bern. et punct. corr. RJ94: ἀπ' αὐτῶν. EB   13 ἴσως] ἔσω Wyt. in app.: εἴσω Bern. ‖ ἀποκρύπτεσθαι] ἀπορρίπτεσθαι Amyot: ἀποθρύπτεσθαι Xyl.   15 περικεραννύμενον] περικρεμαννύμενον ἢ Emp.: περικρεμάμενον corr. et ἢ add. Dübn.: περικορυσσόμενον ἢ Po. ‖ περὶ πόλον B s.l.: περὶ πόλιν E: περὶ πόλλων Β: περιπολοῦν Amyot: περιπολεῖν Dübn.   17 αὐτὸν Xyl.: αὐτῶν EB   18 κάνω κάτω corr. et add. Kepl.: κἂν EB: καὶ pro κἂν et τὰ κάτω ἄνω add. Amyot: τὸ add. ante τὰ ἄνω et καὶ pro κἂν Adler ‖ τραπέντα πάλιν εἶναι] τραπέντα ἀνάπαλιν ἰέναι Wyt. in app.: τραπέντα τἄμπαλιν εἶναι Dübn.: τραπέμπαλιν εἶναι Bern. et alii: τραπέμπαλιν θεῖναι Adler   21 μὲν SR67: μὴ EB   22 κάτω ἄνω suppl. Ch.: lac. 8 lit. EB: μέρος ἄνω RJ94: ἄνω κάτω Amyot: τὸ σῶμα ἄνω ἰέναι Wyt. in app.: σῶμα Emp.: σῶμα ταὐτὸν suppl. et καὶ ἄνω καὶ κάτωθεν καὶ add. ante ἄνωθεν Bern. in app.: σῶμα κάτω χωρεῖν suppl. et corr. Adler: ἀνακύπτειν corr., κατασκαπτόμενον suppl., εἶναι del. et τὸ pro τὸν Purser: κάτω ἄνω σῶμα ταὐτὸν Bens.   23 τις E: τίς Β   24 παραδοξολογιῶν E: παραδόξως λογιῶν Β: παραδόξων λόγων SR67 ‖ πεῖραν] πήραν RJ94 et alii

And after Theon replied that it was Sophocles, I said: "and we shall grant them this procedure out of necessity, but shall not listen to philosophers who want to dismiss paradoxes with paradoxes and who, when struggling with the marvel of certain beliefs, imagine some even more astounding and marvelous, just as do those who introduce the theory of motion to the center: what is there that is not paradoxical? Not that the earth is a sphere despite having such sizeable depths and heights and anomalies in its surface? Not that people live on the antipodes, like worms or geckos, turned upside down, holding on to earth—as we ourselves, not standing straight but at an oblique angle, remain in a leaning position, as if we were drunk—? Not that incandescent masses of thousands of talents which sink into the depths of the earth, when they reach the center, stop there, even though there is nothing to encounter or support them—in fact, if in their downward motion they should exceed the center due to the impulse, they do turn around right away and return of themselves—? Not that pieces of meteors that are sawn off on either side of the earth do not always move downwards but fall upon the earth from without probably force their way through and remain hidden around the center? Not that a tumultuous flow of water flowing downwards, if it should reach the middle point—which they themselves call 'incorporeal'—, stops spreading in a circle around the axis, an incessant swinging and oscillating endlessly? Well, not even by mistake could one force to present some of these paradoxes as possible in his imagination. Indeed this is 'upside down' and everything 'bottoms up', being overturned, if what is up until the center is 'down', but what is under the center gets to be 'up' in turn; so that, if someone should stand having his navel in unison with the center of the very earth, that person would have at the same time head up and feet up too; moreover, if he dug beyond that point, in emerging his ⟨down⟩ is ⟨up⟩, and by digging up he would pull himself down from above; and actually, if someone should be imagined to have walked in the opposite direction to this man, the feet of both are, and so are said, at the same time 'up'.

8. For such a kind and number of strambotic tales there is no proof, by Zeus, but while accepting and lugging in some juggler's pack and frivolity

Lamp.

D ρους φασὶ πελάζειν ἄνω τὴν σελήνην, γῆν οὖσαν, ἐνι|δρύοντας οὐχ ὅπου τὸ μέσον ἐστί· καίτοι γε εἰ πᾶν σῶμα ἐμβριθὲς εἰς τὸ αὐτὸ συννεύει καὶ πρὸς τὸ αὐτοῦ μέσον ἀντερείδει πᾶσι τοῖς μορίοις, οὐχ ὡς μέσον οὖσα τοῦ παντὸς ἡ γῆ μᾶλλον ἢ ὡς ὅλον οἰκειώσεται μέρη αὐτῆς ὄντα τὰ βάρη καὶ τεκμήριον ... ἔσται τῶν ῥεπόντων οὔτι τῆς μεσότητος πρὸς τὸν κόσμον, ἀλλὰ πρὸς τὴν γῆν κοινωνίας τινὸς καὶ συμφυΐας 5
τοῖς ἀπωσμένοις αὐτῆς εἶτα πάλιν καταφερομένοις. Ὡς γὰρ ὁ ἥλιος εἰς ἑαυτὸν ἐπι-
E στρέφει τὰ μέρη ἐξ ὧν συνέστηκε καὶ ἡ γῆ τὸν λίθον, ὥσπερ ⟨αὐτῇ⟩ προσήκοντα, | δέχεται καὶ προσφέρει ἐκεῖνον· ὅθεν ἑνοῦται τῷ χρόνῳ καὶ συμφύεται πρὸς αὐτὴν τῶν τοιούτων ἕκαστον. Εἰ δέ τι τυγχάνει σῶμα τῇ γῇ μὴ προσνενεμημένον ἀπ' ἀρχῆς μηδὲ ἀπεσπασμένον, ἀλλά που καθ' αὑτὸ σύστασιν ἔσχεν ἰδίαν καὶ φύσιν, 10
ὡς φαῖεν ἂν ἐκεῖνοι τὴν σελήνην, τί κωλύει χωρὶς εἶναι καὶ μένειν περὶ αὑτὸ τοῖς αὑτοῦ πεπιεσμένον μέρεσι καὶ συμπεπεδημένον; Οὔτε γὰρ ἡ γῆ μέσον οὖσα δείκνυ-
ται τοῦ παντός, ἥ τε πρὸς τὴν γῆν τῶν ἐνταῦθα συναίρεσις καὶ σύστασις ὑφηγεῖται
F τὸν τρόπον ᾧ μένειν τὰ ἐκεῖ συμπεσόντα πρὸς τὴν σελήνην εἰκός | ἐστιν· ὁ δὲ πάντα τὰ γεώδη καὶ βαρέα συνελαύνων εἰς μίαν χώραν καὶ μέρη ποιῶν ἑνὸς σώματος, οὐχ 15
ὁρῶ διὰ τί τοῖς κούφοις τὴν αὐτὴν ἀνάγκην οὐκ ἀνταποδίδωσιν, ἀλλ' ἐᾷ χωρὶς εἶναι συστάσεις πυρὸς τοσαύτας καὶ οὐ πάντας εἰς τοῦτο συνάγων τοὺς ἀστέρας σαφῶς
925A οἴεται δεῖν καὶ σῶμα κοινὸν εἶναι τῶν ἄνω φορῶν καὶ φλογοειδῶν ἁπάντων. ‖

9. Ἀλλ' ἥλιον μὲν ἀπλέτους μυριάδας ἀπέχειν τῆς ἄνω περιφορᾶς φατε" εἶπον "ὦ φίλε Ἀπολλωνίδη, καὶ φωσφόρον ἐπ' αὐτῷ καὶ στίλβοντα καὶ τοὺς ἄλλους πλάνη- 20
τας ὑφιεμένους τε τῶν ἀπλανῶν καὶ πρὸς ἀλλήλους ἐν διαστάσεσι μεγάλαις φέρε-
σθαι, τοῖς δὲ βαρέσι καὶ γεώδεσιν οὐδεμίαν οἴεσθε τὸν κόσμον εὐρυχωρίαν παρέχειν
ἐν ἑαυτῷ καὶ διάστασιν· ὁρᾶτε ὅτι γελοῖόν ἐστιν, εἰ γῆν οὐ φήσομεν εἶναι τὴν σελή-
νην ὅτι τῆς κάτω χώρας ἀφέστηκεν, ἄστρον δὲ φήσομεν, ὁρῶντες ἀπωσμένην τῆς
ἄνω περιφορᾶς μυριάσι σταδίων τοσαύταις, ὥσπερ βυθόν τινα καταδεδυκυῖαν. Τῶν 25

---

1 πελάζειν] γελοιάζειν RJ94 et alii: πλάζειν Amyot ‖ ἐνιδρύοντας RJ94: ἐνιδρύοντες EB   2 ἐστί·
E: ἐστίν· B ‖ αὑτοῦ] αὐτοῦ Bern. et alii   4 αὐτῆς] αὑτῆς Ch. ‖ lac. 11 lit. E, 16 lit. B: τοῦ ἀνάγκη γίνεσθαι, τὴν ῥοπὴν αὐτοῖς suppl. et ἔσται del. Wyt. in app.: ἐς αὐτὴν suppl. et ἔσται τῶν del. Emp.: ἐκ τῶν βαρέων Bern. in app.: τὸ πάθος suppl. et πρὸς τὸ μέσον add. ante ῥεπόντων Adler: τὸ κατωφερὲς Ch.   4–5 οὔτι τῆς μεσότητος correxi: οὐ τῇ τῆς μεσότητος EB: τῇ del. RJ94: οὐκ αὐτῇ τῆς μεσότητος Amyot: γῇ pro τῇ Emp.: τῇ γῇ pro τῇ τῆς Madv.: γῇ add. post τῇ Adler   6 ἀπωσμέ-
νοις] ἀποσπωμένοις SR67 et alii ‖ αὐτῆς] αὑτῆς B i.t.   7 αὑτῇ suppl. Amyot: lac. 5 lit. E, 9 lit. B: ἴδιον καὶ Wyt. in app.: lac. del. Raing.: αὑτῇ Ch. ‖ προσήκοντα E: προσήκονται B   8 καὶ προσφέ-
ρει ἐκεῖνον· Amyot: καὶ φέρει πρὸς ἐκεῖνον EB: κατωφερῆ πρὸς ἐκείνην, forte probabilius καὶ φέρει πως ἐκεῖνον Wyt. in app.: κατωφερῆ πρὸς τὸ οἰκεῖον Emp.: καὶ φέρει πρὸς τὸ οἰκεῖον Bern. in app.: καὶ φέρει προσκείμενον Kron.: κατωφερῆ πρὸς οἰκεῖον Ch.   9–10 ἀπ' ἀρχῆς Ald. Basil.: ἀπαρχῆς EB   10 που SR67: τοῦ EB   11 αὑτὸ RJ94: αὐτὸ EB   12 αὑτοῦ] αὐτοῦ Wyt. et alii ‖ συμπε-
πεδημένον punct. corr. Steph.: συμπεπεδημένον. EB   17 τοῦτο] ταὐτὸ Amyot et alii ‖ συνάγων] συνάγειν Xyl. ‖ σαφῶς] ἅ φῶς RJ94: καὶ φῶς et δὴ ἓν pro δεῖν Wyt. in app.: ἓν φῶς Kron.   18 καὶ[1] transp. post εἶναι RJ94: del. Wyt. in app. ‖ ἄνω φορῶν SR67: ἀναφορῶν EB: ἀνωφερῶν RJ94: ἀναφόρων Raing.   22 βαρέσι SR67: βαθέσι EB   25 βυθόν] εἰς add. ante βυθόν Wyt. in app. et alii ‖ καταδεδυκυῖαν E: καταδεδυκυίαν; B

they say that other people bring the moon close to the upper region, even though it is earth, by placing it not where the center is. Yet if every heavy body converges to the same point and is compressed with all its parts upon its center, it is no more as center of the sum of things than as a whole that the earth would appropriate the heavy bodies that are parts of it; and ... of falling bodies proves that the earth is by no means in the center of the cosmos but that those bodies which when thrust away from the earth fall back to it again have some affinity and cohesion with it. For such as the sun turns towards itself the parts of that which is made of the same nature, so the earth, as it corresponds ⟨to it⟩, receives and adds the stone, from which it follows that each of these, in due time, becomes one and unites with it. However, if there is a body which has not been assigned to the earth from the beginning nor torn appart from it, but had somehow by itself a constitution and nature of its own, as they would say is the moon, what prevents it to be separate and remain in itself compressed and bound together by its own parts? In fact, it is not even proven that the earth is the center of the universe and the pressing and firmness of things here upon the earth anticipates the way in which it is plausible that things there, falling on the moon, remain there; and so he who pushes together all the earthy and heavy things towards a single place and makes them parts of one single body, I do not see why he does not, out of the same necessity, parallel this in turn with the light things, but allows so many separate concentrations of fire and, while not collecting all the stars towards it, clearly thinks that there must also be a body common to all things that move upwards and are fiery.

9. But the sun is uncountable myriads away from the upper revolution, so you say, Apollonides," said I, "and Phosphorus and Stilbon above it and the rest of planets marching below the fixed stars move at great distances from each other, but still for the heavy and earthy objects you think that the cosmos provides no open space or gaps in itself—you see how ridiculous it is for us to deny that the moon is earth because it stands far from the lower region but to affirm that it is a star, even though we see it driven away from the upper revolution by so many thousands of myriads, as if sunk into an

B  μέν γε ἄστρων κατω|τέρω τοσοῦτόν ἐστιν, ὅσον οὐκ ἄν τις εἴποι μέτρον, ἀλλ' ἐπι-
λείπουσιν ὑμᾶς τοὺς μαθηματικοὺς ἐκλογιζομένους οἱ ἀριθμοί· τῆς δὲ γῆς τρόπον
τινὰ ψαύει καὶ περιφερομένη πλησίον,

ἅρματος ὥσπερ ἀν' ἴχνος ἑλίσσεται,

φησὶν Ἐμπεδοκλῆς,                                                                                       5

ἥ τε παρ' ἄκραν ...

Οὐδὲ γὰρ τὴν σκιὰν αὐτῆς ὑπερβάλλει πολλάκις ἐπὶ μικρὸν αἱρομένην τῷ παμμέ-
γεθες εἶναι τὸ φωτίζον, ἀλλ' οὕτως ἔοικεν ἐν χρῷ καὶ σχεδὸν ἐν ἀγκάλαις τῆς γῆς
περιπολεῖν, ὥστε ἀντιφράττεσθαι πρὸς τὸν ἥλιον ὑπ' αὐτῆς, μὴ ὑπεραίρουσα τὸν
C  σκιερὸν καὶ χθόνιον καὶ νυκτέριον τοῦτον τόπον, ὅς γῆς κλῆρός ἐστι. Διὸ | λεκτέον   10
οἶμαι θαρροῦντας ἐν τῆς γῆς ὅροις εἶναι τὴν σελήνην ὑπὸ τῶν ἄκρων αὐτῆς ἐπιπρο-
σθουμένην.

10. Σκόπει δὲ τοὺς ἄλλους ἀφεὶς ἀπλανεῖς καὶ πλάνητας, ἃ δείκνυσιν Ἀρίσταρ-
χος ἐν τῷ περὶ μεγεθῶν καὶ ἀποστημάτων, ὅτι τὸ τοῦ ἡλίου ἀπόστημα τοῦ ἀποστή-
ματος τῆς σελήνης, ὃ ἀφέστηκεν ἡμῶν, πλέον μὲν ἢ ὀκτωκαιδεκαπλάσιον, ἔλαττον   15
δὲ ἢ εἰκοσαπλάσιόν ἐστι· καίτοι ὁ τὴν σελήνην ἐπὶ μήκιστον αἴρων ἀπέχειν φησὶν
ἡμῶν ἓξ καὶ πεντηκονταπλάσιον τῆς ἐκ τοῦ κέντρου τῆς γῆς· αὕτη δ' ἐστὶ τεσσάρων
μυριάδων καὶ κατὰ τοὺς μέσως ἀναμετροῦντας καὶ ἀπὸ ταύτης συλλογιζομένους
D  ἀ|πέχει ὁ ἥλιος τῆς σελήνης πλέον ἢ τετρακισχιλίας τριάκοντα μυριάδας· οὕτως
ἀπῴκισται τοῦ ἡλίου διὰ βάρος καὶ τοσοῦτο τῇ γῇ προσκεχώρηκεν ὥστε, εἰ τοῖς    20
τόποις τὰς οὐσίας διαιρετέον, ἡ γῆς μοῖρα καὶ χώρα προσκαλεῖται σελήνην καὶ τοῖς
περὶ γῆν πράγμασι καὶ σώμασιν ἐπίδικός ἐστι κατὰ ἀγχιστείαν καὶ γειτνίασιν. Καὶ
οὐθέν, οἶμαι, πλημμελοῦμεν ὅτι τοῖς ἄνω προσαγορευομένοις βάθος τοσοῦτο καὶ
διάστημα διδόντες, ἀπολείπομέν τινα καὶ τῷ κάτω περιδρομὴν καὶ πλάτος ὅσον
ἐστὶν ἀπὸ γῆς ἐπὶ σελήνην· οὔτε γὰρ ὁ τὴν ἄκραν ἐπιφάνειαν τοῦ οὐρανοῦ μόνην    25
E  ἄνω, τἄλλα δὲ κάτω | προσαγορεύων ἅπαντα μέτριός ἐστιν, οὔτε ὁ τῇ γῇ, μᾶλ-
λον δὲ ὁ τῷ κέντρῳ, τὸ κάτω περιγράφων ἀνεκτός· ἀλλὰ καὶ κινητικό(ν) ταύτῃ

---

1 ὅσον ... μέτρον E et B s.l.: ὅσω ... μέτρῳ B    2 ὑμᾶς Xyl.: ἡμᾶς EB    4 ὥσπερ ἀν' ἴχνος ἑλίσσεται
Wyt. in app.: ὥσπερ ἴχνος ἀνελίσσεται EB: ὡς πέρι χνοίη ἑλίσσεται Panz.    6 ἥ τε παρ' DK: ἥ τε
περὶ EB: ἥδε περὶ RJ94: ἡ περὶ Wyt. in app. ‖ lac. 20 lit. E, 26 lit. B: lac. del. Basil.: νύσσαν ἐλαυ-
νομένη vel γαῖαν ἐλ. suppl. DK    7 αἱρομένην RJ94: αἱρομένη EB    10 νυκτέριον E: νυκτερινὸν B
11 ἐν τῆς γῆς ὅροις E s.l.: ἐν τοῖς γῆς ὅροις EB: ἐν τοῖς τῆς γῆς ὅροις Ald. Basil.: ἐν τῆς τοῖς γῆς ὅροις
Dübn.    16 ἀπέχειν B s.l.: ἀπέχει EB    17 αὕτη B: αὐτὴ E    18 συλλογιζομένους] συλλογιζομέ-
νοις Steph. et alii    21 χώρα RJ94: ὥρα EB    27 κινητικὸν suppl. Raing.: κινητικο vac. 2 lit. EB:
κινητικωτάτην καὶ μονιμωτάτην δεῖ ποιεῖν τὴν τάξιν, ἄλλως τε κ.τ.λ. suppl. Wyt. in app.: κινητικοῦ
ταύτῃ διαστήματος Emp.: κἀκείνη τι καὶ pro καὶ κινητικὸ Bern. in app. (sec. Madv. καὶ ἐκείνῃ καὶ)

abyss. It is so far beneath the stars that no one could tell the distance, numbers escape you astronomers when you try to calculate it; in a certain way the moon grazes the earth and revolving close to it,

> 'like a chariot's track reverses the direction of motion,'

Empedocles says,

> 'near the post ...'

Indeed, often the moon does not even surpass the shadow of the earth—which extends very little due to the great size of the illuminating body—but seems to turn around so close and almost within the arms of the earth, so as to be protected from the sun by it, since the moon does not go beyond this shadowy, terrestrial, and nocturnal place that is the earth's share. For this we shall say with confidence, I think, that the moon is within the boundaries of the earth, given that it is obscured/blinded by its edges.

10. But, letting aside the other fixed stars and planets, look at what Aristarchus proves in *On Sizes and Distances*, that 'the distance of the sun in comparison to the distance of the moon—what separates them from us—is more than 18 times and less than 20 times.' However, the highest estimate of the moon's distance from us is 56 times the radius of the earth; this radius is of four myriads according to the mean estimations and, if we calculate from such estimation, the sun is more than four thousand and 30 myriads away from the moon. So far has the moon migrated from the sun due to its weight and so close has it moved to the earth that, if we shall distribute properties according to locations, the share and location of the earth lays litigation against the moon and the latter legally belongs to the affairs and bodies of earth on account of its kinship and vicinity. And I think we do not err at all when, conceding such a height and a distance to the things so-called 'up', we also grant some space to what is 'down' for its revolution and width, as much as the distance from the earth to the moon; because just as the one who calls 'up' only the outermost surface of the heaven and everything else 'down' lacks moderation altogether, so is not tolerable he who delimits what is 'down' to the earth, or rather to its center; but some movable extension must be granted here too, given that the universe permits it

διάστημα τὸ δέον ἐπιχωροῦντος τοῦ κόσμου διὰ μέγεθος· πρὸς δὲ τὸν ἀξιοῦντα πᾶν εὐθὺς ἄνω καὶ μετέωρον εἶναι τὸ ἀπὸ τῆς γῆς, ἕτερος ἀντηχεῖ πάλιν, εὐθὺς εἶναι κάτω τὸ ἀπὸ τῆς ἀπλανοῦς περιφορᾶς.

11. Ὅλως δὲ πῶς λέγεται καὶ τίνος ἡ γῆ μέση κεῖται; Τὸ γὰρ πᾶν ἄπειρόν ἐστι, τῷ δὲ ἀπείρῳ μήτε ἀρχὴν ἔχοντι μήτε πέρας, οὐ προσήκει μέσον ἔχειν· πέρας γάρ τι καὶ τὸ μέσον, ἡ δὲ ἀπειρία περάτων στέρησις. Ὁ δὲ μὴ τοῦ παντὸς ἀλλὰ τοῦ κόσμου

F μέσην εἶναι | τὴν γῆν ἀποφαινόμενος ἡδύς ἐστιν, εἰ μὴ καὶ τὸν κόσμον αὐτὸν ἐνέχεσθαι ταῖς αὐταῖς ἀπορίαις νομίζει· τὸ γὰρ πᾶν οὐδὲ τούτῳ μέσην ἀπέλιπεν, ἀλλὰ

926A ἀνέστιος καὶ ἀνίδρυτός ἐστιν ἐν ἀπείρῳ κενῷ φερόμενος πρὸς οὐδὲν οἰκεῖον, ‖ ⟨ἢ⟩ εἰ ἄλλην τινὰ τοῦ μένειν εὑράμενος αἰτίαν ἔστηκεν, οὐ κατὰ τὴν τοῦ τόπου φύσιν, ὅμοια καὶ περὶ γῆς καὶ περὶ σελήνης εἰκάζειν τινὶ πάρεστιν ὡς ἑτέρᾳ τινὶ ψυχῇ καὶ φύσει μᾶλλον ⟨γίνονται⟩ διαφοραί, τῆς μὲν ἀτρεμούσης ἐνταῦθα, τῆς δ' ἐκεῖ φερομένης. Ἄνευ δὲ τούτων ὅρα μὴ μέγα τι λέληθεν αὐτούς· εἰ γὰρ ὁπωσοῦν καὶ ὅ τι ἂν ἐκτὸς γένηται τοῦ κέντρου τῆς γῆς ἄνω ἐστίν, οὐδέν ἐστι τοῦ κόσμου κάτω μέρος, ἀλλ' ἄνω, καὶ ἡ γῆ καὶ τὰ ἐπὶ γῆς καὶ πᾶν ἁπλῶς σῶμα τὸ κέντρῳ περιεστηκὸς ἢ περικείμενον ἄνω γίνεται, κάτω δέ, μόνον ὄν, ἕν, τὸ ἀσώματον σημεῖον ἐκεῖνο, ὃ

B πρὸς πᾶσαν ἀντικεῖσθαι τὴν τοῦ κόσμου φύσιν ἀναγ|καῖον, εἴ γε δὴ τὸ κάτω πρὸς τὸ ἄνω κατὰ φύσιν ἀντίκειται. Καὶ οὐ τοῦτο μόνον τὸ ἄτοπον, ἀλλὰ καὶ τὴν αἰτίαν ἀπόλλυσι τὰ βάρη δι' ἣν δεῦρο καταρρέπει καὶ φέρεται· σῶμα μὲν γὰρ οὐθέν ἐστι κάτω πρὸς ὃ κινεῖται, τὸ δὲ ἀσώματον οὔτε εἰκός, οὔτε βούλονται τοσαύτην ἔχειν δύναμιν ὥστε πάντα κατατείνειν ἐφ' ἑαυτὸ καὶ περὶ αὐτὸ συνέχειν· ἀλλ' ὅμως ἄλογον εὑρίσκεται καὶ μαχόμενον τοῖς πράγμασι τὸ ἄνω τὸν κόσμον ὅλον εἶναι, τὸ δὲ κάτω μηθέν, ἀλλ' ἢ πέρας ἀσώματον καὶ ἀδιάστατον, ἐκεῖνο δ' εὔλογον, ὡς λέγομεν

C ἡμεῖς, τῷ τε ἄνω χώραν καὶ τῷ κάτω πολλὴν καὶ πλάτος ἔχουσαν διῃρῆ|σθαι.

12. Οὐ μὴν ἀλλὰ θέντες, εἰ βούλει, παρὰ φύσιν ἐν οὐρανῷ τοῖς γεώδεσι τὰς κινήσεις ὑπάρχειν, ἀτρέμα, μὴ τραγικῶς, ἀλλὰ πράως σκοπῶμεν ὅτι τοῦτο τὴν σελήνην οὐ δείκνυσι γῆν μὴ οὖσαν, ἀλλὰ γῆν ὅπου μὴ πέφυκεν οὖσαν· ἐπεὶ καὶ τὸ πῦρ τὸ Αἰτναῖον ὑπὸ γῆν παρὰ φύσιν ἐστίν, ἀλλὰ πῦρ ἐστι, καὶ τὸ πνεῦμα τοῖς ἀσκοῖς περιληφθέν ἐστι μὲν ἀνωφερὲς φύσει καὶ κοῦφον, ἥκει δὲ ὅπου μὴ πέφυκεν ὑπ' ἀνάγκης· αὐτὴ δὲ ἡ ψυχή, πρὸς Διὸς" εἶπον "οὐ παρὰ φύσιν τῷ σώματι συνείρκται, βραδεῖ ταχεῖα καὶ ψυχρῷ πυρώδης, ὥσπερ ὑμεῖς φατε, καὶ ἀόρατος αἰσθητῷ; Διὰ

---

1 τὸ δέον] δοτέον Madv. et alii    4 κεῖται punct. corr. Xyl.: κεῖται. EB: κεῖσθαι; Kepl.    8 τούτῳ SR67: τοῦτο EB: τοῦτον RJ94 ‖ μέσην] μέσον RJ94 et alii    9 ἢ add. ante εἰ Kepl.: ἢ pro εἰ RJ94: δ' add. post εἰ Amyot    10 εὑράμενος αἰτίαν E: αἰτίαν εὑράμενος B    11 τινὶ¹ B et E s.l. ‖ ψυχῇ καὶ] ῥοπῇ καὶ Kepl.: del. Purser: τύχῃ καὶ Po.    12 γίνονται suppl. Raing. in app.: lac. 6 lit. E, 9 lit. B: αἱ Amyot: ψυχικῇ μᾶλλον ἢ φυσικῇ καὶ τοπικῇ, suppl. et διαφορᾷ corr. Wyt. in app.: ἢ τόπου et διαφορᾷ Bern.: ἢ τοπικῇ et διαφορᾷ Ch. ‖ δ ἐκεῖ Madv.: δὲ καὶ EB    13 ὁπωσοῦν] ὁπόσονουν Steph.: ὅτι ἂν καὶ ὁπωσοῦν Wyt. in app.: καὶ transp. ante ὁπωσοῦν Po.    15 τὸ] τῷ Raing.: τὸ τῷ Po. in app.    16 ὄν] del. Madv. et alii    21 αὐτὸ E: αὐτὸ B ‖ ἀλλ' ὅμως] ἄλλως δὲ Wyt. in app.: ἀλλ' ὅλως Dübn. et alii    30 εἶπον E: εἶπεν B

on account of its magnitude. Against he who asserts that everything away from the earth is automatically 'up' and 'suspended in the air', another one responds in turn that what is away from the revolution of the fixed stars is automatically 'down'.

11. All in all, how is the earth said to be situated in the middle and in the middle of what? The universe is infinite, and to the infinite—having no beginning nor boundary—does not pertain to have a middle; as the middle is some sort of boundary as well, but infinity is the privation of boundaries. He who affirms that the earth is not the middle of the universe but of the cosmos is ingenuous, if he does not think that the cosmos itself is also troubled with the same difficulties. In fact, the universe did not grant a middle for the cosmos either, but it is without hearth and base, in an infinite void, moving towards nothing of its own; ⟨or⟩ if it stays in place because it found some other reason to remain still, not because of the nature of its location, the same reasoning is allowed concerning the earth and the moon, as the differences rather ⟨appear⟩ due to another soul or nature, so one is immobile here, and the other is over there moving. This aside, see whether something important has not escaped them: indeed, if what exists, in any way possible, out of the center of the earth is 'up', there is no part of the cosmos 'down', but 'up', and the earth, the things on the earth, and every single body standing or lying around the center become 'up', and 'down' is only a being, one, that incorporeal point which necessarily opposes all nature of the cosmos, if truly 'down' and 'up' oppose each other by nature. And this is not the only nonsense, but it also destroys the cause for which heavy objects descend and move downwards—indeed there is no body 'down' towards which they move, and the incorporeal is neither likely nor would they want it to have such a power that all heavy objects tend towards it and remain around. But all the same, it proves to be illogical and in conflict with the facts for the whole cosmos to be 'up' and nothing 'down' except a boundary, incorporeal and with no extension; what is well reasoned, however, as we ourselves say, is that 'up' and 'down' is divided, each having much ample space.

12. Notwithstanding this, let us assume, if you want, that the motions which earthy objects have at their disposition in heaven are contrary to nature, and so imperturbably, with no drama but calmly, observe that this does not evince that the moon is not earth, but earth placed where it should not naturally be. Then again the fire of Aetna is below earth against nature, but it still is fire, and the air enclosed in goatskins, despite having an upward movement and being light by nature, finds itself there not by nature but out of necessity; and the very soul, by Zeus," I said, "is she not contrarily to nature constrained in a slow, cold, and perceivable body, though she is, as

D τοῦτο | οὖν σώματι ψυχὴν μὴ λέγωμεν εἶναι μηδὲ νοῦν, χρῆμα θεῖον, ὑπὸ βρίθους καὶ πάχους, οὐρανόν τε πάντα καὶ γῆν καὶ θάλασσαν ἐν ταὐτῷ περιπολοῦντα καὶ διιπτάμενον εἰς σάρκας ἥκειν καὶ νεῦρα καὶ μυελοὺς καὶ παθέων μυρίων μεστὰς ὑγρότητας; Ὁ δὲ Ζεὺς ὑμῖν οὗτος, οὐ τῇ μὲν αὑτοῦ φύσει χρώμενος ἕν ἐστι, μέγα πῦρ καὶ συνεχές; Νυνὶ δὲ ὑφεῖται καὶ κέκαμπται καὶ διεσχημάτισται, πᾶν χρῶμα  5
γεγονὼς καὶ γινόμενος ἐν ταῖς μεταβολαῖς· Ὥστε ὅρα καὶ σκόπει, δαιμόνιε, μὴ μεθιστὰς καὶ ἀπάγων ἕκαστον ὅπου πέφυκεν εἶναι διάλυσίν τινα κόσμου φιλοσοφῇς καὶ
E τὸ νεῖκος ἐπάγῃς τὸ | Ἐμπεδοκλέους τοῖς πράγμασι, μᾶλλον δὲ τοὺς παλαιοὺς κινῇς Τιτᾶνας ἐπὶ τὴν φύσιν καὶ Γίγαντας καὶ τὴν μυθικὴν ἐκείνην καὶ φοβερὰν ἀκοσμίαν καὶ πλημμέλειαν ἐπιδεῖν ποθῇς, χωρὶς τὸ βαρὺ πᾶν καὶ χωρὶς ... τὸ κοῦφον.  10

Ἔνθ' οὔτ' ἠελίοιο διείδεται ἀγλαὸν εἶδος·
οὐδὲ μὲν οὐδ' αἴης λάσιον γένος οὐδὲ θάλασσα,

ὥς φησιν Ἐμπεδοκλῆς· οὐ γῆ θερμότητος μετεῖχεν, οὐχ ὕδωρ πνεύματος, οὐκ ἄνω τι τῶν βαρέων, οὐ κάτω τι τῶν κούφων, ἀλλ' ἄκρατοι καὶ ἄστοργοι καὶ μονάδες
F αἱ τῶν ὅλων ἀρχαί, μὴ προσιέμεναι σύγκρισιν ἑτέρου | πρὸς ἕτερον μηδὲ κοινω-  15
νίαν, ἀλλὰ φεύγουσαι καὶ ἀποστρεφόμεναι καὶ φερόμεναι φορᾶς ἰδίας καὶ αὐθάδεις οὕτως εἶχον ὡς ἔχει πᾶν οὗ θεὸς ἄπεστι κατὰ Πλάτωνα· τουτέστιν ὡς ἔχει τὰ σώματα νοῦ καὶ ψυχῆς ἀπολιπούσης, ἄχρις οὗ τὸ ἱμερτὸν ἧκεν ἐπὶ τὴν φύσιν ἐκ
927A προνοίας, φιλότητος ἐγγενομένης καὶ Ἀφροδίτης καὶ ἔρωτος, || ὡς Ἐμπεδοκλῆς λέγει καὶ Παρμενίδης καὶ Ἡσίοδος, ἵνα καὶ τόπους ἀμείψαντα καὶ δυνάμεις ἀπ'  20
ἀλλήλων μεταλαβόντα, καὶ τὰ μὲν κινήσεως, τὰ δὲ μονῆς ἀνάγκαις ἐνδεθέντα καὶ καταβιασθέντα πρὸς τὸ βέλτιον ἐξ οὗ πέφυκεν ἐνδοῦναι καὶ μεταστῆναι ... ἁρμονίαν καὶ κοινωνίαν ἀπεργάσηται τοῦ παντός.

13. Εἰ μὲν γὰρ οὐδ' ἄλλο τι τῶν τοῦ κόσμου μερῶν παρὰ φύσιν ἔσχεν, ἀλλ' ἕκαστον ᾗ πέφυκε κεῖται, μηδεμιᾶς μεθιδρύσεως μηδὲ μετακοσμήσεως δεόμενον, μηδ'  25

---

1 λέγωμεν E: λέγομεν B ∥ εἶναι] ἐνεῖναι Herw. et alii ∥ μηδὲ νοῦν Madv.: μηδὲν οὐ EB: μηδενί RJ94: μηδεμίαν Kepl.: μηδὲ νοῦ Dübn.   1–2 ὑπὸ βρίθους καὶ πάχους] ἢ pro καὶ Ald.: ὑπὸ τοῦ ἀβριθοῦς καὶ ἀπαχοῦς vel ἄπο pro ὑπὸ Emp.: ἀήττητον add. ante ὑπὸ Po.: transp. post μυελοὺς Ch.   2 ταὐτῷ Bern.: ταυτῶ EB   3 διιπτάμενον Wyt. in app.: διιστάμενον EB   3–4 μεστὰς ὑγρότητας et punct. corr. Dübn.: μετὰ ὑγρότητος. EB: αἰτίαν add. Amyot: μετὰ ὑγρότητος; Ch.   4 ὑμῖν Xyl.: ἡμῖν EB ∥ αὑτοῦ E et B i.t.: αὐτοῦ B ∥ ἕν ἐστι E: ἔνεστι B   5 συνεχές] punct. corr. Ald. et alii ∥ Νυνὶ δὲ B: νυνίδε E ∥ χρῶμα] χρῆμα SR67 et alii   6 μεταβολαῖς B: μεταβολαῖς· E   10 lac. 8 lit. E, 4 lit. B: πᾶν suppl. RJ94: forte nil excidit, forte unum διαστήσας Wyt. in app.: τὸ βαρὺ ποιῶν καὶ χωρὶς Emp.: τιθεὶς Bern.: διαστὰν Po. in app.: θεὶς πᾶν Ch.   11 διείδεται Amyot: δεδίττεται EB: δεδίσκεται Karsten   12 γένος] δέμας Karsten: μένος Bergk: σθένος Emp.   18–19 ἐκ προνοίας] ἀπρονοίας Ald.: προνοίας RJ94 Basil.: ὄμμα προνοίας Emp.: ἔργον προνοίας Po. in app.   22 lac. 7 lit. EB: τὴν suppl. Amyot: lac. del. Xyl.1570: ἀρξάμενα Wyt. in app.: τάξιν καὶ Bern. in app.: ταύτην τὴν Raing. in app.: κόσμον καὶ vel σύγκρισιν καὶ Adler: τὰ σώματα Ch.   25 μηδεμιᾶς E: μὴ δὲ μιᾶς B

you people say, fast, fiery, and invisible? Because of this, shall we then deny that soul has body or that intellect, a divine thing, under the influence of weight and density, though it goes around and traverses in an instant heaven, earth, and sea in its flight, has passed into flesh, sinew, nerves, and humidities full of thousands affections? And that Zeus of yours, is it not while in his own nature single, a great and continuous fire? But now he is slackened and subdued and transformed, having become and becoming every color in the course of his changes? Thus look and consider, my dear, when arranging and leading each thing where it naturally corresponds, to not defend a philosophy that brings some sort of dissolution of the cosmos and to bring the strife of Empedocles upon things, or rather to provoke the ancient Titans and Giants against nature and to long to look at that mythical and dreadful disorder and discord, once everything is without what is heavy and without ... what is light.

> 'Hence the bright aspect of the sun is not discerned, | not the dense lineage of earth either, nor sea',

as Empedocles says. Earth did not participate of heat, nor water of air; none of the heavy objects was above, none of the light ones below, but the principles of all things were uncontrolled, disagreeable, and solitary, not going towards a coalition or association with one another, but avoiding each other and taking opposite directions and moving with their particular and arrogant motions, they were in such a condition as everything is from which God is absent, according to Plato—namely, as bodies devoid of intellect and soul. This, until desire came over nature due to providence, thus appearing affection, Aphrodite, and Eros, as Empedocles says, and Parmenides and also Hesiod, so that in exchanging places and trading powers, and by being constrained, some to be in motion and some to be at rest, and compelled to give way and shift from what is natural towards the better, they may produce a concord and community of the whole.

13. In fact, if not a single one of the parts of the cosmos was ever contrary to nature, but each one lies where is natural to it, in need of no shifting or rearrangement, and without having had the need from the beginning either,

ἐν ἀρχῇ δεηθέν, ἀπορῶ τί τῆς προνοίας ἔργον ἐστίν, ἢ τίνος γέγονε ποιητὴς καὶ
πατὴρ δημιουργὸς ὁ Ζεὺς ὁ ἀριστοτέ|χνας. Οὐ γὰρ ἐν στρατοπέδῳ τακτικῶν ὄφε-
λος, εἴπερ εἰδείη τῶν στρατιωτῶν ἕκαστος ἀφ' ἑαυτοῦ τάξιν τε καὶ χώραν καὶ
καιρὸν οὗ δεῖ λαβεῖν καὶ διαφυλάσσειν, οὐδὲ κηπουρῶν οὐδὲ οἰκοδόμων, εἰ πῇ μὲν
αὐτὸ τὸ ὕδωρ ἀφ' αὑτοῦ πέφυκεν ἐπεῖναι τοῖς δεομένοις καὶ κατάρδειν ἐπιρρέον,
πῇ δὲ πλίνθοι καὶ ξύλα καὶ λίθοι ταῖς κατὰ φύσιν χρώμενα τροπαῖς καὶ νεύσεσιν
ἐξ ἑαυτῶν καταλαμβάνειν τὴν προσήκουσαν ἁρμονίαν καὶ χώραν. Εἰ δὲ οὗτος μὲν
ἄντικρυς ἀναιρεῖ τὴν πρόνοιαν ὁ λόγος, τῷ θεῷ δὲ ἡ τάξις τῶν ὄντων προσήκει καὶ
διαιρεῖν, τί θαυμαστὸν οὕτω τετάχθαι καὶ διηρμόσθαι τὴν φύσιν, ὡς | ἐνταῦθα μὲν
πῦρ, ἐκεῖ δὲ ἄστρα, καὶ πάλιν ἐνταῦθα μὲν γῆν, ἄνω δὲ σελήνην ἱδρῦσθαι βεβαι-
οτέρῳ τοῦ κατὰ φύσιν, τῷ κατὰ λόγον δεσμωτηρίῳ ληφθεῖσαν; Ὡς εἴ γε πάντα
δεῖ ταῖς κατὰ φύσιν ῥοπαῖς χρῆσθαι καὶ φέρεσθαι καθὸ πέφυκε, μηδ' ἥλιος κυκλο-
φορείσθω, μήτε φωσφόρος, μηδὲ τῶν ἄλλων ἀστέρων μηδείς· ἄνω γὰρ οὐ κύκλῳ
τὰ κοῦφα καὶ πυροειδῆ κινεῖσθαι πέφυκεν. Εἰ δὲ τοιαύτην ἐξαλλαγὴν ἡ φύσις ἔχει
παρὰ τὸν τόπον, ὥστε ἐνταῦθα μὲν ἄνω φαίνεσθαι φερόμενον τὸ πῦρ, ὅταν δὲ εἰς
τὸν οὐρανὸν παραγένηται τῇ δίνῃ συμπεριστρέφεσθαι, τί θαυμαστὸν εἰ καὶ τοῖς
βαρέσι καὶ | γεώδεσιν ἐκγενομένοις συμβέβηκεν ὡσαύτως εἰς ἄλλο κινήσεως εἶδος
ὑπὸ τοῦ περιέχοντος ἐκνενικῆσθαι; Οὐ γὰρ δὴ τῶν μὲν ἐλαφρῶν τὴν ἄνω φορὰν
ἀφαιρεῖσθαι τῷ οὐρανῷ κατὰ φύσιν ἐστί, τῶν δὲ βαρέων καὶ κάτω ῥεπόντων οὐ
δύναται κρατεῖν, ἀλλ' ... ποτε ἐκεῖνα δυνάμει καὶ ταῦτα μετακοσμήσας ἐχρήσατο
τῇ φύσει αὐτῶν ἐπὶ τὸ βέλτιον.

14. Οὐ μὴν ἀλλ' εἴ γε δεῖ τὰς καταδεδουλωμένας ἕξεις ⟨καὶ⟩ δόξας ἀφέντας ἤδη
τὸ φαινόμενον ἀδεῶς λέγειν, οὐδὲν ἔοικεν ὅλου μέρος αὐτὸ καθ' ἑαυτὸ τάξιν ἢ θέσιν
ἢ κίνησιν ἰδίαν ἔχειν, ᾗ ἄν τις ἁπλῶς κατὰ φύσιν προσαγορεύσειεν· ἀλλ' | ὅταν ἕκα-
στον, οὗ χάριν γέγονε καὶ πρὸς ὃ πέφυκεν ἢ πεποίηται, τούτῳ παρέχῃ χρησίμως
καὶ οἰκείως κινούμενον ἑαυτὸ καὶ πάσχον ἢ ποιοῦν ἢ διακείμενον ὡς ἐκείνῳ πρὸς
σωτηρίαν ἢ κάλλος ἢ δύναμιν ἐπιτήδειόν ἐστι, τότε δοκεῖ τὴν κατὰ φύσιν χώραν
ἔχειν καὶ κίνησιν καὶ διάθεσιν. Ὁ γοῦν ἄνθρωπος, ὡς ἐπὶ τῶν ὄντων ἕτερον κατὰ
φύσιν γεγονώς, ἄνω μὲν ἔχει τὰ ἐμβριθῆ καὶ γεώδη, μάλιστα περὶ τὴν κεφαλήν, ἐν

---

2 Οὐ B: υ E    5 ἀφ αὑτοῦ B: ἀπ' αὐτοῦ E ‖ ἐπεῖναι] ἐπιέναι Amyot et alii: ἐπιρρεῖν RJ94    6 τροπαῖς] ῥοπαῖς RJ94 et alii    9 διαιρεῖν] διαίρεσις Amyot: διαίρεσις vel διάκρισις Kepl.: τὸ διαιρεῖν Dübn. et alii    10 μὲν² om. E    11 δεσμωτηρίῳ ληφθεῖσαν punct. corr. RJ94: δεσμωτηρίῳ ληφθεῖσαν.: δεσμῷ σωτηρίως vel δεσμῷ περιληφθεῖσαν Wyt. in app. (δεσμῷ περιληφθεῖσαν; Dübn. et alii)    12 καθὸ] καθ' ὃ Steph. et alii    15 φαίνεσθαι E: φέρεσθαι B    16 παραγένηται B et E s.l.: γένηται E    17 ἐκγενομένοις] ἐκεῖ γενομένοις Wyt. in app. et alii    18 ἐκνενικῆσθαι punct. corr. RJ94: ἐκνενικῆσθαι· EB    20 vac. 2 lit. EB: ἀλλὰ suppl. Ald. Basil.: ᾗ Kepl.: τῇ αὐτῇ Wyt. in app.    22 καὶ suppl. Xyl.1570: lac. 4 lit. E, 6 lit. B: καὶ τὰς Amyot: forte nil excidit Wyt. in app.: ἕξει pro ἕξεις et lac. del. Dübn.: ἕξει καὶ ἔθει corr. et suppl. Bern. in app. (sec. Madv. ἔθει): ἕξει σαθρᾷ Po. in app.    24 ᾗ] ἣν RJ94 Basil. et alii    25 παρέχῃ SR67: παρέχειν EB: παρέχει Basil.: μέλλῃ add. ante παρέχειν Po.    28 ἐπί] εἴ τι Xyl.1570 et alii    29 τὰ E: τὸν B

I wonder what is the work of providence, or of what is 'maker and demiurge' Zeus 'the master craftsman'. For there is no utility for tactitians in an army, if each one of the soldiers knew by himself the order, place, and moment he must take and maintain, nor for gardeners or builders, if here water all of itself naturally remains with the things that require it and irrigates them with its stream, and there bricks, wood beams, and stones, by following their natural directions and inclinations, assume of themselves the appropriate coordination and position. But if this idea eliminates straightaway providence, and the ordering and division of beings corresponds to God, what marvel is there that nature is so structured and arranged too, so fire is here but the stars there, and in turn earth is here but the moon is established up there by nature, held by the prison of reason, more stable than that of nature? Accordingly, if everything must really attend its natural inclinations and move according to nature, you shall not make the sun travel in circle, nor Phosphorus, nor any of the other stars—because in the upper region it is not natural for light and fiery bodies to move in circles. Now, if nature possesses such a variation depending on the location that fire, even though here manifestly moves upwards, when it has reached heaven goes around with the rotation, what wonder is there if this should happen as well to the heavy and earthy bodies that appeared there, so that they similarly take a different kind of motion when they have been won over by the environment? It surely cannot be the case that it is natural for heaven to eliminate the upward motion of light objects but cannot rule over heavy things with a downward inclination—on the contrary, rearranging with its influence sometimes those and sometimes these, it employed their own nature for the better.

14. Nevertheless, if we are finally to throw off the habits ⟨and⟩ opinions that have enslaved us and to fearlessly say what appears to be the case, no part of a whole all by itself seems to have any order, position, or motion for which someone could call it unconditionally natural; but when each part moves itself in a useful and proper manner owing to that for the sake of which it has been born, for which it has naturally appeared or been made, and suffers, acts or is disposed so that it is convenient to the safeguard, or the beauty, or the power of that thing, then, I think, it has a location, movement and disposition according to nature. In any case, man, who has been born according to nature above any other being, has the heavy and earthy parts above, mainly around the head, and in the middle the warm and fiery parts;

δὲ τοῖς μέσοις τὰ θερμὰ καὶ πυρώδη· τῶν δὲ ὀδόντων, οἱ μὲν ἄνωθεν, οἱ δὲ κάτωθεν
ἐκφύονται καὶ οὐδέτεροι παρὰ φύσιν ἔχουσιν, οὐδὲ τοῦ πυρός, τὸ μὲν ἄνω περὶ τὰ
F ὄμ|ματα ἀποστίλβον κατὰ φύσιν ἐστί, τὸ δ' ἐν κοιλίᾳ καὶ καρδίᾳ παρὰ φύσιν, ἀλλ'
ἕκαστον οἰκείως καὶ χρησίμως τέτακται·

ναὶ μὴν κηρύκων τε λιθορρίνων χελύων τε 5
καὶ παντὸς ὀστρέου φύσιν, ὥς φησιν ὁ Ἐμπεδοκλῆς, καταμανθάνων,
ἔνθ' ὄψει χθόνα χρωτὸς ὑπέρτατα ναιετάουσαν·
καὶ οὐ πιέζει τὸ λιθῶδες οὐδὲ καταθλίβει τὴν ἕξιν ἐπικείμενον,

928A ‖ οὐδέ γε πάλιν τὸ θερμὸν ὑπὸ κουφότητος εἰς τὴν ἄνω χώραν ἀποπτάμενον οἴχε-
ται, μέμικται δέ πως πρὸς ἄλληλα καὶ συντέτακται κατὰ τὴν ἑκάστου φύσιν. 10

15. Ὥσπερ εἰκὸς ἔχειν καὶ τὸν κόσμον, εἴ γε δὴ ζῷόν ἐστι, πολλαχοῦ γῆν ἔχοντα,
πολλαχοῦ δὲ πῦρ καὶ ὕδωρ καὶ πνεῦμα, οὐκ ἐξ ἀνάγκης ἀποτεθλιμμένον, ἀλλὰ
λόγῳ διακεκοσμημένον. Οὐδὲ γὰρ ὀφθαλμὸς ἐνταῦθα τοῦ σώματός ἐστιν ὑπὸ κου-
φότητος ἐκπιεσθείς, οὐδὲ ἡ καρδία τῷ βάρει ὀλισθοῦσα πέπτωκεν εἰς τὸ στῆθος,
ἀλλ' ὅτι βέλτιον ἦν οὕτως ἑκάτερον τετάχθαι. Μὴ τοίνυν μήτε τῶν τοῦ κόσμου 15
B μερῶν νομίζωμεν, μήτε γῆν | ἐνταῦθα κεῖσθαι συμπεσοῦσαν διὰ βάρος, μήτε τὸν
ἥλιον, ὡς ᾤετο Μητρόδωρος ὁ Χῖος, εἰς τὴν ἄνω χώραν ἀσκοῦ δίκην ὑπὸ κουφό-
τητος ἐκτεθλῖφθαι, μήτε τοὺς ἄλλους ἀστέρας, ὥσπερ ἐν ζυγῷ σταθμοῦ, διαφορᾷ
ῥέψαντας ἐν οἷς εἰσι γεγονέναι τόποις· ἀλλὰ τοῦ κατὰ λόγον κρατοῦντος, οἱ μέν,
ὥσπερ ὄμματα φωσφόρα, τῷ προσώπῳ τοῦ παντὸς ἐνδεδεμένοι περιπολοῦσιν, 20
ἥλιος δὲ καρδίας ἔχων δύναμιν, ὥσπερ αἷμα καὶ πνεῦμα, διαπέμπει καὶ διασκε-
δάννυσιν ἐξ ἑαυτοῦ θερμότητα καὶ φῶς, γῇ δὲ καὶ θαλάσσῃ χρῆται κατὰ φύσιν ὁ
C κόσμος ὅσα κοιλίᾳ καὶ κύστει ζῷον. Σελήνη δὲ ἡλίου | μεταξὺ καὶ γῆς, ὥσπερ καρ-
δίας καὶ κοιλίας ἧπαρ ἤ τι μαλθακὸν ἄλλο σπλάγχνον, ἐγκειμένη τήν τε ἄνωθεν
ἀλέαν ἐνταῦθα διαπέμπει καὶ τὰς ἐντεῦθεν ἀναθυμιάσεις πέψει τινὶ καὶ καθάρ- 25
σει λεπτύνουσα περὶ ἑαυτὴν ἀναδίδωσιν· εἰ δὲ καὶ πρὸς ἄλλα τὸ γεῶδες αὐτῆς
καὶ στερέμνιον ἔχει τινὰ πρόσφορον χρείαν, ἄδηλον ἡμῖν· ἐν παντὶ δὲ κρατεῖται
βέλτιον τοῦτο κατηναγκασμένον. Τί γὰρ οὕτω λάβωμεν ἐξ ὧν ἐκεῖνοι λέγουσι,
τὸ εἰκός; Λέγουσι δὲ τοῦ αἰθέρος, τὸ μὲν αὐγοειδὲς καὶ λεπτὸν ὑπὸ μανότητος

---

2 ἐκφύονται E et B s.l.: ἐμφύονται B  5 χελύων τε RJ94: χελωνῶν τε EB: τε χελωνῶν RJ94: τε χελωνῶν τε Amyot  15 μήτε] μηδὲ Dübn. et alii  18 ζυγῷ σταθμοῦ E: ζυγῳ σταθμοῦς B: ζυγοσταθμοῦ Ald. Basil. et alii  19 ῥέψαντας B: ῥέψαντος E  24 σπλάγχνον E: σπλάγχνον B  27–28 κρατεῖται βέλτιον τοῦτο κατηναγκασμένον] τὸ pro τοῦτο SR67: τοῦ κατηναγκασμένου Xyl.[1570]: κρατεῖ τὸ βέλτιον τοῦ κατηναγκασμένου Wyt. in app. et alii  28 γὰρ] εἰ add. post γὰρ Kepl.: οὐχ add. post γὰρ Po.: γὰρ; Raing.  29 εἰκός punct. corr. Wyt.: εἰκός. EB

and concerning the teeth, some grow from above and some from below and neither behaves contrary to nature; nor concerning fire, the one above shining in the eyes is natural yet the one in the belly and in the heart is contrary to nature, but each has been allocated properly and usefully. Now, precisely examining the nature of

'shellfish and turtles with stone-like skin'

and all crustacean, as Empedocles says,

'you shall see earth located above the skin';

and the stony matter does not oppress or crush the constitution which it covers, nor in turn does the heat disappear flying away to the upper region because of its lightness, but they have been mixed with each other somehow and combined according to the nature of each.

15. It is likely that such is the situation for the cosmos also, if it really is a living being, it includes earth in many places, in others fire and water and air, not having been expelled by force but arranged by reason. And so too the eye is not where it is here in the body by having been pressed up by its lightness, nor has the heart fallen in the chest, having slipped down due to its weight, but because it was better to arrange each in this way. Consequently, let us not believe this about the parts of the cosmos, not that earth lies here after having fallen due to its weight, not that the sun, as thought Metrodorus of Chios, was expulsed towards the upper region in the manner of an inflated skin because of its lightness, nor that the remaining stars attained the positions in which they are reclining due to a difference of weight, as in a scale; but, under the rule of reason, some stars, as 'radiant eyes', revolve fixed to the face of the universe, and the sun, having the power of the heart, dispatches and disperses from itself heat and light, as if it were blood and breath, and the cosmos makes use of the earth and the sea according to nature, just as a living being uses its bowels and bladder. And the moon, placed inbetween the sun and the earth, as the liver or one of the other soft viscera between heart and bowels, sends down here the warmth from above and dispatches in turn the exhalations from this region upwards, rarefying them in itself in a sort of fermentation and purification. Whether the earthiness and solidity in it have an appropriate use for other ends as well is unclear to us. In any case, at all times this is much better under control, if need be. So, what probability can we really take from what these people say? They say that the luminous and tenuous part of ether has become sky on account of its subtility and the

οὐρανὸν γεγονέναι, τὸ δὲ πυκνωθὲν καὶ συνειληθέν, ἄστρα· τούτων δὲ τὸ νωθρό-
D  τατον εἶναι τὴν σε|λήνην καὶ θολερώτατον. Ἀλλ' ὅμως ὁρᾶν πάρεστιν οὐκ ἀποκε-
κριμένην τοῦ αἰθέρος τὴν σελήνην, ἀλλ' ἔτι πολλῷ ἐν τῷ περὶ αὐτὴν ἐμφερομένην,
πολλὴν δὲ ὑφ' ἑαυτὴν ἔχουσαν ἀνέμων ⟨δίνην⟩ δινεῖσθαι καὶ κομήτας· οὕτως οὐ ταῖς
ῥοπαῖς σεσήκωται κατὰ βάρος καὶ κουφότητα τῶν σωμάτων ἕκαστον, ἀλλ' ἑτέρῳ    5
λόγῳ κεκόσμηται."
    16. Λεχθέντων δὲ τούτων, κἀμοῦ τῷ Λευκίῳ τὸν λόγον παραδιδόντος ἐπὶ τὰς
ἀποδείξεις βαδίζοντος τοῦ δόγματος, Ἀριστοτέλης μειδιάσας, "μαρτύρομαι" εἶπεν
E  "ὅτι τὴν πᾶσαν ἀντιλογίαν πεποίησαι πρὸς τοὺς αὐτὴν μὲν | ἡμίπυρον εἶναι τὴν
σελήνην ὑποτιθεμένους, κοινῇ δὲ τῶν σωμάτων, τὰ μὲν ἄνω, τὰ δὲ κάτω ῥέπειν ἐξ    10
ἑαυτῶν φάσκοντας· εἰ δ' ἔστι τις ὁ λέγων κύκλῳ τε κινεῖσθαι κατὰ φύσιν τὰ ἄστρα
καὶ πολὺ παρηλλαγμένης οὐσίας εἶναι τῶν τεττάρων, οὐδὲ ἀπὸ τύχης ἦλθεν ἐπὶ
μνήμην ὑμῖν, ὥστε ἐμέ τε πραγμάτων ἀπηλλάχθαι." Καὶ ⟨ὁ⟩ Λεύκιος ... "ὠγαθὲ
εἶπεν "ἀλλὰ τὰ ἄλλα μὲν ἴσως ἄστρα καὶ τὸν ὅλον οὐρανὸν εἴς τινα φύσιν καθα-
ρὰν καὶ εἰλικρινῆ καὶ τῆς κατὰ πάθος ἀπηλλαγμένην μεταβολῆς τιθεμένοις ὑμῖν    15
F  καὶ κύκλον ἄγουσι, δι' οὗ καὶ ἀτελευτήτου | περιφορᾶς ... οὐκ ἄν τις ἔν γε τῷ
νῦν διαμάχοιτο, καίτοι μυρίων οὐσῶν ἀποριῶν· ὅταν δὲ καταβαίνων ὁ λόγος οὕτω
θίγῃ τῆς σελήνης, οὐκέτι φυλάττει τὴν ἀπάθειαν ἐν αὐτῇ καὶ τὸ κάλλος ἐκείνου
τοῦ σώματος, ἀλλ' ἵνα τὰς ἄλλας ἀνωμαλίας καὶ διαφορὰς ἀφῶμεν, αὐτὸ τοῦτο τὸ
διαφαινόμενον πρόσωπον, πάθει τινὶ τῆς οὐσίας ἢ ἀναμίξει πως ἑτέρας ἐπιγέγονε·    20
πάσχει δέ τι καὶ τὸ μιγνύμενον, ἀποβάλλει γὰρ τὸ εἰλικρινὲς βίᾳ τοῦ χείρονος ἀνα-
929A  πιμπλάμενον. ‖ Αὐτῆς δὲ νώθειαν καὶ τάχους ἀμβλύτητα καὶ τὸ θερμὸν ἀδρανὲς
καὶ ἀμαυρόν, ⟨ᾧ⟩ κατὰ τὸν Ἴωνα

    μέλας οὐ πεπαίνεται βότρυς,

---

2–3 ἀποκεκριμένην RJ94 Basil.: ἀποκεκριμένου E: ἀποκεκρυμμένου B    3 ἐν] transp. ante πολλῷ
Amyot: del. Dübn.: μὲν pro ἐν Bens.    4 πολλὴν] πολὺν Amyot (πολλὴν sic) ‖ δίνην supplevi:
lac. 25 lit. EB: αἰθεροειδῆ οὐσίαν τῷ καὶ αὐτοῖς RJ94: χώραν Amyot: βίαν, ὑφ' ἧς ἄλλα τε εἰκός ἐστι
Wyt. in app.: ἀνέμῳ ἐνδινεῖσθαι καὶ κομήταις corr. et lac. del. Emp.: τε ῥιπὰς ὑφ' ὧν (aut αἷς) ἄλλα τε
εἰκὸς Bern. in app.: ᾧ σώματα γεώδη ὑπ' add. ante ἀνέμων et ἀνενεχθέντα πωγωνίας αὐτοί φασιν
συμπεριδινεῖσθαι suppl. Adler: βίαν ὑφ' ὧν ἐκθλιβέντας φασὶν ἐν τῷ αἰθέρι Po. in app.: ἐν ᾧ pro
ἀνέμων (sec. Madv.) et λέγουσιν αὐτοὶ τοὺς πωγωνίας suppl. Ch.    13 ὑμῖν Amyot: ἡμῖν EB ‖ ὁ
suppl. Emp. (sec. Wyt. in app. σέ, ὦ Λεύκιε. καὶ ὁ): lac. 8 lit. E, 10 lit. B: τὸν κλέαρχον ἀλλὰ Amyot:
σὲ τό γε καθ' ἡμᾶς· ὁ δὲ Po. in app.: ὑπολαβὼν ὁ Ch. ‖ lac. 10 lit. EB: ὑπολαβὼν εἶπεν ἄλλα suppl.
et corr. Amyot: οὐκ Wyt. in app.: lac. et ἀλλὰ del. Emp.: ἥκιστα Bern.: οὐδ' ἐλάχιστον Raing. in
app. ‖ ὠγαθὲ Steph.: ὦ' γαθὲ B: ὦ γαθὲ E    14 τὰ] τε Ald. Basil.: τἆλλα Ch.    15 ὑμῖν RJ94: ἡμῖν
EB    16 ἄγουσι] ἄγουσαν Po. in app. Ch. ‖ δι' οὗ] δίου θείου Kepl.: ἀϊδίου Dübn. et alii: δι' ἀϊδίου
Po. in app. ‖ lac. 16 lit. E, 14 lit. B: μετέχουσι suppl. Amyot: κινεῖσθαι Wyt. in app.: τῶν οὐρανίων
Adler: ὁμαλῶς περαινόμενον Po. in app.: οἷόν τε φύσιν ἔχειν Ch.    17 οὕτω] οὗτος Wyt. in app. et
alii    22 νώθειαν E: νωθείαν B    23 ᾧ add. RJ94 Basil.: κατὰ E: καὶ κατὰ B

solid and compressed part has become the stars; and of these the slowest and murkiest is the moon. Yet all the same one can see that the moon whirles about without being separated from the ether, but rather being carried in a large amount that surrounds it, and having beneath much ⟨whirling⟩ of winds and comets. In this way, each of the bodies is not balanced by the inclinations according to its weight and lightness, but is arranged by a different principle."

16. That said, when I was about to give the floor to Lucius—for we were reaching the demonstrations of our teaching—Aristotle, smiling, said: "I bear witness that you have constructed the whole refutation against those who believe that the moon itself is semi-igneous, still say that of all bodies in general some tend to incline by themselves upwards and some downwards; yet if there is someone who says that the stars naturally move in circles and are of a substance radically different from the four elements, that did not by any chance come to your mind, so I myself have been spared trouble." And Lucius said: "my dear ... but for now one would not quarrel with you, who ascribe to the rest of the stars and to the whole heaven a nature that is pure and immaculate and free from qualitative change, and who make it move in a circle, whence also a never-ending revolution ..., despite the myriads of difficulties involved; yet, when this theory descends so as to touch the moon, it no longer preserves the impassivity in it nor the beauty of this body, on the contrary, even without alluding to its other irregularities and differences, this very face that is visible results from some affection of the substance or from a conglomeration with another substance somehow—however, something that is mixed is affected in a way, because it is deprived of its purity by being forcibly sullied by an inferior substance. The moon's torpor and slackness of speed and the weakness and faintness of its heat, ⟨which⟩, according to Ion,

> 'ripes not the grape to duskiness',

Arist.

Lucius

εἰς τί θησόμεθα πλὴν ἀσθένειαν αὐτῆς καὶ πάθος, (εἰ πάθους) ἀιδίῳ σώματι καὶ ὀλυμπίῳ μέτεστιν; Ὅλως γάρ, ὦ φίλε Ἀριστότελες, γῆ μὲν οὖσα, πάγκαλόν τι χρῆμα καὶ σεμνὸν ἀναφαίνεται καὶ κεκοσμημένον, ὡς δὲ ἄστρον ἢ φῶς ἤ τι σῶμα θεῖον καὶ οὐράνιον, δέδια μὴ ἄμορφος ᾖ καὶ ἀπρεπὴς καὶ καταισχύνουσα τὴν καλὴν ἐπωνυμίαν· εἴ γε τῶν ἐν οὐρανῷ τοσούτων τὸ πλῆθος ὄντων, μόνη φωτὸς ἀλλοτρίου δεομένη περίεισι, κατὰ Παρμε|νίδην

ἀεὶ παπταίνουσα πρὸς αὐγὰς ἠελίοιο.

Ὁ μὲν οὖν ἑταῖρος ἐν τῇ διατριβῇ τοῦτο δὴ τὸ Ἀναξαγόρειον ἀποδεικνὺς ὡς ἥλιος ἐντίθησι τῇ σελήνῃ τὸ λαμπρὸν ηὐδοκίμησεν, ἐγὼ δὲ ταῦτα μὲν οὐκ ἐρῶ ἃ παρ' ὑμῶν ἢ μεθ' ὑμῶν ἔμαθον· ἔχων δὲ τοῦτο πρὸς τὰ λοιπὰ βαδιοῦμαι. Φωτίζεσθαι τοίνυν τὴν σελήνην οὐχ ὡς ὕελον ἢ κρύσταλλον ἐλλάμψει καὶ διαφαύσει τοῦ ἡλίου, πιθανόν ἐστιν, οὔτ' αὖ κατὰ σύλλαμψίν τινα καὶ συναυγασμόν, ὥσπερ αἱ δᾷδες, αὐξομένου τοῦ φωτός. Οὕτω γὰρ οὐδὲν ἧττον ἐν νουμηνίαις ἢ διχομηνίαις ἔσται πανσέληνος ἡμῖν, εἰ μὴ στέγει μηδὲ ἀντιφράττει τὸν ἥλιον, ἀλλὰ δίεισιν ὑπὸ μανό|τητος ἢ κατὰ σύγκρασιν εἰσλάμπει καὶ συνεξάπτει περὶ αὐτὴν τὸ φῶς· οὐ γὰρ ἔστιν ἐκκλίσεις οὐδὲ ἀποστροφὰς αὐτῆς, ὥσπερ ὅταν ᾖ διχότομος καὶ ἀμφίκυρτος ἢ μηνοειδής, αἰτιᾶσθαι περὶ τὴν σύνοδον, ἀλλὰ κατὰ στάθμην, φησὶ Δημόκριτος, ἱσταμένη τοῦ φωτίζοντος ὑπολαμβάνει καὶ δέχεται τὸν ἥλιον, ὥστε αὐτήν τε φαίνεσθαι καὶ διαφαίνειν ἐκεῖνον εἰκὸς ἦν. Ἡ δὲ πολλοῦ δεῖ τοῦτο ποιεῖν· αὐτή τε γὰρ ἄδηλός ἐστι τηνικαῦτα κἀκεῖνον ἀπέκρυψε καὶ ἠφάνισε πολλάκις,

ἀπεσκέδασεν δ' οἱ αὐγάς,

ὥς φησιν Ἐμπεδοκλῆς,

ἔστ' αἶαν καθύπερθεν, ἀπεσκνίφωσε δὲ γαίης
τόσσον ὅσον τ' εὖρος γλαυκώπιδος ἔπλετο μήνης·

---

1 αὐτῆς] αὑτῆς; punct. corr. Xyl. ‖ εἰ πάθους add. post πάθος SR67: ὧν οὐδετέρου add. RJ94: καὶ ὁ Ἀριστοτέλης· πάθος ἄρα ἀιδίῳ corr. et add. Xyl.¹⁵⁷⁰: εἰ πάθος add. Steph.: πάθος; πόθεν οὖν πάθους corr. et add. Po. 2 μέτεστιν punct. corr. Ald. Basil.: μέτεστιν. EB 6 περίεισι E et B s.l.: περίεστι B 10 παρ' ὑμῶν B: παρυμῶν E ‖ ἔχων δὲ τοῦτο E: ἔχων δὲ B: ἑκὼν δὲ SR67 et alii: ἐχόμενος δὲ τούτου Po. in app.: ἐῶν Görg. 11 ὕελον B: ὕελλον E et B s.l. 14 δίεισιν] διήισιν Madv. et alii 15 εἰσλάμπει] ἐκλάμπει Sandb. et alii ‖ αὐτήν] αὑτήν RJ94 18 αὐτή B et E i.t.: αὑτήν E 19 αὐτή E: αὕτη B: αὕτη Steph. 21 ἀπεσκέδασεν Xyl.¹⁵⁷⁰: ἀπεσκεύασε EB 24 τόσσον E et B s.l.: τόσον B ‖ γλαυκώπιδος ἔπλετο μήνης E: ἔπλετο γλαυκώπιδος μήνης B: γλαυκώπιδι μήνῃ RJ94

to what shall we attribute them but to weakness and affection, if an eternal and celestial body can take part of an affection? Well, in a word, dear Aristotle, as earth, the moon appears to be something absolutely beautiful, dignified, and neat, as a star or light or a divine and celestial body, differently, I fear it is malformed and embarrassing and soils its noble title—if indeed, among the high number of beings in heaven, it alone goes around in need of 'foreign light', according to Parmenides,

> 'always seeking with its sight the rays of the sun'.

Our comrade was honored in his lecture by proving this very proposition of Anaxagoras, namely that

> 'the sun conveys brilliance to the moon',

but I certainly will not speak about the things which I learned from you or with you, so having it this way, I will proceed to the remaining issues. Well then, it is plausible that the moon is illuminated, not as glass or ice would be, by the brightness and shining of the sun through it, and not in turn because of some concentration of light or convergence of rays, like torches, where the light increases. For in this case, there would be a full moon for us, no less at the beginning of the month than in the middle of the month, if the moon does not conceal and obstruct the sun, but its light goes through because of the moon's subtility or as a result of a combination, and it shines in and joins in kindling when around the moon. Indeed, it is not the moon's declins or detours what causes its invisibility when it is in conjunction—as they are when it is at the half and gibbous or crescent—, but 'aligned', says Democritus,

> 'in standing with the source of light, it seizes and receives the sun',

so that it would be likely for the moon to shine and to let the sun shine through. However, it is far from doing this: the moon is itself invisible then, during conjunction, and it concealed and hid the sun frequently,

> 'it scattered the sun's rays',

as says Empedocles,

> 'from above down to the earth it cast in shade as much of the earth as the width of the bright-eyed moon';

D | καθάπερ εἰς νύκτα καὶ σκότος οὐκ εἰς ἄστρον ἕτερο(ν) τοῦ φωτὸς ἐμπεσόντος. Ὃ δὲ λέγει Ποσειδώνιος ὡς ὑπὸ βάθους τῆς σελήνης οὐ περαιοῦται δι᾽ αὐτῆς τὸ τοῦ ἡλίου φῶς πρὸς ἡμᾶς, ἐλέγχεται καταφανῶς· ὁ γὰρ ἀὴρ ἄπλετος ὢν καὶ βάθος ἔχων πολλαπλάσιον τῆς σελήνης ὅλος ἐξηλιοῦται καὶ καταλάμπεται ταῖς αὐγαῖς. Ἀπολείπεται τοίνυν τὸ τοῦ Ἐμπεδοκλέους, ἀνακλάσει τινὶ τοῦ ἡλίου πρὸς τὴν σελήνην  5
γίνεσθαι τὸν ἐνταῦθα φωτισμὸν ἀπ᾽ αὐτῆς, ὅθεν οὐδὲ θερμὸν οὐδὲ λαμπρὸν ἀφικνεῖται πρὸς ἡμᾶς, ὥσπερ ἦν εἰκὸς ἐξάψεως καὶ μίξεως ⟨τῶν⟩ φώτων γεγενημένης,
E ἀλλ᾽ οἷον αἵ τε φωναὶ | κατὰ τὰς ἀνακλάσεις ἀμαυροτέραν ἀναφαίνουσι τὴν ἠχὼ τοῦ φθέγματος, αἵ τε πληγαὶ τῶν ἀφαλλομένων βελῶν μαλακώτεραι προσπίπτουσιν,

ὡς αὐγὴ τύψασα σεληναίης κύκλον εὐρὺν  10

ἀσθενῆ καὶ ἀμυδρὰν ἀνάρροιαν ἴσχει πρὸς ἡμᾶς διὰ τὴν κλάσιν ἐκλυομένης τῆς δυνάμεως."

17. Ὑπολαβὼν δὲ ὁ Σύλλας "ἀμέλει ταῦτα" εἶπεν "ἔχει τινὰς πιθανότητας· ὃ δὲ ἰσχυρότατόν ἐστι τῶν ἀντιπιπτόντων πότερον ἔτυχέ τινος παραμυθίας ἢ παρῆλθεν ἡμῶν τὸν ἑταῖρον;" "Τί τοῦτο" ἔφη "λέγεις" ὁ Λεύκιος "ἢ τὸ πρὸς τὴν διχότομον  15
F ἀπορούμενον;" "Πάνυ μὲν οὖν" ὁ Σύλλας εἶπεν "ἔχει γὰρ τινα λόγον τὸ | πάσης ἐν ἴσαις γωνίαις γινομένης ἀνακλάσεως, ὅταν ἡ σελήνη διχοτομοῦσα μεσουρανῇ, μὴ φέρεσθαι τὸ φῶς ἐπὶ γῆς ἀπ᾽ αὐτῆς, ἀλλὰ ὀλισθαίνειν ἐπέκεινα τῆς γῆς· ὁ γὰρ
930A ἥλιος ἐπὶ τοῦ ὁρίζοντος ὢν ἅπτεται τῇ ἀκτῖνι τῆς σελήνης· ‖ διὸ καὶ κλασθεῖσα πρὸς ἴσα ἐπὶ θάτερον ἐκπεσεῖται πέρας καὶ οὐκ ἀφήσει δεῦρο τὴν αὐγήν, ἢ δια-  20
στροφὴ μεγάλη καὶ παράλλαξις ἔσται τῆς γωνίας, ὅπερ ἀδύνατόν ἐστι." "Ἀλλὰ νὴ Δία" εἶπεν ὁ Λεύκιος "καὶ τοῦτο ἐρρήθη." Καὶ πρός γε Μενέλαον ἀποβλέψας ἐν τῷ διαλέγεσθαι τὸν μαθηματικόν, "αἰσχύνομαι μὲν" ἔφη "σοῦ παρόντος, ὦ φίλε Μενέλαε, θέσιν ἀναιρεῖν μαθηματικὴν ὥσπερ θεμέλιον τοῖς κατοπτρικοῖς ὑποκειμένην πράγμασιν· ἀνάγκη δὲ εἰπεῖν ὅτι τὸ πρὸς ἴσας τείνεσθαι γωνίας ἀνάκλασιν πᾶσαν,  25
B οὔτε φαινόμενον αὐτόθεν οὔτε ὁμολογούμενόν ἐστιν, ἀλλὰ διαβάλλεται μὲν | ἐπὶ τῶν κυρτῶν κατόπτρων, ὅταν ἐμφάσεις ποιῇ μείζονας ἑαυτῶν πρὸς ἓν τὸ τῆς ὄψεως σημεῖον, διαβάλλεται δὲ τοῖς διπτύχοις κατόπτροις, ὡς ἐπικλιθέντων πρὸς ἄλληλα

---

1 ἕτερον suppl. SR67: ἕτερο vac. 3 lit. EB: ἑτεροειδὲς RJ94: αἰθηρ (sic) vel ἕτερον RJ94: ἕτερον τοιοῦτον Wyt. in app.: ἑτεροῖον Bern. in app.: ἑτερόν τι Papabas.   2 δι αὐτῆς B: διαυτῆς E   4 ὅλος E: ὅλως B   7 τῶν suppl. SR67: lac. 5 lit. E, 3 lit. B: lac. del. Xyl.: τινός Wyt. in app.: δύο Raing.: δυοῖν Po.   8 ἀμαυροτέραν E: ἀμαυρωτέραν B   10 αὐγή SR67: αὐτὴ EB ‖ εὐρὺν E: εὔρυν B   15 ἑταῖρον punct. corr. Wyt.: ἑταῖρον. EB   17 διχοτομοῦσα] διχότομος οὖσα Wyt. in app. et alii ‖ μεσουρανῇ] μεσουρανία Ald. Basil.: μεσουρανεῖ Amyot Xyl.1570: μεσουρανήσῃ Kepl.   20 ἴσα] ἴσας Bens. et alii   25 εἰπεῖν Wyt. in app.: εἶπεν EB ‖ τείνεσθαι] γίνεσθαι RJ94 et alii   28 ὡς]: ὢν RJ94 et alii ‖ ἐπικλιθέντων RJ94: ἐπικριθέντων EB

just as if light would fall into night and darkness and not upon another star. Moreover, what Posidonius says, namely that on account of the depth of the moon the light of the sun cannot pierce through it towards us, this is manifestly refuted: indeed, the air, while being unlimited and having a depth many times larger than that of the moon, is illuminated and enlightened by the rays. There remains then the theory of Empedocles that the moonlight down here results from a reflection of the sun onto the moon, that is why there is neither warmth nor brilliance that reaches us, as we should expect if there had been an ignition and mixture of ⟨their⟩ lights, but just as voices show an echo fainter than the original sound when they are reflected, and ricochets make the impact of missiles softer,

'so too a ray that strucks the broad disk of the moon',

retains a weak and faint refluence when back to us, having its force loose because of the refraction."

17. Here Sulla interrupted him and said: "Without any doubt this has some plausibility; but that which is the strongest of the pitfalls, did it found some persuasion or did it escape our comrade's attention?" "What do you mean," said Lucius, "or is it about the difficulty regarding the half-moon?" "Precisely that," said Sulla, "because there is some reason in the fact that, since all reflection occurs at equal angles, whenever the moon at the half reaches the middle point in the sky, the light cannot move towards the earth from it, but glides beyond the earth—as the sun, being on the horizon, reaches the moon with its ray, reason why, being reflected equally, the ray would fall onto the opposite limit of the horizon and would not send forth its brightness here, otherwise there would be great distortion and dislocation of the angle, which is impossible." "Well, yes, by Zeus," said Lucius, "this was discussed too." And, looking at Menelaus the astronomer while still speaking, he said: "I am ashamed, in your presence, dear Menelaus, to refute a mathematical thesis which serves as a foundation on which rests the subject of catoptrics; nevertheless, it is necessary to say that the axiom 'all reflection occurs at equal angles', is neither self-evident nor a fact on which everyone agrees: in fact, it is overthrown, on the one hand, by convex mirrors, when the point of the visual ray creates bigger images in one respect; and it is refuted, on the other, by folding mirrors, as each of the planes inclined to

    Sulla

    Lucius
    Sulla

    Lucius
    Men.

καὶ γωνίας ἐντὸς γενομένης, ἑκάτερον τῶν ἐπιπέδων διττὴν ἔμφασιν ἀποδίδωσι καὶ ποιεῖ τέτταρας εἰκόνας ἀφ' ἑνὸς προσώπου, δύο μὲν ἀντιστρόφους τοῖς ἔξωθεν ἐναργεστέρας μέρεσι, δύο δὲ δεξιοφανεῖς ἀμαυρὰς ἐν βάθει τῶν κατόπτρων· ὧν τῆς γενέσεως τὴν αἰτίαν Πλάτων ἀποδίδωσιν· εἴρηκε γὰρ ὅτι τοῦ κατόπτρου ἔνθεν καὶ
C ἔνθεν ὕ|ψος λαβόντος ὑπαλλάττουσιν αἱ ὄψεις τὴν ἀνάκλασιν ἀπὸ τῶν ἑτέρων ἐπὶ θάτερα μεταπίπτουσαν. Εἴπερ οὖν τῶν ὄψεων εὐθὺς πρὸς ἡμᾶς ⟨αἱ μὲν⟩ ἀνατρέχουσιν, αἱ δὲ ἐπὶ θάτερα μέρη τῶν κατόπτρων ὀλισθαίνουσαι πάλιν ἐκεῖθεν ἀναφέρονται πρὸς ἡμᾶς, οὐ δυνατόν ἐστιν ἐν ἴσαις γωνίαις γίνεσθαι πάσας ἀνακλάσεις· ὅσας ὁμόσε χωρεῖν ὁρῶντες ἀξιοῦσιν αὐτοῖς τοῖς ἀπὸ τῆς σελήνης ἐπὶ γῆν φερομένοις ῥεύμασι τὴν ἰσότητα τῶν γωνιῶν ἀναιρεῖν, πολλῷ τοῦτο ἐκείνου πιθανώτερον εἶναι νομίζοντες. Οὐ μὴν ἀλλὰ εἰ δεῖ τοῦτο χαρίζεσθαι τῇ πολλὰ δὴ φίλῃ γεωμετρίᾳ
D καὶ δοῦναι, πρῶ|τον μὲν ἀπὸ τῶν ἠκριβωμένων ταῖς λειότησι συμπίπτειν ἐσόπτρων εἰκός ἐστιν· ἡ δὲ σελήνη πολλὰς ἀνωμαλίας ἔχει καὶ τραχύτητας ὥστε τὰς αὐγὰς ἀπὸ σώματος μεγάλου προσφερομένας ὕψεσιν ἀξιολόγοις ἀντιλάμψεις καὶ διαδόσεις ἀπ' ἀλλήλων λαμβάνουσιν, ἀνακλᾶσθαί τε παντοδαπῶς καὶ περιπλέκεσθαι καὶ συνάπτειν αὐτῇ ἑαυτῇ τὴν ἀνταύγειαν οἷον ἀπὸ πολλῶν φερομένην πρὸς ἡμᾶς κατόπτρων. Ἔπειτα κἂν πρὸς αὐτῇ τῇ σελήνῃ τὰς ἀντανακλάσεις ἐν ἴσαις γωνίαις ποιῶμεν, οὐκ ἀδύνατον φερομένας ἐν διαστήματι τοσούτῳ τὰς αὐγὰς κλάσεις
E ἴσχειν καὶ περιολισθήσεις ὡς συγ|χεῖσθαι καὶ κάμπτειν τὸ φῶς. Ἔνιοι δὲ καὶ δεικνύουσι γράφοντες ὅτι πολλὰ τῶν φώτων ἐπὶ γῆν ἀφίησι κατὰ γραμμὴν ὑπὸ τὴν κεκλιμένην ὑποτεθεῖσαν· σκευωρεῖσθαι δὲ ἅμα λέγοντι διάγραμμα καὶ ταῦτα πρὸς πολλοὺς οὐκ ἐνῆν.

18. Τὸ δ' ὅλον" ἔφη "θαυμάζω πῶς τὴν διχότομον ἐφ' ἡμᾶς κινοῦσιν ἐμπίπτουσαν μετὰ τῆς ἀμφικύρτου καὶ τῆς μηνοειδοῦς· εἰ γὰρ αἰθέριον ὄγκον ἢ πύρινον ὄντα τὸν τῆς σελήνης ἐφώτιζεν ὁ ἥλιος, οὐκ ἂν ἀπέλειπεν αὐτῇ σκιερὸν ἀεὶ καὶ ἀλαμπὲς ἡμισφαίριον πρὸς αἴσθησιν, ἀλλ' εἰ καὶ κατὰ μικρὸν ἔψαυε περιιών, πολλὴν ἀνα-
F πίμπλασθαι καὶ δι' ὅλης τρέφε|σθαι τῷ φωτὶ πανταχόσε χωροῦντι δι' εὐπετείας

---

1 διττὴν I.22: διττῆς EB    2 τοῖς] ἐν add. ante τοῖς Dübn. et alii    3 ἐναργεστέρας Raing.: ἀριστεροῖς EB: ἀριστεροῖς del. Dübn. et alii ‖ δεξιοφανεῖς] ἀλλ' add. post δεξιοφανεῖς Po. ‖ ἐν βάθει] τῷ βάθει Emp. ‖ τῶν κατόπτρων· iteratio sententiae ὅταν ἐμφάσεις ... διαβάλλεται δὲ et lac. 14 lit. E, 11 lit. B    6 τῶν ὄψεων] αἱ μὲν add. post τῶν ὄψεων SR67 ‖ αἱ μὲν suppl. Amyot: lac. 19 lit. E, 14 lit. B: aut nihil excidit aut ἀπὸ τῶν κατόπτρων Wyt. in app.: αἱ μὲν ἐκ τῶν ἔξωθεν Adler: αἱ μὲν κατ ἀνάκλασιν Po. in app.: αἱ μὲν ἀπὸ τῶν ἐπιπέδων Ch.    9 ὅσας] ὥστε SR67 et alii: οἷς οἱ vel οἷς τινες Po. in app.: ὥστε pro ὅσας et ἔνιοι μὲν τοῖς μαθηματικοῖς add. Ch. ‖ χωρεῖν ὁρῶντες Prickard: χωροῦντες EB: τοῖς add. ante ἀξιοῦσιν et ἀναιρῶμεν pro ἀναιρεῖν Emp.: ὥστε τοῦθ' οἱ μὴ συγχωροῦντες pro ὅσας ὁμόσε χωροῦντες Adler    10 ῥεύμασι B: ῥήμασι E    15 ἀνακλᾶσθαί τε B: ἀνακλᾶσθαι τὲ E    16 ἑαυτῇ E: ἑαυτῆ B    19 συγχεῖσθαι Amyot: συγκεῖσθαι EB ‖ κάμπτειν Emp.: λάμπειν EB    20 γραμμὴν] γραμμῆς Wyt. in app.    20–21 ὑπὸ τὴν κεκλιμένην] ὑπὸ τὴν κεκλασμένην Emp.: ἀπὸ τῆς ἐκκεκλιμένης Ch.    21 ὑποτεθεῖσαν RJ94: ὑποτεθείσης EB    25 αὐτῇ] αὐτῆς Wyt. in app.: ἐν αὐτῇ Raing. in app    26 περιιών SR67: περὶ ὧν EB: περὶ ἣν I.22: περιών RJ94: περίοδον Kepl. ‖ πολλὴν] ὅλην I.22 et alii    27 τρέφεσθαι] τρέπεσθαι RJ94 et alii

each other and having formed an inner angle exhibits a double image and creates four likenesses of a single object: two reversed, clearer in the outer parts, and two straight, dim in the depth of the mirrors. Plato provides the cause of the origin of these: for he has said that in the cases where a mirror is elevated on each side the visual rays alternate the reflection due to their shifting from one side to the other. So, if of the visual rays ⟨some⟩ return straight to us while others bounce to the opposite sides of the mirrors and from there they return back to us, it is not possible that all reflections occur at equal angles. They observe that these images meet in one point and claim that the equality of the angles is refuted when it comes to the streams of light that move from the moon to the earth, considering this to be much more plausible than that axiom. Notwithstanding this, if we must please and conceed this axiom to the dearly beloved geometry, then, firstly, this would likely happen in mirrors that are polished evenly with precision; but the moon has numerous irregularities and roughnesses, so the rays from a large body approaching considerable heights which get from one another reflections and diffusions of light, are reflected in every direction and intertwined, and the very reflection converges with itself, as if it were moving towards us from many mirrors. Secondly, even if we pretend that the reflections on the moon itself occur at equal angles, it is not impossible that the rays, moving across such a great distance, suffer refractions and deflections, to the point of blurring and bending their light. Some people even prove in their writings that many of the moon's beams of light reach the earth along a line stretched under the inclined surface; but it was not possible to implement a geometrical diagram while talking, more so in front of so many people.

18. All in all," he said, "I am surprised by how they raise against us the moon's light falling upon us at its half as well as at the gibbous and the crescent phases; after all, if the mass of the moon that the sun illuminates was ethereal or fiery, the sun would not leave in it a hemisphere that is always shadowy and unilluminated to sense-perception; on the contrary, if, when revolving, the sun minimally grazed it, the moon should be very much saturated and cherished entirely, giving in to the light proceeding abundantly in

ἦν προσῆκον· ὅπου γὰρ οἶνος ὕδατος θιγὼν κατὰ πέρας καὶ σταγὼν αἵματος εἰς
ὑγρὸν ἐμπεσόντος ἀνέχρωσε πᾶν ἅμα ... φοινιχθέν· αὐτὸν δὲ τὸν ἀέρα λέγουσιν οὐκ
ἀπορροίαις τισὶν οὐδὲ ἀκτῖσι μεμιγμέναις, ἀλλὰ τροπῇ καὶ μεταβολῇ κατὰ νύξιν ἢ
ψαῦσιν ἀπὸ τοῦ φωτὸς ἐξηλιοῦσθαι, πῶς ἄστρον ἄστρου καὶ φῶς φωτὸς ἁψάμε-
931A νον οἴονται μὴ κεράννυσθαι μηδὲ σύγχυσιν ποιεῖν δι' ὅλου καὶ μεταβολήν, ‖ ἀλλ'    5
ἐκεῖνα φωτίζειν μόνον ὧν ἅπτεται κατὰ τὴν ἐπιφάνειαν· "Ὃν γὰρ ὁ ἥλιος περιιὼν
κύκλον ἄγει καὶ περιστρέφει περὶ τὴν σελήνην, νῦν μὲν ἐπιπίπτοντα τῷ διορίζοντι
τὸ ὁρατὸν αὐτῆς καὶ τὸ ἀόρατον, νῦν δὲ ἀνιστάμενον πρὸς ὀρθὰς ὥστε τέμνειν ἐκεῖ-
νον ὑπ' ἐκείνου τε τέμνεσθαι, ἄλλαις κλίσεσι καὶ σχέσεσι τοῦ λαμπροῦ πρὸς τὸ
σκιερὸν ἀμφικύρτους καὶ μηνοειδεῖς ἀποδιδόντα μορφὰς ἐν αὐτῇ· παντὸς μᾶλλον   10
ἐπιδείκνυσιν οὐ σύγκρασιν ἀλλ' ἐπαφήν, οὐδὲ σύλλαμψιν ἀλλὰ περίλαμψιν αὐτῆς
ὄντα τὸν φωτισμόν. Ἐπεὶ δὲ οὐκ αὐτὴ φωτίζεται μόνον, ἀλλὰ καὶ δεῦρο τῆς αὐγῆς
B ἀνα|πέμπει τὸ εἴδωλον, ἔτι καὶ μᾶλλον ἰσχυρίσασθαι τῷ λόγῳ περὶ τῆς οὐσίας δίδω-
σιν. Αἱ γὰρ ἀνακλάσεις γίνονται πρὸς οὐδὲν ἀραιὸν οὐδὲ λεπτομερές, οὐδὲ ἔστι φῶς
ἀπὸ φωτὸς ἢ πῦρ ἀπὸ πυρὸς ἀφαλλόμενον, ἢ νοῆσαι ῥᾴδιον, ἀλλὰ δεῖ τὸ ποιῆσον   15
ἀντιτυπίαν τινὰ καὶ κλάσιν ἐμβριθὲς εἶναι καὶ πυκνόν, ἵνα πρὸς αὐτὸ πληγὴ καὶ
ἀπ' αὐτοῦ φορὰ γένηται· τὸν γοῦν αὐτὸν ἥλιον ὁ μὲν ἀὴρ διίησιν οὐ παρέχων ἀνα-
κοπὰς οὐδὲ ἀντερείδων, ἀπὸ δὲ ξύλων καὶ λίθων καὶ ἱματίων εἰς φῶς τιθεμένων,
πολλὰς ἀντιλάμψεις καὶ περιλάμψεις ἀποδίδωσιν. Οὕτω δὲ καὶ τὴν γῆν ὁρῶμεν
C ὑπ' | αὐτοῦ φωτιζομένην· οὐ γὰρ εἰς βάθος ὥσπερ ὕδωρ οὐδὲ δι' ὅλης ὥσπερ ἀὴρ   20
διίησι τὴν αὐγήν, ἀλλ' οἷος τὴν σελήνην περιστείχει κύκλος αὐτοῦ καὶ ὅσον ὑπο-
τέμνεται μέρος ἐκείνης, τοιοῦτος ἕτερος περίεισι τὴν γῆν καὶ τοσοῦτον φωτίζων
ἀεὶ καὶ ἀπολείπων ἕτερον ἀφώτιστον· ἡμισφαιρίου γὰρ ὀλίγῳ δοκεῖ μεῖζον εἶναι τὸ
περιλαμπόμενον ἑκατέρας. Δότε δή μοι γεωμετρικῶς εἰπεῖν πρὸς ἀναλογίαν· ὡς εἰ
τριῶν ὄντων οἷς τὸ ἀφ' ἡλίου φῶς πλησιάζει· γῆς, σελήνης, ἀέρος, ὁρῶμεν οὐχ ὡς ὁ   25
ἀὴρ μᾶλλον ἢ ὡς ἡ γῆ φωτιζομένην τὴν σελήνην, ἀνάγκη φύσιν ἔχειν ὁμοίαν ἃ τὰ
D αὐτὰ πάσχειν ὑ|πὸ τοῦ αὐτοῦ πέφυκεν."

19. Ἐπεὶ δὲ πάντες ἐπῄνεσαν τὸν Λεύκιον, "εὖ γε" ἔφην "ὅτι καλῷ λόγῳ καλὴν
ἀναλογίαν προσέθηκας· οὐ γὰρ ἀποστερητέον σε τῶν ἰδίων." Κἀκεῖνος ἐπιμειδιά-
σας, "οὐκοῦν" ἔφη "καὶ δεύτερον ἀναλογίᾳ προσχρηστέον, ὅπως μὴ ⟨τῷ⟩ τὰ αὐτὰ   30
πάσχειν ὑπὸ τοῦ αὐτοῦ μόνον, ἀλλὰ καὶ τῷ ταὐτὰ ποιεῖν ταὐτόν, ἀποδείξωμεν τῇ γῇ
τὴν σελήνην προσεοικυῖαν· ὅτι μὲν γὰρ οὐδὲν οὕτως τῶν περὶ τὸν ἥλιον γινομένων

---

1 θιγὼν Dübn.: θίγων EB ‖ κατὰ B: ατὰ E    2 ἅμα RJ94: αἷμα EB ‖ lac. 8 lit. E, 6 lit. B: τὸ suppl.
RJ94: αἵματι Amyot: lac. del. Wyt. in app.: διαφοινιχθέν Bern. in app.: αἱματώδης ἅμα corr. et suppl.
Purser: τῷ ψαύειν vel τῷ θιγεῖν Adler    3 κατὰ νύξιν E: κατάνυξιν B    4 ἐξηλιοῦσθαι E: ἐξηλλοι-
οῦσθαι B: ἐξαλλοιοῦσθαι RJ94    5 οἴονται B et E i.t.: οἴονται E ‖ κεράννυσθαι E: κεράννισθαι B ‖
δι ὅλου E: διόλου B    6 ἐπιφάνειαν punct. corr. Steph.: ἐπιφάνειαν· EB    7 περὶ E: πρὸς B    9 τε
B et E s.l.    10 μηνοειδεῖς B: νοειδεῖς E    11 ἐπιδείκνυσιν RJ94: ἐπιδεικνύουσιν EB    12 δεῦρο B:
εὖρο E    15 ἀπὸ φωτὸς E: ἀποφωτός B ‖ ἢ] del. SR67 et alii    21 αὐτοῦ SR67: αὐτῶν EB: αὐτὴν
I.22    22 τοσοῦτον E: τοσοῦτο B    30 τῷ add. Basil.

all directions. Since wine that just touches water at its surface and a drop of blood fallen into liquid at the very instant stains all the liquid red ..., they say that the air itself shines with the sun, not by mixing with some sort of emanations or rays, but by an alteration and mutation resulting from an impact or contact with the light, how can they believe that a star can graze another star and light can graze another light and not fuse together or produce a complete blend and alteration, but instead they illuminate only the parts which are attained on the surface? As a matter of fact, the sun in its revolution makes a circle and whirls around the moon, which now falls onto the circle, dividing the moon's visible and invisible parts and now stands at a right angle to it so as to cut it and be cut by it, with different inclinations and correlations of the bright part with respect to the dark one, producing in it the gibbous and crescent shapes: this, more than anything, demonstrates that the moon's illumination results not of a mixture but of contact, not of a concentration of inner light but of a radiation of surrounding light. And since it not only is illuminated itself, but also sends the semblance of the sun's illumination back here, this gives even more strength to our theory of the moon's substance. After all, reflections do not appear from anything rarefied or subtle, and there is no light rebounding from light or fire from fire—or at least easy to imagine—but it is necessary for whatever causes some repercussion or reflection to be heavy and solid, in order that the blow coming against it may be moved away from it; in any case, this very same sunlight that the air allows to go through without providing any impediment or resistance, gives back many reflections and radiations from woods, stones, and clothes being exposed to the light. And this way also we see the earth being illuminated by the sun: for it does not let the ray of light go through to a certain depth, as water does, nor fully, as air does either, but just as the circle of the sun moves around the moon and as much part of the moon as it intercepts, such another circle moves around the earth as well, always illuminating so much of it and leaving another part unlit—the illuminated section in each of them, indeed, seems to be somewhat bigger than a hemisphere. Please, allow me to say it in geometrical terms with an analogy: if, given three things which the light from the sun approaches—earth, moon, air—we see the moon being illuminated not as the air is more than as the earth, necessity naturally demands that things suffering the same effects by the same agent have a resembling nature."

19. When everyone had praised Lucius, I said: "Very well, you have added to a fine narration a fine analogy; you should not be deprived of what belongs to you." And he said, smiling: "Well then, an analogy must be used a second time, so that we may prove that the moon resembles the earth, not only

Lucius

Lucius

ὅμοιόν ἐστιν ὡς ἔκλειψις ἡλίου δύσει, δότε μοι, ταύτης ἔναγχος τῆς συνόδου μνη-
E σθέντες, ἣ πολλὰ μὲν ἄστρα πολλαχόθεν τοῦ οὐρανοῦ διέφηνεν εὐθὺς ἐκ | μεσημ-
βρίας ἀρξαμένη, κρᾶσιν δὲ οἵαν τὸ λυκαυγὲς τῷ ἀέρι παρέσχεν. Εἰ δὲ μή, Θέων ἡμῖν
οὗτος τὸν Μίμνερμον ἐπάξει καὶ τὸν Κυδίαν καὶ τὸν Ἀρχίλοχον, πρὸς δὲ τούτοις τὸν
Στησίχορον καὶ τὸν Πίνδαρον ἐν ταῖς ἐκλείψεσιν ὀλοφυρομένους τὸν φανερώτατον 5
κλεπτόμενον καὶ μέσῳ ἄματι τὴν νύκτα γινομένην καὶ τὴν ἀκτῖνα τοῦ ἡλίου σκό-
τους ἀτραπὸν ⟨ἐσσυμέναν⟩ φάσκοντας, ἐπὶ πᾶσι δὲ τὸν Ὅμηρον νυκτὶ καὶ ζόφῳ
τὰ πρόσωπα κατέχεσθαι τῶν ἀνθρώπων λέγοντα καὶ τὸν ἥλιον ἐξαπολωλέναι τοῦ
F οὐρανοῦ περὶ τὴν σελήνην καὶ ... τοῦτο γίνεσθαι | πεφυκέναι, τοῦ μὲν φθίνοντος
μηνός, τοῦ δὲ ἱσταμένου. Τὰ λοιπὰ δὲ οἶμαι ταῖς μαθηματικαῖς ἀκριβείαις εἰς τὸν ... 10
ἐξῆχθαι καὶ βέβαιον· ὡς ἥ γε νύξ ἐστι σκιὰ γῆς, ἡ δὲ ἔκλειψις τοῦ ἡλίου σκιὰ σελή-
νης, ὅταν ἡ ὄψις ἐν αὐτῇ γένηται· δυόμενος γὰρ ὑπὸ τῆς γῆς ἀντιφράττεται πρὸς
932A τὴν ὄψιν, ἐκλιπὼν δὲ ὑπὸ τῆς σελήνης· || ἀμφότεραι δέ εἰσιν ἐπισκοτήσεις· ἀλλ' ἡ
μὲν δυτικὴ τῆς γῆς, ἡ δὲ ἐκλειπτικὴ τῆς σελήνης τῇ σκιᾷ καταλαμβανούσης τὴν
ὄψιν· ἐκ δὲ τούτων εὐθεώρητον τὸ γινόμενον· εἰ γὰρ ὅμοιον τὸ πάθος, ὅμοια τὰ ποι- 15
οῦντα· τῷ γὰρ αὐτῷ τὰ αὐτὰ συμβαίνειν ὑπὸ τῶν αὐτῶν ἀναγκαῖόν ἐστιν· εἰ δὲ οὐχ
οὕτω τὸ περὶ τὰς ἐκλείψεις σκότος βύθιόν ἐστιν οὐδὲ ὁμοίως τῇ νυκτὶ πιέζει τὸν
ἀέρα, μὴ θαυμάζωμεν· οὐσία μὲν γὰρ ἡ αὐτὴ τοῦ τὴν νύκτα ποιοῦντος καὶ τοῦ τὴν
ἔκλειψιν σώματος, μέγεθος δὲ οὐκ ἴσον. Ἀλλὰ Αἰγυπτίους μὲν ἑβδομηκοστόδυον,
B οἶμαι, φάναι μόριον εἶναι τὴν σελήνην, Ἀναξαγόραν δέ, ὅση Πελοπόννη|σος. Ἀρί- 20
σταρχος δὲ τὴν διάμετρον τῆς σελήνης λόγον ἔχουσαν ἀποδείκνυσιν, ὃς ἐλάττων
μὲν ἢ ἑξήκοντα πρὸς δεκαεννέα, μείζων δέ πως ⟨ἢ⟩ ἑκατὸν ὀκτὼ πρὸς τεσσα-
ράκοντα τρία ἐστίν. Ὅθεν ἡ μὲν γῆ παντάπασι τῆς ὄψεως τὸν ἥλιον ἀφαιρεῖται
διὰ μέγεθος, μεγάλη γὰρ ἡ ἐπιπρόσθησις καὶ χρόνον ἔχουσα τὸν τῆς νυκτός· ἡ δὲ
σελήνη κἂν ὅλον ποτὲ κρύψῃ τὸν ἥλιον, οὐκ ἔχει χρόνον οὐδὲ πλάτος ἡ ἔκλειψις, 25
ἀλλὰ περιφαίνεταί τις αὐγὴ περὶ τὴν ἴτυν οὐκ ἐῶσα βαθεῖαν γενέσθαι τὴν σκιὰν

---

1 ταύτης ἔναγχος τῆς συνόδου B: ταύτης ἔναγχος συνόδου E: ταύτης τῆς ἔναγχος συνόδου Po.   3
Θέων SR67: θεῶν EB     4 τὸν Μίμνερμον I.22 SR67 (vel Μίμερμνον): ἐργομίμναμον EB: ἔργῳ
μίμνερμον RJ94   5 τὸν φανερώτατον] τὸν φανερώτατον θεόν Wyt. in app.: ἄστρον φανερώτατον
Bergk   6 ἄματι τὴν νύκτα SR67 (ἄματι sic): ἄμα τὴν νύκτα EB: ἄματι (sic) νύκτα Wyt.   6–7
σκότους B: σκότος E: σκότου Bergk   7 ἐσσυμέναν suppl. Adler: lac. 16 lit. EB: ἱεμένην Amyot:
ὑποδῦναι Xyl.1570: forte nihil excidit Wyt. in app.   8 πρόσωπα Xyl.1570: πρῶτα EB   9 lac. 12
lit. EB: ὅτι suppl. Amyot: lac. del. Xyl.1570: περὶ τὴν σελήνης σύνοδον suppl. Wyt. in app.: παρὰ τὴν
σελήνην καὶ ὡς ἐν συνόδῳ corr. Bern. in app.: ἡλίου σύνοδον suppl. Adler: περὶ τὴν σύνοδον καὶ ἐπι-
στάμενον ὅτι τοῦτο Po. in app.: αἰνιττόμενον ὡς Ch.: προσδηλοῦντα ὡς Görg.: τελείεσθαι conieci ||
πεφυκέναι RJ94: πέφυκε EB   10 lac. 8 lit. EB: ἀποδεικτικὸν λόγον suppl. Amyot: ἀσφαλῆ λόγον
Wyt. in app.: τὸ pro τὸν et πιστὸν suppl. Emp.: τὸ πιθανὸν Herw.: τὸ νημερτὲς vel τὸ νητρεκὲς Adler:
σαφῆ λόγον Ch.   20 τὴν σελήνην] γῆς add. ante τὴν σελήνην RJ94 || Πελοπόννησος B: Πελοπό-
νησος E   21 τὴν διάμετρον] τὴν διάμετρον τῆς γῆς πρὸς add. ante τὴν διάμετρον Bern.   22
δεκαεννέα SR67: δὲ, καὶ ἐννέα EB: δέκα καὶ ἐννέα Xyl. || ἢ add. RJ94: δ' ἢ ὡς Bern.   22–23 τεσ-
σαράκοντα] τριάκοντα Kepl.

because they both suffer the same effects by the same agent, but also because they cause the same effects on the same patient. After all, among the things that happen to the sun, nothing resembles its setting as much as a solar eclipse; grant me this, by recalling this recent conjunction which showed many stars from many parts of the sky, beginning just after midday, and provided to the air a temperature like that of twilight. If not, Theon here will cite us Mimnermus, Cydias, Archilochus, and beside also Stesichorus and Pindar, who during eclipses bewail 'the capture of the brightest' and 'the appearance of night right in the middle of the day', and say that the beam of the sun '⟨is sped⟩ the path of shade'; and above all Homer, who says 'with night' and gloom 'the faces' of men are covered and 'the sun has perished from the heaven' surrounding the moon and ... that this naturally occurs 'from waning month to waxing month'. For the rest, I think that it has been reduced by the precision of mathematics to the certain and ..., precisely night is the shadow of the earth, and the eclipse of the sun is the shadow of the moon, when our vision comes to be on it; in fact, when it sets it is intercepted by the earth from our vision and when it is eclipsed, by the moon; both are obscurations: while the vespertine is obscuration by the earth, the ecliptic is that by the moon, with the shadow intercepting our vision. From this it is easy to understand what is happening: if the affection is similar, so are the agents—indeed it must be by the same agents that the same things occur to the same subject. But if the darkness during eclipses is not as deep or oppresses the air in the same way as night does, we shall not marvel at this, for the nature of the body that produces night and that which produces the eclipse is the same, but their size is not equal. For their part, Egyptians say, I believe, that the moon is one seventy-second part of the earth, but Anaxagoras says that it is the size of the Peloponnesus. Aristarchus, differently, establishes that the diameter of the earth to that of the moon has a proportion which is smaller than 60 to 19 but somewhat greater than 108 to 43. Therefore, the earth completely removes the sun from our sight due to its size, because the obstruction is vast and has the length of night; yet even if the moon sometimes conceals the sun entirely, the eclipse does not have duration or prolongation, but a kind of brightness is visible around the edge not allowing the shadow to become

καὶ ἄκρατον. Ἀριστοτέλης δὲ ὁ παλαιὸς αἰτίαν τοῦ πλεονάκις τὴν σελήνην ἐκλεί-
C πουσαν ἢ | τὸν ἥλιον καθορᾶσθαι, πρὸς ἄλλαις τισὶ καὶ ταύτην ἀποδίδωσιν· ἥλιον
γὰρ ἐκλείπειν σελήνης ἀντιφράξει, σελήνην δὲ (γῆς). Ὁ δὲ Ποσειδώνιος ὁρισά-
μενος οὕτως· τόδε τὸ πάθος ἔκλειψίς ἐστιν ἡλίου, σύνοδος σκιᾶς σελήνης οἷς τὴν
ἔκλειψιν (πάθουσιν·) ἐκείνοις γὰρ μόνοις ἔκλειψίς ἐστιν ὧν ἂν ἡ σκιὰ τῆς σελήνης    5
καταλαβοῦσα τὴν ὄψιν ἀντιφράξῃ πρὸς τὸν ἥλιον· ὁμολογῶν δὲ σκιὰν τῆς σελήνης
φέρεσθαι πρὸς ἡμᾶς, οὐκ οἶδα ὅτι λέγειν ἑαυτῷ καταλέλοιπεν. Ἄστρου δὲ σκιὰν
D ἀδύνατον γενέσθαι· τὸ γὰρ ἀφώτιστον σκιὰ λέγεται, τὸ | δὲ φῶς οὐ ποιεῖ σκιὰν ἀλλ'
ἀναιρεῖν πέφυκεν.

20. Ἀλλὰ δὴ τί" ἔφη "μετὰ τοῦτο τῶν τεκμηρίων ἐλέχθη;" Κἀγὼ "τὴν αὐτὴν"    10
ἔφην "ἐλάμβανεν ἡ σελήνη ἔκλειψιν." "Ὀρθῶς" εἶπεν "ὑπέμνησας· ἀλλὰ δὴ πότε-
ρον ὡς πεπεισμένων ὑμῶν καὶ τιθέντων ἐκλείπειν τὴν σελήνην ὑπὸ τοῦ σκιάσματος
ἁλισκομένην ἤδη τρέπωμαι πρὸς τὸν λόγον, ἢ βούλεσθε μελέτην ποιήσωμαι καὶ
ἀπόδειξιν ὑμῖν τῶν ἐπιχειρημάτων ἕκαστον ἀπαριθμήσας;" "Νὴ Δία" εἶπεν ὁ Θέων
"τούτοις ἐμμελέτησον· ἐγὼ δὲ καὶ πειθοῦς τινος δέομαι ταύτῃ μόνον ἀκηκοὼς ὡς    15
E ἐπὶ μίαν [μὲν] εὐθεῖαν τῶν τριῶν σωμάτων γινομένων, γῆς | καὶ ἡλίου καὶ σελήνης,
αἱ ἐκλείψεις συντυγχάνουσιν· ἡ γὰρ γῆ τῆς σελήνης ἢ πάλιν ἡ σελήνη τῆς γῆς ἀφαι-
ρεῖται τὸν ἥλιον. Ἐκλείπει γὰρ οὗτος μὲν σελήνης, σελήνη δὲ γῆς ἐν μέσῳ τῶν τριῶν
ἱσταμένης· ὧν γίνεται, τὸ μὲν ἐν συνόδῳ, τὸ δὲ ἐν διχομηνίᾳ." Καὶ ὁ Λεύκιος ἔφη
"σχεδὸν μέντοι τῶν λεγομένων κυριώτατα ταῦτ' ἐστί. Πρόλαβε δὲ πρῶτον, εἰ βού-    20
λει, τὸν ἀπὸ τοῦ σχήματος τῆς σκιᾶς λόγον· ἔστι γὰρ κῶνος, ἅτε ἢ μεγάλου πυρὸς ἢ
φωτὸς σφαιροειδοῦς ἐλάττονα, σφαιροειδὴ δέ, περιβάλλοντος ὄγκον. Ὅθεν ἐν ταῖς
F ἐκλείψεσι τῆς σελήνης αἱ περιγραφαὶ τῶν μελαινομένων πρὸς τὰ λαμ|πρὰ τὰς ἀπο-
τομὰς περιφερεῖς ἴσχουσιν· ἃς γὰρ ἂν στρογγύλον στρογγύλῳ προσμίξαν ἢ δέξηται

---

3 γῆς *suppl.* RJ94: *lac.* 30 *lit.* E, 23 *lit.* B: γῆς πολλῷ μείζονος Amyot: γῆς, ἣν πολὺ μείζονα οὖσαν
πλεονάκις ἀποκρύπτειν τὴν σελήνην Wyt. *in app.*: γῆς πλεονάκις, μείζονος οὔσης Bern. *in app.*:
γῆς, πολλῷ μείζονος οὔσης Adler    4 τόδε τὸ πάθος B *et* E *s.l.*: τὸ δὲ πάθος E ‖ οἷς E *i.t.*: ἧς EB
4–5 τὴν ἔκλειψιν] *del.* Prickard: *transp. cum* τόδε τὸ πάθος Purser    5 πάθουσιν *supplevi: lac.* 22
*lit.* E, 11 *lit.* B: ὁρισάμενος, ὅτι τόδε τὸ πάθος τῆς ὄψεως ἔστιν οὐχ ἡλίου, καὶ σύνοδος σκιᾷ σελήνης ἣν
δὴ ἔκλειψιν ἡλίου καλοῦμεν· ὁμολογῶν γε *corr. et suppl.* Wyt. *in app.*: σκιᾷ *pro* σκιᾶς *et* ἢ σελήνης
σκιᾷ γῆς *add. ante* τὴν ἔκλειψιν *et* οὐκ ὀρθῶς ὡρίσατο *suppl. et* κέ *pro* γὰρ Bern. *in app.*: σύνοδος
σελήνῃ, ἧς σκιὰ τὴν ἔκλειψιν *corr. et* τοῖς ἀφωτίστοις τῆς γῆς μέρεσι ποιεῖ ὀρθῶς μὲν μείζονα τὴν γῆν
εἶναι τῆς ὑπέθετο *suppl.* Adler: ἂν ᾖ ταὐτό πως λέγει Purser: ἂν γῆς μέρεσι κατασκιάζῃ Ch.: σύνοδος
*del. et* σκιᾷ *pro* σκιᾶς *et* ποιεῖ, τούτοις ἐπισκοτοῦσα *suppl.* Görg.    6 ἀντιφράξῃ RJ94: ἀντιφράξαι
EB ‖ δὲ] γε Wyt. *in app.*: δὴ Ch.    8 ποιεῖ E: ποιεῖν B    10 δὴ τί E: τί δὴ B ‖ ἐλέχθη *punct. corr.*
Ald. Basil.: ἐλέχθη· EB    11 ὑπέμνησας B: ὑπομνήσας E    12 πεπεισμένων E: πεποιημένων B    13
τρέπωμαι Wyt. *in app.*: τρέπονται EB: τρέπομαι SR67: τρεπόμεθα RJ94 ‖ ποιήσωμαι] ποιήσωμεν
B *s.l.*    14 ὑμῖν Ald. Basil.: ὑμῶν EB ‖ ἀπαριθμήσας *punct. corr.* Ald. Basil.: ἀπαριθμήσας· EB:
ἀπαριθμῆται RJ94: ἀπαριθμήσασθαι Amyot    16 μὲν *secl.* Wyt. *in app.*    19 διχομηνίᾳ] διχοτομίᾳ
Ald. Basil. *et alii*    20 μέντοι B (τοι *s.l.*): μέν τι E ‖ Πρόλαβε] πρόσλαβε RJ94 *et alii*    21 κῶνος
Amyot Xyl.[1570]: κοινὸς EB ‖ ἢ Raing.: μὴ EB: καὶ Ald. Basil.: δὴ Po. Ch.

deep and pure. And the ancient Aristotle gives this as a reason among some others for the fact that the moon is seen eclipsed more frequently than the sun, for the sun is eclipsed by interposition of the moon but the moon by that ⟨of the earth⟩." Posidonius explained it this way: this circumstance is an eclipse of the sun, a conjunction of the shadow of the moon with those who ⟨suffer⟩ the eclipse; for there is an eclipse only for those whom the shadow of the moon screens from the sun by intercepting their vision; given that he admits that a shadow of the moon moves towards us, I do not know what is left for him to say. There cannot be shadow from a star, because the unlighted is called shadow, and light cannot produce shadow but destroys it by nature.

20. But, well then," he said, "which of the proofs was introduced after this one?" And I said, "the moon is subject to the same eclipse." "You have reminded me correctly;" he said, "but shall I turn now to my argument assuming that you are convinced and hold that the moon is eclipsed because it is caught in the shadow or do you want me to give a report and demonstration ennumerating each of the arguments?" "By Zeus," said Theon, "please, give these gentlemen a report. I, for my part, also need some persuasion, for I have only heard about this that when the three bodies come to be in straight line—earth, sun, and moon—eclipses happen: the earth occults the sun from the moon or the moon, in turn, from the earth. Indeed, the sun is eclipsed when the moon stands in the middle of the three, and the moon when it is the earth; of these phenomena, one happens at conjunction and the other at the middle of the month." And so Lucius said: "These are about the main ideas of what is said on the matter. But first include, if you will, the argument resulting from the shape of the shadow: it is a cone, as is the case when a great, spherical fire or light encircles a smaller, still spherical mass. This is the reason why during the eclipses of the moon the limits of the darkened portions obtain curved sections against the bright ones—indeed, whenever a round mass is joined to another round mass the cuts they either receive or cause, wherever they take place, turn out to be round. Secondly, I

Lamp.
Lucius

Theon

Lucius

τομὰς ἢ παράσχῃ, πανταχόσε χωροῦσαι δι' ὁμοιότητα γίνονται κυκλοτερεῖς· δεύτερον οἶμαί σε γινώσκειν ὅτι, σελήνης μὲν ἐκλείπει πρῶτα μέρη τὰ πρὸς ἀπηλιώτην, ἡλίου δὲ τὰ πρὸς δύσιν· κινεῖται δέ, ἡ μὲν σκιὰ τῆς γῆς ἐπὶ τὴν ἑσπέραν ἀπὸ τῶν ἀνατολῶν, ἥλιος δὲ καὶ σελήνη τοὐναντίον ἐπὶ τὰς ἀνατολάς. ‖ Ταῦτα γὰρ ἰδεῖν τε παρέχει τῇ αἰσθήσει τὰ φαινόμενα κἀκ λόγων οὐ πάνυ τι μακρῶν μαθεῖν ἔστιν. Ἐκ δὲ τούτων ἡ αἰτία βεβαιοῦται τῆς ἐκλείψεως· ἐπεὶ γὰρ ἥλιος μὲν ἐκλείπει καταλαμβανόμενος, σελήνη δὲ ἀπαντῶσα τῷ ποιοῦντι τὴν ἔκλειψιν, εἰκότως, μᾶλλον δὲ ἀναγκαίως, ὁ μὲν ὄπισθεν ἁλίσκεται πρῶτον, ἡ δ' ἔμπροσθεν· ἄρχεται γὰρ ἐκεῖθεν ἡ ἐπιπρόσθησις, ὅθεν πρῶτον [μὲν] ἐπιβάλλει τὸ ἐπιπροσθοῦν. Ἐπιβάλλει δέ, ἐκείνῳ μὲν ἀφ' ἑσπέρας, ἡ σελήνη πρὸς αὐτὸν ἁμιλλωμένη, ταύτῃ δὲ ἀπὸ τῶν ἀνατολῶν, ὡς πρὸς τοὐναντίον ὑποφερομένη. Τρίτον τοίνυν ἔτι τὸ τοῦ χρόνου λάβε καὶ τὸ τοῦ μεγέθους | τῶν ἐκλείψεων αὐτῆς, ὑψηλὴ μὲν ἐκλείπουσα καὶ ἀπόγειος ὀλίγον ἀποκρύπτεται χρόνον, πρόσγειος δὲ καὶ ταπεινὴ αὐτὸ τοῦτο παθοῦσα σφόδρα πιέζεται καὶ βραδέως ἐκ τῆς σκιᾶς ἄπεισι· καίτοι ταπεινὴ μὲν οὖσα τοῖς μεγίστοις χρῆται κινήμασιν, ὑψηλὴ δὲ τοῖς ἐλαχίστοις· ἀλλὰ τὸ αἴτιον ἐν τῇ σκιᾷ τῆς διαφορᾶς ἐστιν· εὐρυτάτη γὰρ οὖσα περὶ τὴν βάσιν, ὥσπερ οἱ κῶνοι, συστελλομένη τε κατὰ μικρὸν εἰς ὀξὺ τῇ κορυφῇ καὶ λεπτὸν ἀπολήγει πέρας· ὅθεν ἡ σελήνη ταπεινὴ μὲν ἐμπεσοῦσα τοῖς μεγίστοις λαμβάνεται κύκλοις ὑπ' αὐτῆς καὶ διαπερᾷ τὸ βύθιον καὶ σκοτωδέστατον, ἄνω δέ, οἷον ἐν τενάγει, | διὰ λεπτότητα τοῦ σκιεροῦ χρανθεῖσα ταχέως ἀπαλλάττεται. Παρίημι δὲ ὅσα χωρὶς ἰδίᾳ πρὸς τὰς βάσεις καὶ διαφορήσεις ἐλέχθη· καὶ γὰρ ἐκεῖναι μέχρι γε τοῦ ἐνδεχομένου προσίενται τὴν αἰτίαν, ἀλλὰ ἐπανάγω πρὸς τὸν ὑποκείμενον λόγον ἀρχὴν ἔχοντα τὴν αἴσθησιν. Ὁρῶμεν γὰρ ὅτι πῦρ ἐκ τόπου σκιεροῦ διαφαίνεται καὶ διαλάμπει μᾶλλον εἴτε παχύτητι τοῦ σκοτώδους ἀέρος οὐ δεχομένου τὰς ἀπορρεύσεις καὶ διαχύσεις, ἀλλὰ συνέχοντος ἐν ταὐτῷ τὴν οὐσίαν καὶ σφίγγοντος, εἴτε τῆς αἰσθήσεως τοῦτο πάθος ἐστίν, ὡς τὰ θερμὰ παρὰ τὰ ψυχρά, θερμότερα, καὶ τὰς ἡδονὰς παρὰ τοὺς πόνους, σφοδροτέρας· οὕτω τὰ λαμπρὰ φαίνεσθαι παρὰ τὰ σκοτεινὰ φανερά, τοῖς διαφόροις πάθεσιν ἀντεπιτείνοντα τὴν φαντασίαν. Ἔοικε δὲ πιθανώτερον εἶναι τὸ πρότερον, ἐν | γὰρ ἡλίῳ πᾶσα πυρὸς φύσις, οὐ μόνον τὸ λαμπρὸν ἀπόλλυσιν, ἀλλὰ τῷ εἴκειν γίνεται δύσεργος καὶ ἀμβλυτέρα· σκίδνησι γὰρ ἡ θερμότης καὶ διαχέει τὴν δύναμιν. Εἴπερ οὖν ἡ σελήνη πυρὸς εἴληχε βληχροῦ καὶ ἀδρανοῦς, ἄστρον οὖσα θολερώτερον, ὥσπερ αὐτοὶ λέγουσιν, οὐθὲν ὧν πάσχουσα φαίνεται νῦν, ἀλλὰ τὰ ἐναντία πάντα πάσχειν αὐτὴν προσῆκόν ἐστι· φαίνεσθαι μὲν ὅτε κρύπτεται, κρύπτεσθαι δὲ ὁπηνίκα φαί-

---

5 τι E: τοι B    8 ὁ Wyt. in app.: τὸ EB: τὸν RJ94 ‖ ἡ Steph.: ἢ EB: τὴν RJ94    9 μὲν secl. Wyt. in app.    10 ταύτῃ] ταύτη Ald.: ἡ γῆ add. post ταύτη δ' Madv. ‖ ἀνατολῶν] ἡ σκιὰ τῆς γῆς add. post ἀνατολῶν Adler    11 λάβε om. B    12–13 ἀποκρύπτεται E et B s.l.: ἀπολείπεται B    16 εὐρυτάτη E: εὐρυτάτῃ B    20 ἰδίᾳ E: ἰδίους B: ἰδίων RJ94    23 εἴτε SR67: ἐπὶ EB ‖ παχύτητι RJ94 Basil.: ταχύτητι EB: ταχυτῆτι B s.l.    24 ἀπορρεύσεις E: ἀπορεύσεις B    31 βληχροῦ E et B i.t.: βαηχροῦ B

believe you know that the first parts of the moon to be eclipsed are eastward, and of the sun, westward; and that while the shadow of the earth moves towards the west from east, the sun and the moon, reversedly, towards the east. This is what the phenomena make visible to sense-perception and it does not take long to learn. From these the cause of the eclipse is firmly established; after all, given that the sun is eclipsed by being caught up and the moon by catching what causes the eclipse, it is likely, or rather necessary, that the sun is taken first from behind and the moon from the front—as the obstruction begins at the place which the obstructing body invades first. It tosses over the sun from the west, the moon hastening eagerly towards it, and over the moon, from the east, as the moon is taken from under in the opposite direction. Thirdly, take into account even more the issue of the duration and the dimension of lunar eclipses, when it is eclipsed high and far from the earth, it is concealed for a little time, but when it undergoes this very phenomenon near the earth and low, it is strongly gripped and slowly walks away from the shadow—even though when the moon is low it makes use of its amplest motions and when it is high of the slightest. Yet the reason for the difference is in the shadow: as it is largest at the base, just like cones, being gradually reduced it ends at the peak in a sharp and fine tip. From this it follows that if the moon falls in the shadow when being low, it is taken by it in its largest circles and crosses the deep and darkest section, but when high, like in shallow water because of the tenuousness of the shadow being just slightly grazed, the moon moves away quickly. I pass over everything which was said except to the phases and variations in particular, because these also, as far as possible, admit the cause of our argument; however, I turn back to what lies under our argument, which has its origin in sense-perception. Indeed we see that fire shines and glows more intensely from a shadowy place, whether as a result of the shadowy air that does not allow the emanations and diffusions due to its density—but encloses and holds the substance in one place—, or as a result of an affection of our senses, just as warm bodies next to cold ones seem hotter, and pleasures next to pains, more intense, similarly bright things next to dark ones seem brighter, the impression being heightened by the different affections. It seems that the first option is more plausible, since every type of fire, in sunlight, not only loses its brightness but in so doing becomes ineffective and weaker; after all, the sun's heat disperses and dissipates its power. Therefore, if the moon is endowed with a faint and languid fire, thus being a quite impure star, as they themselves affirm, it should show none of the phenomena that it now undergoes, but it would be appropriate for the moon to suffer all of the opposite: to be visible when it is in fact hidden and to hide whenever it

νεται· τουτέστι κρύπτεσθαι μὲν τὸν ἄλλον χρόνον ὑπὸ τοῦ περιέχοντος αἰθέρος ἀμαυρουμένην, ἐκλάμπειν δὲ καὶ γίνεσθαι καταφανῆ δι' ἓξ μηνῶν καὶ πάλιν διὰ πέντε τῇ | σκιᾷ τῆς γῆς ὑποδυομένην· αἱ γὰρ πέντε καὶ ἑξήκοντα καὶ τετρακόσιαι περίοδοι τῶν ἐκλειπτικῶν πανσελήνων, τὰς τέσσαρας καὶ τετρακοσίας ἑξαμήνους ἔχουσι, τὰς δὲ ἄλλας πενταμήνους. Ἔδει τοίνυν διὰ τοσούτων χρόνων φαίνεσθαι τὴν σελήνην ἐν τῇ σκιᾷ λαμπρυνομένην, ἡ δέ, ἐν ⟨αὐτῇ⟩ μὲν ἐκλείπει καὶ ἀπόλλυσι τὸ φῶς, ἀναλαμβάνει δὲ αὖθις ὅταν ἐκφύγῃ τὴν σκιάν, καὶ φαίνεταί γε πολλάκις ἡμέρας, ὡς πάντα μᾶλλον ἢ πύρινον οὖσα σῶ|μα καὶ ἀστεροειδές."

21. Εἰπόντος δὲ τοῦτο τοῦ Λευκίου, συνεξέδραμον ἅμα πως τῷ ⟨λέγειν⟩ ὅ τε Φαρνάκης καὶ ὁ Ἀπολλωνίδης· εἶτα τοῦ Ἀπολλωνίδου παρέντος, ὁ Φαρνάκης εἶπεν ὅτι τοῦτο καὶ μάλιστα τὴν σελήνην δείκνυσιν ἄστρον ἢ πῦρ οὖσαν· οὐ γάρ ἐστι παντελῶς ἄδηλος ἐν ταῖς ἐκλείψεσιν, ἀλλὰ διαφαίνει τινὰ χρόαν ἀνθρακώδη καὶ βλοσυράν, ἥτις ἴδιός ἐστιν αὐτῆς. Ὁ δὲ Ἀπολλωνίδης ἐνέστη περὶ τῆς σκιᾶς· ἀεὶ γὰρ οὕτως ... ὀνομάζειν τοὺς μαθηματικοὺς τὸν ἀλαμπῆ τόπον ... σκιάν τε μὴ δέχεσθαι τὸν οὐρανόν. ‖ Ἐγὼ δέ, "τοῦτο μὲν" ἔφην "πρὸς τοὔνομα μᾶλλον ἐριστικῶς ἢ πρὸς τὸ πρᾶγμα φυσικῶς καὶ μαθηματικῶς ἐνισταμένου· τὸν γὰρ ἀντιφραττόμενον ὑπὸ τῆς γῆς τόπον εἰ μὴ σκιάν τις ἐθέλοι καλεῖν ἀλλ' ἀφεγγὲς χωρίον, ὅμως ἀναγκαῖον ἐν αὐτῷ τὴν σελήνην γενομένην ... Καὶ ὅλως" ἔφην "εὔηθές ἐστιν ἐκεῖ μὴ φάναι τῆς γῆς ἐξικνεῖσθαι τὴν σκιὰν ⟨ὅθεν⟩ ἡ σκιὰ τῆς σελήνης ἐπιπίπτουσα τῇ ὄψει καὶ ... πρὸς τὴν γῆν ἔκλειψιν ἡλίου ποιεῖ. Πρὸς σὲ δέ, ὦ Φαρνάκη, τρέψομαι· τὸ γὰρ ἀνθρακῶδες ἐκεῖνο καὶ διακαὲς χρῶμα τῆς σελήνης ὃ φῂς ἴδιον | αὐτῆς εἶναι, σώματός ἐστι πυκνότητα καὶ βάθος ἔχοντος· οὐθὲν γὰρ ἐθέλει τοῖς ἀραιοῖς ὑπόλειμμα φλογὸς οὐδ' ἴχνος ἐμμένειν οὐδ' ἔστιν ἀνθρακογένεσις οὐ μὴ στερέμνιον σῶμα δεξάμενον διὰ βάθους τὴν πύρωσιν καὶ σῴζον, ὥς που καὶ Ὅμηρος εἴρηκεν·

---

6 αὐτῇ suppl. Ch. in app.: lac. 5 lit. EB: σκιᾷ RJ94: τῇ σκιᾷ Wyt. in app.    9 λέγειν suppl. Po. in app. Ch.: lac. 7 lit. E, 5 lit. B: αὐτῷ RJ94: λόγῳ ἐπιβαλλόμενοι Amyot: λόγῳ Wyt. in app.: λήγοντι Raing. in app.    10 παρέντος SR67: παρόντος EB    13 βλοσυράν I.22: βλοσσυράν EB    14 vac. 3 lit. E: lac. 6 lit. post ὀνομάζειν B: πάντα suppl. RJ94: ὄντως Amyot: lac. del. Kepl.: ἐξονομάζειν Raing. in app.: μόνον vel δεῖν γὰρ οὕτως ὀν. κατὰ Po. in app. ‖ lac. 4 lit. E, 7 lit. B: lac. del. Ald. Basil.: ἐπὶ γῆς vel μόνον Po.    16 ἐνισταμένου RJ94: ἐνισταμένους EB    18 lac. 30 lit. E, 34 lit. B: μᾶλλον λάμπειν καὶ διαφαίνεσθαι suppl. RJ94: ἐξαμαυροῦσθαι vel ἐκκλείψαι Amyot: σκοτοῦσθαι Wyt. in app.: σκοτοῦσθαι καὶ ἀμαυροῦσθαι Bern. in app.: ἐπιπροσθεῖσθαι ὑπὸ τῆς γῆς καὶ ἐκλείπειν Adler: εἴ γε γῆ τίς ἐστι, ἀφεγγῆ καὶ ἀλαμπῆ γενέσθαι Purser: καὶ ἐπισκοτουμένην ἄστρον μὴ εἶναι vel εἴ γ' ἄστρον ἐστίν, καὶ μᾶλλον ἐκλάμπειν Po. in app.: ἐπισκοτεῖσθαι τοῦ ἡλιακοῦ φωτὸς στερομένην Ch.    19 φάναι Ald. Basil.: φᾶναι EB ‖ ὅθεν suppl. Amyot: lac. 11 lit. E, 8 lit. B: ὅπου RJ94: ἔνθαπερ Bern. in app.: ὁπόθεν καὶ Purser: ὅθεν ἔοικεν Po. in app.    20 lac. 7 lit. EB: διήκουσα suppl. RJ94: ἀντερείδουσα vel φερομένη Amyot ‖ ποιεῖ RJ94: ποιεῖν EB    22 ἀραιοῖς RJ94: ἀρχαίοις EB    23 οὐ μὴ Wyt.: οὐ μὴν EB: εἰ μὴ I.22: ὅπου μὴ Xyl.$^{1570}$: ὅπου οὐδὲ Kepl.    24 σῴζον Xyl.$^{1570}$: σόλων EB: ψόλον Amyot

is visible—namely, to hide any other time when it is obscured by the surrounding ether, and to shine and become visible every six months or in turn every five, when it sinks into the shadow of the earth—because of 465 ecliptic full moons, 404 have a six-months cycle, and the rest a five-months one. It should have been at such times that the moon appears resplendent in the shadow, whereas in ⟨it⟩ the moon is eclipsed and loses its light, and receives it back as soon as it escapes the shadow and appears often during the day, so the moon is all but a fiery and star-like body."

21. When Lucius said this, almost simultaneously Pharnaces and Apollonides sprang forth in order ⟨to speak⟩. After Apollonides gave way to Pharnaces, the latter said that this demonstrates, above all, that the moon is a star or a fire, given that it is not fully invisible during eclipses, but shows a kind of smouldering and dreadful color which is characteristic of it. And Apollonides raised the issue concerning the shadow on the grounds that astronomers always give this name to the space with no light, and heaven does not admit shadow. And I said: "this comes from who objects naggingly to the terminology rather than to the facts like a natural philosopher or an astronomer. If one does not want to call the place screened by the earth 'shadow' but 'unlit', all the same the moon must ... when it gets there. And in general too," I said, "it is naive to deny that the shadow of the earth reaches that point ⟨whence⟩ the shadow of the moon, by impinging upon sight and ... to the earth, produces a solar eclipse. Towards you, Pharnaces, I shall turn now: as a matter of fact, that smouldering and scorching color of the moon that you say is characteristic of it is that of a body which possesses density and depth; for no rest of flame nor trace is able to remain in rarefied bodies and no incandescence is possible where there is not a solid body capable of receiving and sustaining the ignition in depth, as somewhere also Homer said:

Pharn.

Apoll.

Lamp.

αὐτὰρ ἐπεὶ πυρὸς ἄνθος ἀπέπτατο· παύσατο δὲ φλὸξ
ἀνθρακιὴν στορέσας.

Ὁ γὰρ ἄνθραξ ἔοικεν οὐ πῦρ ἀλλὰ σῶμα πεπυρωμένον εἶναι καὶ πεπονθὸς ὑπὸ
πυρὸς στερεῷ καὶ ῥίζαν ἔχοντι προσμένοντος ὄγκῳ καὶ προσδιατρίβοντος· αἱ δὲ
φλόγες ἀραιάς εἰσιν ἔξαψις καὶ ῥεύματα τροφῆς καὶ ὕλης ταχὺ δι' ἀσθένειαν ἀνα- 5
C λυομένης· ὥστε οὐδὲν | ἂν ὑπῆρχε τοῦ γεώδη καὶ πυκνὴν εἶναι τὴν σελήνην ἕτερον
οὕτως ἐναργὲς τεκμήριον, εἴπερ αὐτῆς ἴδιον ἦν, ὡς χρῶμα τὸ ἀνθρακῶδες. Ἀλλ'
οὐκ ἔστιν, ὦ φίλε Φαρνάκη, πολλάς, τὰς ἐκλειπούσας χρόας ἀμείβειν, καὶ διαιροῦ-
σιν αὐτὰς οὕτως οἱ μαθηματικοὶ κατὰ χρόνον καὶ ὥραν ἀφορίζοντες· ἂν ἀφ' ἑσπέρας
ἐκλείπῃ, φαίνεται μέλαινα δεινῶς ἄχρι τρίτης ὥρας καὶ ἡμισείας· ἂν δὲ μέσῃ, τοῦτο 10
δὴ τὸ ἐπιφοινίσσον ἵησι [καὶ πῦρ] καὶ πυρωπόν· ἀπὸ δὲ ἑβδόμης ὥρας καὶ ἡμι-
σείας, ἀνίσταται τὸ ἐρύθημα· καὶ τέλος ἤδη πρὸς ἕω, λαμβάνει χρόαν κυανοειδῆ καὶ
D χαροπὴν ἀφ' ἧς δὴ καὶ μάλιστα γλαυ|κῶπιν αὐτὴν οἱ ποιηταὶ καὶ Ἐμπεδοκλῆς ἀνα-
καλοῦνται. Τοσαύτας οὖν χρόας ἐν τῇ σκιᾷ τὴν σελήνην λαμβάνουσαν ὁρῶντες, οὐκ
ὀρθῶς ἐπὶ μόνον καταφέρονται τὸ ἀνθρακῶδες, ὃ μάλιστα φῆσαι τις ἂν ἀλλότριον 15
αὐτῆς εἶναι καὶ μᾶλλον ὑπόμιγμα καὶ λεῖμμα τοῦ φωτὸς διὰ τῆς σκιᾶς περιλάμ-
ποντος, ἴδιον δὲ τὸ μέλαν καὶ γεῶδες. Ὅπου δὲ πορφυρίσιν ἐνταῦθα καὶ φοινικίσι
λίμναις τε καὶ ποταμοῖς δεχομένοις ἥλιον ἐπίσκια χωρία γειτνιῶντα συγχρώζεται
καὶ περιλάμπεται διὰ τὰς ἀνακλάσεις, ἀποδιδόντα πολλοὺς καὶ διαφόρους ἀπαυγα-
E σμούς, τί θαυμαστὸν εἰ ῥεῦμα πολὺ σκιᾶς | ἐμβάλλον ὥσπερ εἰς πέλαγος οὐράνιον 20
οὐ σταθεροῦ φωτὸς οὐδὲ ἠρεμοῦντος, ἀλλὰ μυρίοις ἄστροις περιελαυνομένου μίξεις
τε παντοδαπὰς καὶ μεταβολὰς λαμβάνοντος, ἄλλην ἄλλοτε χρόαν ἐκματτόμενον
ἀπὸ τῆς σελήνης ἐνταῦθα ἀποδίδωσιν; Ἄστρον μὲν γὰρ ἢ πῦρ οὐκ ἂν ἐν σκιᾷ δια-
φανείη μέλαν ἢ γλαυκὸν ἢ κυανοειδές, ὄρεσι δὲ καὶ πεδίοις καὶ θαλάσσαις, πολλαὶ
μὲν ἀφ' ἡλίου μορφαὶ χρωμάτων ἐπιτρέχουσι καὶ σκιαῖς καὶ ὁμίχλαις, οἵας φαρμά- 25
κοις γραφικοῖς, μιγνύμενον ἐπάγει βαφὰς τὸ λαμπρόν. Ὧν τὰ μὲν τῆς θαλάττης
F ἐπικεχείρηκεν ἀμωσγέπως ἐξονομά|ζειν Ὅμηρος, ἰοειδέα καλῶν καὶ οἴνοπα πόν-
τον, αὖθις δὲ πορφύρεον κῦμα γλαυκήν τε ἄλλως θάλασσαν καὶ λευκὴν γαλήνην,
τὰς δὲ περὶ τὴν γῆν διαφορὰς τῶν ἄλλοτε ἄλλως ἐπιφαινομένων χρωμάτων παρῆ-
κεν, ὡς ἀπείρους τὸ πλῆθος οὔσας. Τὴν δὲ σελήνην οὐκ εἰκὸς ὥσπερ τὴν θάλασσαν 30
μίαν ἔχειν ἐπιφάνειαν, ἀλλὰ ἐοικέναι μάλιστα τῇ γῇ τὴν φύσιν, ἣν ἐμυθολόγει
935A Σωκράτης ὁ παλαιός, ‖ εἴτε δὴ ταύτην αἰνιττόμενος, εἴτε δὴ ἄλλην τινὰ διηγούμε-
νος. Οὐ γὰρ ἄπιστον οὐδὲ θαυμαστὸν εἰ μηδὲν ⟨ἐν⟩έχουσα διεφθορὸς ἑαυτῇ μηδὲ

---

2 στορέσας] στορέσασα B s.l.   6 τοῦ om. B   8 τὰς] γὰρ RJ94 et alii ‖ ἐκλειπούσας] ἐκλειπού-
σαι Ald.: ἐκλείπουσα RJ94 et alii: ἐκλειπούσης Kepl. ‖ ἀμείβειν] ἀμείβει RJ94 et alii   11 ἵησι B i.t.:
ἵησι EB ‖ καὶ πῦρ secl. Dübn. ‖ καὶ² E et B s.l.   12 ἤδη B: ἤδη E ‖ λαμβάνει SR67: λαμβάνειν
EB   21 περιελαυνομένου E: ἐλαυνομένου B   23 ἀποδίδωσιν punct. corr. Steph.: ἀποδίδωσιν. EB
28 κῦμα B: κύμα E   30 ὥσπερ om. B   33 ἐνέχουσα Raing.: ἔχουσα EB: ἐν add. ante ἑαυτῇ
Emp. et alii

'yet when fire's bloom flew away and flame ceased, | he put down the embers ...'

Well, it appears that coal is not fire but a body ignited and affected by fire, which adheres to and remains with a solid mass possessing a foundation, whereas flames are kindling and emanations of rarefied nourishment or matter that is quickly dissolved as a result of its weakness; so nothing else would serve so clearly as proof that the moon is earthy and dense, if it really was characteristic of it, as the smouldering color. However, dear Pharnaces, it is not possible, for they are many, to change the colors in the eclipse, and astronomers classify them by delimiting them in this way: according to time or hour—if the moon is eclipsed in the evening it appears awfully black until half past the third hour; if at midnight, it lets go this reddish and fiery tone; after half past the seventh hour, red color takes place; and finally, if dawn is already near, it takes on a bluish or azure shade, precisely from which the poets and Empedocles call it above all 'sparkling-eyed'. Then, when such are the colorations, we see the moon taking in the shadow, it is not correct to reduce them to only the smouldering color, especially the one someone could say is foreign to it and more of a mixture and a remnant of the light shining through the shadow, while characteristic of the moon would be black and earthy. Since here shadowy locations close to lakes and rivers receiving the sun take on the color and brilliance of the purples and reds that shade them, as a result of the reflections returning many and diverse effulgences, what marvel is there if a great emanation of shade debouching as it were into a heavenly sea—not of calm light or at rest but one that is pushed around by myriads of stars and that takes on mixtures and alterations of all sorts—, receiving from the moon the impression of one shade or another, sends them back here? In fact, a star or fire could not shine black, glaucous or bluish in the shadow, but on mountains, plains, and seas various shades of colors spread from the sun, and its brilliance, blended with shadows and mists, produces tones such as if blended with the colors for painting. Of these, Homer undertook somehow the task of naming the ones concerning the sea, calling it 'violet' and 'winey' and again 'purple wave' and 'glaucous sea' elsewhere and 'white tranquility;' yet the variations of colors around the earth, differing now and then, he passed over on account of their number being infinite. However, it is unlikely that the moon, like the sea, has one single surface, but resembles essentially the earth in nature, that which the ancient Socrates discussed in a myth—whether he really meant this one enigmatically or described some other. Well, it is not incredible or surprising that the moon, if containing nothing corrupted or muddy itself but garner-

ἰλυῶδες, ἀλλὰ φῶς τε καρπουμένη καθαρὸν ἐξ οὐρανοῦ καὶ θερμότητος, οὐ δια-
καοῦς οὐδὲ μανικοῦ πυρός, ἀλλὰ νοτεροῦ καὶ ἀβλαβοῦς καὶ κατὰ φύσιν ἔχοντος,
οὖσα πλήρης κάλλη τε θαυμαστὰ κέκτηται τόπων, ὄρη τε φλογοειδῆ καὶ ζώνας
ἁλουργοὺς ἔχει χρυσόν τε καὶ ἄργυρον οὐκ ἐν βάθει διεσπαρμένον, ἀλλὰ πρὸς τοῖς
πεδίοις ἐξανθοῦντα πολὺν ἢ πρὸς ὕψεσι λείοις περιφερόμενον. Εἰ δὲ τούτων ὄψις 5
B ἀφικνεῖται διὰ τῆς σκιᾶς ἄλλοτε ἄλλη πρὸς ἡμᾶς | ἐξαλλαγῇ καὶ διαφορᾷ τινι τοῦ
περιέχοντος, τό γε μὴν τίμιον οὐκ ἀπόλλυσι τῆς δόξης οὐδὲ τὸ θεῖον ἡ σελήνη·
ἥτις ... ἱερὰ πρὸς ἀνθρώπων νομιζομένη, μᾶλλον ἢ πῦρ θολερόν, ὥσπερ οἱ Στωι-
κοὶ λέγουσι, καὶ τρυγῶδες· πῦρ μέν γε παρὰ Μήδοις καὶ Ἀσσυρίοις βαρβαρικὰς
ἔχει τιμάς· οἳ φόβῳ τὰ βλάπτοντα θεραπεύουσι πρὸ τῶν σεμνῶν ἀφοσιούμενοι· τὸ 10
δὲ γῆς ὄνομα παντί που φίλον Ἕλληνι καὶ τίμιον καὶ πάτρῳον ἡμῖν ὥσπερ ἄλλον
τινὰ θεῶν σέβεσθαι. Πολλοῦ δὲ δέομεν ἄνθρωποι τὴν σελήνην, γῆν οὖσαν ὀλυμπίαν,
C ἄψυχον ἡγεῖσθαι σῶμα καὶ ἄνουν καὶ ἄμοιρον ὧν θεοῖς | ἀπάρχεσθαι προσήκει νόμῳ
τε τῶν ἀγαθῶν ἀμοιβὰς τίνοντας καὶ κατὰ φύσιν σεβομένους τὸ κρεῖττον ἀρετῇ καὶ
δυνάμει καὶ τιμιώτερον. Ὥστε μηδὲν οἰώμεθα πλημμελεῖν γῆν αὐτὴν θέμενοι· τὸ 15
δὲ φαινόμενον τουτὶ πρόσωπον αὐτῆς, ὥσπερ ἡ παρ᾽ ἡμῖν ἔχει γῆ κόλπους τινὰς
μεγάλους, οὕτως ἐκείνην ἀνεπτύχθαι βάθεσι μεγάλοις καὶ ῥήξεσιν ὕδωρ ἢ ζοφε-
ρὸν ἀέρα περιέχουσιν· ὧν ἐντὸς οὐ καθίησιν οὐδὲ ἐπιψαύει τὸ τοῦ ἡλίου φῶς, ἀλλὰ
ἐκλείπει καὶ διεσπασμένην ἐνταῦθα τὴν ἀνάκλασιν ἀποδίδωσιν."

22. Ὑπολαβὼν δὲ ὁ Ἀπολλωνίδης, "εἶτα, ὦ πρὸς αὐτῆς" ἔφη "τῆς σελήνης, δυνα- 20
D τὸν εἶναι δοκεῖ | ὑμῖν ῥηγμάτων τινῶν ἢ φαράγγων εἶναι σκιὰς κἀκεῖθεν ἀφικνεῖσθαι
δεῦρο πρὸς τὴν ὄψιν, ἢ τὸ συμβαῖνον οὐ λογίζεσθε κἀγὼ τουτὶ εἴπω; Ἀκούοιτε δὲ
καίπερ οὐκ ἀγνοοῦντες· ἡ μὲν διάμετρος τῆς σελήνης δυοκαίδεκα δακτύλους ἔχει
τὸ φαινόμενον ἐν τοῖς μέσοις ἀποστήμασι μέγεθος, τῶν δὲ μελάνων καὶ σκιερῶν
ἕκαστον ἡμιδακτυλίου φαίνεται μεῖζον, ὥστε τῆς διαμέτρου μεῖζον ἢ εἰκοστοτέ- 25
ταρτον εἶναι· καὶ μήν, εἰ μόνων ὑποθοίμεθα τὴν περίμετρον τῆς σελήνης τρισμυρίων
σταδίων, μυρίων δὲ τὴν διάμετρον, κατὰ τὸ ὑποκείμενον οὐκ ἔλαττον ἂν εἶναι πεν-
E τακοσίων σταδίων ἐν | αὐτῇ τῶν σκιερῶν ἕκαστον. Ὅρα δὴ πρῶτον ἂν ᾖ δυνατὸν
τῇ σελήνῃ τηλικαῦτα βάθη καὶ τηλικαύτας εἶναι τραχύτητας, ὥστε σκιὰν ποιεῖν
τοσαύτην· ἔπειτα πῶς οὖσαι τηλικαῦται τὸ μέγεθος ὑφ᾽ ἡμῶν οὐχ ὁρῶνται." Κἀγὼ 30
μειδιάσας πρὸς αὐτὸν "εὖ γε" ἔφην "ὅτι τοιαύτην ἐξεύρηκας ἀπόδειξιν, ὦ Ἀπολλω-

---

4 ἁλουργοὺς E: ἁλουργὰς B    5 περιφερόμενον] περιχεόμενον Amyot: περιφαινόμενον Bern. in
app.: προφερόμενον Adler    6 τινι B: τινὶ E    8 ἥτις et lac. 10 lit. E, 13 lit. B: γῆ suppl. RJ94: γῆ τις
(sic) corr. et ὀλύμπια καὶ suppl. Amyot: ἤ τις corr. et θεὸς διατελεῖ καὶ suppl. Wyt. in app.: γῆ τις
et lac. del. Emp.: γῆ τις corr. et οὖσα πάγκαλος suppl. Adler ‖ μᾶλλον ἢ RJ94: ἢ μᾶλλον EB    12
θεῶν E: θεὸν B et alii ‖ δέομεν RJ94 Basil.: δεῖ οἵ μὲν E: δεῖ οἱ μὲν B    15 γῆν RJ94 Basil.: τὴν EB
22 εἴπω punct. corr. RJ94: εἴπω· EB ‖ Ἀκούοιτε δὲ E: ἀκούοιτε δὲ post καίπερ οὐκ ἀγνοοῦντες B:
ἀκούητε δὴ SR67: ἀκούοιτε δὴ RJ94    27 ἂν εἶναι] ἂν εἴη RJ94 et alii

ing pure light from heaven and being filled with warmth, not a blazing or raging fire but wet and innocuous and in accordance to nature, possesses marvellous beauties in its regions and flame-like mountains, and has purple areas as well as gold and silver not disseminated in depth but blooming abundantly on the plains or moving around on the smooth heights. If sight of these reaches us through the shadow, at variance now and then due to some diversity and difference of the surrounding air, the moon does not lose the honor nor the divinity of its reputation, because it is held by men to be sacred, rather than a murky and residual fire, as Stoics say. After all, fire receives barbaric honors among the Medes and Assyrians, who out of fear worship deceiving powers instead of the venerable ones by way of propitiatory rites; but the name of earth is to all Greeks dear and respectable, and our native tradition too, to be worshipped like any other of the gods. So we men are far from thinking that the moon, being a celestial earth, is a souless and mindless body and without its share in what it is our duty to consecrate to the gods by law as retribution for the goods received and we should worship according to nature what is better and more honorable both in virtue and power. Accordingly, we shall think that we make no mistake when supposing that the moon is earth, and regarding this face which appears to be its, in the same way that around us the earth has some great gulfs, so also the moon unfolds with great depths and clefts containing water or gloomy air—into these the light of the sun does not descend and does not touch the interior, but goes astray and sends back here a dispersed reflection."

22. Breaking in at this moment, Apollonides said: "then by the moon itself, do you folks believe it is possible that any of those clefts or cliffs cast shadows which attain from there our sight down here, or do you not evaluate the implications and shall I explain this myself? Please listen, even though you are not unaware of it: the diameter of the moon has an apparent size of twelve digits at its mean distance, and of the black and shadowy stains each appears to be greater than half a digit, therefore it is greater than one twenty-fourth of the diameter. Really, if we suppose the circumference of the moon to be thirty thousand stades only, and the diameter to be ten thousand, according to this supposition each of the shadowy spots in it would be of no less than five hundred stades. See, firstly, whether it would be possible that such sizable depths and ridges exist in the moon so as to cast a shadow that big; and, secondly, how come, despite being so great in size, we do not see them." Then, while smiling, I told him: "very well, you have discovered such a demonstration, Apollonides, with which you can demonstrate that you and I

Apoll.

Lamp.

80                                                                                                    DE FACIE

νίδη, δι' ἧς κἀμὲ καὶ σαυτὸν ἀποδείξεις τῶν Ἀλωαδῶν ἐκείνων εἶναι μείζονας, οὐκ
ἐν ἅπαντι μέντοι χρόνῳ τῆς ἡμέρας, ἀλλὰ πρωῒ μάλιστα καὶ δείλης, (εἰ) οἴει, τὰς
σκιὰς ἡμῶν τοῦ ἡλίου ποιοῦντος ἠλιβάτους, τὸν καλὸν τοῦτον αἰσθήσει παρέχειν
F   συλλογισμόν, | ὡς εἰ μέγα τὸ σκιαζόμενον, ὑπερμέγεθες τὸ σκιάζον. Ἐν Λήμνῳ μὲν
οὐδέτερος ἡμῶν εὖ οἶδ' ὅτι γέγονε, τουτὶ μέντοι τὸ θρυλούμενον ἰαμβεῖον ἀμφότεροι    5
πολλάκις ἀκηκόαμεν,

            Ἄθως καλύψει πλευρὰ Λημνίας βοός·

936A  ἐπιβάλλει γὰρ ἡ σκιὰ τοῦ ὄρους ὡς ἔοικε χαλκέῳ τινὶ βοϊδίῳ, ‖ μῆκος ἀποτείνουσα
διὰ τῆς θαλάττης οὐκ ἔλαττον ἑπτακοσίων σταδίων (οὐ) διὰ τὸ κατασκιάζον ὕψος
εἶναι τὴν αἰτίαν (ἀλλ') ὅτι πολλαπλασίους αἱ τοῦ φωτὸς ἀποστάσεις τῶν σωμάτων    10
τὰς σκιὰς ποιοῦσι. Δεῦρο δὴ θεῶ καὶ τῆς σελήνης ὅτε πάμμηνός ἐστι καὶ μάλιστα
τὴν ἰδέαν ἔναρθρον τοῦ προσώπου βαθύτητι τῆς σκιᾶς ἀποδίδωσι, τὸ μέγιστον ἀπέ-
χοντα διάστημα τὸν ἥλιον· ἡ γὰρ ἀπόστασις τοῦ φωτὸς αὐτὴ τὴν σκιὰν μεγάλην, οὐ
τὰ μεγέθη τῶν ὑπὲρ τὴν σελήνην ἀνωμαλιῶν πεποίηκε. Καὶ μὴν οὐδὲ τῶν ὀρῶν τὰς
B   ὑπεροχὰς ἐῶσι μεθ' ἡμέραν αἱ περιαυγαὶ τοῦ ἡλίου καθορᾶσθαι· τὰ μέντοι βα|θέα    15
καὶ κοῖλα φαίνεται καὶ σκιώδη πόρρωθεν. Οὐδὲν οὖν ἄτοπον εἰ καὶ τῆς σελήνης
τὴν ἀντίλαμψιν καὶ τὸν ἐπιφωτισμὸν οὐκ ἔστι καθορᾶν ἀκριβῶς· αἱ δὲ τῶν σκιε-
ρῶν παραθέσεις παρὰ τὰ λαμπρὰ τῇ διαφορᾷ τὴν ὄψιν οὐ λανθάνουσιν.

      23. Ἀλλ' ἐκεῖνο μᾶλλον" ἔφην "ἐλέγχειν δοκεῖ τὴν λεγομένην ἀνάκλασιν ἀπὸ τῆς
σελήνης, ὅτι τοὺς ἐν ταῖς ἀνακλωμέναις αὐγαῖς ἑστῶτας οὐ μόνον συμβαίνει τὸ    20
φωτιζόμενον ὁρᾶν, ἀλλὰ καὶ τὸ φωτίζον. Ὅταν γάρ, αὐγῆς ἀφ' ὕδατος πρὸς τοῖ-
χον ἁλλομένης, ὄψις ἐν αὐτῷ τῷ πεφωτισμένῳ κατὰ τὴν ἀνάκλασιν τόπῳ γένηται,
C   τὰ τρία καθορᾷ· τήν τ' ἀνακλωμένην αὐ|γήν, καὶ τὸ ποιοῦν ὕδωρ τὴν ἀνάκλασιν,
καὶ τὸν ἥλιον αὐτόν, ἀφ' οὗ τὸ φῶς τῷ ὕδατι προσπίπτον ἀνακέκλασται. Τού-
των δὲ ὁμολογουμένων καὶ φαινομένων, κελεύουσι τοὺς ἀνακλάσει φωτίζεσθαι τὴν    25
γῆν ὑπὸ τῆς σελήνης ἀξιοῦντας ἐπιδεικνύναι νύκτωρ ἐμφαινόμενον τῇ σελήνῃ τὸν

---

1 Ἀλωαδῶν Dübn.: ἀλωάδων E: ἀλωάδων B: Ἀλωείδων Xyl.: ἀλωαδῶν Raing. ‖ ἐκείνων B: ἐκεῖν
E ‖ εἶναι μείζονας E: μείζονας εἶναι B    2 εἰ add. Dübn.: ὅτε add. et παρέχει pro παρέχειν Wyt. in
app.: ὃς add. Purser: εἴ γ' add. Po.    5 θρυλούμενον Ch.: τεθρυλημένον E: θρυλούμενον B: τεθρυ-
λημένον Dübn.    7 πλευρὰ Ald. Basil.: πλευρᾶς EB: πλευρᾷ B i.t.: σκιάζει νῶτα pro καλύψει
πλευρᾶς Xyl.¹⁵⁷⁰    9–10 οὐ ... ἀλλ add. et transp. Amyot: τὸ κατασκιάζον ὕψος εἶναι διὰ τὴν αἰτίαν
EB: τῷ pro τὸ RJ94: σὺ δ' οὖν add. ante τὸ κατασκιάζον et διανοήσῃ pro διὰ et οὐδὲ μεμνήσῃ add.
ante ὅτι Wyt. in app.: τὸ δὲ κατασκιάζον ὕψος ἐννέα· διὰ τίνα αἰτίαν; ὅτι corr. Emp.: ὧν τὸ κατασκ.
ὕψος εἶναι δεῖ τὴν αἰτίαν κέ Bern. in app.: ἀλλ' οὐ φήσομεν τοσούτων σταδίων add. post σταδίων
Adler: γελοῖος δ' ὁ φάσκων τοσούτων σταδίων add. post σταδίων Po. in app.: ἀλλ' οὐ χρὴ δήπου-
θεν ἑπτακοσίων σταδίων add. post σταδίων Ch. (sec. Purser οὐ χρὴ δὲ ἑπτακοσίων σταδίων)    14
ὀρῶν B: ὁρῶν E    15 μεθ ἡμέραν Steph.: μεθημέραν EB    17 τὴν B et E s.l. ‖ ἀντίλαμψιν Amyot:
ἀντίληψιν EB    26 ἐπιδεικνύναι E: ἐπιδεικνῦναι B

are both bigger than those Aloades, mind you not at all times during the day but exclusively in the morning and in the evening, ⟨if⟩ you pretend, because the sun makes our shadows huge, to supply this charming argument with sense-perception: if the shadow cast is great, what casts the shadow is exaggeratedly greater. Neither of us, that I know well, has been in Lemnos, yet this iamb repeated over and over we have both often heard:

'Athos will cover the flanks of the Lemnian calf'.

Because the shadow of the mountain, as it appears, throws over some bronze calf extending over the sea no less than seven hundred stades, the reason ⟨not⟩ being that what casts the shadow is elevated, ⟨but⟩ because the distances of the light source make the shadows of the bodies many times larger. Here, in fact, observe that it is at full moon when the moon gives back most articulately the semblance of the face as a result of the depth of the shadow, the sun standing at the greatest distance from it; for it is the remoteness of the light source itself which has made the shadow large, not the size of the irregularities over the moon. Even more so, the light beams of the sun do not allow the peaks of mountains to be seen in broad daylight; yet the deep, hollow, and shadowy parts are visible from afar. So there is nothing odd if of the moon as well it is not possible to accurately distinguish the reflection and illumination, while the juxtapositions of the shadowy parts next to the brilliant ones do not escape our sight because of the contrast.

23. But what about that argument," I said, "that seems to refute more strongly the alleged reflection from the moon: it happens to those who are placed among the reflected rays that they see not only the object illuminated but also the illuminating object. Well, if a ray bounces off of the water towards a wall, whenever the vision comes to be in the spot that is itself illuminated by the reflection, it distinguishes the three realities: the reflected ray, the water that causes the reflection, and the sun itself, from where light has been reflected by falling upon the water. Because of these approved and apparent facts, they command those who believe that the earth is illuminated with reflected light by the moon to point out the sun appearing in the

ἥλιον, ὥσπερ ἐμφαίνεται τῷ ὕδατι μεθ' ἡμέραν ὅταν ἀνάκλασις ἀπ' αὐτοῦ γένηται·
μὴ φαινομένου δὲ τούτου, κατ' ἄλλον οἴονται τρόπον οὐκ ἀνακλάσει γίνεσθαι τὸν
φωτισμόν· εἰ δὲ μὴ τοῦτο, μηδὲ γῆν εἶναι τὴν σελήνην." "Τί οὖν" ἔφη "πρὸς αὐτοὺς
D λεκτέον;" ὁ Ἀπολλωνίδης. "Κοινὰ γὰρ | ἔοικε καὶ πρὸς ἡμᾶς εἶναι τὰ τῆς ἀνακλά-
σεως." "Ἀμέλει τρόπον τινὰ" ἔφην ἐγὼ "κοινά, τρόπον δὲ ἄλλον οὐ κοινά. Πρῶτον 5
δὲ ὅρα τὰ τῆς εἰκόνος, ὡς ἄνω ποταμῶν καὶ τραπὲν πάλιν λαμβάνουσιν. Ἐπὶ γῆς
γάρ ἐστι καὶ κάτω τὸ ὕδωρ, ὑπὲρ γῆς δὲ σελήνη καὶ μετέωρος· ὅθεν ἀντίστροφον
αἱ κεκλασμέναι τὸ σχῆμα τῆς γωνίας ποιοῦσι, τῆς μὲν ἄνω πρὸς τῇ σελήνῃ, τῆς δὲ
κάτω πρὸς τῇ γῇ τὴν κορυφὴν ἐχούσης. Μὴ ἅπασαν οὖν ἰδέαν κατόπτρου, μηδὲ ἐκ
πάσης ἀποστάσεως ὁμοίαν ἀνάκλασιν ποιεῖν ἀξιούτωσαν, ἐπεὶ μάχονται πρὸς τὴν 10
E ἐνάργειαν. Οἱ δὲ σῶμα μὴ λεπτὸν μηδὲ λεῖον ὥσπερ | ἐστὶ τὸ ὕδωρ ἀποφαίνοντες
τὴν σελήνην, ἀλλὰ ἐμβριθὲς καὶ γεῶδες, οὐκ οἶδα ὅπως ἀπαιτοῦνται τοῦ ἡλίου τὴν
ἔμφασιν ἐν αὐτῇ πρὸς τὴν ὄψιν· οὐδὲ γὰρ τὸ γάλα τοὺς τοιούτους ἐσοπτρισμοὺς
ἀποδίδωσιν, οὐδὲ ποιεῖ τῆς ὄψεως ἀνακλάσεις διὰ τὴν ἀνωμαλίαν καὶ τραχύτητα
τῶν μορίων. Πόθεν γε τὴν σελήνην δυνατόν ἐστιν ἀναπέμπειν ἀφ' ἑαυτῆς τὴν ὄψιν, 15
ὥσπερ ἀναπέμπει τὰ λειότερα τῶν ἐσόπτρων; Καίτοι καὶ ταῦτα δήπουθεν, ἐὰν
ἀμυχή τις ἢ ῥύπος ἢ τραχύτης καταλάβῃ τὸ σημεῖον [ἂν] ἀφ' οὗ πέφυκεν ἡ ὄψις
F ἀνακλᾶσθαι τυποῦται, καὶ βλέπεται μὲν αὐτά, | τὴν δὲ ἀνταύγειαν οὐκ ἀποδίδωσιν.
Ὁ δὲ ἀξιῶν ἢ καὶ τὴν ὄψιν ἡμῶν ἐπὶ τὸν ἥλιον ἢ μηδὲ τὸν ἥλιον ἐφ' ἡμᾶς ἀνακλᾶν
ἀφ' ἑαυτῆς τὴν σελήνην ἡδύς ἐστι, τὸν ὀφθαλμὸν ἥλιον ἀξιῶν εἶναι, φῶς δὲ τὴν ὄψιν, 20
οὐρανὸν δὲ τὸν ἄνθρωπον. Τοῦ μὲν γὰρ ἡλίου δι' εὐτονίαν καὶ λαμπρότητα πρὸς τῇ
σελήνῃ γινομένην μετὰ πληγῆς τὴν ἀνάκλασιν φέρεσθαι πρὸς ἡμᾶς εἰκός ἐστιν,
ἡ δὲ ὄψις, ἀσθενὴς οὖσα καὶ λεπτὴ καὶ ὀλιγοστή, τί θαυμαστὸν εἰ μήτε πληγὴν
ἀνακρουστικὴν ποιεῖ μήτε ἀφαλλομένης τηρεῖ τὴν συνέχειαν, ἀλλὰ θρύπτεται καὶ
937A ἀπολείπει, πλῆθος οὐκ ἔχουσα φωτὸς ‖ ὥστε μὴ διασπᾶσθαι περὶ τὰς ἀνωμαλίας 25
καὶ τραχύτητας; Ἀπὸ μὲν γὰρ ὕδατος καὶ τῶν ἄλλων ἐσόπτρων ἰσχύουσαν ἔτι τῆς
ἀρχῆς ἐγγὺς οὖσαν ἐπὶ τὸν ἥλιον ἅλλεσθαι τὴν ἀνάκλασιν, οὐκ ἀδύνατόν ἐστιν· ἀπὸ
δὲ τῆς σελήνης κἂν γίνωνταί τινες ὀλισθήσεις αὐτῆς, ἀσθενεῖς ἔσονται καὶ ἀμυ-
δραὶ καὶ προαπολείπουσαι διὰ τὸ μῆκος τῆς ἀποστάσεως. Καὶ γὰρ ἄλλως τὰ μὲν
κοῖλα τῶν ἐσόπτρων, εὐτονωτέραν ποιεῖ τῆς προηγουμένης αὐγῆς τὴν ἀνακλωμέ- 30
νην, ὥστε καὶ φλόγας ἀναπέμπειν πολλάκις, τὰ δὲ κυρτὰ καὶ τὰ σφαιροειδῆ, τῷ μὴ

---

1 μεθ ἡμέραν E: μεθημέραν B ‖ ἀπ αὐτοῦ Wyt. *in app.*: ὑπ' αὐτοῦ EB: ὑπ' αὐτῶν Ald. Basil.    4
λεκτέον *punct. corr.* Raing.: λεκτέον EB    5 οὐ E: οὐδὲ B *et alii*    6 τραπὲν πάλιν] τραπέμπαλιν
Meineke *et alii*    7 γάρ ἐστι Kepl.: πάρεστι EB ‖ καὶ E *et* B *s.l.*    9 τῇ γῇ τὴν κορυφήν E *et*
B *s.l.*: τὴν κορυφὴν τῇ γῇ B ‖ κατόπτρου Po. *in app.* Ch.: κάτοπτρον EB: κάτοπτον Amyot: κατό-
πτρων Dübn.    11 ἐνάργειαν SR67: ἐνέργειαν EB    16 ἐσόπτρων *punct. corr.* Steph.: ἐσόπτρων·
E: ἐσόπτρων· B    17 ἂν *secl.* Wyt. *in app.*    18 ἀνακλᾶσθαι Kepl.: ἀνακλασθὲν EB: ἀνακλασθεῖσα
Amyot: ἀνακλασθῆναι Dübn. ‖ τυποῦται καὶ] τυποῦσθαι *et* καὶ *del.* Amyot: τυφλοῦται καὶ Dübn.
*et alii*    26 τραχύτητας *punct. corr.* Dübn.: τραχύτητας· EB    27 ἥλιον] σφαῖραν *add. post* ἥλιον
l.22: ὀφθαλμὸν *pro* ἥλιον l.25 ‖ ἅλλεσθαι E: ἄλλεσθαι B    31 τὰ *om.* B

moon at night, just as it appears in water during the day every time there is a reflection of the sun off the water; given that it does not appear on the moon, they believe that the illumination originates in different fashion, not by reflection—yet, without this, the moon is not earth either." "What then," said Apollonides, "must be said to them? To be sure, it seems that the issues about reflection are common for us too." "Definitely common in a way, yes," said I, "but in another way not common. Firstly, look at how they take the problem of the image, like rivers flowing upwards and back. Because water is on earth and below, but the moon is over the earth and suspended on high, which is why the reflected rays produce a reverse form of the angle, one having the top above at the moon, the other below at the earth. Not every type of mirror, then, nor from any distance, can they require to produce a similar reflection, since then they fight against the evidence. Differently, those who declare that the moon is a body not tenuous or smooth, as water is, but heavy and earthy, I do not see why they are asked for the image of the sun to be visible in the moon; for milk does not return such mirrorings either nor produces reflections of the visual ray by reason of the irregularity and roughness of its parts. How could it be possible then that the moon sends the visual ray back from itself, just as the smoother mirrors send it back? Yet even these, clearly, if a scratch or dirt or roughness catches the point from which the visual ray is naturally reflected, get the imprint, and while they are seen they do not return the reflection. One who requires that the moon reflects either our vision also to the sun or else not even the sun to us is simple minded, for he sustains that the eye is a sun, the visual ray light, and man a heaven. The fact is that as a result of the sun's vigor and brightness, which reaches the moon with a blow, it is plausible that the reflection moves towards to us; but the visual ray, which is weak, tenuous, and of little significance, what marvel is there if it does not make any impact with a rebound or when bouncing off does not preserve the continuity, but breaks and gives up, as it does not possess enough light so as to not be torn apart around the irregularities and corrugations? Well, from water and from other kinds of mirrors, given that it still has strength by being near to its origin, it is not impossible for the reflection to rebound to the sun; but from the moon, even if some rays manage to slide off, they will be weak, blurry, and hastily dispersed due to the dimension of the distance. And for the rest, those mirrors which are concave make the reflection of the ray more intense than it was before, so that it sends away flames; and those which are convex and spherical by not putting pressure equally from all points make it weak and

Apoll.

Lamp.

B πανταχόθεν ἀντερείδειν ἀσθενῆ καὶ ἀμαυ|ράν. ... ὁρᾶται δήπουθεν, ὅταν ἴριδες δύο
φανῶσι, νέφους νέφος ἐμπεριέχοντος, ἀμαυρὰν ποιοῦσαν καὶ ἀσαφῆ τὰ χρώματα
τὴν περιέχουσαν· τὸ γὰρ ἐκτὸς νέφος ἀπωτέρω τῆς ὄψεως κείμενον οὐκ εὔτονον
οὐδὲ ἰσχυρὰν τὴν ἀνάκλασιν ἀποδίδωσι. Καὶ τί δεῖ πλείονα λέγειν; Ὅπου γὰρ τὸ
τοῦ ἡλίου φῶς ἀνακλώμενον ἀπὸ τῆς σελήνης, τὴν μὲν θερμότητα πᾶσαν ἀποβάλ- 5
λει, τῆς δὲ λαμπρότητος αὐτοῦ λεπτὸν ἀφικνεῖται μόλις πρὸς ἡμᾶς καὶ ἀδρανὲς
λείψανον, ἦ που τῆς ὄψεως τὸν ἴσον φερομένης δίαυλον, ἐνδέχεται μόριον ὁτιοῦν
C λείψανον ἐξικέσθαι πρὸς | τὸν ἥλιον ἀπὸ τῆς σελήνης; Ἐγὼ μὲν οὐκ οἶμαι. Σκο-
πεῖτε δὲ" εἶπον "καὶ ὑμεῖς, εἰ τὰ αὐτὰ πρὸς τὸ ὕδωρ καὶ τὴν σελήνην ἔπασχεν ἡ
ὄψις, ἔδει καὶ γῆς καὶ φυτῶν καὶ ἀνθρώπων καὶ ἄστρων ἐμφάσεις ποιεῖν τὴν παν- 10
σέληνον, οἵας τὰ λοιπὰ ποιεῖται τῶν ἐσόπτρων· εἰ δὲ οὐ γίνονται πρὸς ταῦτα τῆς
ὄψεως ἀνακλάσεις δι' ἀσθένειαν αὐτῆς ἢ τραχύτητα τῆς σελήνης, μηδὲ πρὸς τὸν
ἥλιον ἀπαιτῶμεν.

24. Ἡμεῖς μὲν οὖν" ἔφην "ὅσα μὴ διαπέφευγε τὴν μνήμην τῶν ἐκεῖ λεχθέντων
ἀπηγγέλκαμεν. Ὥρα δὲ καὶ Σύλλαν παρακαλεῖν, μᾶλλον δὲ ἀπαιτεῖν τὴν διήγησιν, 15
D οἷον ἐπὶ ῥη|τοῖς ἀκροατὴν γεγενημένον· ὥστε εἰ δοκεῖ, καταπαύσαντες τὸν περί-
πατον καὶ καθίσαντες ἐπὶ τῶν βάθρων, ἑδραῖον αὐτῷ παράσχωμεν ἀκροατήριον."
Ἔδοξε δὴ ταῦτα καὶ καθισάντων ἡμῶν, ὁ Θέων "ἐγώ τοι, ὦ Λαμπρία," εἶπεν "ἐπι-
θυμῶ μὲν οὐδενὸς ἧττον ὑμῶν ἀκοῦσαι τὰ λεχθησόμενα· πρότερον δὲ ἂν ἡδέως
ἀκούσαιμι περὶ τῶν οἰκεῖν λεγομένων ἐπὶ τῆς σελήνης, οὐκ εἰ κατοικοῦσί τινες, 20
ἀλλ' εἰ δυνατὸν ἐκεῖ κατοικεῖν· εἰ γὰρ οὐ δυνατόν, ἄλογον καὶ τὸ γῆν εἶναι τὴν σελή-
νην. Δόξει γὰρ πρὸς οὐθὲν ἀλλὰ μάτην γεγονέναι, μήτε καρποὺς ἐκφέρουσα, μήτε
E ἀνθρώ|ποις τισὶν ἕδραν παρέχουσα καὶ γένεσιν καὶ δίαιταν· ὧν ἕνεκα καὶ ταύτην
γεγονέναι φαμὲν κατὰ Πλάτωνα

τροφὸν ἡμετέραν, ἡμέρας τε καὶ νυκτὸς ἀτρεκῆ φύλακα καὶ δημιουργόν. 25

Ὁρᾷς δὲ ὅτι πολλὰ λέγεται καὶ σὺν γέλωτι καὶ μετὰ σπουδῆς περὶ τούτων; Τοῖς μὲν
γὰρ ὑπὸ τὴν σελήνην οἰκοῦσιν ὥσπερ Ταντάλοις ὑπὲρ κεφαλῆς ἐκκρέμασθαί φασι·
τοὺς δὲ οἰκοῦντας αὖ πάλιν ἐπ' αὐτῆς ὥσπερ Ἰξίονας ἐνδεδεμένους ῥύμῃ τόσῃ ...

---

1 lac. 13 lit. E, 17 lit. B: ποιεῖ suppl. Amyot: ἀποδίδωσιν Bern. in app.: αὐτὴν ἀναδίδωσιν Adler:
αὐγὴν ἀποδίδωσιν Raing. in app.: μᾶλλον ἀποδίδωσιν Po. in app. ‖ ὁρᾶται] ὁρᾶτε RJ94 et alii   2
ἀμαυρὰν] ἀμαυρὰ Amyot (ἄμαυρα sic) et alii   4 λέγειν punct. corr. Steph.: λέγειν· EB   7 ἢ
που B: ἢ που E ‖ τὸν ἴσον B s.l.: τὴν ἴσην EB   8 λείψανον] ἢ add. ante λείψανον Po. in app.:
λειψάνου Ch. ‖ ἀπὸ τῆς σελήνης Wyt. in app.: ὑπὸ τῆς σελήνης EB   10 ἔδει RJ94: ὃ δὴ EB: ὅτι
ἔδει Amyot   25 τροφὸν SR67: τροφὴν EB   27 ὑπὲρ SR67: ἐκ EB   28 τόσῃ et lac. 42 lit. E, 32
lit. B: περικινεῖσθαι ὥστε μὴ πεσεῖν suppl. Amyot.: τοσαύτῃ corr. et δινεῖσθαι suppl. Wyt. in app.:
τοσαύτῃ περιδινεῖσθαι, ὥστ' ἐκπεσεῖν μὴ δύνασθαι Bern. in app.: τοσαύτῃ κινουμένης ἀεὶ περιδινεῖ-
σθαι Adler: τοσαύτῃ καὶ δίνῃ περιφερομένους μὴ ἐκπεσεῖν Purser: τοσαύτῃ περιδινουμένης οὐδέποτ'
ἐν ἀσφαλεῖ βεβηκέναι (vel ἡσυχίαν ἄγειν) Po. in app.: τοσαύτῃ, τῆς καταφορᾶς κωλύειν τὴν κύκλῳ
περιδίνησιν Ch.: τοσαύτῃ πληγαῖς τοῦ περιέχοντος ἀέρος ἀεὶ χειμάζεσθαι Görg.

faint. Whenever two rainbows appear because one cloud encloses another, it is doubtless apparent that the encompassing rainbow, being faint, produces colors that are also indistinct—because the outer cloud, being farther from vision returns a reflection that is not intense or strong. Then, what else needs to be said? Indeed, when the light of the sun that is reflected from the moon loses all its heat, and only a delicate and faint remnant of its brilliance reaches us, to what extent is it possible that, of the sight moving the same double-course, any remnant whatsoever could reach the sun from the moon? Well, I personally do not think so. And you too, folks," I said, "look at this, if in the same way the visual ray was affected by water and by the moon, it would also be necessary that the full moon makes reflections of the earth, of plants, of men, and of the stars, just as the rest of mirrors do; yet, if reflections of the visual ray do not happen to these objects, either due to the feebleness of the ray or the roughness of the moon, let us not demand such reflections to the sun either.

24. Now, certainly," said I, "all what has not escaped our memory we have reported from the things discussed there. And so it is time to call upon Sulla, or rather to demand his narration, as this was the condition for him to become a listener; thus, if you agree, let us conclude our promenade and sit on the benches, so as to offer him a settled audience." They agreed to this and once we were seated, Theon said: "While I, Lamprias, desire no less than any of you to hear the things about to be said, first I would gladly hear about those which are said to dwell on the moon—not if some really do live there, but whether it is possible to live there; because if it is not possible, it is unreasonable also to say that the moon is earth. Indeed the moon would seem to have been created for nothing, rather pointlessly, neither producing fruit nor providing for certain men an abode, an origin, and means of life; on account of which we say, together with Plato, that ours came into being

Theon

> 'our nurse, firm guardian and creator of day and night'.

Do you see that many things are being said both jokingly and seriously about these matters? Indeed they say that for those who live under the moon it is suspended over their heads, like (the stone) for Tantalus; and those who live on it, in turn, fixed like Ixions, with such a speed ... The fact is that the

Καίτοι μίαν οὐ κινεῖται κίνησιν, ἀλλ', ὥς που καὶ λέγεται τριοδῖτις ἐστίν, ἅμα μῆκος
F ἐπὶ τοῦ ζῳδιακοῦ καὶ πλάτος φερομένη καὶ βάθος· ὧν | τὴν μὲν περιδρομήν, τὴν δὲ
ἕλικα, τὴν δὲ οὐκ οἶδα πῶς ἀνωμαλίαν ὀνομάζουσιν οἱ μαθηματικοί, καίπερ οὐδε-
μίαν ὁμαλὴν οὐδὲ τεταγμένην ταῖς ἀποκαταστάσεσιν ὁρῶντες ἔχουσαν· οὐκ εἰ λέων
τις ἔπεσεν ὑπὸ ῥύμης εἰς Πελοπόννησον ἄξιόν ἐστι θαυμάζειν, ἀλλ' ὅπως οὐ μυρία 5
ὁρῶμεν ἀεὶ

πεσήματα ἀνδρῶν καὶ ἀπολακτισμοὺς βίων

938A ἐκεῖθεν οἷον ἐκκυβιστώντων καὶ περιτραπέντων. ‖ Καὶ γὰρ γελοῖον περὶ μονῆς τῶν
ἐκεῖ διαπορεῖν εἰ μὴ γένεσιν μηδὲ σύστασιν ἔχειν δύναται· ὅπου γὰρ Αἰγύπτιοι καὶ
Τρωγλοδύται, οἷς ἡμέρας μιᾶς ἀκαρὲς ἵσταται κατὰ κορυφὴν ὁ ἥλιος ἐν τροπαῖς, 10
εἶτα ἄπεισιν, ὀλίγον ἀπέχουσι τοῦ κατακεκαῦσθαι ξηρότητι τοῦ περιέχοντος, ἤπου
τοὺς ἐπὶ τῆς σελήνης εἰκός ἐστι δώδεκα θερείας ὑπομένειν ἔτους ἑκάστου, κατὰ
μῆνα τοῦ ἡλίου πρὸς κάθετον αὐτοῖς ἐφισταμένου καὶ στηρίζοντος, ὅταν ᾖ πανσέ-
ληνος; Πνεύματά γε μὴν καὶ νέφη καὶ ὄμβρους, ὧν χωρὶς οὔτε γένεσις φυτῶν ἔστιν
B οὔτε σωτηρία γενομένοις, ἀμήχανον ἐκεῖ διανοηθῆναι συνιστάμενα διὰ | θερμότητα 15
καὶ λεπτότητα τοῦ περιέχοντος· οὐδὲ γὰρ ἐνταῦθα τῶν ὀρῶν τὰ ὑψηλὰ δέχεται
τοὺς ἀγρίους καὶ ἐναντίους χειμῶνας· ἀλλ' ... ἤδη καὶ σάλον ἔχων ὑπὸ κουφότητος
ὁ ἀὴρ ἐκφεύγει τὴν σύστασιν ταύτην καὶ πύκνωσιν· εἰ μὴ νὴ Δία φήσομεν ὥσπερ
ἡ Ἀθηνᾶ τῷ Ἀχιλλεῖ νέκταρός τι καὶ ἀμβροσίας ἐνέσταξε μὴ προσιεμένῳ τροφήν,
οὕτω τὴν σελήνην, Ἀθηνᾶν λεγομένην καὶ οὖσαν, τρέφειν τοὺς ἄνδρας ἀμβροσίαν 20
ἀνιεῖσαν αὐτοῖς ἐφημέριον, ὡς Φερεκύδης ὁ παλαιὸς οἴεται σιτεῖσθαι αὐτοὺς ⟨τοὺς⟩
C θεούς. Τὴν μὲν γὰρ Ἰνδικὴν ῥίζαν, ἥν φησι Μεγασθένης τοὺς μήτε πί|νοντας, ἀλλ'
ἀστόμους ὄντας ὑποτύφειν καὶ θυμιᾶν καὶ τρέφεσθαι τῇ ὀσμῇ, πόθεν ἄν τις ἐκεῖ
φυομένην λάβοι μὴ βρεχομένης τῆς σελήνης;"

---

2 φερομένη E: ἐπιφερομένη B: *unde forte legendum* ἅμα ἐπὶ μῆκος τοῦ ζ. κ. πλ. φερομένη Wyt. *in app.*: ἀντιφερομένη Ch. ‖ δὲ[1] B: δεὸν E    3–4 οὐδεμίαν ὁμαλὴν οὐδὲ τεταγμένην] οὕτως *add. post* τεταγμένην Amyot: οὐδὲν ἀνώμαλον οὐδὲ τεταραγμένον *corr.* Wyt. *in app.*: ὁμοίως *add. ante* ὁμαλὴν Adler    4 ἔχουσαν· B: ἐχούσαις E: ἐνοῦσαν Po. *in app.* ‖ οὐκ] οὔκουν SR67 *et alii*    5 Πελοπόννησον B: Πελοπόνησον E ‖ ὅπως SR67: ὅμως EB: ὅτι RJ94    7 βίων B: υἷων E: ζώων Amyot    8 περιτραπέντων Amyot: περιτρεπόντων EB: περιρρεπόντων Apelt: περιτρεπομένων Po. ‖ γὰρ *om.* E: μὴν Dübn. ‖ μονῆς Basil.: μόνης EB    9 δύναται· B: δύναται E: δύνανται Wyt. *in app. et alii*    13–14 πανσέληνος *punct. corr.* Dübn.: πανσέληνος· EB    17 *lac.* 10 *lit.* EB: εἰλικρινὴς ὢν ἤδη καὶ σάλον οὐκ ἔχων *suppl. et corr.* Amyot: λεπτότητα Wyt. *in app.*: γαλήνην ἀσάλευτον ἔχον *suppl. et corr.* Emp.: λεπτὸς (*vel* ἀραιὸς) ὢν Bern. *in app.*: μάνωσιν Purser: καθαρὸς ὢν (*vel* διάχυσιν) Po. *in app.*    21 ἀνιεῖσαν Dübn.: ἀνεῖσαν EB ‖ τοὺς *add. post* αὐτοὺς Wyt. *in app.* (τοὺς *pro* αὐτοὺς *i.t.*): αὖ τοὺς *pro* αὐτοὺς Raing.    22 τοὺς μήτε πίνοντας] μήτε ἐσθίοντας *add. post* τοὺς SR67: τοὺς *del. et* μήτε ἐσθίοντας *add.* Steph.    23 ἀστόμους l.22 SR67: εὐστόμους EB    24 σελήνης *punct. corr.* Steph.: σελήνης· EB

moon does not move in a single movement, but, as somewhere they call it, it is the 'three-ways goddess', moving through the zodiac at the same time in longitude, latitude, and depth. Of these, astronomers call one movement 'revolution', another 'spiral', and the last one, I do not know why, 'anomaly', even though we see it does not have a single motion that is uniform or systematic in its revolutions. There is no reason to wonder if a lion were to fall on the Peloponnese due to its impulse, yet how is it that we are not always seeing thousands of

'falls of men and lives spurned way',

as if plunging headlong from up there and turned upside down. Moreover, it is laughable to raise the question regarding the dwelling of those there if it is not possible to have an origin or subsistence; indeed, when Egyptians and Troglodytes, for whom the sun remains vertically at the top just for an instant of the day during the solstice and then sets forth, are not far from being completely burnt by the aridity of the environment, is it then likely that those on the moon undergo twelve summers each year, where each month the sun is placed and fixed over them vertically when there is full moon? Yet winds, clouds, and rains, without which there can be no growth or preservation of plants, cannot be conceived to arise there, due to the warmth and delicateness of the environment. Because not even down here do the top of the mountains receive fierce and clashing storms, but the air ..., already and having a rolling swell due to its lightness, escapes this compaction and condensation; or else, by Zeus, we shall say that just as Athena infused Achilles with some nectar and ambrosia when he would not come near food, so the moon, which is Athena by name and fact, nourishes men by sending forth ambrosia everyday, as the ancient Pherecydes believes the gods themselves are nourished. For the Indian root, which Megasthenes says that those who do not even drink but, not having a mouth, ignite, burn and inhale for their nourishment, how could it be supposed to grow there if the moon is not irrigated by rain?"

25. Ταῦτα τοῦ Θέωνος εἰπόντος, "⟨κάλλιστά⟩ γε" ἔφην "καὶ ἄριστα τῇ παι-
διᾷ τοῦ λόγου τὰς ὀφρῦς ... ἃ καὶ θάρσος ἡμῖν ἐγγίνεται πρὸς τὴν ἀπόκρισιν, μὴ
πάνυ πικρὰν μηδὲ αὐστηρὰν εὐθύνην προσδοκῶσι· καὶ γὰρ ὡς ἀληθῶς τῶν σφό-
δρα πεπεισμένων τὰ τοιαῦτα διαφέρουσιν, οἱ σφόδρα δυσκολαίνοντες αὐτοῖς καὶ
διαπιστοῦντες, ἀλλὰ μὴ πράως τὸ δυνατὸν καὶ τὸ ἐνδεχόμενον ἐθέλοντες ἐπισκο-
πεῖν. Εὐθὺς οὖν τὸ πρῶτον οὐκ ἀναγκαῖόν ἐστιν, εἰ μὴ κατοικοῦσιν ἄνθρωποι τὴν
σελή|νην, μάτην γεγονέναι καὶ πρὸς μηθέν· οὐδὲ γὰρ τήνδε τὴν γῆν δι' ὅλης ἐνερ-
γὸν οὐδὲ προσοικουμένην ὁρῶμεν, ἀλλὰ μικρὸν αὐτῆς μέρος, ὥσπερ ἄκραις τισὶν
ἢ χερρονήσοις ἀνεχούσης ἐκ βυθοῦ, γόνιμόν ἐστι ζῴων καὶ φυτῶν· τῶν δὲ ἄλλων,
τὰ μὲν ἔρημα καὶ ἄκαρπα χειμῶσι καὶ αὐχμοῖς, τὰ δὲ πλεῖστα κατὰ τῆς μεγάλης
δέδυκε θαλάσσης. Ἀλλὰ σὺ τὸν Ἀρίσταρχον ἀγαπῶν ἀεὶ καὶ θαυμάζων, οὐκ ἀκούεις
Κράτητος ἀναγινώσκοντος,

Ὠκεανός, ὅσπερ γένεσις πάντεσσι τέτυκται
ἀνδράσιν ἠδὲ θεοῖς, πλείστην ἐπὶ γαῖαν ἵησιν.

Ἀλλὰ πολλοῦ δεῖ μάτην ταῦτα γεγονέναι· καὶ γὰρ ἀναθυμιάσεις ἡ θάλασσα μαλα|
κὰς ἀνίησι καὶ τῶν πνευμάτων τὰ ἥδιστα θέρους ἀκμάζοντος ἐκ τῆς ἀοικήτου καὶ
κατεψυγμένης αἱ χιόνες ἀτρέμα διατηκόμεναι χαλῶσι καὶ διασπείρουσιν ἡμέρας
τε καὶ νυκτὸς ἕστηκεν ἀτρεκὴς ἐν μέσῳ φύλαξ, κατὰ Πλάτωνα, καὶ δημιουργός.
Οὐδὲν οὖν κωλύει καὶ τὴν σελήνην, ζῴων μὲν ἔρημον εἶναι, παρέχειν δὲ ἀνακλά-
σεις [τε] τῷ φωτὶ περὶ αὐτὴν διαχεομένῳ καὶ συρροὴν ταῖς τῶν ἀστέρων αὐγαῖς
ἐν αὐτῇ καὶ σύγκρασιν, ᾗ συνεκπέττει τε τὰς ἀπὸ τῆς γῆς ἀναθυμιάσεις ἅμα τε
καὶ τοῦ ἡλίου τὸ ἔμπυρον ἄγαν καὶ σκληρὸν ἀφίησι· καί πού τι καὶ παλαιᾷ φήμῃ
διδόντες Ἄρτεμιν αὐ|τὴν νομισθῆναι φήσομεν ὡς παρθένον καὶ ἄγονον, ἄλλως δὲ
βοηθητικὴν καὶ ὠφέλιμον. Ἐπεὶ τῶν γε εἰρημένων οὐδέν, ὦ φίλε Θέων, ἀδύνατον
δείκνυσι τὴν λεγομένην ἐπ' αὐτῆς οἴκησιν· ἥ τε γὰρ δίνη πολλὴν ἔχουσα πραότητα
καὶ γαλήνην ἐπιλεαίνει τὸν ἀέρα καὶ διαμένει συγκατακοσμούμενον, ‖ ὥστε μηδὲν

---

1 κάλλιστά suppl. Wyt. in app.: lac. 8 lit. EB: δεξιώτατα Amyot: καλῶς γε suppl. et καθαιρεῖς pro καὶ ἄριστα Emp.: εὐκαίρως Raing.: ὑπέρευ Ch.   2 lac. 16 lit. E, 12 lit. B: ἀφήρηκας suppl. et ᾗ pro ἃ Amyot: ἡμῶν ἀνῆκας, δι' suppl. et θάρσον pro θάρσος Wyt.: ἡμῶν ἔλυσας· δι' Bern.: ἡμῶν καθῆκας, δι' Ch.   3 πικρὰν B s.l.: μικρὰν EB   4 διαφέρουσιν] οὐχ add. post διαφ. Amyot: οὐδὲν add. ante διαφ. Kepl.: οὐδὲν add. post διαφ. Dübn.   8 ἄκραις I.22: ἄκροις EB: ἄκρως Ald.   9 χερρονήσοις E: χερονήσοις B: χερρονήσοις RJ94 ‖ ἀνεχούσης P.J.: ἀνέχουσιν EB: ἀνέχον RJ94: ἀνεχούσαις Emp.   12 ἀναγινώσκοντος E: ἀναγινώσκων B   14 ἵησιν Bern.: ἵησιν EB   20 τε om. B   21 τε om. E   22 τοῦ ἡλίου Wyt. in app.: τῷ ἡλίῳ EB ‖ ἀφίησι] ἀνίησι Wyt. in app. et alii ‖ πού Wyt. in app.: πολύ EB   23 αὐτὴν B: αὐτ lac. 4 lit. E ‖ ἄλλως] ἄλλοις Wyt. in app.: ἄλλας Raing.: ἄλλαις Ch.   24 ὦ φίλε Amyot Xyl.1570: ὠφελεῖν EB   26 διαμένει] διαχέει Amyot: διανέμει Wyt. in app.

25. After Theon had so spoken, I said "⟨beautifully⟩ and splendidly by the playfulness of your speech the brows ..., wherefore there is confidence in us to reply, since we expect no bitter or severe correction at all. Truly, those who are vehemently convinced about these things really differ from those who are terribly annoyed by them and disbelieve them, unwilling to examine calmly what is possible and what admisible. In point of fact, firstly, it is not necessary that the moon has become, if men do not inhabit it, pointless and without any purpose, for we see that our earth is not productive and inhabited entirely either, but only a small part of it, as it were rising out of the deep with some peaks and peninsulas, is fertile with animals and plants, while of the remaining parts, some are desolate and fruitless due to storms and droughts, and the majority are submerged under the great sea. But you, always so fond of and admirative of Aristarchus, do not listen to Crates when he acknowledges that

> 'ocean, which is source that generates all | of men and gods, spreads over most of earth'.

Yet it is not in the slightest necessary that these parts have come to be in vain: in fact the sea sends away gentle exhalations and the softest winds are released and dispersed when, summer being at its heightest point, snows slowly melt from the uninhabited and frozen region; and

> 'a guardian and demiurge of day and night',

according to Plato, remains firm in the center. Certainly nothing prevents that the moon as well, if bereft of living beings, provides reflections for the light that is dispersed around it and a point of confluence and of convergence in itself for the rays of the stars, whereby it both attenuates the exhalations from the earth as well as it sends back what is excessively scalding and scorching of the sun; and perhaps giving some credit to the ancient tradition, we shall say that the moon is thought to be Artemis owing to its virginity and sterility, but is nontheless helpful and useful. Secondly, none of the things so far said, dear Theon, demonstrates the alleged inhabitation on it to be impossible: well, the rotation, possessing such a gentleness and tranquility, softens the air and keeps it well arranged, so that there is no dan-

Lamp.

εἶναι δέος ἐκπεσεῖν καὶ ἀποσφαλῆναι τοὺς ἐκεῖ βεβιωκότας· εἰ δὲ μὴ δι' ἑαυτὴν
καὶ τὸ ποικίλον τοῦτο τῆς φορᾶς καὶ πεπλανημένον οὐκ ἀνωμαλίας οὐδὲ ταραχῆς
ἐστιν, ἀλλὰ θαυμαστὴν ἐπιδείκνυνται τάξιν ἐν τούτοις καὶ πορείαν οἱ ἀστρολόγοι
κύκλοις τισὶ περὶ κύκλους ἑτέρους ἐξελιττομένοις συνάγοντες αὐτήν· οἱ μὲν ἀτρε-
μοῦσαν, οἱ δὲ λείως καὶ ὁμαλῶς ἀεὶ τάχεσι τοῖς αὐτοῖς ἀνθυποφερομένην· αὗται　5
γὰρ αἱ τῶν κύκλων ἐπιβάσεις καὶ περιαγωγαὶ καὶ σχέσεις πρὸς ἀλλήλους καὶ πρὸς
ἡμᾶς τὰ φαινόμενα τῆς κινήσεως ὕψη καὶ βάθη καὶ τὰς κατὰ πλάτος παραλλάξεις
B　ἅμα ταῖς κατὰ μῆ|κος αὐτῆς περιόδοις ἐμμελέστατα συμπεραίνουσι. Τὴν δὲ πολ-
λὴν θερμότητα καὶ συνεχῆ πύρωσιν ὑπὸ ἡλίου οὐ παύσῃ φοβούμενος ἂν πρῶτον
μὲν ἀντιθεὶς ταῖς ⟨ἐνθάδε⟩ ἕνδεκα θερινὰς ⟨σὺν⟩ συνόδοις τὰς πανσελήνους, εἴσῃ　10
δὲ τὸ συνεχὲς τῆς μεταβολῆς ταῖς ὑπερβολαῖς χρόνον οὐκ ἐχούσαις πολὺν ἐμποιεῖν
κρᾶσιν οἰκείαν καὶ τὸ ἄγαν ἑκατέρας ἀφαιρεῖν· ἐκ μέσου δὲ τούτων ὡς εἰκὸς ὥραν
ἔαρι προσφορωτάτην ἔχουσιν. Ἔπειτα πρὸς μὲν ἡμᾶς καθίησι δι' ἀέρος θολεροῦ καὶ
συνεπερείδοντος θερμότητα ταῖς ἀναθυμιάσεσι τρεφομένην, ἐκεῖ δὲ λεπτὸς ὢν καὶ
C　διαυγὴς ὁ ἀὴρ σκίδνησι καὶ δια|χεῖ τὴν αὐγὴν ὑπέκκαυμα καὶ σῶμα μηδὲν ἔχου-　15
σαν. Ὕλην δὲ καὶ καρπούς, αὐτόθι μὲν ὄμβροι τρέφουσιν, ἑτέρωθι δέ, ὥσπερ ἄνω
περὶ Θήβας παρ' ὑμῖν καὶ Συήνην, οὐκ ὄμβριον ὕδωρ ἀλλὰ γηγενὲς ἡ γῆ πίνουσα
καὶ χρωμένη πνεύμασι καὶ δρόσοις οὐκ ἂν ἐθελήσειεν, οἶμαι, τῇ πλεῖστον ὑομένῃ
πολυκαρπίᾳ συμφέρεσθαι δι' ἀρετήν τινα καὶ κρᾶσιν· τὰ δὲ αὐτὰ φυτὰ τῷ γένει,
παρ' ἡμῖν μὲν ἐὰν σφόδρα πιεσθῇ χειμῶσιν ἐκφέρει πολὺν καὶ καλὸν καρπόν· ἐν　20
δὲ Λιβύῃ καὶ παρ' ὑμῖν ἐν Αἰγύπτῳ δύσριγα κομιδῇ καὶ δειλὰ πρὸς χειμῶνάς ἐστι·
D　τῆς δὲ Γεδρωσίας καὶ Τρωγλοδύτιδος, ἣ καθήκει πρὸς τὸν ὠκεα|νόν, ἀφόρου διὰ
ξηρότητα καὶ ἀδένδρου παντάπασιν οὔσης, ἐν τῇ παρακειμένῃ καὶ περικεχυμένῃ
θαλάττῃ θαυμαστὰ μεγέθη φυτῶν τρέφεται καὶ κατὰ βυθοῦ τέθηκεν· ὧν τὰ μὲν
ἐλαίας, τὰ δὲ δάφνας, τὰ δὲ Ἴσιδος τρίχας καλοῦσιν· οἱ δὲ ἀνακαμψέρωτες οὗτοι　25
προσαγορευόμενοι τῆς γῆς ἐξαιρεθέντες οὐ μόνον ζῶσι κρεμάμενοι χρόνον ὅσον

---

1 βεβιωκότας·] βεβηκότας RJ94 *et alii* ‖ εἰ δὲ μὴ δι ἑαυτὴν *correxi*: εἰ δὲ μὴ δὲ αὐτή EB: εἰ μὴ καὶ αὐτὴ Amyot: ἔτι δὲ, νὴ Δι', αὐτό γε *corr. et* καὶ *del*. Wyt. *in app*.: Ἡ δὲ μεταλλαγὴ Dübn.: Ἡ τε μεταλλαγὴ Bern.: ἥ τε μὴ διὰ μιᾶς κίνησις αὕτη Po. *in app.*: εἰ δὲ μηδ' ἁπλῆ Ch.　3 ἐπιδείκνυνται Basil.: ἐπιδείκνυται EB　8 συμπεραίνουσι RJ94 Basil.: συμπαραινοῦσι EB　9 ἡλίου οὗ B *et* E *s.l.*: ἡλίου E: οὗ *del*. RJ94 Basil. *et alii*　10 ἀντιθεὶς B: ἀντιθῇς E ‖ ταῖς ... πανσελήνους *conieci*: ταῖς—θερινὰῖς συνόδοις τὰς πανσελήνους EB: τὰς—θερινὰς συνόδους ταῖς πανσελήνοις Bern. *in app.*: ταῖς—θερινὰῖς πανσελήνοις τὰς συνόδους Adler ‖ ἐνθάδε *ante* ἕνδεκα *addidi*: δώδεκα *pro* ἕνδεκα Amyot *et alii*: ἐνθάδε *pro* ἕνδεκα Prickard ‖ εἴσῃ] εἶτα Basil.: εἰκὸς Po. *in app.*: ὑποθῇ Ch. 11 ἐχούσαις E: ἐχούσας B: ἐχούσης Ald. Basil. *et alii*　12 ἐκ μέσου *correxi*: ἀμέσου EB: τὰ μέσα Basil.: διὰ μέσου Adler: ἀνὰ μέσον Po. *in app*.　13 προσφορωτάτην Ald. Basil. (προσφορωτάτην *sic*): προσφορωτάτων EB　14 συνεπερείδοντος θερμότητα Dübn.: συνεπερείδων τὴν θερμότητα EB: συνεπερείδα τὴν θερμότητα Amyot: συνεπερείδοντος τὴν θερμότητα Emp.　16 αὐτόθι Amyot: αὐτοὶ EB: αὐτοῦ Wyt. *in app*. ‖ ἑτέρωθι Amyot: ἑτέρως EB　17 ἡ γῆ I.22: ἥ γε EB　19 συμφέρεσθαι I.22 SR67: συμφαίνεσθαι EB: συμφύρεσθαι Steph.　20 ἐὰν Bern.: εἰ EB ‖ χειμῶσιν] χιόσιν E *s.l.*　21 Λιβύῃ E: λιβύι B　22 Γεδρωσίας B: γε δροσίας E ‖ Τρωγλοδύτιδος E: τρωγλοδίτιδος B

ger that those who live there may fall and slip off. And if not by the rotation itself, also this variation of movement and wandering is not attributable to irregularity or confusion, rather astronomers show a marvelous order and progression in them, conducting the moon in circles that unroll about other circles—although some assume that the moon remains immobile and others that it regresses smoothly and evenly with steady speed—; for the very juxtapositions, revolutions, and dispositions of the circles to one another and to us accomplish most harmoniously the visible variations of motion in altitude and depth and the alternations in latitude as well as its revolutions in longitude. In what regards to the great heat and continual scorching of the sun, you will not stop fearing it, first of all, when contrasting to those ⟨here⟩ eleven summer full moons with their conjunctions, but suppose that the continuity of change produces in the extremes, which do not last for long, a propitious temperature and removes the excess from either; inbetween these it is likely that inhabitants have a season most resembling to spring. Moroever, while the sun sends towards us through dim and oppressive air the warmth that is nourished by the exhalations, there, because it is delicate and limpid, the air scatters and dissipates the ray, which has no matter or body. Rain nourishes on the spot woods and fruits, but elsewhere, as among you up there around Thebes and Syene, the land, drinking not rain-water but water springing from earth and making use of winds and dews, would not want, I think, to be associated with the best harvest of fruits produced by rains, because of a certain excellence and temperament. Even plants of the same sort in our region, if they are strongly gripped during winter-storms, they produce abundant and good fruits, but in Libya and in your Egypt are terribly sensitive to cold and fearful of winter; and, while Gedrosia and Ethiopia, which extends up until the ocean, are sterile and altogether without trees due to the aridity, in the nearby and surrounding sea plants of stunning dimensions grow and blossom from the deep, of which they call some 'olives', 'laurels', and 'hair of Isis'; and those called 'love-restorers' when pulled out of the earth not only survive when hung up for as

βούλεταί τις, ἀλλὰ βλαστάνουσιν ... Σπείρεται δέ, τὰ μὲν πρὸς χειμῶνος, τὰ δὲ θέρους ἀκμάζοντος, ὥσπερ σήσαμον καὶ μελίνη· τὸ δὲ θύμον ἢ τὸ κενταύριον ἂν εἰς ἀγαθὴν καὶ πίονα σπαρῇ χώραν καὶ βρέχηται καὶ ἄρδηται τῆς κατὰ φύσιν
E ἐξίσταται ποιότητος καὶ ἀποβάλλει τὴν δύναμιν, αὐχμῷ δὲ χαίρει καὶ πρὸς | τὸ οἰκεῖον ἐπιδίδωσιν· εἰ δὲ, ὥς φασιν, οὐδὲ τὰς δρόσους ἀνέχεται, καθάπερ τὰ πλεῖστα τῶν Ἀραβικῶν, ἀλλ' ἐξαμαυροῦται διαινόμενα καὶ φθείρεται· τί δὴ θαυμαστόν ἐστιν εἰ γίνονται περὶ τὴν σελήνην ῥίζαι καὶ σπέρματα καὶ ὗλαι μηθὲν ὑετῶν δεόμεναι μήτε χιόνων, ἀλλὰ πρόσφορον ἀέρα καὶ λεπτὸν εὐφυῶς ἔχουσαι; Πῶς δὲ οὐκ εἰκὸς ἀνιέναι τε πνεύματα θαλπόμενα τῇ σελήνῃ καὶ τῷ σάλῳ τῆς περιφορᾶς αὔρας τε παρομαρτεῖν ἀτρέμα καὶ δρόσους καὶ ὑγρότητας ἐλαφρὰς περιχεούσας καὶ διασπειρομένας ἐπαρκεῖν τοῖς βλαστάνουσιν· αὐτὴ δὲ τῇ κράσει μὴ πυρώδη
F μηδὲ αὐχμηράν, | ἀλλὰ μαλακὴν καὶ ὑδροποιὸν εἶναι; Ξηρότητος μὲν γὰρ οὐδὲν ἀφικνεῖται πάθος ἀπ' αὐτῆς πρὸς ἡμᾶς, ὑγρότητος δὲ πολλὰ καὶ θηλύτητος· αὐξήσεις φυτῶν, σήψεις κρεῶν, τροπαὶ καὶ ἀνέσεις οἴνων, μαλακότητες ξύλων, εὐτοκίαι
940A γυναικῶν. Δέδοικα δὲ ἡσυχάζοντα Φαρνάκην αὖθις ἐρεθίζειν καὶ κινεῖν, ‖ ὠκεανοῦ τε πλημμύρας, ὥς λέγουσιν αὐτοί, καὶ πορθμῶν ἐπιδόσεις διαχεομένων καὶ αὐξανομένων ὑπὸ τῆς σελήνης τῷ ἀνυγραίνεσθαι παρατιθέμενος· διὸ πρὸς σὲ τρέψομαι μᾶλλον, ὦ φίλε Θέων· λέγεις γὰρ ἡμῖν ἐξηγούμενος ταυτὶ τὰ Ἀλκμᾶνος

(Διὸς) θυγάτηρ Ἔρσα τρέφει καὶ Σελάνας,

ὅτι νῦν τὸν ἀέρα καλεῖ καὶ Δία, φησὶν αὐτὸν ὑπὸ τῆς σελήνης καθυγραινόμενον εἰς δρόσους τρέπεσθαι. Κινδυνεύει γάρ, ὦ ἑταῖρε, πρὸς τὸν ἥλιον ἀντιπαθῆ φύσιν ἔχειν· εἴ γε μὴ μόνον ὅσα πυκνοῦν καὶ ξηραίνειν ἐκεῖνος, αὐτὴ μαλάσσειν καὶ
B διαχεῖν πέφυκεν, ἀλλὰ καὶ τὴν ἀπ' ἐκεί|νου θερμότητα καθυγραίνειν καὶ καταψύχειν προσπίπτουσαν αὐτῇ καὶ συμμιγνυμένην. Οἵ τε δὴ τὴν σελήνην ἔμπυρον σῶμα καὶ διακαὲς εἶναι νομίζοντες ἁμαρτάνουσιν· οἵ τε τοῖς ἐκεῖ ζῴοις ὅσα τοῖς ἐνταῦθα πρὸς γένεσιν καὶ τροφὴν καὶ δίαιταν ἀξιοῦντες ὑπάρχειν, ἐοίκασι καὶ θεαταῖς τῶν περὶ τὴν φύσιν ἀνωμαλιῶν, ἐν αἷς μείζονας ἔστι καὶ πλέονας πρὸς ἄλληλα

---

1 *lac.* 21 *lit.* EB: *nil excidisse* Wyt. *in app.*: καὶ νέα βλαστήματα *suppl.* Bern. *in app.*: ἄλλα δ' ἄλλης δεῖται τροφῆς Po. *in app.*   2 τὸ¹ E: τὸν B   5 εἰ SR67: οἱ EB: τὰ Basil.: ἔνια Paton   6 διαινόμενα RJ94: λειαινόμενα EB ‖ δὴ SR67: δὲ EB   7 ὗλαι B: ὕλαι E   7–8 δεόμεναι RJ94: δεόμενα EB   8 πρόσφορον *correxi*: πρόσθερον EB: πρὸς θερινὸν SR67: πρὸς θερινὸν καὶ ξηρὸν RJ94: πρὸς θέρειον Bern. *in app.*: πρὸς θερμὸν Raing. *in app.* ‖ ἔχουσαι *punct. corr.* Steph.: ἔχουσαι· EB: ἔχουσα RJ94   11 αὐτῇ] αὐτὴν Kepl. *et alii*   12 εἶναι *punct. corr.* Steph.: εἶναι· EB   15–16 ὠκεανοῦ τε Basil.: ὥστε καὶ ἀνοιγαί EB: ὥστε ἢ ἀναγώγαι RJ94: ἀνάγει *pro* ἀνοιγαί RJ94 ‖ ὠκεανοῦ τε πλημμύρας ὡς *conieci*:   18 ταυτὶ Bern.: ταύτῃ EB: ταῦτα Steph.   19 Διὸς *suppl.* Steph.: *lac.* 7 *lit.* E, 12 *lit.* B: οἷα Δίος Xyl.¹⁵⁷⁰ ‖ Ἔρσα I.22: ἔργα EB   20 καὶ Δία] δία τὸν ἀέρα καλεῖ, καὶ φησὶν (sic) Xyl.¹⁵⁷⁰: διάφυσιν Steph.: δία καὶ φησιν Kepl.   24 δὴ SR67: δὲ EB   26–27 ἐοίκασι καὶ θεαταῖς] ἐοίκασι οὐκ θεαταῖς I.22: ἐοίκασιν ἀθεάτοις Xyl.¹⁵⁷⁰: ἐοίκασι ἀθεάτοι Steph.   27 τὴν *om.* B ‖ πλέονας E: πλείονας B

long as you want but they also germinate. Some plants are sown towards winter and some during the peak of summer, like sesame and millet; differently, thyme or centaury, if cultivated in a good and rich land and watered and irrigated, turn away from their natural quality and lose their strength, but are pleased with droughts and then spread properly; but if, as they say, not even dew they stand—as is the case of most Arabian plants—but are weakened and ruined when moistened, what wonder is there then if on the moon there grow roots, seeds, and trees in need of no rain or snow, but which have conveniently adapted to a suitable and rarefied air? And why is it not possible that winds, heated up by the moon, arise and that breezes steadily accompany the stir of its revolution and so dews and light moisture, scattered all around and disseminated, promote the sprouts—because the very composition of the moon is not fiery nor arid, but soft and humidifying? After all, no effect of dryness reaches us from it, but rather many of humidity and femininity: the growth of plants, the decomposition of meats, the aging and alterations of wine, the softening of wood, and easy childbirth for women. I fear to provoke and incite again Pharnaces, now that he is calm, if I resort to, as they themselves say, the tides of the ocean and the rise of waters in the straits which are dispersed and increased by the liquefying action of the moon; consequently, I shall rather turn to you, dear Theon, for when explaining to us these words of Alcman,

'Dew, daughter ⟨of Zeus⟩ and the moon, nourishes',

you say that, because now he calls the air also 'Zeus', he says that by being liquefied by the moon he turns into dew. There is the risk then, my friend, that the moon has a nature contrary to the sun; if everything that the sun condenses and dries, the moon not only naturally softens and dissolves, but also humidifies and cools down the sun's heat, when it falls onto the moon and mixes with it. Therefore, those who think that the moon is a fiery and burning body are mistaken, and those who hold that there should be for the animals there all what there is for the ones here in what regards origin, growth, and way of life, seem to be observant of the differences in nature, among which it is possible to discern more and greater dissimilarities and variations between living beings than between them and inanimate objects.

τῶν ζῴων ἢ πρὸς τὰ μὴ ζῷα διαφορὰς καὶ ἀνομοιότητας εὑρεῖν. Καὶ σύστομοι μὲν ἄνθρωποι καὶ ὀσμαῖς τρεφόμενοι μὴ ἔστωσαν, εἰ μὴ ⟨Θέωνι ἄστο⟩μοι δοκοῦσι, τὴν δὲ ἀτμῶν οὓς ἡμῖν αὐτὸς ἐξηγεῖτο δύναμιν ᾐνίξατο μὲν Ἡσίοδος εἰ|πών·

    οὐδ' ὅσον ἐν μαλάχῃ τε καὶ ἀσφοδέλῳ μέγ' ὄνειαρ.

Ἔργῳ δὲ ἐμφανῆ παρέσχεν Ἐπιμενίδης διδάξας, ὅτι μικρῷ παντάπασιν ἡ φύσις ὑπεκκαύματι ζωπυρεῖ καὶ συνέχει τὸ ζῷον, ἂν ὅσον ἐλαίας μέγεθος λάβῃ, μηδεμιᾶς ἔτι τροφῆς δεόμενον. Τοὺς δὲ ἐπὶ τῆς σελήνης, εἴπερ εἰσίν, εὐσταλεῖς εἶναι τοῖς σώμασι καὶ διαρκεῖς ὑπὸ τῶν τυχόντων τρέφεσθαι πιθανόν ἐστι· καὶ γὰρ αὐτὴν τὴν σελήνην, ὥσπερ τὸν ἥλιον ζῷον ὄντα πύρινον καὶ τῆς γῆς ὄντα πολλαπλάσιον, ἀπὸ τῶν ὑγρῶν φασι τῶν ἐπὶ τῆς γῆς τρέφεσθαι καὶ τοὺς ἄλλους ἀστέρας ἀπείρους ὄντας· οὕτως ἐλαφρὰ καὶ λιτὰ τῶν ἀναγκαίων | φέρειν ζῷα τὸν ἄνω τόπον ὑπολαμβάνουσιν. Ἀλλ' οὔτε ταῦτα συνορῶμεν οὔτε ὅτι καὶ χώρα καὶ φύσις καὶ κρᾶσις ἄλλη πρόσφορός ἐστιν αὐτοῖς· ὥσπερ οὖν εἰ τῇ θαλάττῃ μὴ δυναμένων ἡμῶν προσελθεῖν μηδὲ ἅψασθαι, μόνον δὲ τὴν θέαν αὐτῆς πόρρωθεν ἀφορώντων καὶ πυνθανομένων ὅτι πικρὸν καὶ ἄποτον καὶ ἁλμυρὸν ὕδωρ ἐστίν, ἔλεγέ τις ὡς ζῷα πολλὰ καὶ μεγάλα καὶ παντοδαπὰ ταῖς μορφαῖς τρέφει κατὰ βάθους καὶ θηρίων ἐστὶ πλήρης ὕδατι χρωμένων ὅσαπερ ἡμεῖς ἀέρι, μύθοις ἂν ὅμοια καὶ τέρασιν ἐδόκει περαίνειν, οὕτως ἐοίκαμεν ἔχειν καὶ τούτοις ἀσκεῖν πρὸς τὴν σε|λήνην, ἀπιστοῦντες ἐκεῖ τινας ἀνθρώπους κατοικεῖν. Ἐκείνους δ' ἄν, οἴομαι, πολὺ μᾶλλον ἀποθαυμάσαι τὴν γῆν, ἀφορῶντας οἷον ὑποστάθμην καὶ ἰλὺν τοῦ παντὸς ἐν ὑγροῖς καὶ ὁμίχλαις καὶ νέφεσι διαφαινομένην ἀλαμπὲς καὶ ταπεινὸν καὶ ἀκίνητον χωρίον, εἰ ζῷα φύει καὶ τρέφει μετέχοντα κινήσεως, ἀναπνοῆς, θερμότητος· κἂν εἴ ποθεν αὐτοῖς ἐγγένοιτο τῶν Ὁμηρικῶν τούτων ἀκοῦσαι,

    σμερδαλέ' εὐρώεντα τά τε στυγέουσι θεοί περ

καὶ

    τόσσον ἔνερθ' Ἀίδαο ὅσον οὐρανός ἐστ' ἀπὸ /γαίης·

---

1 σύστομοι] ἄστομοι I.22 SR67: εὔστομοι Dübn.    2 Θέωνι ἄστομοι *supplevi et correxi: lac.* 9 *lit. et* μὴ EB: ζῆν ἄσιτοι δυνάμενοι *suppl.* Amyot: οἳ μηδὲ εἶναι μοι *suppl. et corr.* Wyt. *in app.*: ὑπάρχειν *et* δὴ *pro* μὴ Purser: Θέωνι γ' εἶναι Adler (1933): εἶναι Θέωνι *suppl. et corr.* Po.: οἳ Μεγασθένει γ' εἶναι *suppl. et corr.* Ch. (*sec.* Adler 1910 καὶ Μεγασθένει δοκοῦσι εἶναι)    2–3 τὴν δὲ ἀτμῶν οὓς *conieci* (τὴν δὲ Kepl.): τήν τε ἄμμονος EB: ἥν γε ἄμμονος RJ94: ἣν δ' ἀμμώνιος Amyot: ἣν δὲ ἄμμεως Adler (1910): τὴν δ' ἄλιμον, ἧς Po. Ch. (*sec.* Adler 1933 τὴν δ' ἄλιμον *et* ἣν *add. post* δύναμιν)    7 ἔτι B: ἐπὶ E    16 παντοδαπὰ E: πανταδοπὰ B    18 τούτοις ἀσκεῖν E: τούτους ἀσκεῖν B: οὕτω διακεῖσθαι Amyot: τὸ αὐτὸ πάσχειν Wyt. *in app.*: τοῦτο πάσχειν Raing.    26 ὅσον E: ὅσσον B

And let there not be 'narrow-mouthed' men nourished by odors, if ⟨Theon⟩ does not think they are ⟨'mouthless'⟩, yet the power of vapors, which he himself just explained to us, also Hesiod pointed at when he said: 'Nor as much benefit as in mallow and squill'. And in fact Epimenides made it manifest when he demonstrated that nature rekindles and sustains, with quite minimal fuel, the living being, who, when consuming the size of an olive, needs no more nourishment. It is plausible that those on the moon, if they do exist, are slight of body and adapted so as to be fed by whatever they come across; and so they say that the moon itself, just like the sun too, which is a fiery living being and many times larger than the earth, is nourished by the humidity on earth, and so are the other the stars too, which are countless; so they believe that the beings that inhabit the upper region are light and simple in their needs. However, we do not understand these beings, nor that a different location, nature, and temperature is suited to them; just as if, not being ourselves able to approach or touch the sea but only to contemplate the view from afar and know that its water is bitter, undrinkable, and salty, someone told us that many and large animals and of all sorts of shapes grow in its depths and that it is full of beasts which make use of water in the same way we use air, he would seem to conclude his reasoning with myths and wonders, such dispositions we seem to have and train in them with respect to the moon, when we distrust that some men inhabit there. Yet, they, I think, would be much more astonished that the earth—looking at it as the dregs and dirt of cosmos, glimpsing through moisture, steam, and clouds as an unlit, low, and immobile place—might generate and nourish living beings that take part in motion, breathing, and warmth; and if they happened to hear these Homeric verses somewhere:

> 'terrible and humide, which even the gods loathe',

and

> 'as much below Hades as below heaven is | the earth',

ταῦτα φήσουσιν ἀτεχνῶς περὶ τοῦ χωρίου τούτου λέγεσθαι καὶ τὸν Ἅιδην
F ἐνταῦθα καὶ τὸν | Τάρταρον ἀπῳκίσθαι· γῆν δὲ μίαν εἶναι τὴν σελήνην, ἴσον ἐκείνων
τῶν ἄνω καὶ τῶν κάτω τούτων ἀπέχουσαν."

26. Ἔτι δέ μου σχεδὸν λέγοντος, ὁ Σύλλας ὑπολαβὼν "ἐπίσχες" εἶπεν "ὦ Λαμ-
πρία, καὶ παραβαλοῦ τὸ θυρίον τοῦ λόγου, μὴ λάθῃς τὸν μῦθον, ὥσπερ εἰς γῆν
941A ἐξοκείλας, καὶ συγχέῃς τὸ δρᾶμα τοὐμὸν ἑτέραν ἔχον σκηνὴν καὶ διάθεσιν. || Ἐγὼ
μὲν οὖν ὑποκριτής εἰμι, πρότερον δὲ αὐτοῦ φράσω τὸν ποιητὴν ἡμῖν εἰ μή τι κωλύει
καθ' Ὅμηρον ἀρξάμενον,

Ὠγυγίη τις νῆσος ἀπόπροθεν εἰν ἁλὶ κεῖται,

δρόμον ἡμερῶν πέντε Βρεττανίας ἀπέχουσα πλέοντι πρὸς ἑσπέραν· ἕτεραι δὲ τρεῖς
ἴσον ἐκείνης ἀφεστῶσαι καὶ ἀλλήλων πρόκεινται μάλιστα κατὰ δυσμὰς ἡλίου θερι-
νάς. Ὧν ἐν μιᾷ τὸν Κρόνον οἱ βάρβαροι καθεῖρχθαι μυθολογοῦσιν ὑπὸ τοῦ Διός,
τόνδε ὡς υἱὸν ἔχοντα φρουρόν, τῶν τε νήσων ἐκείνων καὶ τῆς θαλάττης ἣν Κρόνιον
πέλαγος ὀνομάζουσι παρακάτω κεῖσθαι. Τὴν δὲ μεγάλην ἤπειρον, ὑφ' ἧς ἡ μεγάλη
B πε|ριέχεται κύκλῳ θάλαττα, τῶν μὲν ἄλλων ἔλαττον ἀπέχειν, τῆς δὲ Ὠγυγίας
περὶ πεντακισχιλίους σταδίους κωπήρεσι πλοίοις κομιζομένῳ· βραδύπορον γὰρ
εἶναι καὶ πηλῶδες ὑπὸ πλήθους ῥευμάτων τὸ πέλαγος· τὰ δὲ ῥεύματα τὴν μεγά-
λην ἐξιέναι γῆν καὶ γίνεσθαι προσχώσεις ἀπ' αὐτῶν καὶ βαρεῖαν εἶναι καὶ γεώδη
τὴν θάλατταν, ᾗ καὶ πεπηγέναι δόξαν ἔσχε. Τῆς δὲ ἠπείρου τὰ πρὸς τῇ θαλάττῃ
κατοικεῖν Ἕλληνας περὶ κόλπον οὐκ ἐλάττονα τῆς Μαιώτιδος, οὗ τὸ στόμα τῷ
στόματι τοῦ Κασπίου πελάγους μάλιστα κατ' εὐθεῖαν κεῖσθαι· καλεῖν δὲ καὶ νομί-
C ζειν ἐκείνους ἠπειρώτας μὲν αὑτούς | ταύτην τὴν γῆν κατοικοῦντας, ὡς καὶ κύκλῳ
περίρρυτον ⟨οὐκ⟩ οὖσαν ὑπὸ τῆς θαλάσσης. Οἴεσθαι δὲ τοῖς Κρόνου λαοῖς ἀναμι-
χθέντας ὕστερον τοὺς μεθ' Ἡρακλέους παραγενομένους καὶ ὑπολειφθέντας, ἤδη
σβεννύμενον τὸ Ἑλληνικὸν ἐκεῖ καὶ κρατούμενον γλώττῃ τε βαρβαρικῇ καὶ νόμοις
καὶ διαίταις οἷον ἀναζωπυρῆσαι πάλιν ἰσχυρὸν καὶ πολὺ γενόμενον· διὸ τιμὰς ἔχειν
πρώτας τὸν Ἡρακλέα, δευτέρας δὲ τὸν Κρόνον. Ὅταν οὖν ὁ τοῦ Κρόνου ἀστήρ, ὃν
Φαίνοντα μὲν ἡμεῖς ἐκείνους δὲ Νυκτοῦρον ἔφη καλεῖν, εἰς Ταῦρον παραγένηται δι'
ἐτῶν τριάκοντα, παρασκευασαμένους ἐν χρόνῳ πολλῷ τὰ περὶ τὴν θυσίαν καὶ τὸν

---

2 ἐνταῦθα] dupl. B ‖ ἀπῳκίσθαι· E: ἀποκεῖσθαι B    7 ἡμῖν] ὑμῖν Steph. et alii ‖ κωλύει] κωλύοι
B s.l.    8 ἀρξάμενον] ἀρξάμενος Amyot et alii    9 τις Dübn.: τίς EB ‖ ἀπόπροθεν RJ94: ἀπό-
προσθεν EB    13 τόνδε ὡς υἱὸν correxi: τὸν δὲ, ὡς υἱὸν (sic) EB: τὸν δὲ ἄγυον Amyot: τὸν δὲ ὡς
ὕπνον Wyt. in app.: Βριάρεων δὲ τὸν υἱὸν Adler: τὸν δ' ὑπνώδως Purser: τὸν δὲ Βριάρεων Kalt.: τὸν
δ' Ὤγυγον Apelt: τὸν δὲ Βριάρεων ὡς υἱὸν Po. in app. ‖ φρουρόν] φρουρὰν Kalt. et alii    14 παρα-
κάτω κεῖσθαι] παρακατακεῖσθαι Amyot: πέραν κατῳκίσθαι Dübn.: παρακατῳκίσθαι Apelt    15
ἀπέχειν Basil.: ἀπέχει EB    18 προσχώσεις Xyl.: προχώσεις EB    19 ᾗ] ᾖ Xyl. et alii    21 κεῖσθαι·
E: κινεῖσθαι B    22 αὑτοὺς I.22: αὐτοὺς EB: νησιώτας δὲ add. post αὑτοὺς Basil.: τοὺς add. post
νησιώτας δὲ Wyt. in app.    23 οὐκ addidi    27 οὖν E: δὲ B: δὲ οὖν Raing.

they would simply state that this is what is said about this place and that Hades and Tartarus have been placed here; so that only the moon is earth, since it is at an equal distance from those regions above and these ones below."

26. I was still talking when Sulla broke in and said: "Hold on, Lamprias, and lock the door of your discourse lest you unintentionally run the myth aground, as it were, and trouble my drama, which has a different setting and disposition. Well, I am only the narrator, and I will firstly say, if nothing prevents it, that its author began for us by quoting Homer:

'An isle, Ogygia, lies away in the sea',

at a five-day distance from Britain sailing westward; and there are three other islands equally distant from it and from one another lying mainly in the direction of the summer sunset. In one of these, the natives narrate that Cronus is confined by Zeus, having him, as son, as his guardian, and below the ground of those islands and of the sea that they call 'Cronian' he is settled. The great continent, by which the great ocean is surrounded, does not lie far from the other islands, but about five thousand stades from Ogygia for he who travels in ships with oars, for the sea is slow to traverse and muddy due to the numerous streams; the streams flow from the great land and from them alluvial deposits are produced, thus the sea appears to be thick and earthy, which is also thought to be frozen. Greeks inhabit the coast of the continent, by a gulf no smaller than the Maeotis, whose inlet lies precisely on the same parallel as that of the Caspian sea. And they call and regard as continentals precisely those who inhabit this land, as if it was ⟨not⟩ completely surrounded by the sea. They believe that those who arrived at a later time together with Heracles and were left behind by him, having mingled with the tribes of Cronus, rekindled again, so to say, the Greek spark strongly and vigorously, which was already being smothered and governed by the barbaric tongue, and laws and customs. This is the reason why Heracles has the first honors and Cronus the second. Now when the star of Cronus, which we call 'Phaenon' but, as he said, they call 'Nycturus,' enters the sign of Taurus every thirty years, having spent a long time preparing the sacrifice and the ...

<sub>Sulla</sub>

D ἃ ... | ἐκπέμπειν κλήρῳ λαχόντας ἐν πλοίοις τοσούτοις θεραπείαν τε πολλὴν καὶ παρασκευὴν ἀναγκαίαν μέλλουσι πλεῖν πέλαγος τοσοῦτον εἰρεσίᾳ καὶ χρόνον ἐπὶ ξένης βιοτεύειν πολὺν ἐμβαλλομένους. Ἀναχθέντας οὖν χρῆσθαι τύχαις, ὡς εἰκός, ἄλλους ἄλλαις, τοὺς δὲ διασωθέντας ἐκ τῆς θαλάττης πρῶτον μὲν ἐπὶ τὰς προκειμένας νήσους οἰκουμένας δὲ ὑφ᾽ Ἑλλήνων κατίσχειν καὶ τὸν ἥλιον ὁρᾶν κρυπτόμενον 5 ὥρας μιᾶς ἔλαττον ἐφ᾽ ἡμέρας τριάκοντα· καὶ νύκτα τοῦτο εἶναι, σκότος ἔχουσαν ἐλαφρὸν καὶ λυκαυγὲς ἀπὸ δυσμῶν περιλαμπόμενον. Ἐκεῖ δὲ διατρίψαντας ἡμέρας ἐνενήκοντα καὶ μετὰ τιμῆς καὶ φιλοφροσύνης ἱεροὺς νομιζομένους καὶ προσ-
E αγορευομένους, | ὑπὸ πνευμάτων ἤδη περαιοῦσθαι· μηδὲ ἄλλους τινὰς ἐνοικεῖν ἢ σφᾶς τε αὐτοὺς καὶ τοὺς πρὸ αὐτῶν ἀποπεμφθέντας. Ἐξεῖναι μὲν γὰρ ἀποπλεῖν 10 οἴκαδε τοὺς τῷ θεῷ τὰ τρὶς δέκ᾽ ἔτη συλλατρεύσαντας, αἱρεῖσθαι δὲ τοὺς πλείστους ἐπιεικῶς αὐτόθι κατοικεῖν· τοὺς μὲν ὑπὸ συνηθείας, τοὺς δὲ ὅτι πόνου δίχα καὶ πραγμάτων ἄφθονα πάρεστι πάντα πρὸς θυσίαις καὶ χορηγίαις, οἳ περὶ λόγους τινὰς αἰεὶ καὶ φιλοσοφίαν διατρίβουσι. Θαυμαστὴν γὰρ εἶναι τῆς τε νήσου τὴν φύσιν καὶ τὴν πραότητα τοῦ περιέχοντος ἀέρος· ἐνίοις δὲ καὶ τὸ θεῖον ἐμποδὼν γίνεσθαι δια- 15
F νοηθεῖσιν ἀποπλεῖν ὥσπερ συν|ήθεσι καὶ φίλοις ἐπιδεικνύμενον, οὐκ ὄναρ μόνον οὐδὲ διὰ συμβόλων, ἀλλὰ καὶ φανερῶς ἐντυγχάνειν πολλοὺς ὄψεσι δαιμόνων καὶ φωναῖς· αὐτὸν μὲν γὰρ τὸν Κρόνον ἐν ἄντρῳ βαθεῖ περιέχεσθαι πέτρας χρυσοειδοῦς καθεύδοντα, τὸν γὰρ ὕπνον αὐτῷ μεμηχανῆσθαι δεσμὸν ὑπὸ τοῦ Διός, ὄρνιθας δὲ τῆς πέτρας κατὰ κορυφὴν εἰσπετομένους ἀμβροσίαν ἐπιφέρειν αὐτῷ καὶ τὴν νῆσον 20
942A εὐωδίᾳ κατέχεσθαι πᾶσαν, ὥσπερ ἐκ πηγῆς σκιδναμένη τῆς πέτρας. || Τοὺς δὲ δαίμονας ἐκείνους περιέπειν καὶ θεραπεύειν τὸν Κρόνον, ἑταίρους αὐτῷ γενομένους ὅτε δὴ θεῶν καὶ ἀνθρώπων ἐβασίλευσε· καὶ πολλὰ μὲν ἀφ᾽ ἑαυτῶν μαντικοὺς ὄντας προλέγειν, τὰ δὲ μέγιστα καὶ περὶ τῶν μεγίστων ὡς ὀνείρατα τοῦ Κρόνου κατιόντας ἐξαγγέλλειν· ὅσα γὰρ ὁ Ζεὺς προδιανοεῖται, ταῦτα ὀνειροπολεῖν τὸν Κρόνον, 25 εἶναι δὲ ἀνάστασιν τὰ τιτανικὰ πάθη καὶ κινήματα τῆς ψυχῆς ⟨ἕως⟩ ἂν αὐτῷ παν-

---

1 ἃ et lac. 23 lit. E, 17 lit. B: ἀπόπλουν Amyot Xyl.¹⁵⁷⁰: ἀπὸ τῆς οἰκείας πλοῦν Bern. in app.: ἀποπλοῦν ἐπὶ τὴν Κρόνου νῆσον Po. in app.: ἀπόστολον θεωροὺς ἱκανοὺς Ch.: ἀναπλοῦν conieci  2 παρασκευὴν B: vac. 3 lit. σκευὴν E  3 ἐμβαλλομένους Kepl.: ἐμβάλλομεν οὓς EB: ἐμβαίνοντας οὖν καὶ Amyot ‖ οὖν Wyt.: οὐ EB: οὐ del. RJ94 ‖ χρῆσθαι Amyot Xyl.¹⁵⁷⁰: χρὴ EB  8 καὶ¹ om. E  9 ἤδη] οἳ δεῖ Bern. in app. et alii  11 τὰ τρὶς δέκ ἔτη Bern.: τῷ τρισκαιδεκάτῳ EB: τρισκαίδεκα ἔτη vel τριάκοντα SR67  13 οἳ] ἢ RJ94 et alii  18 πέτρας] ἐπὶ πέτρας I.22 et alii  20 εἰσπετομένους Madv.: οὓς πετομένους EB: πετομένους Wyt. in app.  23 ἐβασίλευσε·] ἐβασίλευε Emp. 25 ἐξαγγέλλειν· E: ἐξαγγέλειν B ‖ προδιανοεῖται E: προσδιανοεῖται B: ὕπαρ διανοεῖται Wyt. in app. 26 εἶναι δὲ ἀνάστασιν] κατ᾽ ἀνάστασιν Kepl.: αὐτοῦ add. post ἀνάστασιν Wyt. in app.: εἶναι δ᾽ ἐν ἀναστάσει corr. Herw.: ἐπειδὰν στασιάσαντα Po. (sec. ἐπειδὰν παύσῃ Madv.): εἶναι δ᾽ ἀνάστασιν Ch.: ἔχειν δ᾽ οὕτως ἵνα vel εἶναι δὲ τοῦτο ἵνα Do. ‖ ἕως ἂν add. et corr. Ch. (sec. Bern. in app. ἕως ἂν ἐν): ἐν EB: ᾇ κατευνάζων pro ἐν αὐτῷ παντάπασιν Wyt. in app.: πάντα ἕως ἂν πᾶσιν et αὐτῷ del. Herw. 26–100.1 παντάπασιν] πάντα παύσῃ Bern. in app.: πάλιν ἀνάπαυσιν Ch.

after choosing it by lot they send it forth in so many ships with a large escort and provisions as necessary for men who are going to sail so much sea by oar and live for such a long time abroad. Those who have been sent, as is logical, have different fortunes, and those who escape from the sea occupy in the first place the outlying islands, inhabited by Greeks, and see the sun concealed for less than an hour in thirty days—and this is night, because it has a slight and crepuscular darkness illuminated by the sunset. There they stay for 90 days and, with honor and friendliness, are considered and called 'holy men', then from here they are carried away by the winds. No one else inhabits there but themselves and those who have been sent forth before them. For it is granted to those who have served the god during a period of thirty years to sail back home, but most of them opportunely prefer to dwell there—some out of habit, others because without labor and hustle have plenty of everything for sacrifices and religious festivities, who then always employ their time among various studies and philosophy. Indeed, the nature of the island is astounding and so is the softness of the surrounding air; in fact, for some who intend to sail away, the divinity presents itself as an obstacle, showing up as family members and friends, not only as a dream or by means of portents, but many also clearly encounter visions and voices of daemons. Well, Cronus himself is locked in a deep cave of golden rock, sleeping—for sleep has been devised as a bond for him by Zeus—, and birds bring ambrosia to him, flying in over the top of the rock, and so the entire island possesses a delightful fragrance, spreading from the rock as if from a fountain. And those daemons take care and serve Cronus, having been his comrades precisely when he governed over gods and men. And because they are seers, they prophesy by themselves, but they reveal the greatest prophecies and those concerning the greatest matters as dreams of Cronus by coming down; for everything that Zeus premeditates, this Cronus dreams, and the titanic passions and commotions of his soul are a destabilization ⟨until⟩ sleep com-

τάπασιν ὁ ὕπνος ... καὶ γένηται τὸ βασιλικὸν καὶ θεῖον αὐτὸ καθ' ἑαυτὸ καθαρὸν καὶ ἀκήρατον. Ἐνταῦθα δὴ κομισθείς, ὡς ἔλεγεν ὁ ξένος, καὶ θεραπεύων τὸν θεὸν ἐπὶ
B σχολῆς, ἀ|στρολογίας μὲν ἐφ' ὅσον γεωμετρήσαντι πορρωτάτω προελθεῖν δυνατόν ἐστιν, ἐμπειρίαν ἔσχε φιλοσοφίας δὲ τῆς ἄλλης τῷ φυσικῷ χρώμενος. Ἐπιθυμίαν δέ τινα καὶ πόθον ἔχων γενέσθαι τῆς μεγάλης νήσου θεατής, οὕτω γὰρ ὡς ἔοικε          5
τὴν παρ' ἡμῖν οἰκουμένην ὀνομάζουσιν, ἐπεὶ δὲ τὰ τριάκοντα ἔτη διῆλθεν, ἀφικομένων τῶν διαδόχων οἴκοθεν, ἀσπασάμενος τοὺς φίλους ἐξέπλευσε, τὰ μὲν ἄλλα κατεσκευασμένος εὐσταλῶς, ἐφόδιον δὲ συχνὸν ἐν χρυσοῖς ἐκπώμασι κομίζων. Ἃ μὲν οὖν ἔπαθε καὶ ὅσους ἀνθρώπους διῆλθεν, ἱεροῖς τε γράμμασιν ἐντυγχάνων ἐν
C τελεταῖς τε πά|σαις τελούμενος, οὐ μιᾶς ἡμέρας ἔργον ἐστὶ διελθεῖν, ὡς ἐκεῖνος          10
ἡμῖν ἀπήγγελλεν εὖ μάλα καὶ καθ' ἕκαστον ἀπομνημονεύων· ὅσα δὲ οἰκεῖα τῆς ἐνεστώσης διατριβῆς ἐστιν, ἀκούσατε. Πλεῖστον γὰρ ἐν Καρχηδόνι χρόνον διέτριψεν, ἅτε δὴ παρ' ἡμῖν μεγάλας ἔχοντος ⟨τιμὰς⟩ καὶ τινὰς ὅτε ἡ προτέρα πόλις ἀπώλλυτο διφθέρας ἱερὰς ὑπεκκομισθείσας κρύφα καὶ διαλαθούσας πολὺν χρόνον ἐν γῇ κειμένας ἐξεῦρεν. Τῶν τε φαινομένων θεῶν ἔφη χρῆναι, καί μοι παρεκελεύετο, τιμᾶν          15
D διαφερόντως τὴν σελήνην, ὡς τοῦ βίου κυριωτάτην οὖσαν ... | ἐχομένην.

27. Θαυμάζοντος δέ μου ταῦτα καὶ δεομένου σαφέστερον ἀκοῦσαι, "πολλὰ" εἶπεν "ὦ Σύλλα, περὶ θεῶν οὐ πάντα δὲ καλῶς λέγεται παρ' Ἕλλησιν, οἷον εὐθὺς ὀρθῶς Δήμητραν καὶ Κόρην ὀνομάζοντες, οὐκ ὀρθῶς ὁμοῦ καὶ περὶ τὸν αὐτὸν ἀμφοτέρας εἶναι τόπον νομίζουσιν. Ἡ μὲν γὰρ ἐν γῇ καὶ κυρία τῶν περὶ γῆν ἐστιν, ἡ δὲ ἐν          20
σελήνῃ καὶ τῶν περὶ σελήνην, Κόρη τε καὶ Φερσεφόνη κέκληται, τὸ μὲν ὡς φωσφόρος οὖσα, Κόρη δὲ ὅτι καὶ τοῦ ὄμματος ἐν ᾧ τὸ εἴδωλον ἀντιλάμπει τοῦ βλέποντος,
E ὥσπερ τὸ ἡλίου φέγγος ἐνορᾶται τῇ σελήνῃ, κόρην προσαγορεύομεν. Τοῖς τε | περὶ τὴν πλάνην καὶ τὴν ζήτησιν αὐτῶν λεγομένοις ἔνεστιν ... τὸ ἀληθές· ἀλλήλων γὰρ ἐφίενται χωρὶς οὖσαι καὶ συμπλέκονται περὶ τὴν σκιὰν πολλάκις· τὸ δὲ νῦν μὲν ἐν          25
οὐρανῷ καὶ φωτί, νῦν δὲ ἐν σκότῳ καὶ νυκτὶ γενέσθαι περὶ τὴν Κόρην ψεῦδος μὲν οὐκ ἔστιν, τοῦ δὲ χρόνου τῷ ἀριθμῷ πλάνην παρέσχηκεν· οὐ γὰρ ἓξ μῆνας, ἀλλὰ

---

1 *lac.* 10 *lit.* E, 13 *lit.* B: συστέλλει, ἕως κοσμηθῇ *suppl.* Wyt. *in app.*: καὶ κατακοσμήσῃ *suppl.* Bern. *in app.*: *lac. et* καὶ *del.* Herw.: κατακοιμήσῃ Po.: καταστήσῃ Ch.    6 ἐπεὶ δὲ] ἐπεί γε Wyt. *in app.*: ἐπεὶ δὴ Raing. (sec. Madv. ἐπειδή)    7 ἀσπασάμενος E: ἀσπασαμένους B    8 εὐσταλῶς RJ94: εὐσταθῶς EB ‖ ἐν *om.* B    10 τε *om.* B: τε *transp. ante* τελεταῖς Emp.    13 τιμὰς *addidi*: μεγάλης *corr. et* τιμὰς *pro* τινὰς Basil.: τυχὼν ἀξιώσεως καὶ τιμῆς *corr.* Amyot: τοῦ Κρόνου *add. et* τιμὰς· καὶ *pro* καὶ τιμάς Wyt. *in app.*: τοῦ Κρόνου *add. et* τιμάς, καὶ τινὰς *corr.* Emp.: τοῦ Κρόνου τιμὰς *transp. ante* ἔχοντος Bern. *in app.*    15 ἐξεῦρεν Adler: ἐξευρεῖν EB: ἐξευρὼν Basil.    16 *lac.* 30 *lit.* E, 25 *lit.* B: ἡγεμόνα· τὴν δὲ γῆν *suppl.* Wyt. *in app.*: ἡγεμόνα· ταύτης δὲ τὴν γῆν Bern. *in app.*: πλεῖστά τε μετὰ τῆς μητρὸς ἀγαθὰ παρεχομένεν Po. *in app.*: καὶ τοῦ θανάτου, τῶν Ἅιδου λειμώνων Ch.    18 εἶπεν I.22: εἰπεῖν EB    21 περὶ σελήνην E: περὶ τὴν σελήνην B ‖ Φερσεφόνη Dübn.: Περσεφόνη EB    21–22 φωσφόρος E: φωσφόρος B    24 ἔνεστιν *et lac.* 8 *lit.* E, ἔνεστι *et lac.* 10 *lit.* B: *lac. del. et* τι *pro* τὸ Xyl.1570: ἐπιεικῶς σὺν τῷ μυθώδει καὶ *suppl.* Wyt. *in app.*: ὡς ἔοικε *suppl. et* τι *pro* τὸ Bern. *in app.*: μέν τι καὶ Po.: ἠνιγμένον Ch.: ὄντως καὶ *supplevi*    25 τὸ Basil.: δ EB    27 τοῦ δὲ χρόνου Raing.: οὐδὲ χρόνου EB: ὁ δὲ χρόνος SR67

pletely ... him and his royal and divine status becomes pure and unmixed in itself. He was dispatched precisely there, as the Stranger said, and while serving the god, he studied astronomy for pleasure, going as far as it is possible for he who practices geometry, and with the rest of philosophy as far as it is possible for the natural philosopher. But growing sort of a desire and longing to be able to see the great island—so they seem to call the part of the world inhabited by us—after the thirty years were gone, the ensuing party of servants having arrived from the homeland, greeting his friends he sailed away, for the rest travelling light but carrying abundant supplies in golden cups. Now, all what he experienced and whomever he met—finding sacred writings and being initiated in all mystery rites—is not a task that can be recounted in a single day, as he recited it to us perfectly and remembering it in detail; but listen to what is relevant to the present discussion. Well then, he spent a lot of time in Carthage, as he received great ⟨honors⟩ among us, and he found sacred parchments from when the earlier city was destroyed, which had been secretly taken away and had remained hidden for a long time in the ground. Of the visible gods he said that one should honor the moon above all, and he ordered me to do so, inasmuch as it is the highest sovereign over life ... has.

27. When I showed my astonishment for these things and asked to hear about it more clearly, he said: "Sulla, many things are said about the gods among the Greeks, but not everything is correct: for instance, while they call Demeter and Cora correctly, they wrongly believe that both are at the same time in the same place. As a matter of fact, the former is on earth and is the ruler of terrestrial affairs, and the latter is on the moon and ruler of lunar affairs, and she is called both Cora and Persephone, the latter as 'carrier of light', and Cora because we call 'pupil' the part of the eye in which shines the image of the one who looks into it, just as the light of the sun is seen in the moon. And among the stories about the wanderings and searching between them there is ... some truth, in fact when they are apart they tend to each other and they often unite in the shadow; it is not false that Cora appears now in the sky and with light, then in darkness and at night, but this has caused an error in the computation of time: for not during six

παρ' ἓξ μῆνας ὁρῶμεν αὐτὴν ὑπὸ τῆς γῆς, ὥσπερ ὑπὸ τῆς μητρός, τῇ σκιᾷ λαμβα-
νομένην, ὀλιγάκις δὲ τοῦτο διὰ πέντε μηνῶν παθοῦσαν ἐπεὶ τόν γε Ἅιδην ἀπολιπεῖν
F ἀδύνατόν ἐστιν αὐτήν, τοῦ Ἅιδου περ οὖσαν· ὥσπερ καὶ Ὅμη|ρος ἐπικρυψάμενος
οὐ φαύλως τοῦτο εἶπεν

ἀλλὰ ἐς Ἠλύσιον πεδίον καὶ πείρατα γαίης. 5

Ὅπου γὰρ ἡ σκιὰ τῆς γῆς ἐπινεμομένη παύεται, τοῦτο τέρμα τῆς γῆς ἔθετο καὶ
πέρας. Εἰς δὲ τοῦτο φαῦλος μὲν οὐδεὶς οὐδὲ ἀκάθαρτος ἄνεισιν, οἱ δὲ χρηστοὶ μετὰ
τὴν τελευτὴν κομισθέντες αὐτόθι, ῥᾷστον μὲν οὕτω βίον, οὐ μὴν μακάριον οὐδὲ
θεῖον ἔχοντες ἄχρι τοῦ δευτέρου θανάτου διατελοῦσι.
28. Τίς δὲ οὗτός ἐστιν, ὦ Σύλλα, μὴ περὶ τούτων ἔρῃ, μέλλω γὰρ αὐτὸς διηγεῖ- 10
943A σθαι. ‖ Τὸν ἄνθρωπον οἱ πολλοὶ σύνθετον μὲν ὀρθῶς ἐκ δυοῖν δὲ μόνων σύνθετον
οὐκ ὀρθῶς ἡγοῦνται. Μόριον γὰρ εἶναί πως ψυχῆς οἴονται τὸν νοῦν, οὐδὲν ἧττον
ἐκείνων ἁμαρτάνοντες οἷς ἡ ψυχὴ δοκεῖ μόριον εἶναι τοῦ σώματος· νοῦς γὰρ ψυχῆς,
ὅσῳ ψυχὴ σώματος, ἄμεινόν ἐστι καὶ θειότερον. Ποιεῖ δὲ ἡ μὲν ψυχῆς (καὶ σώματος
τὸ ἄλογον καὶ τὸ παθητικόν, ἡ δὲ νοῦ καὶ ψυχῆς) σύνοδος, λόγον· ὧν τὸ μὲν ἡδονῆς 15
ἀρχὴ καὶ πόνου, τὸ δὲ ἀρετῆς καὶ κακίας. Τριῶν δὲ τούτων συμπαγέντων, τὸ μὲν
σῶμα ἡ γῆ, τὴν δὲ ψυχὴν ἡ σελήνη, τὸν δὲ νοῦν ὁ ἥλιος παρέσχεν εἰς τὴν γένεσιν
B ... ὥσπερ αὖ τῇ σελήνῃ τὸ φέγγος. Ὃν δὲ ἀποθνήσκομεν θάνατον, ὁ μὲν ἐκ | τριῶν
δύο ποιεῖ τὸν ἄνθρωπον, ὁ δὲ ἓν ἐκ δυοῖν, καὶ ὁ μέν ἐστιν ἐν τῇ τῆς Δήμητρος ⟨γῇ⟩
... ἐν αὐτῇ τελεῖν καὶ τοὺς νεκροὺς Ἀθηναῖοι δημητρείους ὠνόμαζον τὸ παλαιόν, 20
⟨ὁ⟩ δὲ ἐν τῇ σελήνῃ τῆς Φερσεφόνης· καὶ σύνοικός ἐστι τῆς μὲν χθόνιος ὁ Ἑρμῆς,
τῆς δὲ οὐράνιος. Λύει δὲ αὕτη μὲν ταχὺ καὶ μετὰ βίας τὴν ψυχὴν ἀπὸ τοῦ σώματος,
ἡ δὲ Φερσεφόνη πράως καὶ χρόνῳ πολλῷ τὸν νοῦν ἀπὸ τῆς ψυχῆς, καὶ διὰ τοῦτο
μονογενὴς κέκληται· μόνον γὰρ γίνεται τὸ βέλτιστον τοῦ ἀνθρώπου διακρινόμενον

---

2 παθοῦσαν Wyt. *in app.*: παροῦσαν EB: πάσχουσαν Kepl. ‖ ἐπεὶ SR67: ἐπὶ EB    3 περ οὖσαν·] πέρας οὖσαν RJ94 *et alii*: περοῦσαν Steph.    11 μόνων E: μόνον B    14–15 καὶ σώματος τὸ ἄλογον καὶ τὸ παθητικόν ἡ δὲ νοῦ καὶ ψυχῆς addidi (sec. Bern. καὶ σώματος μῖξις τὸ ἄλογον καὶ τὸ παθητικόν ἡ δὲ νοῦ καὶ ψυχῆς): μετὰ νοῦ λόγον, μετὰ δὲ σώματος πάθος *add. post* σύνοδος *et* λόγον *del.* Amyot: καὶ σώματος σύνοδος πάθος, ἡ δέ νοῦ καὶ ψυχῆς *add. et* σύνοδος *del.* Wyt. *in app.*: καὶ σώματος μῖξις αἴσθησιν ἡ δὲ νοῦ καὶ ψυχῆς Raing.: ποιεῖ δὲ ἡ μὲν ψυχῆς καὶ σώματος μῖξις αἴσθησιν ἡ δὲ νοῦ καὶ ψυχῆς Po.    18 *lac.* 8 *lit.* E, 11 *lit.* B: παρέχει δὲ τῇ ψυχῇ τὸν λόγον ὁ νοῦς *suppl. et* ὥσπερ τῇ σελήνῃ τὸ φέγγος ὁ ἥλιος *corr.* Amyot: καὶ γὰρ καὶ ἡ σελήνη παρέχει τῇ γῇ ὑγρότητα γόνιμον καὶ φέγγος *suppl. et* ὥσπερ αὖ ὁ ἥλιος τῇ σελήνῃ τὸ φέγγος *corr.* Wyt. *in app.*: τἀνθρώπῳ Bern. *in app. (sec. transl.* Amyot) ‖ αὖ E: οὖν B: αὐτῇ Raing. *in app.*    19 ἐν τῇ τῆς] γῇ *add. ante* τῆς Madv.: γῇ *pro* τῇ Raing. ‖ γῇ *supplevi: lac.* 21 *lit.* E, 26 *lit.* B: χώρᾳ *suppl.* Amyot: μοίρᾳ· ὅθεν τὸ μυεῖσθαι, παρωνύμως τῷ τελευτᾶν Wyt. *in app.*: διὸ προσέοικε τῷ τελευτᾶν Bern. *in app.*: ὅθεν τὸ τελευτᾶν ὁμωνύμως *et* λέγεται τῷ *pro* ἐν αὐτῇ Adler: ὅθεν αὐτῇ τελεῖσθαί φαμεν καὶ τὸν βίον Po. *in app.*: διὸ τελευτᾶν λέγεται τὸν βίον *suppl. et* ἐν *del.* Ch.    21 ὁ *add.* Amyot ‖ Φερσεφόνης·] Περσεφόνης E *s.l.*    22 αὕτη Bern.: αὐτὴ EB    24 μόνον I.22 SR67: μόνη EB

months but every six months we see her being taken under the shadow of the earth, as it were by her mother, and occasionally she experiences this every five months, given that she cannot abandon Hades, precisely because she belongs to Hades, and so Homer said it faultlessly in concealed words:

'but to the Elysian plain and the confines of earth'.

Because where the shadow of the earth ceases to expand, this he set as the end and limit of the earth. To this place no one foul or impure ascends, but the excellent ones are sent there after their ending, leading a comfortable life, but certainly not blessed or divine, until they reach the second death.

28. And what is this, Sulla, do not ask about these things, for I intend to explain them in detail myself. Most people think, rightly, that man is composite, but wrongly that he is composed of two components only. For they believe that the intellect is somehow part of the soul, thus being no less mistaken than those who believe that the soul is part of the body: in fact, just as soul in relation to the body, so the intellect in relation to the soul is better and more divine. While the combination of soul ⟨and body⟩ produces ⟨the irrational and the affective, that of intellect and soul⟩ produces reason; and of these, one is the principle of pleasure and pain, and the other, of virtue and vice. In the constitution of these three components, earth provides the body, the moon provides the soul, and the sun provides the intellect to the generation ... as in turn light to the moon. And concerning the death we die, one turns man from three components into two, the other from two into one; and the former happens in the ⟨earth⟩ of Demeter ... to finish in it and Athenians used in the old times to call the dead 'Demetrians', ⟨the latter⟩ in the moon of Persephone; and while Hermes the terrestrial is associated with the former, so is Hermes the celestial with the latter. She detaches the soul from the body quickly and violently, and Persephone the intellect from the soul softly and taking her time, and that is why she is called 'single-born'—because the best component of man becomes 'single' when detached ⟨by⟩ her. Each death

C ⟨ὑπ'⟩ αὐτῆς. Συντυγχάνει δὲ οὕτως κατὰ φύσιν ἑκάτερον· πᾶσαν ψυχήν, ἄνουν | τε
καὶ σὺν νῷ, σώματος ἐκπεσοῦσαν εἱμαρμένον ἐστὶν ⟨ἐν⟩ τῷ μεταξὺ γῆς καὶ σελή-
νης χωρίῳ πλανηθῆναι χρόνον οὐκ ἴσον, ἀλλ' αἱ μὲν ἄδικοι καὶ ἀκόλαστοι δίκας
τῶν ἀδικημάτων τίνουσι, τὰς δὲ ἐπιεικεῖς ὅσον ἀφαγνεῦσαι καὶ ἀποπνεῦσαι ⟨τοὺς⟩
ἀπὸ τοῦ σώματος, ὥσπερ αἰτίου πονηροῦ, μιασμοὺς ἐν τῷ πραοτάτῳ τοῦ ἀέρος, ὃν    5
λειμῶνας Ἅιδου καλοῦσι, δεῖ γίνεσθαι χρόνον τινὰ τεταγμένον, ⟨ἐν ᾧ⟩ οἷον ἐξ ἀπο-
δημίας ἀνακομιζόμεναι φυγαδικῆς εἰς πατρίδα γεύονται χαρᾶς οἷον οἱ τελούμενοι
μάλιστα θορύβῳ καὶ πτοήσει συγκεκραμένῃ μετ' ἐλπίδος ἰδίας ἔχουσι. Πολλὰς γὰρ
D ἐξωθεῖ καὶ ἀποκυματίζει γλι|χομένας ἤδη τῆς σελήνης, ἐνίας δὲ καὶ τῶν ἐκεῖ περι-
κάτω τρεπομένας, οἷον εἰς βυθὸν αὖθις, ὁρῶσι καταδυομένας. Αἱ δὲ ἄνω γενόμεναι  10
καὶ βεβαίως ἱδρυθεῖσαι πρῶτον μέν, ὥσπερ οἱ νικηφόροι, περιίασιν ἀναδούμεναι
στεφάνοις πτερῶν εὐσταθείας λεγομένοις, ὅτι τῆς ψυχῆς τὸ ἄλογον καὶ τὸ παθητι-
κὸν εὐήνιον ἐπιεικῶς τῷ λόγῳ καὶ κεκοσμημένον ἐν τῷ βίῳ παρέσχοντο. Δεύτερον
⟨δὲ⟩ ἀκτῖνι τὴν ὄψιν ἐοικυῖαι, περὶ δὲ τὴν φύσιν ἄνω κουφιζομένην ὥσπερ ἐνταῦθα
τῷ περὶ τὴν σελήνην αἰθέρι, καὶ τόνον ἀπ' αὐτοῦ καὶ δύναμιν οἷον τὰ στομούμενα  15
E βαφὴν ἴσχουσι· τὸ γὰρ ἀραιὸν ἔτι καὶ διακεχυμένον ῥώννυται καὶ | γίνεται στα-
θερὸν καὶ διαυγές, ὥστε ὑπὸ τῆς τυχούσης ἀναθυμιάσεως τρέφεσθαι· καὶ καλῶς
Ἡράκλειτος εἶπεν ὅτι

αἱ ψυχαὶ ὀσμῶνται καθ' Ἅιδην.

29. Ἐφορῶσι δὲ πρῶτον μὲν αὐτῆς σελήνης τὸ μέγεθος καὶ τὸ κάλλος καὶ τὴν φύσιν    20
οὐχ ἁπλῆν οὐδὲ ἄμικτον ἀλλ' οἷον ἄστρου σύγκραμα καὶ γῆς οὖσαν· ὡς γὰρ ἡ γῆ
πνεύματι μεμιγμένη καὶ ὑγρῷ μαλακὴ γέγονε καὶ τὸ αἷμα τῇ σαρκὶ παρέχει τὴν
αἴσθησιν ἐγκεκραμένον, οὕτω τῷ αἰθέρι λέγουσι τὴν σελήνην ἀνακεκραμένην διὰ
βάθους, ἅμα μὲν ἔμψυχον εἶναι καὶ γόνιμον, ἅμα δὲ ἰσόρροπον ἔχειν τὴν πρὸς τὸ
F βαρὺ συμμετρίαν τῆς κουφότητος. Καὶ γὰρ αὐ|τὸν οὕτω τὸν κόσμον ἐκ τῶν ἄνω    25
καὶ τῶν κάτω φύσει φερομένων συνηρμοσμένον ἀπηλλάχθαι παντάπασι τῆς κατὰ
τόπον κινήσεως. Ταῦτα δὲ καὶ Ξενοκράτης ἔοικεν ἐννοῆσαι θείῳ τινὶ λογισμῷ, τὴν

---

1 ὑπ add. I.22   2 ἐν add. Wyt. in app.   4 τοὺς add. Dübn.   5 αἰτίου] ἀτμοῦ Emp. et alii ‖
ὃν B et E s.l.   6 ἐν ᾧ addidi: εἶτα add. Basil.: μεθ' ὃν add. Bern. in app.: ἔνθ' add. Po.   8 συγκε-
κραμένῃ] συγκεκραμένην Amyot et alii ‖ ἰδίας] ἡδείας Xyl.¹⁵⁷⁰ (transl.) et alii   9–10 περικάτω
Madv.: περὶ κάτω EB: περὶ τὰ κάτω Kepl.: κάτω περιτρεπομένας Purser   10 καταδυομένας E:
καταγινομένας B: κάτω γινομένας Raing. in app.   11 ἱδρυθεῖσαι Wyt. in app.: ἱδρύθησαν EB ‖
περιίασιν RJ94: περιίστασιν E: περιστᾶσιν B ‖ ἀναδούμεναι Hutten: ἀναδούμενοι EB   14 δὲ add.
SR67 ‖ ἐοικυῖαι Wyt. in app.: ἐοικέναι EB ‖ περὶ δὲ τὴν φύσιν Ch. (sec. Sandb. πυρὶ δὲ τὴν φύσιν):
περὶ δὲ τὴν ψυχὴν EB: πυρὶ δὲ τὴν ψυχὴν Wyt. in app.   ‖ ὥσπερ ἐνταῦθα] ὥσπερ ἐντετάσθαι Amyot:
τῷ ἀέρι add. post ὥσπερ ἐνταῦθα Sandb.: ἐξομοιοῦνται vel ἐνδιαιτῶνται Po. in app.: del. Lern.   15
ἀπ αὐτοῦ Wyt. in app.: ἀφ' αὑτοῦ EB   16 βαφὴν] βαφῇ Bern. in app.: ἀπὸ βαφῆς Lern.   22
ὑγρῷ et lac. del. Ald. Basil.: luc. 5 lit. EB: ὑγρότητι suppl. Papabas.   25–26 ἐκ τῶν ἄνω καὶ τῶν
κάτω SR67: ἐν τῷ ἄνω καὶ τῷ κάτω EB: ἐν τῶν ἐκ τῷ ἄνω καὶ τῶν κάτω Raing.

happens by nature this way: every soul that has been detached from the body, with or without mind, is destined to wander ⟨in⟩ the space between the earth and the moon not during the same amount of time, while the unjust and indisciplined souls pay the price of their faults, the righteous souls must remain for a set amount of time in the softest regions of the air, which they call 'meads of Hades', enough for them to purify and blow away ⟨the⟩ stains from the body, as from a grievous origin. ⟨During this time⟩, as if brought home from banishment abroad, they savor joy most like that of initiates, with confusion and excitement commingled with a particular expectation. For many who already desire the moon, it rejects and waves away, and they see a few that are already there turning upside down, as if diving back into an abyss. Those that have got up and are firmly settled, firstly, like victors, go around crowned with crowns of feathers called 'of steadfastness'—because what is irrational and affective in the soul was conveniently docile to reason and commanded by it during their lifetime. And secondly, resembling in appearance a ray of light but in respect to their nature, which is lightweight up there as it is here, resembling the ether around the moon, they get from it both tension and strength, as instruments get their temper, so what is still light and dispersed is strengthened and becomes steady and limpid, in such a way that souls are nourished by whichever exhalation they come across; Heraclitus too nicely said that

'souls inhale in Hades'.

29. They first contemplate size, beauty, and the nature of the moon itself, which is not simple or unalloyed but sort of a mixture of star and earth; for just as the earth, being mixed with air and moisture has become soft and as blood mixed with the flesh provides it with sense-perception, they say that so too the moon having been deeply commingled with ether is at once animated and fruitful and also has a well-balanced proportion of lightness to heaviness. Even more, the universe itself, being assembled out of some things that naturally move upwards and some downwards, has completely escaped local motion. And it appears that Xenocrates also thought of this by

ἀρχὴν λαβὼν παρὰ Πλάτωνος. Πλάτων γάρ ἐστιν ὁ καὶ τῶν ἀστέρων ἕκαστον ἐκ γῆς καὶ πυρὸς συνηρμόσθαι διὰ τῶν ⟨δυοῖν⟩ μεταξὺ φύσεων ἀναλογίᾳ δοθεισῶν ἀποφηνάμενος· οὐδὲν γὰρ εἰς αἴσθησιν ἐξικνεῖσθαι ᾧ μή τι γῆς ἐμμέμικται καὶ φωτός. Ὁ δὲ Ξενοκράτης, τὰ μὲν ἄστρα καὶ τὸν ἥλιον ἐκ πυρός φησι καὶ τοῦ πρώτου πυκνοῦ συγκεῖσθαι, ‖ τὴν δὲ σελήνην ἐκ τοῦ δευτέρου πυκνοῦ καὶ τοῦ ἰδίου ἀέρος, τὴν δὲ γῆν ἐξ ὕδατος [καὶ ἀέρος] καὶ τοῦ τρίτου τῶν πυκνῶν· ὅλως δὲ μήτε τὸ πυκνὸν αὐτὸ καθ' αὑτὸ μήτε τὸ μανὸν εἶναι ψυχῆς δεκτικόν. Καὶ ταῦτα μὲν περὶ οὐσίας σελήνης. Εὖρος δὲ καὶ μέγεθος οὐχ ὅσον οἱ γεωμέτραι λέγουσιν, ἀλλὰ μεῖζον πολλάκις ἐστί· καταμετρεῖ δὲ τὴν σκιὰν τῆς γῆς ὀλιγάκις τοῖς ἑαυτῆς μεγέθεσιν οὐχ ὑπὸ σμικρότητος, ἀλλὰ θερμότητι ἐπείγει τὴν κίνησιν, ὅπως ταχὺ διεκπερᾷ τὸν σκοτώδη τόπον ὑπεκφέρουσα ⟨τὰς⟩ τῶν ἀγαθῶν σπευδούσας καὶ βοώσας· οὐκέτι γὰρ ἐξακούουσιν ἐν τῇ σκιᾷ γενόμεναι τῆς περὶ | τὸν οὐρανὸν ἁρμονίας· ἅμα δὲ καὶ κάτωθεν αἱ τῶν κολαζομένων ψυχαὶ τηνικαῦτα διὰ τῆς σκιᾶς ὀδυρόμεναι, ἀλαλάζουσαι προσφέρονται, διὸ καὶ κροτεῖν ἐν ταῖς ἐκλείψεσιν εἰώθασιν οἱ πλεῖστοι χαλκώματα καὶ ψόφον ποιεῖν καὶ πάταγον ἐπὶ τὰς φαύλας. Ἐκφοβεῖ δὲ αὐτὰς καὶ τὸ καλούμενον πρόσωπον, ὅταν ἐγγὺς γένωνται, βλοσυρόν τι καὶ φρικῶδες ὁρώμενον. Ἔστι δὲ οὐ τοιοῦτον, ἀλλ' ὥσπερ ἡ παρ' ἡμῖν ἔχει γῆ κόλπους βαθεῖς καὶ μεγάλους, ἕνα μὲν ἐνταῦθα διὰ στηλῶν Ἡρακλείων ἀναχεόμενον εἴσω πρὸς ἡμᾶς, ἔξω δὲ τὸν Κάσπιον καὶ τοὺς περὶ τὴν Ἐρυθρὰν θάλατταν, οὕτω βάθη ταῦτα τῆς σελήνης ἐστὶ καὶ κοιλώματα. Καλοῦσι δὲ αὐτῶν | τὸ μὲν μέγιστον Ἑκάτης μυχόν, ὅπου καὶ δίκας διδόασιν αἱ ψυχαὶ καὶ λαμβάνουσιν ὧν ἂν ἤδη γεγενημέναι δαίμονες ἢ πάθωσιν ἢ δράσωσι, τὰ δὲ δύο Μακάρων· περαιοῦνται γὰρ αἱ ψυχαὶ δι' αὐτῶν, νῦν μὲν εἰς τὰ πρὸς οὐρανὸν τῆς σελήνης, νῦν δὲ πάλιν εἰς τὰ πρὸς γῆν· ὀνομάζεται δὲ τὰ μὲν πρὸς οὐρανὸν τῆς σελήνης Ἠλύσιον πεδίον, τὰ δ' ἐνταῦθα Φερσεφόνης [οὐκ ἀντίχθονος].

---

2 δυοῖν *suppl.* Po.: *lac.* 5 *lit.* EB: τούτων Adler: δυεῖν *vel* διττῶν Purser ‖ δοθεισῶν] δεθεισῶν SR67 *et alii* 3 οὐδὲν SR67: οὐδένα EB 6 καὶ ἀέρος *secl.* Ch.: καὶ ἀέρος E: καὶ πυρὸς B ‖ τοῦ E *et* B *s.l.* 8 Εὖρος Steph.: εὖρος E: εὖρος B 9 πολλάκις] πολλῷ SR67 (πολλῶ sic) *et alii* ‖ ἑαυτῆς E: ἑαυτοῦ B 10 ἀλλὰ θερμότητι ἐπείγει B: ἀλλὰ θερμ *lac.* 7 *lit.* ἐπείγει E: ἀναθερμότητα ἐπάγει Ald.: ἀλλὰ θερμότατα ἐπάγει I.22: ἀλλὰ θερμοτάτην ἐπάγει SR67: ἀλλὰ θερμότερον ἐπείγει Arnim: ἀλλὰ θερμότητος, ᾗ κατ' ἐπείγει Po. (*sec.* Wyt. *in app.* ἀλλὰ θερμότητος, ᾗ ἐπείγει): ἀλλὰ θερμοτάτην ἐπείγει Ch. 11 τὰς *addidi* (*sec.* SR67 τὰς τῶν ἀγαθῶν ψυχάς): ψυχὰς *add. ante* τῶν ἀγαθῶν Basil.: τὰς ψυχὰς *add. post* βοώσας Bern.: τὰς ψυχὰς *add. post* τῶν ἀγαθῶν Po. 13–14 ὀδυρόμεναι ἀλαλάζουσαι προσφέρονται] ὀδυρόμεναι, ἀλαλάζουσαι (sic) προσφέροντας Ald.: ὀδυρόμεναι, ἀλαλάζουσι (sic) διαφερόντως SR67 *et alii*: ὀδυρόμεναι, καὶ ἀλαλάζουσαι προσφέρονται Basil. 15 φαύλας Po.: φυλὰς EB: ψυχὰς I.22 SR67 *et alii* 16 βλοσυρόν Steph.: βλοσσυρόν EB 22 τὰ δὲ δύο Μακάρων· P.J.: τὰς δὲ δύο Μακράς EB: τὰ δὲ δύο μικρὰ SR67: τὰ δὲ δύο μακρὰ Dübn.: ὁδοὺς *add. post* τὰς δὲ δύο Μακράς Raing. *in comm.*: τὰ δὲ δύο μακρὰ *corr. et* τὰς Πύλας *add.* Ch. 23 ὀνομάζεται Kepl.: ὀνομάζεσθαι EB 24 πεδίον B: παιδίον E 25 οὐκ ἀντίχθονος *del.* Amyot: οἶκος ἀντίχθονος Ch. (*sec.* Arnim ὀνομάζεσθαι ... οἶκον ἀντίχθονος)

a kind of divine thinking, taking the basis from Plato. Indeed, it is Plato who declared that each of the stars is composed by earth and fire through the two intermediate natures given in proportion; for nothing can be perceived by the senses if it is not commingled with some earth and light. Xenocrates, differently, says that the stars and the sun are composed of fire and the first kind of density, the moon of the second density and its particular air, and the earth of water and the third kind of density; and overall neither density nor tenuousness all by themselves are capable of receiving a soul. But enough about the substance of the moon. Its width and size are not what geometers say, but many times bigger. It measures off the earth's shadow with few of its own magnitudes not because the shadow is small but because with warmth the moon hastens its motion in order that it may cross the shadowy place fast, bearing away ⟨those⟩ of the good which urge it on and cry out, as they can no longer hear the harmony of the universe when they find themselves in the shadow. And all together, from below, the souls of the punished approach then through the shadow, moaning and howling—this is why during eclipses the majority of people are accustomed to beat brasses and to make noise and fuss against the souls. These are frightened also by the so called 'face', when they get close, because of its frightening and hair-raising aspect. However, it is not so, but just as our earth includes deep and large gulfs—one here extending through the pillars of Heracles inside towards us, another outside the Caspian and the surroundings of the Red sea—just the same are these depths and cavities of the moon. They call the largest of these 'recess of Hecate', where the souls suffer and pay fines for whatever they endured or committed after having already become daemons, and the other two 'of the Blessed'; because the souls proceed through them, either towards the side of the moon facing heaven or back to the side facing earth; and the side of the moon facing heaven is called the 'Elysian plain' and the one facing here '(plain) of Persephone'.

30. Οὐκ ἀεὶ δὲ διατρίβουσιν ἐπ' αὐτὴν οἱ δαίμονες, ἀλλὰ χρηστηρίων δεῦρο κατίασιν ἐπιμελησόμενοι καὶ ταῖς ἀνωτάτω συμπάρεισι καὶ συνοργιάζουσι τῶν τελετῶν, | κολασταί τε γίνονται καὶ φύλακες ἀδικημάτων καὶ σωτῆρες ἔν τε πολέμοις καὶ κατὰ θάλατταν ἐπιλάμπουσιν. Ὅ τι δ' ἂν μὴ καλῶς περὶ ταῦτα πράξωσιν, ἀλλὰ ὑπ' ὀργῆς ἢ πρὸς ἄδικον χάριν ἢ φθόνῳ, δίκην τίνουσιν· ὠθοῦνται γὰρ αὖθις ἐπὶ γῆν συρρηγνύμενοι σώμασιν ἀνθρωπίνοις. Ἐκ δὲ τῶν βελτιόνων ἐκείνων οἵ τε περὶ τὸν Κρόνον ὄντες ἔφασαν αὐτοὺς εἶναι, καὶ πρότερον ἐν τῇ Κρήτῃ τοὺς Ἰδαίους Δακτύλους ἔν τε Φρυγίᾳ τοὺς Κορύβαντας γενέσθαι, καὶ τοὺς περὶ Βοιωτίαν ἐν αὐλῶνι Τροφωνιάδας καὶ μυρίους ἄλλους πολλαχόθι τῆς οἰκουμένης· ὧν ἱερὰ καὶ τιμαὶ καὶ προσηγο|ρίαι διαμένουσιν, αἱ δὲ δυνάμεις ἐνίων εἰς ἕτερον τόπον τῆς ἀρίστης ἐξαλλαγῆς τυγχανόντων. Τυγχάνουσι δέ, οἱ μὲν πρότερον, οἱ δὲ ὕστερον, ὅταν ὁ νοῦς ἀποκριθῇ τῆς ψυχῆς· ἀποκρίνεται δὲ ἔρωτι τῆς περὶ τὸν ἥλιον εἰκόνος, δι' ἧς ἐπιλάμπει τὸ ἐφετὸν καὶ καλὸν καὶ θεῖον καὶ μακάριον, οὗ πᾶσα φύσις ἄλλη δὲ ἄλλως ὀρέγεται. Καὶ γὰρ αὐτὴν τὴν σελήνην ἔρωτι τοῦ ἡλίου περιπολεῖν δεῖ καὶ συγγίνεσθαι, ὀρεγομένην ἀπ' αὐτοῦ τὸ γονιμώτατον. Λείπεται δὲ ἡ τῆς ψυχῆς φύσις ἐπὶ τὴν σελήνην, οἷον ἴχνη τινὰ βίου καὶ ὀνείρατα διαφυλάττουσα· καὶ περὶ ταύτης ὀρθῶς ἡγοῦ λελέ|χθαι, τὸ

ψυχὴ δ' ἠΰτ' ὄνειρος ἀποπταμένη πεπότηται.

Οὐδὲ γὰρ εὐθὺς οὐδὲ τοῦ σώματος ἀπαλλαγεῖσα τοῦτο πέπονθεν, ἀλλὰ ὕστερον ὅταν ἔρημος καὶ μόνη τοῦ νοῦ ἀπαλλαττομένη γένηται· καὶ Ὅμηρος ὧν εἶπε πάντων μάλιστα δὴ κατὰ θεὸν εἰπεῖν ἔοικε περὶ τῶν καθ' Ἅιδου

τὸν δὲ μετ' εἰσενόησα βίην Ἡρακληείην,
εἴδωλον· αὐτὸς δὲ μετ' ἀθανάτοισι θεοῖσιν.

Αὐτός τε γὰρ ἕκαστος ἡμῶν οὐ θυμός ἐστιν· οὐδὲ φόβος οὐδὲ ἐπιθυμία, καθάπερ οὐδὲ σάρκες οὐδὲ ὑγρότητες, ἀλλ' ὃ διανοούμεθα καὶ φρονοῦμεν· ‖ ἥ τε ψυχή, τυπουμένη μὲν ὑπὸ τοῦ νοῦ, τυποῦσα δὲ τὸ σῶμα καὶ περιπτύσσουσα πανταχόθεν

---

1 χρηστηρίων SR67: χρηστηρίῳ EB    2 ἀνωτάτω B: ἀνωτάταις E    5 ὑπ' ὀργῆς SR67: ὑπὲρ γῆς EB
6 συρρηγνύμενοι] συνειργνύμενοι RJ94 et alii    7 αὐτοὺς] αὑτοὺς Bern. et alii    7–8 Ἰδαίους Ald.
Basil.: ἰδίους EB    8 περὶ B: πε E    9 ἐν αὐλῶνι P.J.: ἐν Οὐδώρᾳ EB: ἐνουδώσα Ald.: ἐν λεβαδείᾳ
SR67: ἐν λεβαδίᾳ Basil.: ἐν οὐδ' ὥρας corr. et μιᾶς πολὺ πλέον ἐντεῦθεν ἀπέχοντι χωρίῳ add. Po. in
app.: ἐνιδρυμένους vel ἐνιδρυθέντας vel ἐνιδρύοντας Lehnus    10 ἐνίων] ἀπολείπουσιν add. post
ἐνίων SR67: ἔτι·ἀπολείπουσιν add. et δ' αἱ pro αἱ δὲ Bern.: ἐξέλιπον add. ante ἐνίων Po.: ἔνευον pro
ἐνίων Apelt    14 περιπολεῖν B: περιπεριπολεῖν E ‖ δεῖ Ch.: ἀεὶ EB    15 γονιμώτατον] δέχεσθαι
vel λαμβάνειν add. post γονιμώτατον Wyt. in app.: τῷ γονιμωτάτῳ Emp.: τοῦ γονιμωτάτου et φασίν.
ἵεται pro λείπεται Bern. in app.    21 καθ' Ἅιδου Amyot: καθόλου EB    22 Ἡρακληείην Steph.:
ἡρακλείην EB    24 οὐ θυμός l.22 SR67: εὔθυμός EB    25 ὃ] ᾧ SR67 et alii    26 περιπτύσσουσα
E: περιπτύσσου B: περὶ πτύπου Ald. Basil.

30. But daemons do not spend their time forever on the moon, they descend here so as to look after oracles and they assist and take part in the highest mystery cults, they act as chastisers, as guardians against injustices, and as saviors too, and they shine in wars and on the sea. For what they perform regarding these issues not fairly but inspired by wrath or for an unjust end or out of envy they are penalized, for they are cast back upon earth smashed in human bodies. To the former class of better daemons, the attendants of Cronus said they belong, as did before the Idaean Dactyls in Crete and the Corybants in Phrygia, as well as are the Trophoniads in a cave near Boeotia and thousands of others in many parts of the world, whose rites, honors, and apellations endure, and of a few even the powers, when the supreme alteration towards another location is attained. They attain it, some sooner and some later, when the intellect has been separated from the soul; and it is separated by love for the image around the sun, through which shines forth the desirable, beautiful, divine, and blessed, for which all nature in one way or another yearns. Indeed, the moon itself by love for the sun must turn around and be with it, yearning for the ultimate impregnation from it. And the nature of the soul is left behind on the moon, as if retaining certain traces and dreams from life; and regarding her, you should think that it has rightly been said:

> 'Soul like a dream has flown floating away'.

Well, this does not happen right away nor when the soul has parted the body, but after a while, when separated from the intellect, she becomes isolated and alone; and Homer, of all the things he said, seems to have been especially divinely inspired in what regards those in Hades:

> 'together with the strength of Heracles I noticed | his shade; but he is with the immortal gods'.

In fact the true self of each of us is not desire, nor fear or passion, just as it is not flesh or fluids either, but that by which we think and understand; and the soul, shaped by the intellect and shaping and enfolding the body all around,

ἐκμάττεται τὸ εἶδος, ὥστε κἂν πολὺν χρόνον χωρὶς ἑκατέρου γένηται, διατηροῦσα
τὴν ὁμοιότητα καὶ τὸν τύπον, εἴδωλον ὀρθῶς ὀνομάζεται. Τούτων δὲ ἡ σελήνη,
καθάπερ εἴρηται, στοιχεῖόν ἐστιν. Ἀναλύονται γὰρ εἰς ταύτην, ὥσπερ εἰς τὴν γῆν
τὰ σώματα τῶν νεκρῶν, ταχὺ μὲν αἱ σώφρονες μετὰ σχολῆς, ἀπράγμονα καὶ φιλό-
σοφον στέρξασαι βίον, ἀφεθεῖσαι γὰρ ὑπὸ τοῦ νοῦ καὶ πρὸς οὐθὲν ἔτι χρώμεναι  5
B   τοῖς πάθεσιν ἀπομαραίνονται. Τῶν δὲ φιλοτί|μων καὶ πρακτικῶν, ἐρωτικῶν τε περὶ
σώματα καὶ θυμοειδῶν, αἱ μέν, οἷον ἐν ὕπνῳ, ταῖς τοῦ βίου μνημοσύναις ὀνείρασι
χρώμεναι, διαφέρονται καθάπερ ἡ τοῦ Ἐνδυμίωνος· ἐπεὶ δ' αὐτὰς τὸ ἄστατον καὶ
τὸ ἀπειθὲς ἐξίστησι καὶ ἀφέλκει τῆς σελήνης πρὸς ἄλλην γένεσιν, οὐκ ἐᾷ ... ἀλλ'
ἀνακαλεῖται καὶ καταθέλγει. Μικρὸν γὰρ οὐδὲν οὐδὲ ἥσυχον, οὐδὲ ὁμολογούμε- 10
νον ἔργον ἐστίν, ὅταν ἄνευ νοῦ τῷ παθητικῷ σώματος ἐπιλάβωνται. Τιτυοὶ δὲ καὶ
Τυφῶνες, ὅ τε Δελφοὺς κατασχὼν καὶ συνταράξας τὸ χρηστήριον ὕβρει καὶ βίᾳ
C   τύφων, ἐξ ἐκείνων ἄρα τῶν ψυχῶν ἦσαν, ἐρή|μων λόγου καὶ τύφῳ πλανηθέντι τῷ
παθητικῷ χρησαμένων· χρόνῳ δὲ κἀκείνας κατέδησεν εἰς αὑτὴν ἡ σελήνη καὶ κατε-
κόσμησεν. Εἶτα τὸν νοῦν αὖθις ἐπισπείραντος τοῦ ἡλίου τῷ ζωτικῷ δεχομένη, νέας 15
ποιεῖ ψυχάς, ἡ δὲ γῆ τρίτον σῶμα παρέσχεν. Οὐδὲν γὰρ αὕτη δίδωσι μετὰ θάνατον
ὅσα λαμβάνει πρὸς γένεσιν· ἥλιος δὲ λαμβάνει μὲν οὐδέν, ἀπολαμβάνει δὲ τὸν νοῦν
διδούς, σελήνη δὲ καὶ λαμβάνει καὶ δίδωσι καὶ συντίθησι καὶ διαιρεῖ καὶ κατ' ἄλλην
καὶ ἄλλην δύναμιν, ὧν Εἰλείθυια μὲν ἡ συντίθησιν, Ἄρτεμις δὲ ἡ διαιρεῖ, καλεῖται.
D   Καὶ τριῶν Μοιρῶν, ἡ μὲν Ἄτροπος περὶ τὸν ἥλιον ἱδρυμένη | τὴν ἀρχὴν ἐνδίδωσι τῆς 20
γενέσεως, ἡ δὲ Κλωθώ, περὶ τὴν σελήνην φερομένη, συνδεῖ καὶ μίγνυσιν, ἐσχάτη
δὲ συνεφάπτεται περὶ γῆν ἡ Λάχεσις, ᾗ πλεῖστον τύχης μέτεστι. Τὸ γὰρ ἄψυχον
ἄκυρον αὐτὸ καὶ παθητὸν ὑπ' ἄλλων, ὁ δὲ νοῦς ἀπαθὴς καὶ αὐτοκράτωρ, μικτὸν δὲ
καὶ μέσον ἡ ψυχή, καθάπερ ἡ σελήνη τῶν ἄνω καὶ κάτω σύμμιγμα καὶ μετακέρας
ὑπὸ τοῦ θεοῦ γέγονε, τοῦτον ἄρα πρὸς ἥλιον ἔχουσα τὸν λόγον, ὃν ἔχει γῆ πρὸς 25
σελήνην. Ταῦτ'" εἶπεν ὁ Σύλλας "ἐγὼ μὲν ἤκουσα τοῦ ξένου διεξιόντος, ἐκείνῳ δὲ οἱ
E   τοῦ Κρόνου κατευνασταὶ καὶ θεράποντες, ὡς ἔλεγεν αὐτός, ἐξήγγειλαν. | Ὑμῖν δέ,
ὦ Λαμπρία, χρῆσθαι τῷ λόγῳ πάρεστιν ᾗ βούλεσθε."

---

1 κἂν πολὺν χρόνον χωρὶς ἑκατέρου γένηται B: κἂν χωρὶς ἑκατέρου γένηται, πολὺν χρόνον E: πολὺν
χρόνον *del.* Lern.    2 τύπον] SR67: τόπον EB    9 ἀπειθὲς *conieci*: ἀπαθὲς EB: εὐπαθὲς SR67:
εὐπαθὲς *vel* ἀειπαθὲς Kepl.: ἐμπαθὲς Wyt. *in app.*: ἀπαγὲς P.J.   ‖ *lac.* 13 *lit.* E: 11 *lit.* B: οὐδ' *corr. et*
πρὸς τοὺς σώφρονας βίους τρέπεσθαι, ἀλλὰ πρὸς τοὺς ἀκολάστους *suppl. et* ἀλλ' *del.* Wyt. *in app.*:
καταμένειν Bern. *in app.* (*sec. transl.* Amyot): καθησυχάζειν Po.: νεύειν ἐπὶ γῆν Ch.    10 κατα-
θέλγει E *et* B *i.l.*: ἀναθέλγει B    13 τύφων *corr.* P.J.: τυφῶν EB: Πύθων Kalt. *et alii*  ‖ ἐρήμων Kepl.:
ἔρημοι EB: ἐρημία Wyt. *in app.* ‖ λόγου Wyt. *in app.*: λόγῳ EB    14 κατέδησεν] P.J.: κατέδειξεν
EB: κατεδεξαμένη I.22: κατεδέξατο SR67: κατέδεξεν Basil.: δεξαμένη Steph.  ‖ αὑτὴν B *i.t.*: αὐτὴν
EB    16 δίδωσι] τοῖς ἄλλοις δυσί, ἀλλ' ἀποδίδωσι *add. post* δίδωσι Wyt. *in app.*: ἀλλ' ἀποδίδωσι
*add.* Dübn.: ἀποδίδουσα *add. post* γένεσιν Ch.    18 καὶ⁴] *del.* Basil. *et alii*    19 Εἰλείθυια E:
εἰλήθυια B    22 μέτεστι E: μετέστι B    24 σύμμιγμα E *et* B *s.l.*: σύμιγμα B  ‖ μετακέρας P.J.:
μέγα κέρας EB: μέγα κέρασμα Amyot Xyl.¹⁵⁷⁰: μέγα τέρας Kepl.: μετακέρασμα *vel* σύγκριμα Wyt.
*in app.*

receives the impression of its shape, in such a way that even if it happens to be separated for a long time from either one, because it retains the likeness and the imprint, it is properly called 'image'. Of these, as already said, the moon is the element. Indeed they are dissolved into it, like the bodies of the dead into earth, quickly the wise souls who welcomed a life of leisure, untroubled, and philosophical, for once they have been left behind by the intellect and no longer make any use of passions they fade away. Differently, of the ambitious and busy, and those infatuated by the body and impetuous, some spend their time as in sleep, making use of ther memories of life as dreams, just like the soul of Endymion; but, when what is uncertain and disobedient in them excites them and draws them away from the moon to another birth, the moon does not allow it, but invokes and enchants them back. In fact it is not a negligible, gentle, or agreed upon matter when souls with the affective part bereft of reason take hold of a body. Creatures like Tityus, Typhon, and the one who after occupying Delphi and confusing the oracle covered it in smoke with its insolence and violence, all belonged to this class of souls, void of reason and subject to the affective part wandering about blinded by the smoke; but also these in due time the moon tied to itself and set in order. Then, receiving once again the intellect that the sun with its vital force has sown, the moon creates new souls, and earth in the third place contributes with a body. In fact, the earth gives nothing after death, only as much as it takes for the generation, and the sun takes nothing but regains the intellect that it gives, whereas the moon both takes and gives, and unites and separates, and is denominated according to each power, of which Eileithyia is the one that unites and Artemis the one that separates. And of the three Moirai, Atropos, enthroned around the sun, grants the principle of generation; Clotho, moving around the moon, joins and mingles; and the last one, Lachesis, contributes to the task around earth, for which she partakes the most in chance. For that which is inanimate is itself powerless and impressionable by others and the intellect is impassible and self-governed, but the soul is composite and intermediate, just as the moon has been made by god a blend and compound of stuff from above and below, thus having the same ratio with respect to the sun which earth has with respect to the moon. This," said Sulla, "I heard when the Stranger narrated it, and to him the servitors and caretakers of Cronus reported it, as he himself said. It is upon you and your companions, Lamprias, to make use of the narration as you will."

# Commentary to the Critical Edition

The commentary is organized to both illustrate and solve the difficulties within *De facie*. In general, a passage is included in the commentary when it presents one or more of the following aspects:
– The manuscripts have a physical lacuna or a lacuna is deducted by the context, affecting the understanding of a passage.
– The passage has serious syntactic or semantic difficulties.
– This edition proposes a new correction or conjecture.

Each heading normally keeps the following structure: first, in includes the text of the present edition, accompanied by the reading transmitted in the manuscripts; second, a summary of the problems that are involved in the passage; third, plausible solutions proposed by previous scholarship, and fourth, the plausible solution adopted in the present edition.[1]

With a view to avoiding the overload of footnotes in the commentary, previous proposals are referred to by means of the editor's name. Their interventions in the text are easily traceable, since the section *"Editores citati"* provides full references. Differently, when emendations are not included in an edition but in specific studies, a full reference is provided in the footnotes.

920B 1    … Ὁ μὲν οὖν Σύλλας ταῦτα εἶπε· "τῷ γὰρ ἐμῷ μύθῳ προσήκει κἀκεῖ-
θέν ἐστιν·"

EB    Ὀαυνοσυλλας E / ὁ μὲν οὖν σύλλας B ταῦτα εἶπε. τῷ γὰρ ἐμῷ μύθῳ προσήκει· κἀκεῖθέν ἐστιν·

The beginning of the treatise is plausibly lost.[2] With most editions, I accept B's reading for the first sentence (Ὁ μὲν οὖν σύλλας), against the corrupted reading of E (Ὀαυνοσυλλας). Raingeard and Cherniss preferred to start directly with ὁ Σύλλας; and Pohlenz, in his edition, maintained the corrupted form of E, preceded by the *crux philologica*, and suggested (in the apparatus) the conjecture ἀκούσωμεν οὖν ὁ Σύλλας.

B's reading, interestingly, coincides with the beginning of *Quaest. conv.* 3.4, which also starts by referring to the same Sulla: Ὁ μὲν οὖν Σύλλας ταῦτ᾽ εἶπεν. B's beginning might consequently be an attempt to correct the incomprehensible

---

[1] Translation of singular terms is not provided unless the issue at stake is precisely the meaning of the words transmitted by the manuscripts.
[2] L. Lesage Gárriga, *Plutarch's Moon*, in preparation.

form of E into an existing form found elsewhere in Plutarch's work.[3] However, it must be kept in mind that the current beginning most probably was not the original beginning of *De facie*.

E's reading ('Οαυνοσυλλας) could be explained as a corruption of ὁ οὖν followed by an erroneous repetition of the article: ὁ οὖν ὁ Σύλλας. Without the erroneous repetition, this construction is used elsewhere in Plutarch for the introduction of a character.[4]

The plausible loss of the beginning has caused different interpretations of the first sentences' syntax. The pronoun ταῦτα could allude to the previous words, from the lost part of the treatise, thus functioning as object of the verb εἶπε (... Σύλλας ταῦτα εἶπε.); or the pronoun ταῦτα could be part of Sulla's following words, thus functioning as subject of the verbs προσήκει and ἐστιν, which would make the whole sentence as object of εἶπε (... Σύλλας "ταῦτα" εἶπε "τῷ γὰρ ἐμῷ μύθῳ προσήκει κἀκεῖθέν ἐστιν"). The first option is the one transmitted by the manuscripts—according to their punctuation—and was maintained both in 16th century editions and by Raingeard and Cherniss, but it has the inconvenience of leaving the second part of the sentence without a subject.[5] The second option, however, places γάρ in the middle of the sentence, something which goes against the laws that govern the position of particles in Greek.[6] This problem was easily solved by an annotation in RJ94, which simply eliminated the problematic particle. Wyttenbach differently changed γάρ into γ' and suggested (in the critical apparatus) a further option: '*poterat item* τῷ παρ' ἐμοὶ μύθῳ *corrigi*.' Johann Nicolas Madvig proposed to replace τῷ γὰρ ἐμῷ with τῷ παραμέσῳ.[7] Given the uncertain state of the text as it has reached us, these corrections do not seem to be fully justified.

| | |
|---|---|
| 920B 4–5 | "Τί δὲ οὐκ ἐμέλλομεν" εἶπον "ὑπὸ τῆς ἐν τούτοις ἀπορίας ἐπ' ἐκεῖνα ἀπωσθέντες;" |
| EB | τί δὲ οὐκ ἐμέλλομεν εἶπον ὑπὸ τῆς ἐν τούτοις ἀπορίας ἐπ' ἐκείνους ἀπωσθέντες. |

---

[3] Prickard, *Plutarch on The Face*, 52.

[4] See *Sept. sap. conv.* 151F (ὁ οὖν Νειλόξενος ἡσυχῇ πρὸς ἐμέ "πολλά γ'," εἶπεν.) and *De comm. not.* 1069B (ὁ οὖν Ὀδυσσεύς).

[5] Cherniss, "Concerning the Face," 3 n. a, dismissed the modifications introduced in the rest of the sentence by other scholars on the grounds that the copyist of B might have corrected E's reading.

[6] J.D. Denniston, *The Greek Particles* (Oxford: Clarendon Press, ²1981 [1934]) LVIII–LXI, and 56–114 for the uses of γάρ.

[7] J.N. Madvig, *Adversaria critica ad scriptores graecos*, vol. 1 (Copenhagen: J.H. Schultz, 1871) 664.

The demonstrative pronouns τούτοις and ἐπ' ἐκείνους—in both manuscripts—are without clear antecedents, which makes Lamprias' words ambiguous and unclear. If ἐν τούτοις refers to the traditional opinions just mentioned above by Sulla (920B, τὰς ἀνὰ χεῖρα ταύτας καὶ διὰ στόματος πᾶσι δόξας) it should be seen as neuter. This, in turn, would imply that the expression ἐπ' ἐκείνους refers to another kind of opinion, namely innovative and unconventional δόξας that could help to solve the problematic nature of the moon. However, ἐπ' ἐκείνους is masculine and cannot refer to the feminine noun δόξα.

An annotation in RJ94 tried to solve this difficulty by changing the form into ἐπ' ἐκείνας, but this change adds another problem, since it is then necessary to modify ἐν τούτοις as well, for it can only be masculine or neuter. Later, Wyttenbach (in the apparatus) accepted RJ94's modification into ἐπ' ἐκείνας and furthermore changed τούτοις into ταύταις. However, Pohlenz substituted ἐπ' ἐκείνους for the neuter plural ἐπ' ἐκεῖνα, which has now the same gender as ἐν τούτοις: both are neuter plural designating "opinions," ordinary the former and extravagant the latter.

Pohlenz stated that this correction was found in "ς"—siglum which he used to refer to 16th century scholars. However, I have not been able to find it in any of the handwritten corrections by the 16th century scholars, nor in the editions published during that century.[8] Consequently, I attribute the correction to him.[9]

The corruption of the manuscripts' reading ἐπ' ἐκείνους could be explained by the attraction of the preceding pronoun (τούτοις), which may have been interpreted by the copyist as a masculine. Another possible interpretation, however, is that both ἐν τούτοις and ἐπ' ἐκείνους are indeed masculine pronouns, in cataphoric function anticipating the syntagma κοινοὶ λόγοι that appears a few lines after. However, this syntagma is placed too far for the reader to remember the connection; consequently, it is more probable that we are dealing with a scribal mistake.

920C 10–12   ὁρᾷς γὰρ εὐθὺς ὡς ἄτοπος ὁ λέγων τὸ φαινόμενον εἶδος ἐν τῇ σελήνῃ πάθος εἶναι τῆς ὄψεως ὑπεικούσης τῇ λαμπρότητι δι' ἀσθένειαν, ὃ ⟨πρόσωπον⟩ καλοῦμεν,[10]

---

[8] See Pohlenz, "De facie in orbe lunae," xii.
[9] Other instances of this same phaenomenon occur in headings 921D, 940A, 944BC, and 945B.
[10] I owe the punctuation of this sentence to the *Basiliensis* edition, which corrected the interrogation mark that appears in both manuscripts.

EB    ὁρᾷς γὰρ εὐθὺς ὡς ἄτοπος ὁ λέγων τὸ φαινόμενον εἶδος ἐν τῇ σελήνῃ πάθος εἶναι τῆς ὄψεως ὑπεικούσης τῇ λαμπρότητι δι' ἀσθένειαν ὃ ... καλοῦμεν;

Both manuscripts transmit a lacuna of seven letters, which obviously should have included the object of the verb καλοῦμεν. Many scholars have proposed various ways to complete the text: an annotation in RJ94 proposed ὅπερ ἀνάκλασιν; Amyot, ἀμβλυωπίαν; Xylander (in the commentary to his translation), ἀμβλυώττειν; Wyttenbach (in the apparatus), μαραυγεῖν; Raingeard, μαρμαρυγάς; Pohlenz, μαρμαρυγήν; and Cherniss, μαραυγίαν.[11] It is easy to see that all proposals resemble each other, but Plutarch's custom is to combine this verb with a substantive and never with an infinitive, which allows us to reduce the possibilities.[12]

Even if all scholars chose a technical term for the phaenomenon described, in my view, it is plausible that Plutarch may have employed precisely the common term we usually use to refer to the irregularities of the moon's surface, namely 'face' (πρόσωπον). This noun fits into the lacuna and is the simplest solution for the missing term.

920D 20-22    ἔδει γάρ, οἶμαι, τοὐναντίον εἴπερ ἡττωμένου πά⟨θημα⟩ ὄμματος ἐποίει τὴν φαντασίαν, ὅπου τὸ πάσχον ἀσθενέστερον, ⟨σαφέστερον⟩ εἶναι τὸ φαινόμενον.

EB    ἔδει γὰρ οἶμαι τοὐναντίον εἴπερ ἡττωμένου πά ... ὄμματος ἐποίει τὴν φαντασίαν, οπου E/ ὅπου B τὸ πάσχον ἀσθενέστερον εἶναι τὸ φαινόμενον·

The difficulty of this passage lies in its two lacunae: the first is a physical blank of about five letters after πά in both manuscripts, the second is assumed from the context.

Regarding the first lacuna, the Aldine edition, perhaps by mistake, transformed the syllable πά into the article neuter plural τά, and the following editions of Basel, Stephanus and Xylander maintained this reading. This conditioned some of the emendations that took τά as a starting point: RJ94, for instance, has an annotation correcting the article into neuter genitive singular (τοῦ) in order to match it with the first word after the lacuna (ὄμματος). Amyot, after accepting τά, conjectured πάθη. Later corrections took the manuscripts'

---

11    Xylander, *Plutarchi Chaeronensis*, 717.
12    According to the *TLG*, in 39 uses of the verbal form καλοῦμεν none appears with an infinitive as object.

reading πά as starting point. Wyttenbach proposed πά⟨θος⟩—, building on Amyot's correction but with an eye on the manuscripts—; Raingeard proposed πάθημά τι. Given that πάθημα alone fits the space provided by EB better than πάθος, but that the indefinite pronoun τι adds no specific value to the sentence, I supply the lacuna only with the noun.

A bit further in the same passage, the lack of coherence seems to point to the existence of another lacuna. In the previous sentence, Lamprias disproved the idea that the image of a face in the moon is caused by an affection of sight because those with great and acute sight distinguish the figure very clearly. In this sentence, he seems to be making the same statement, but uses the opposite reasoning: if the image was indeed created by a weak sight, those with deficient sight should perceive it more distinctly. However, as it has come to us (ὅπου τὸ πάσχον ἀσθενέστερον εἶναι τὸ φαινόμενον), the sentence leaves the second part of the comparison incomplete: it lacks, at least, a comparative in correspondence with the second nominalized participle.

Amyot wrote on the margin of his *Basiliensis* the correction τὸ πάσχον ἀσθενὲς σαφέστερον and added the alternative reading ἐναργέσθερον. Wyttenbach—with no reference to his predecessor—proposed the conjecture ἐστιν σαφέστερον after ἀσθενέστερον. Hutten simplified Wyttenbach's conjecture by omitting the copulative verb. I agree with Hutten in that only σαφέστερον is necessary and the addition of the verb only complicates the explanation of the corruption: without ἐστιν, the copyist, having two adjectives in comparative form with the same endings, following one another, would have jumped from the first directly to what comes after the second.

920EF 6-9   ὄντως γὰρ ὑποδύεται περιιόντα τοῖς λαμπροῖς τὰ σκιερὰ καὶ πιέζει, πάλιν ὑπ' αὐτῶν καὶ ἀποκοπτόμενα, καὶ ὅλως πέπλεκται δι' ἀλλήλων ⟨ὥστε⟩ γραφικὴν τὴν δια⟨τύπωσιν⟩ εἶναι τοῦ σχήματος. ⟨Τοῦτο δὲ⟩ καὶ πρὸς Κλέαρχον, ὦ Ἀριστότελες, οὐκ ἀπιθάνως ἐδόκει λέγεσθαι τὸν ὑμέτερον.

EB   ὄντως γὰρ ὑποδύεται περιόντα τοῖς λαμπροῖς τὰ σκιερά· καὶ πιέζει πάλιν ὑπ' αὐτῶν καὶ ἀποκοπτόμενα· καὶ ὅλως πέπλεκται δι' ἀλλήλων ... γραφικὴν τὴν δια ... εἶναι τοῦ σχήματος ... καὶ πρὸς κλέαρχον ὦ ἀριστότελες οὐκ ἀπιθάνως ἐδόκει λέγεσθαι τὸν ὑμέτερον.

This passage presents three difficulties: a) there is a verb whose meaning does not fit in the context; b) something seems to be missing in the sentence from ὄντως γάρ to δι' ἀλλήλων, even though neither of the manuscripts records a lacuna; and c) there are three lacunae following one another very closely in the final part of the passage.

As far as the first issue is concerned, both manuscripts report the form περιόντα, participle of περίειμι, 'to be situated around.' Since the passage is referring to the shadowy parts that penetrate into the luminous ones (ὑποδύεται [...] τοῖς λαμπροῖς τὰ σκιερά), it seems necessary to switch this participle for a verb of movement, such as περίειμι, 'to go around,' whose participle is περιιόντα. This form was proposed for the first time by an annotation on the margin of RJ94.[13]

Regarding the second issue, the alleged lacuna in the text, the sentence explains how the shadowy and luminous parts are intermingled with one another in order to form the figure perceived from the earth (καὶ πιέζει πάλιν ὑπ' αὐτῶν καὶ ἀποκοπτόμενα καὶ ὅλως πέπλεκται δι' ἀλλήλων). As it is nowadays, the text includes a verb in 3rd person present active voice (πιέζει), a present participle medium-passive (ἀποκοπτόμενα), an agent separated from what could be its verb—the medium-passive participle—by the conjunction καί, and another verb in 3rd person present but in passive voice (πέπλεκται). Consequently, most scholars thought that the text is incomplete.

The Aldine RJ94 noted the simplest solution: suppressing the conjunction that separates participle and agent. Centuries later, Bernardakis suggested adding καὶ πιέζεται before καὶ πιέζει; Adler proposed the addition of ἐκεῖνα καὶ πιέζεται after καὶ πιέζει; Purser, the addition of καὶ ἀποκόπτοντα after ἀποκοπτόμενα; and both Pohlenz and Cherniss presented as their own the correction πιεζόμενα after καὶ πιέζει.[14] All of them supposed the presence of a polyptoton in the passage and explained the corruption as caused by an omission of one of the verbs.

I believe there is no need to alter the text, since a slight change in the punctuation solves the problems. When placing πάλιν ὑπ' αὐτῶν καὶ ἀποκοπτόμενα between commas, καί, before the participle ἀποκοπτόμενα, functions as an adverb. The two other καί—one before πιέζει and one before ὅλως πέπλεκται—both function as conjunction and link the following verbs.

Regarding the third issue, the three lacunae closely following one another referred to above (καὶ ὅλως πέπλεκται δι' ἀλλήλων ... γραφικὴν τὴν δια ... εἶναι τοῦ σχήματος ... καὶ πρὸς Κλέαρχον), the first occupies a space of five letters in E and around eight in B; the second approximately the same space; and the third about seven letters in both manuscripts. For the first lacuna, Amyot suggested ὥστε εἰκόνα αὐτῶν; Wyttenbach simplified this conjecture and kept the conjunction only; and Pohlenz (in the apparatus) suggested ὡς μονονού. I accept

---

13  Admittedly, the participle of this verb can, on occasion, also be written with a single iota—which would agree with the reading of EB—but that is only allowed when prosodic needs apply, which is not the case.
14  Adler, *Dissertationes philologae Vindobonenses*, 90; Purser, "Mr. Prickard's Translation," 310.

the conjecture ὥστε based on the presence of the infinitive εἶναι a bit later in the same sentence, for they form a construction rather common to express consequence, ⟨ὥστε⟩ [...] εἶναι ('in order to make [...]').[15]

In the second lacuna, after the article τήν, the text seems to require a noun in the accusative, beginning with δια-: RJ94 conjectured δια⟨γραφικήν⟩; Amyot, δια⟨γραφῆν⟩; and Kepler wrote down δια⟨τύπωσιν⟩.[16] I accept Kepler's conjecture, since a bit further in the text Plutarch uses the verb διετύπωσαν ('to represent,' or 'to describe') to refer to the forms drawn on the moon's surface by the luminous and shadowy layers (921BC, αἱ τῶν φωτεινῶν ἐπιβολαὶ τοῖς σκοτεινοῖς, ὕψους εἰκόνα καὶ βάθος λαμβάνουσαι, τὰς περὶ τὰ ὄμματα καὶ τὰ χείλη εἰκόνας φαινομένας ὁμοιότατα διετύπωσαν).

For the third lacuna, Amyot suggested προσωπου (sic), which might fit nicely if EB did not include a strong punctuation after τοῦ σχήματος. Wyttenbach suggested (in the apparatus) ὅθεν αὐτὸ τοῦτο; Bernardakis proposed τοῦτο δέ; Raingeard (also in the apparatus), αὐτὰ δὲ ταῦτα; and Pohlenz, ταὐτὸ δέ. Based on the frequency of each of these proposals in Plutarch's work, I include τοῦτο δέ in the main text with the idea that it may reflect Plutarch's style.[17]

| | |
|---|---|
| 921C 11–13 | εἰ τῆς οἰκουμένης εὖρος ἰσοῖς καὶ μῆκος ἐνδέχεται πᾶσαν ὡσαύτως ἀπὸ τῆς σελήνης ὄψιν ἀνακλωμένην ἐπιθιγγάνειν τῆς θαλάσσης |
| EB | εἰ τῆς οἰκουμένης εὖρος ἴσης καὶ μῆκος, ἐνδέχεται πᾶσαν ὡσαύτως ἀπὸ τῆς σελήνης ὄψιν ἀνακλωμένην ἐπιθιγγάνειν τῆς θαλάσσης, |

The text of EB (εἰ τῆς οἰκουμένης εὖρος ἴσης καὶ μῆκος) does not seem to match reality, given that the inhabited world was not equal in width and length. Several editors corrected the form ἴσης: first, Leonicus suggested ἐχούσης; later on, Bernardakis proposed a combination of the transmitted text and Leonicus' correction, ἴσον ἐχούσης—which does not solve the problem of sense—; finally, Pohlenz offered the conjecture τοσαύτης.

Lamprias begins his statement with a false conditional clause that also includes a false consequence. Perhaps the false condition can be maintained

---

15  J. Morwood, *Oxford Grammar of Classical Greek* (Oxford: Oxford University Press, 2001) 177–178. In *De facie* this construction is used elsewhere, for instance: 925B, ὥστε ἀντιφράττεσθαι πρὸς τὸν ἥλιον ὑπ' αὐτῆς; 926B, ὥστε πάντα κατατείνειν ἐφ' ἑαυτὸ καὶ περὶ αὐτὸ συνέχειν; and 935E, ὥστε σκιὰν ποιεῖν τοσαύτην.

16  Kepler, *Ioh. Keppleri Mathematici*, 101. Kelper's conjecture was later used by Wyttenbach as his own.

17  According to the *TLG*, ὅθεν αὐτὸ τοῦτο: 0 occurrences; τοῦτο δέ: 63 occurrences; αὐτὰ δὲ ταῦτα: 0 occurrences; and ταὐτὸ δέ: 4 occurrences.

if we interpret that he does not speak for himself, but attributes it to his interlocutor, Apollonides. This conjecture is plausible, given that in the preceding sentence Lamprias was indeed speaking directly to Apollonides (921C, Ἐκεῖνο μὲν γὰρ ἐρωτᾶν ἀσφαλέστερόν ἐστιν ἢ ἀποφαίνεσθαι *σοῦ παρόντος*). The only intervention necessary is the correction of ἴσης into a verb in 2nd person singular. This is possible with the verb ἰσόω (ἰσοῖς, 'you make equal'), and the corruption can be explained as due to iotacism.

921D 17–19   καίτοι γε φίλε πρίαμ ... ἀλλὰ πολλοῖς οὐκ ἀρέσκει φυσιολογῶν περὶ τῆς ὄψεως ⟨ὡς⟩ αὐτὴν ὁμοπαθῆ κρᾶσιν ἴσχειν καὶ σύμπηξιν εἰκός ἐστι μᾶλλον ἢ πληγάς τινας καὶ ἀποπηδήσεις οἵας ἔπλαττε τῶν ἀτόμων Ἐπίκουρος.

EB   καίτοι γε φίλε πρίαμ ... ἀλλὰ πολλοῖς οὐκ ἀρέσκει φυσιολογῶν περὶ τῆς ὄψεως αὐτὴν ὁμοπαθῆ κρᾶσιν ἴσχειν καὶ σύμπηξιν, εἰκός ἐστι μᾶλλον, ἢ πληγάς τινας καὶ ἀποπηδήσεις οἵας ἔπλαττε τῶν ἀτόμων ἐπίκουρος.

Two issues are at stake in this passage: firstly, there is a short lacuna at the beginning; and secondly, the syntax of the sentence that explains the way vision functions is unclear.

As far as the former is concerned, both manuscripts transmit a blank of three letters after φίλε πρίαμ. The first attempts to emend it come from annotations in the Aldine RJ94, one contributor with φίλε πρίαμε and another with φίλε λαμπρία, and in Amyot's *Basiliensis* with φίλε λαμπρίας. They all are problematic: while the first one introduces a character (Priame) who is not part of the dialogue, the other two proposals make no sense, since it is Lamprias who speaks at the moment.[18] Later editions tried to offer more suitable conjectures: Wyttenbach suggested φίλος γ' ἀνήρ; Otto Apelt, ὤφειλε προτιμᾶσθαι; Pohlenz, φιλοπράγμων ἀνήρ; Cherniss, ἐφιλέργει ἀνήρ.[19] Adler, on his turn, suggested a rather daring option: to correct φίλε πρίαμ and supply the lacuna with ἔφη, ὦ Λαμπρία, τοῦδ' ἔστιν, implying, in this way, that Apollonides intervenes here and that Lamprias resumes his discourse afterwards.[20] However, as Purser already noticed, there is no indication whatsoever in the text for such a possibility, and the treatise always clearly marks switches of interlocutors.[21] The best

---

18   On the participants in *De facie*, see above "Characters," 10–22.
19   O. Apelt, "Zu Plutarch und Plato," in *Jahresbericht über das Gymnasium Carolo-Alexandrinum zu Jena* (Jena: Universitäts-Buchdruckerei G. Neuenhahn, 1905) 16.
20   Adler, *Dissertationes philologae Vindobonenses*, 91–92.
21   Purser, "Mr. Prickard's Translation," 311.

solution, appears to be the combination of emendation and conjecture offered by Pohlenz. His correction not only provides a good sense for the passage—it would refer to Hipparchus, mentioned a few lines above—but it is also palaeographically explainable. However, given that possibilities are innumerable, to maintain the lacuna seems preferable.

Concerning the syntactic problem, the section that refers to Hipparchus' work on vision (οὐκ ἀρέσκει φυσιολογῶν περὶ τῆς ὄψεως αὐτὴν ὁμοπαθῆ κρᾶσιν ἴσχειν καὶ σύμπηξιν εἰκός ἐστι μᾶλλον) lacks a subject for εἰκός ἐστι. To solve the problem, scholars have modified τῆς ὄψεως αὐτήν in the attempt to include the missing subject in accusative: Wyttenbach (in the apparatus) proposed ὄψεως αὐτῆς, ἥν; Jacob Johann Hartman, ὄψεως ἥν; Raingeard, ὄψεως. Αὐτήν; and Pohlenz, ὄψεως ὡς αὐτήν.[22] Some scholars, however, not only tried to include a subject in that part of the passage, but also interpreted that vision itself cannot be the subject, rather the subject should be "the ray." They consequently offered various solutions: Dübner, ὄψεως αὐγή; Bernardakis (in the apparatus), ὄψεως αὐγῇ γὰρ ταύτην; Adler accepted Wyttenbach's ὄψεως αὐτῆς, ἥν and added τῇ αὐγῇ after ὁμοπαθῆ.[23]

Adding αὐγῇ does not have significant value, because vision is the topic of discussion and can perfectly function as the subject of the sentence. Of the remaining proposals, I find Pohlenz's conjecture the most convincing. In that case, ὡς relates to the participle φυσιολογῶν, whose subject is Hipparchus, and its loss would be the result of a simple haplography (ὄψεως ὡς). Furthermore, with this solution, the pronoun αὐτήν transmitted by EB can be maintained.

| | |
|---|---|
| 921D 21–22 | τοιαύτῃ τὴν ὄψιν ἢ θραύειν προσήκει ⟨ἢ⟩ καὶ ἀποστρέφειν |
| EB | τοιαύτῃ τὴν ὄψιν ἢ θραῦσιν προσήκει καὶ ἀποστρέφειν.[24] |

As is transmitted, the text presents both syntactical and semantic difficulties. Concerning the former, the copulative conjunction καί cannot link a verb in personal form (προσήκει) with the infinitive that follows (ἀποστρέφειν). Therefore, some editions such as the *Basiliensis* or Xylander changed the verb into an infinitive (προσήκειν). This modification forced them in turn to transform the

---

22  J.J. Hartman, *De Plutarcho scriptore et philosopho* (Leiden: Brill, 1916) 561.
23  Adler, *Dissertationes philologae Vindobonenses*, 92.
24  While the context requires a dative, Stephanus and Wyttenbach include the nominative τοιαύτη. Whether this change results from a conscious decision or from inadvertance, given that the manuscripts do not transmit the subscribed iotas, we cannot know. On this issue and its implications, see "Editorial Criteria" and footnote 4.

initial τοιαύτῃ into an accusative (τοιαύτην τὴν ὄψιν ἢ θραῦσιν προσήκειν καὶ ἀποστρέφειν). Raingeard offered a simpler solution, he removed the conjunction (τοιαύτῃ τὴν ὄψιν ἢ θραῦσιν προσήκει ἀποστρέφειν).

In regards to the semantic difficulties, the substantive ὄψιν should not be linked to θραῦσιν due to the meaning of the latter ('slaughter,' or 'destruction') which hardly collaborates with the contextual word "vision." The first to offer a solution to this problem was one of the contributors to RJ94, who eliminated ἢ and corrected θραῦσιν into an infinitive, θραύειν. Thus, the other infinitive (ἀποστρέφειν) can be attached to θραύειν by the copulative conjunction καί. Another of the contributors of the same Aldine copy proposed to change ἢ θραῦσιν into οὐ θραύειν, perhaps in an attempt to account for the disjunctive, instead of simply eliminating it.

Later on, Pohlenz accepted Wyttenbach's addition of the particle δέ after the demonstrative adjective τοιαύτῃ, RJ94's modification of θραῦσιν into θραύειν, but also maintained the disjunctive ἢ that preceeds it—instead of eliminating it or changing it into οὐ. Pohlenz strangely attributed the correction ἢ θραύειν to RJ94. This, however, is not the case: RJ94's correction links two infinitives through καί and for this to be possible the disjunctive construction must have been previously eliminated. In fact, in the Aldine copy both the disjunctive conjunction and the noun θραῦσιν are underlined, while only the infinitive is written on the margin as correction. Pohlenz, then, is responsible for maintaining ἢ before the infinitive, and he was able to do so only because he also added another disjunctive conjunction.[25] He substituted the copulative conjunction καί for a second disjunctive before the second infinitive: τοιαύτῃ δὲ τὴν ὄψιν ἢ θραύειν προσήκει ἢ ἀποστρέφειν.

I believe it is not necessary to modify the text to such an extent. The only compulsory changes are the following: θραῦσιν must be turned into an infinitive (θραύειν) to avoid its connection with ὄψιν and to allow the copulative conjunction to link two identical verbs (θραύειν and ἀποστρέφειν); another disjunctive conjunction (ἤ) should be added before the copulative one in order to preserve the first disjunctive conjunction and καί in adverbial function. In this case, the textual corruption can easily be explained: the infinitive was turned into an accusative due to the proximity of ὄψιν followed by the disjunction; the second disjunctive conjunction was lost due to the ease for monosyllabic words to disappear and to iotacism—the diphthong of the last syllable of the preceding word (προσήκει) was pronounced the same as ἤ.

---

25  See footnote 9, above, for other occurrences in which a conjecturer erroneously attributed his innovation to previous scholars.

| | |
|---|---|
| 921E 2–3 | Ἀλλ ... πρὸς τὸν Λεύκιον ἔφην ἀποβλέψας "ὃ πρῶτον ἐλέχθη τῶν ἡμετέρων ὑπόμνησον." |
| EB | ἀλλ ... πρὸς τὸν λεύκιον. ἐφ' ὧν ἀποβλέψας ὃ πρῶτον ἐλέχθη τῶν ἡμετέρων ὑπόμνησον· |

This sentence includes two complications: a lacuna at the beginning and a missing main verbal form.

Both manuscripts transmit a lacuna of 16 letters that, despite the length, does not affect the sense. The annotation found in the Aldine RJ94 merely added the alpha lacking in ἀλλ, which seems to indicate that the scholar eliminated the lacuna. Some editors, however, completed it with different variants of pronouns: Amyot suggested ἔγω; Wyttenbach (in the apparatus) σύ γε. Adler is the only editor to offer a conjecture that fits the available space: ἐάσωμεν ταῦτα, καὶ σύ.[26] As said, however, the sense can be understood without intervening in the text, and, consequently, to simply note the lacuna seems preferable.

In what regards the lack of the verbal form, editors modified the suspiciously corrupted ἐφ' ὧν of EB in an attempt to fix the syntax of the section: indeed, the passage includes no plural that could be the precedent of the relative pronoun ὧν, which appears to be completely out of place. One of the contributors to the Aldine RJ94 corrected it into εἶπον; Amyot offered ἔφην. Based on two reasons I accept Amyot's correction: statistically, the imperfect ἔφην appears more often when Lamprias is speaking (10 times vs. 7 εἶπον); and, palaeographically, the corruption from ἔφην to ἐφ' ὧν is easier to explain.[27]

| | |
|---|---|
| 923A 19–22 | ὥσπερ Ἀρίσταρχον ᾤετο δεῖν Κλεάνθης τὸν σάμιον ἀσεβείας προσκαλεῖσθαι τοὺς Ἕλληνας, ὡς κινοῦντα τοῦ κόσμου τὴν ἑστίαν, ὅτι ⟨τὰ⟩ φαινόμενα σώζειν ἀνὴρ ἐπειρᾶτο, μένειν τὸν οὐρανὸν ὑποτιθέμενος, |
| EB | ὥσπερ ἀρίσταρχος ᾤετο δεῖν κλεάνθη τὸν σάμιον ἀσεβείας προκαλεῖσθαι τοὺς ἕλληνας. ὡς κινοῦντα τοῦ κόσμου τὴν ἑστίαν· ὅτι φαινόμενα σώζειν ἀνὴρ ἐπειρᾶτο, μένειν τὸν οὐρανὸν ὑποτιθέμενος· |

This passage presents several problems. The main issue concerns the syntactical function of the people involved in the accusation for impiety (Aristarchus and Cleanthes); the other three issues are of minor relevance, they concern both the syntax and the semantics of the infinitive προκαλεῖσθαι, the participle φαινόμενα, and the noun ἀνήρ.

---

26  Adler, *Dissertationes philologae Vindobonenses*, 93.
27  See for a detailed analysis Pérez Jiménez, "Gestos, palabras y actitudes," 66–68.

Concerning the prosecution for impiety regarding Aristarchus and Cleanthes, EB state that Aristarchus wanted the Greeks to sue Cleanthes, but associate the adjective in accusative τὸν σάμιον to Cleanthes, even if the figure in question here is most probably the famous Cleanthes of Assos. The first intervention in the text appears in RJ94, which replaced τὸν σάμιον with τὸν ἄσσιον. In the 17th century, Gilles Ménage switched the order of elements of EB: Cleanthes becomes the subject and Aristarchus the object of the accusation.[28] In this correction, the adjective τὸν σάμιον refers to Aristarchus. Raingeard, differently, maintained EB's reading, claiming (in his commentary) that there is no need to assume that the text refers to Cleanthes of Assos and that it might very well be a countryman of Aristarchus, also from Samos.[29] While Lucio Russo and Silvio Medaglia kept both the subject and the object of EB, they assumed a corruption elsewhere to explain the problematic adjective.[30] They suggested replacing τὸν σάμιον with τοὺς σαμίους and adding the preposition εἰς before τοὺς Ἕλληνας. The adjective now refers to Aristarchus' countrymen, which would be the subject of the dependent substantive clause, while τοὺς Ἕλληνας would in turn be a complement (ὥσπερ Ἀρίσταρχος ᾤετο δεῖν Κλεάνθη τοὺς σαμίους ἀσεβείας προσκαλεῖσθαι εἰς τοὺς Ἕλληνας).

While RJ94's correction is rather efficient and simple, it does not provide an explanation for the corruption. Ménage's emendation, however, is backed up by some facts. Firstly, there is a mention, by Diogenes Laertius, of a work supposedly written by Cleanthes called Πρὸς Ἀρίσταρχον, which points to a polemic involving Cleanthes as the prosecutor of Aristarchus.[31] Secondly, with the correction there becomes a parallel structure between this passage and the previous: in the previous passage, Lucius asks a Stoic thinker (Pharnaces) not to lay suit against them; in the current passage, he uses as an example a Stoic thinker (Cleanthes) that laid a suit against someone (Aristarchus). I am not very convinced by Raingeard's denial that the text is referencing Cleanthes of Assos. Lastly, Russo and Medaglia need too many interventions just to maintain the syntactic function of Aristarchus and Cleanthes as transmitted by EB. Therefore, I accept Ménage's emendation.

---

28  In Th., Aldobrandini, *Laertii Diogenis De vitis dogmatis et apophthegmatis eorum qui in philosophia claruerunt; libri x. Thoma Aldobrandino interprete, cum annotationibus eiusdem. Quibus accesserunt annotationes H. Stephani, & Utriusque Casavboni; cum uberrimis Aegidii Menagii observationibus* (London: Typis Tho. Radcliffe, 1664) 226, he wrote ἀρίσταρχον τὸν σάμιον ᾤετο δεῖν κλεάνθης.

29  Raingeard, *Le peri toy prosopoy*, 69.

30  L. Russo & S.M. Medaglia, "Sulla presunta accusa di impietà ad Aristarco di Samo," *QUCC* 53 (1996) 120.

31  Aldobrandini, *Laertii Diogenis De vitis dogmatis*, 206.

Concerning the minor difficulties, the first one affects the meaning of the infinitive προκαλεῖσθαι ('to be challenged'). It was modified by the Aldine RJ94 into προσκαλεῖσθαι, given that προσκαλέω does not have a passive value but means 'to summon into court,' which is the meaning required by the context.

The second difficulty is related to the participle φαινόμενα, given that Plutarch never uses this participle in the sense of "the phenomena" without the article. Consequently, RJ94 added τά, which seems to be a mandatory intervention.

The third difficulty concerns ἀνήρ, which lacks its corresponding article. Dübner corrected the problem with a crasis between the article and the noun: he simply corrected the breathing of the manuscripts' reading into the rough form (ἁνήρ).[32]

| | |
|---|---|
| 923BC 3–5 | περὶ δὲ τῆς γῆς ἴσως Αἰσχύλος ἡμᾶς πέπεικεν ὡς ὁ Ἄτλας ἕστηκε κίων οὐρανοῦ τε καὶ χθονός ὤμοις ἐρείδων ἄχθος οὐκ εὐάγκαλον· |
| EB | περὶ δὲ τῆς γῆς ἴσως αἰσχύλος ἡμᾶς πέπεικεν ὡς ὁ ἄτλας ἕστηκε κίων οὐρανοῦ τε καὶ χθονός· ὤμοις ἐρείδων ἄχθος οὐκ εὐάγκαλον· |

Two modifications are introduced in the passage: the first one concerns the pronoun transmitted by the manuscripts (ἡμᾶς) and the other concerns Aeschylus' quote.[33] In my view, however, these changes are not necessary.

The pronoun ἡμᾶς was modified into the 2nd person plural by Stephanus, a correction always accepted ever since, with the exception of Raingeard. The confusion between pronouns was easy to happen, since both sounded the same due to iotacism, and in fact, the confusion occurs elsewhere in the treatise.[34] Here, Lucius is talking to Pharnaces—he first used σκόπει—and by extension to all Stoics—he then used the 2nd person plural δεδοίκατε. But this does not compel him to only use the 2nd person. The reference to a specific belief and the association of such belief with an authoritative composer could very well be in 1st person plural, in which case the idea is transformed into a general statement that involves Lucius' audience as a whole.

---

32   He made the same correction in 920F. There is another occurrence, also in 920F, but in that case Dübner suggested ὁ ἀνήρ, and it was Bernardakis to suggest ἁνήρ.

33   *Prometheus Vinct.* 350–351.

34   For instances where EB read a pronoun, either 1st or 2nd person plural, that must be changed, see the headings corresponding to 926D and 928EF. Notwithstanding this, I believe scholars have had a slight tendency to switch pronouns, modifying a text that perhaps did not need any intervention; see, beside this case, the entry on 941A.

The verses of Aeschylus, even if being grammatically correct, as quoted by Plutarch, were corrected by an annotation in Turnebus' Aldine copy, which transformed the word κίων into the accusative κίον'—an emendation accepted by most editors afterwards. The change is due to the fact that it appears under this form in Aeschylus, in which it is interpreted as the object of Atlas' action. While the correction is plausible, I prefer to maintain κίων, since the transmitted text is, in principle, correct, and we do not know whether Plutarch made a mistake quoting from memory or whether he knew the verse under a form unknown to us. It is also possible, as Raingeard suggests (in his commentary), that Plutarch might have consciously altered the text to highlight the architectural role of Atlas.[35]

923C 7–10   καὶ διὰ τοῦτο Φαρνάκης αὐτὸς μὲν ἐν ἀδείᾳ τοῦ πεσεῖν τὴν γῆν ἐστιν, οἰκτείρει δὲ τοὺς ὑποκειμένους τῇ μεταφορᾷ τῆς σελήνης Αἰθίοπας ἢ Ταπροβηνούς, μὴ βάρος αὐτοῖς ἐμπέσῃ τοσοῦτον.
EB   καὶ διατοῦτο φαρνάκης αὐτὸς μὲν ἐν ἀδείᾳ τοῦ πεσεῖν τὴν γῆν ἐστιν· οἰκτείρει δὲ τοὺς ὑποκειμένους τῇ μεταφορᾷ τῆς σελήνης αἰθίοπας· ἢ ταπροβηνοὺς, μὴ βάρος EB / βορός B s.l. αὐτοῖς ἐμπέσῃ τοσοῦτον·[36]

The text, despite not presenting much trouble content wise, has been modified in four different places. While three of them are minor changes, one of them affects the interpretation of the passage.

Let us start with the minor revisions. Firstly, Bernardakis—followed by Pohlenz and Cherniss—changed the verb οἰκτείρει, transmitted by EB, into its attic equivalent οἰκτίρει. Secondly, the Aldine edition read αὐτῆς, instead of αὐτοῖς. Given that the nouns to which the pronoun refers are Αἰθίοπας ἢ Ταπροβηνούς, it can be easily explained as an erratum due to iotacism. Most of the handwritten annotations of different Aldine copies corrected it into dative plural. Thirdly, Pohlenz closed the passage with a question mark (τοσοῦτον;). I do not adopt any of these changes, since they either are unnecessary or mistakes.

Concerning the fourth and more interesting modification to the text, the noun μεταφορᾷ has been replaced because of its meaning: 'transport,' or 'change.'[37] An annotation in the Aldine RJ94 reads καταφορᾷ, which means

---

35   Raingeard, Le peri toy prosopoy, 72.
36   Both E and B read βάρος ('weight'), B adds supra lineam βορός, an adjective meaning "gluttonous" that obviously nobody accepted. See the emendation in Appendix 2.
37   LSJ provides also the meaning "phase of the moon" and refers to this passage specifically. This seems not to be appropriate, as Cherniss already pointed out in "Notes on Plutarch's De facie," 139.

'fall;' Cherniss suggested περιφορᾷ, meaning 'circular movement.' Both of these changes provide the text with a more suitable substantive. In this case, Pharnaces expresses his fear for those who are placed either under the moon's path or under the trajectory of its fall. Both options are supported by their appearance a few lines below: that of RJ94, in 923C, ὥσπερ ὅσα ταῖς σφενδόναις ἐντεθέντα τῆς καταφορᾶς κώλυσιν ἴσχει τὴν κύκλῳ περιδίνησιν; that of Cherniss, in 923D, διὸ τὴν σελήνην οὐκ ἄγει τὸ βάρος ὑπὸ τῆς περιφορᾶς τὴν ῥοπὴν ἐκκρουόμενον.

Despite the apparent support it has, I do not think the correction is necessary. To begin with, the presence of these nouns later in the text does not imply their repetition here; furthermore, even if it may not be that technical, the reference to μεταφορᾷ is coherent, since it reinforces Lucius' statement that it is precisely the moon's shifting that prevents it from falling.

923E 22–24 "Πάνυ μὲν οὖν" εἶπεν ὁ Φαρνάκης "τὸν οἰκεῖον καὶ κατὰ φύσιν τόπον ἔχουσαν, ὥσπερ αὐτῇ τὸν μέσον, οὗτος γάρ ἐστι περὶ ὃν ἀντερείδει πάντα τὰ βάρη ῥέποντα καὶ φέρεται καὶ συννεύει πανταχόθεν."[38]

EB πάνυ μὲν οὖν εἶπεν ὁ φαρνάκης. τὸν οἰκεῖον καὶ κατὰ φύσιν τόπον ἔχουσαν. ὥσπερ αὐτὴ τὸν μέσον. οὗτος γάρ ἐστι περὶ ὃν ἀντερείδει πάντα τὰ βάρη ῥέποντα. καὶ φέρεται. καὶ συννεύει πανταχόθεν.

In this passage, Pharnaces defends the theories of natural positions in the cosmos and the earth's central position in it. The section in which the latter issue is defended is corrupt (ὥσπερ αὐτὴ τὸν μέσον). The pronoun αὐτή should refer to the earth, the nearest feminine (γῆν in Lucius' last sentence, and ἔχουσαν in Pharnaces' reply), and τὸν μέσον should refer to τὸν [...] τόπον.

Whether intentionally or not, the Aldine and the *Basiliensis* editions transformed the pronoun into the neuter αὐτό. This, in turn, implies the replacement of the following article into a neuter as well (τό), a correction found in the Aldine belonging to Leonicus and the *Basiliensis*. The resulting text (ὥσπερ αὐτὸ τὸ μέσον) was accepted by Stephanus, Xylander and Wyttenbach. Amyot— whose *Basiliensis* already read ὥσπερ αὐτὸ τὸ μέσον—proposed to correct the adverb ὥσπερ into the relative pronoun ὅπερ. Wyttenbach suggested (in his critical apparatus) to reform the whole sentence into τὸν μέσον τόπον ἔχουσαν ὥσπερ αὐτῇ οἰκεῖον καὶ κατὰ φύσιν—which seems to be an unnecessary and excessive correction. Adolf Emperius introduced the syntagma ἡ γῆ between ὥσπερ and αὐτὸ τὸ μέσον; Hans von Arnim, followed by Cherniss, proposed to transform

---

38   The passage has been transmitted with many errata by the first editions: the Aldine edition replaced Φαρνάκης with Φανάκης, ὃν with ὂν, and ἀντερείδει with ἀνερείδει; the edition of Basel and that of Xylander transformed the adverb πανταχόθεν into πανταχώθεν.

ὥσπερ into the relative pronoun in masculine—it modifies τόπος—, corrected the feminine pronoun into a dative and maintained EB's reading τὸν μέσον: ὅσπερ αὐτῇ τὸν μέσον; and Pohlenz simply switched αὐτή for αὕτη.[39]

The adverb of manner ὥσπερ poses no problem and is an acceptable reading, and τὸν μέσον is correct, given that it refers to the masculine ὁ τόπος. The only mandatory modification affects, therefore, the pronoun αὐτή: I accept Von Arnim's dative, which fits the grammar and whose corruption into the nominative is understandable.

924C 21–22   κἂν μὲν διασκάπτῃ τὸν ἐπέκεινα τόπον, ἀνακύπτον αὐτοῦ τὸ ⟨κάτω ἄνω⟩ εἶναι καὶ κάτω ἄνωθεν ἕλκεσθαι τὸν ἀνασκαπτόμενον·

EB   κἂν μὴ διασκάπτῃ τὸν ἐπέκεινα τόπον ἀνακύπτον αὐτοῦ τὸ ... εἶναι καὶ κάτω ἄνωθεν ἕλκεσθαι τὸν ἀνασκαπτόμενον·

Lamprias suggests a hypothetical scenario in which a man would lie in perfect consonance with the earth's centre, and, from there, he constructs a whole series of implications. The present text concerns one of those implications, namely which parts of his body would be up or down if the man digs the ground up. It has been modified due to the complexity of the implication at stake and to the presence of a lacuna, of around eight letters in both manuscripts, that further complicates the proper understanding of the passage.

In the first place, Leonicus replaced the negative μή transmitted by EB with the particle μέν. Raingeard maintained the text of EB, interpreting that there would be no need to dig further, for the result would still be the same. Leonicus' intervention, however, was accepted by most scholars, including myself, who saw a better syntax after the inclusion of the particle—κἂν μέν here, εἰ δέ in the next sentence—, and thus interpreted the text as an affirmative in order to provide meaning to the rhetorical and difficult to imagine situation that Lamprias describes.

Regarding the lacuna, the syntax of the sentence points to the loss of the object of the participle ἀνακύπτον, which must have had as its complement the pronoun αὐτοῦ. The first conjecture is an annotation in Turnebus' Aldine copy, μέρος ἄνω; then that of Amyot, ἄνω κάτω. From Wyttenbach onwards, most propositions include the noun σῶμα: Wyttenbach suggested (in the apparatus) τὸ σῶμα ἄνω and the correction of εἶναι into ἰέναι; Emperius, simply σῶμα; Gustave Edward Benseler, ταὐτόν, and he also deleted the following κάτω; Bernar-

---

39   A. Emperius, *Opuscula Philologica et Historica* (Göttingen: F.G. Schneidewin, 1874) 288; *SVF* II, 646.

dakis suggested (in the apparatus) σῶμα ταὐτόν, but also added an excessively reworked correction of the rest of the text: καὶ κάτω καὶ ἄνω καὶ κάτωθεν καὶ ἄνωθεν ἕλκεσθαι; Adler added σῶμα κάτω and corrected εἶναι into χωρεῖν; and, lastly, Cherniss suggested κάτω ἄνω.[40] Those who introduced σῶμα were compelled to correct the article in front of the last participle (ἀνασκαπτόμενον) into a neuter: Wyttenbach stated "αὐτόν vel αὐτό (scilicet σῶμα)," and Emperius, Benseler, and Purser simply replaced τόν with τό.[41]

It is not justified to modify the transmitted text according to a conjecture. The use of σῶμα only complicates the text, since it compels further arrangements and also represents a redundant addition: if a part of someone emerges (ἀνακύπτον αὐτοῦ) it is obviously a part of his body, without the need of explicitly using the noun. Consequently, the best conjecture is that of Cherniss, which not only fits into the space of the lacuna and does not require further modifications, but it also offers a clear sentence and forms a chiastic structure common in Plutarch's style: participle + down/up (ἀνακύπτον [...] κάτω ἄνω) and down/up + participle (κάτω ἄνωθεν [...] τὸν ἀνασκαπτόμενον).[42]

| | |
|---|---|
| 924D 2–6 | καίτοι γε εἰ πᾶν σῶμα ἐμβριθὲς εἰς τὸ αὐτὸ συννεύει καὶ πρὸς τὸ αὐτοῦ μέσον ἀντερείδει πᾶσι τοῖς μορίοις, οὐχ ὡς μέσον οὖσα τοῦ παντὸς ἡ γῆ μᾶλλον ἢ ὡς ὅλον οἰκειώσεται μέρη αὐτῆς ὄντα τὰ βάρη καὶ τεκμήριον ... ἔσται τῶν ῥεπόντων οὔτι τῆς μεσότητος πρὸς τὸν κόσμον, ἀλλὰ πρὸς τὴν γῆν κοινωνίας τινὸς καὶ συμφυΐας τοῖς ἀπωσμένοις αὐτῆς εἶτα πάλιν καταφερομένοις. |
| EB | καίτοι γε εἰ πᾶν σῶμα ἐμβριθὲς εἰς τὸ αὐτὸ συννεύει· καὶ πρὸς τὸ αὐτοῦ μέσον ἀντερείδει πᾶσι τοῖς μορίοις, οὐχ ὡς μέσον οὖσα τοῦ παντὸς ἡ γῆ μᾶλλον, ἢ ὡς ὅλον, οἰκειώσεται μέρη αὐτῆς ὄντα τὰ βάρη· καὶ τεκμήριον· ... ἔσται τῶν ῥεπόντων οὐ τῇ τῆς μεσότητος πρὸς τὸν κόσμον, ἀλλὰ πρὸς τὴν γῆν κοινωνίας τινὸς καὶ συμφυΐας τοῖς ἀπωσμένοις αὐτῆς· EB / αὐτοῖς· B i.t. εἶτα πάλιν καταφερομένοις. |

---

40  Emperius, *Opuscula*, 289; G.E. Benseler, *De hiatu in oratoribus Atticis et historicis Graecis, libri duo* (Freiberg: J.G. Engelhardt, 1841) 517; and Adler, *Dissertationes philologae Vindobonenses*, 96.

41  Purser, "Mr. Prickard's Translation," 312. He modified the whole passage excessively: ἀνακύπτειν αὐτοῦ τὸ ⟨κατασκαπτό⟩μενον καὶ κάτω ἄνωθεν ἕλκεσθαι τὸ ἀνασκαπτόμενον.

42  For the use of chiasmi see A. Pérez Jiménez, "Plutarch and Transgressions of Nature: Stylistic Analysis of *De facie in orbe lunae* 926CD," in M. Meeusen & L. van der Stockt (eds.), *Natural Spectaculars. Aspects of Plutarch's Philosophy of Nature* (Leuven: Leuven University Press, 2015) 215–226.

A few textual difficulties appear in the passage: a) the manuscripts report a lacuna, of approximately 11 letters in E and 16 in B; b) there is an incomplete syntagma, τῇ τῆς μεσότητος; and c) E and B differ in one word, namely the second occurrence of the pronoun αὐτῆς, which B corrects into αὐτοῖς. Beside these, scholarship has intervened in several places: they have modified the pronouns εἰς τὸ αὐτό, τὸ αὐτοῦ and the first occurrence of αὐτῆς, and the participle τοῖς ἀπωσμένοις was changed from ἀπωθέω into ἀποσπάω.

Let us begin with the lacuna. The syntagma preceding the blank (καὶ τεκμήριον) seems to start a new argument, since the previous sentence is complete. Wyttenbach (in the apparatus) significantly rearranged the sentence up until the negative οὐ—something usual to his style: τοῦ ἀνάγκη γίνεσθαι, τὴν ῥοπὴν αὐτοῖς; Emperius conjectured ἐς αὐτήν; Bernardakis proposed (in the apparatus) ἐκ τῶν βαρέων; and Cherniss suggested to supply a subject for the sentence, τὸ κατωφερές.[43]

It is evident from the variety of conjectures that the syntax of the passage is complex. I personally agree with Cherniss' choice to interpret τεκμήριον as the attribute of the verb following the lacuna (ἔσται) and thus look for a subject. However, given the uncertainty of the sentence's construction, it is preferable to include the different options in the apparatus and not to integrate any in the body of text.

Next, the problem concerned with τῇ τῆς μεσότητος seems to reflect the loss of a noun in dative that should have been modified by τῇ. The simplest solution of deleting the problematic article was proposed by RJ94, but it is rather difficult to explain how the article would have found its way into the text. The text deals with the earth, but the reference to the earth is now far—placed before the lacuna. Remaining suggestions added the noun or a reference to it: Amyot transformed the article into a pronoun, αὐτῇ τῆς μεσότητος; Emperius replaced the article with the noun, γῇ τῆς μεσότητος; Madvig replaced the second article instead, τῇ γῇ μεσότητος; and Von Arnim added the noun, τῇ γῇ τῆς μεσότητος.[44] While they all are acceptable variants, I suggest that the text does not require the clarification of the noun "earth." A plausible solution might be to see οὐ τῇ as a corruption for οὔτι. The adverb's meaning, 'not at all,' or 'by no means,' fits into the context and the corruption is explainable through iotacism, given that its last syllable is pronounced as the article.

---

43  Emperius, *Opuscula*, 289.
44  Emperius, *Opuscula*, 289; Madvig, *Adversaria critica*, 664; *SVF* II, 646. For the confusion between gamma and tau, see West, *Textual Criticism and Editorial Technique*, 25. This confusion appears elsewhere in *De facie*: 922D with αὐγή corrupted into αὕτη; or 945D with μέγα κέρας for μετακέρας.

Then, we have the pronoun issue to deal with from the latter part of the text (τοῖς ἀπωσμένοις αὐτῆς εἶτα πάλιν καταφερομένοις) where EB read αὐτῆς. B corrects it *in textu* into the form αὐτοῖς, constructing a syntagma with the preceding participle τοῖς ἀπωσμένοις.[45] The antecedent of the pronoun, however, is not the participle but ἡ γῆ, mentioned a few lines above: the pronoun must be maintained in feminine singular.

In regards to the transmission of pronouns, while both manuscripts often transmit the same form, whether the demonstrative or the attic contracted form of the reflexive personal, it seems that they lack a criterion and often mix their use. This is a matter that has caused recurrent problems for editors who tried to systematize them.[46] In this passage, there are three examples.

The first part of the passage deals with every heavy body (εἰ πᾶν σῶμα ἐμβριθές). The first syntagma depends on the verb συννεύει ('to converge'), thus its complement can be εἰς τὸ αὐτό ('towards the same point'), which is the form transmitted by EB. Wyttenbach, however, suggested the correction εἰς ἑαυτό ('towards itself'). The second syntagma depends on the verb ἀντερείδει ('to compress,' or 'to pressure'), and, again, the form of EB τὸ αὑτοῦ can be maintained, as a heavy body compresses with all its parts (πᾶσι τοῖς μορίοις) upon its center. Bernardakis, however, proposed to change it into τὸ αὑτοῦ ('upon its own center').

The second part of the passage deals with one specific heavy body, the earth (ἡ γῆ), which appropriates heavy bodies (οἰκειώσεται μέρη [...] τὰ βάρη) not as the center but as a whole (οὐχ ὡς μέσον οὖσα τοῦ παντὸς ἡ γῆ μᾶλλον ἢ ὡς ὅλον). EB's reading αὐτῆς was changed by Cherniss into αὑτῆς with the idea that the earth appropriates things that are "of herself." The use of a reflexive pronoun is not compulsory here either, given that the pronoun transmitted by the manuscripts provides the meaning requested by the context: the earth appropriates things that are "of the same" nature, to wit, earthy bodies.

Finally, the participle ἀπωσμένοις (from ἀπωθέω, 'to thrust away') was changed into ἀποσπωμένοις (from ἀποσπάω, 'to drag away') by an annotation in Leonicus' Aldine exemplar, which is a correction accepted by most of the 16th century scholars and Wyttenbach. The modification, however, does not improve the passage, since it is merely conditioned by the presence of this verb a few lines below (924E, Εἰ δέ τι τυγχάνει σῶμα τῇ γῇ μὴ προσνενεμημένον ἀπ' ἀρχῆς μηδὲ ἀπεσπασμένον).

---

45    See B's emendation in Appendix 2.
46    See footnote 34, above, for the same issue regarding the alternation between pronouns in 1st and 2nd person plural.

924DE 6-8  Ὡς γὰρ ὁ ἥλιος εἰς ἑαυτὸν ἐπιστρέφει τὰ μέρη ἐξ ὧν συνέστηκε καὶ ἡ γῆ τὸν λίθον, ὥσπερ ⟨αὐτῇ⟩ προσήκοντα, δέχεται καὶ προσφέρει ἐκεῖνον·

EB  ὡς γὰρ ὁ ἥλιος εἰς ἑαυτὸν ἐπιστρέφει τὰ μέρη ἐξ ὧν συνέστηκε. καὶ ἡ γῆ τὸν λίθον ὥσπερ ... προσήκοντα E / προσήκονται B δέχεται καὶ φέρει πρὸς ἐκεῖνον,

Besides a lacuna, this passage presents a semantic difficulty with καὶ φέρει πρὸς ἐκεῖνον at the end in the sentence.

The lacuna reported by the manuscripts is enough for approximately five letters in E, which is then followed by προσήκοντα; in B, there is room for nine letters, which is followed by προσήκονται. The verbal form in plural of B is certainly out of place, because it affects only the earth's behaviour, not that of the sun and the earth together. Various conjectures have been suggested to complete the lacuna: Amyot proposed αὐτῇ; Wyttenbach (in the apparatus), ἴδιον καί; Cherniss, αὐτῇ. Differently, Raingeard thought that if one deletes the lacuna the sentence seems to lack nothing.

Concerning the semantic problem in the last sentence (καὶ φέρει πρὸς ἐκεῖνον), the earth does not move towards the stony body, but rather attracts it. The first scholar to suggest a solution was Amyot with καὶ προσφέρει ἐκεῖνον; then Wyttenbach (in the apparatus) wrote "κατωφερῆ πρὸς ἐκείνην: *forte probabilius* καὶ φέρει πως ἐκεῖνον;" Emperius proposed καταφερῆ πρὸς τὸ οἰκεῖον; Bernardakis (also in the apparatus), καὶ φέρει πρὸς τὸ οἰκεῖον; and A.J. Kronenberg, καὶ φέρει προσκείμενον.[47]

I chose both of Amyot's proposals, because in the first case αὐτῇ provides more precision to the modal construction and in the second the corruption is easy to explain: a simple transposition that transforms the preverb into a preposition.

924F 16-18  ἀλλ' ἐᾷ χωρὶς εἶναι συστάσεις πυρὸς τοσαύτας καὶ οὐ πάντας εἰς τοῦτο συνάγων τοὺς ἀστέρας σαφῶς οἴεται δεῖν καὶ σῶμα κοινὸν εἶναι τῶν ἄνω φορῶν καὶ φλογοειδῶν ἁπάντων.

EB  ἀλλ' ἐᾷ χωρὶς εἶναι συστάσεις πυρὸς τοσαύτας· καὶ οὐ πάντας εἰς τοῦτο συνάγων τοὺς ἀστέρας σαφῶς οἴεται δεῖν· καὶ σῶμα κοινὸν εἶναι τῶν ἀναφορῶν καὶ φλογοειδῶν ἁπάντων·

---

47  Emperius, *Opuscula*, 289; A.J. Kronenberg, "Ad Plutarchi *Moralia* (Continued)," *Mnemosyne* 10 (1941) 41.

Some grammatical issues need attention in this sentence: a) the pronoun transmitted by EB, b) the participle ἀναφορῶν, and c) the obscure syntactical construction of the passage, which scholars have tried to solve by modifying different parts of the sentence.

Regarding the pronoun, scholars have claimed that the passage offers the idea that all bodies sharing the same nature are driven towards the same spot, not towards an undefined place, which would, in their view, be the reading transmitted by EB (εἰς τοῦτο). Consequently, Amyot was the first to correct the pronoun into ταὐτό, in order to provide the right meaning, namely 'to the same place.' The reading of the manuscripts, however, may be maintained if we accept τοῦτο as referring to fire. Fire is mentioned in the previous sentence, and it represents the same substance that creates the stars and is the substance towards which stars are driven.

Concerning the problem with the participle of the verb ἀναφορέω (ἀναφορῶν), its transitive use does not fit into the sentence ('to take up'). The form transmitted by EB has been changed since the 16th century: an annotation in Leonicus' Aldine copy reads ἄνω φορῶν ('moving in the upper region'); another in the Aldine exemplar of Turnebus reads ἀνωφερῶν ('that tends to move upwards'). The latter option is accepted by all modern scholars except Raingeard, who read ἀναφόρων, which he himself explained is a hapax constructed on the models of κατάφορος and διάφορος ("ce qui s'élève," in his translation).[48] The modification into a compound—of adverb and φορέω, frequentative of φέρω, or into an adjective—solves the problem; thus, to replace the transmitted text with a hapax seems unnecessarily risky. The reason why I accept Leonicus' correction is that it is better from the point of view of textual corruption, since it only requires the modification of EB in one letter.

The remaining modifications are due to the obscure syntax of the sentence: while the main verbs, ἐᾷ and οἴεται, are united by the first καί, the second conjunction appears to have no linking function: there is no verb in personal form after it, nor a noun before that could be coordinated with σῶμα, nor an infinitive to be coordinated with εἶναι.

An annotation in RJ94 relocated καί after εἶναι, in order to create the structure "both this and that" (καὶ τῶν ἀναφορῶν καὶ φλογοειδῶν ἁπάντων); Xylander solved the problem by turning the participle (συνάγων) into an infinitive (συνάγειν), thus coordinating it by means of καί with εἶναι; Wyttenbach offered two solutions (in the critical apparatus): (1) he simply deleted the conjunction, or (2) corrected and reorganized great part of the sentence (καὶ φῶς οἴεται δὴ ἐν

---

48  Raingeard, *Le peri toy prosopoy*, 81.

καί); Bernardakis (in the apparatus) in the line of the second suggestion proposed δεῖν εἶναι σῶμα κοινὸν τῶν ἀνωφερῶν.[49] Others corrected a word preceding καί, in order to coordinate it with the noun that follows (σῶμα κοινόν): an annotation in RJ94 transformed the adverb σαφῶς into ἅ φῶς; and Kronenberg corrected it into ἓν φῶς.[50] Sandbach suggested that πάντας εἰς τοῦτο συνάγων τοὺς ἀστέρας σαφῶς is altogether "an intrusive explanation from the margin."[51]

Although these corrections simplify the grammar of the text, I believe none of them is actually mandatory: οὐ πάντας εἰς τοῦτο συνάγων τοὺς ἀστέρας is an aside, it does not have to be coordinated with the rest and needs no intervention. The word σαφῶς does not suppose a complication in itself, its modification is merely motivated to solve textual problems elsewhere in the sentence. The problem with καί, then, can be solved by interpreting it as an adverb and not as conjunction.

| | |
|---|---|
| 925B 2–6 | τῆς δὲ γῆς τρόπον τινὰ ψαύει καὶ περιφερομένη πλησίον, |
| | ἅρματος ὥσπερ ἀν᾽ ἴχνος ἑλίσσεται, |
| | φησὶν Ἐμπεδοκλῆς, |
| | ἥ τε παρ᾽ ἄκραν ... |
| EB | τῆς δὲ γῆς τρόπον τινὰ ψαύει. καὶ περιφερομένη πλησίον, ἅρματος ὥσπερ ἴχνος ἀνελίσσεται φησὶν ἐμπεδοκλῆς. ἥ τε περὶ ἄκραν ... |

When Plutarch deals with the movement of the moon revolving very close to the earth, he quotes a verse from Empedocles in order to introduce a comparison with a chariot (B 46 DK). The quotation presents several problems: to begin with, the verse is incomplete, since EB present a lacuna after ἄκραν of approximately 20 letters in the case of E and 26 letters in the case of B; then it presents some textual problems. The first part of the verse, ἅρματος ὥσπερ ἴχνος ἀνελίσσεται, was modified by Wyttenbach (in the apparatus) into ὥσπερ ἀν᾽ ἴχνος ἑλίσσεται; and by Panzerbieter into ὡς πέρι χνοίη ἑλίσσεται.[52] The latter's motivation seems to be that the meaning of the noun and verb transmitted by the manuscripts are not suitable: the noun χνοίη, meaning 'axle-box,' would fit better in the context of the turning of a chariot than 'track,' or 'footstep;' and the verb ἑλίσσω, meaning 'to turn round or about' would be better than 'to unroll,' or 'to roll back.' Wyttenbach's correction, however, maintains both the noun

---

49   Oddly, he attributed this modification to Dübner.
50   Kronenberg, "Ad Plutarchi *Moralia*," 41.
51   F.H. Sandbach, "Second Meeting," *Proceedings of the Cambridge Philological Society* (1943) 15.
52   According to DK, vol. 1, 331.

and the verb of EB, with the only modification that the latter is separated from its preverb by the noun. With this simple intervention, Wyttenbach solves the problem of the metrical form of the verse.

Concerning the second part of the verse, ἤ τε was altered by an annotation in RJ94 into ἤδε; and Wyttenbach deleted τε. The lacuna was deleted by the *Basiliensis* edition and by Xylander; Hermann Diels proposed to correct περὶ ἄκραν into παρ' ἄκραν and supplied two variants, either νύσσαν ἐλαυνομένη or γαῖαν ἐλαυνομένη.[53] The beginning of this second part of the verse does not need any intervention, and the lacuna cannot be successfully supplied given that no other testimony of such a verse has been preserved. I do, however, accept Diels's replacement of περὶ ἄκραν with παρ' ἄκραν based on metrical grounds: as with the first part of the verse, the text transmitted by EB does not provide part of a hexameter.

| | |
|---|---|
| 926A 9–12 | (ἢ) εἰ ἄλλην τινὰ τοῦ μένειν εὑράμενος αἰτίαν ἔστηκεν, οὐ κατὰ τὴν τοῦ τόπου φύσιν, ὅμοια καὶ περὶ γῆς καὶ περὶ σελήνης εἰκάζειν τινὶ πάρεστιν ὡς ἑτέρᾳ τινὶ ψυχῇ καὶ φύσει μᾶλλον ⟨γίνονται⟩ διαφοραί,[54] |
| EB | εἰ ἄλλην τινὰ τοῦ μένειν εὑράμενος αἰτίαν E / αἰτίαν εὑράμενος B ἔστηκεν, οὐ κατὰ τὴν τοῦ τόπου φύσιν, ὅμοια καὶ περὶ γῆς καὶ περὶ σελήνης εἰκάζειν τινὶ πάρεστιν ὡς ἑτέρᾳ τινὶ B E s.l. ψυχῇ καὶ φύσει μᾶλλον ... διαφοραί· |

This passage presents a few minor grammatical issues and a lacuna of six letters in E and of nine in B.

Firstly, while the sentence is related to the previous one, no link between them has been transmitted. Consequently, the beginning has been modified in order to provide one: an annotation in RJ94 transformed the conditional εἰ into the disjunctive ἤ; Amyot added the particle δέ (εἰ δ' ἄλλην); and Kepler added the disjunctive before the conditional (ἢ εἰ).[55]

While the preceding sentence simply rejects the theory of natural positions by affirming that the universe has no fixed position (925F, ἀνέστιος καὶ ἀνίδρυτός ἐστιν ἐν ἀπείρῳ κενῷ φερόμενος πρὸς οὐδὲν οἰκεῖον), the current sentence envisages a new condition: after evaluating the possibility that the universe is unmoved, the text nevertheless denies that this is due to the theory of natural positions. I believe, therefore, that Kepler's suggestion fits in the passage perfectly: a disjunctive opposing this sentence to the previous together with a

---

[53] DK, vol. 1, 331.
[54] The Aldine edition, I reckon by a mistake, omitted καὶ περὶ γῆς.
[55] Kepler, *Ioh. Keppleri Mathematici*, 112.

conditional that introduces the new condition. Furthermore, the fall of ἤ can easily be explained by the frequent loss of monosyllables and by the identical sonority of both words (ἤ εἰ) due to iotacism.

Another grammatical issue concerns the different readings included by our two manuscripts. E reads εὑράμενος αἰτίαν, while B reads αἰτίαν εὑράμενος. B's transposition was probably intended in order to avoid the syntagma ἄλλην τινὰ αἰτίαν being separated by both τοῦ μένειν and εὑράμενος. While E's reading is perfectly acceptable, B introduces a *lectio facilior* that is not mandatory.[56]

The last grammatical issue regards the manuscripts' reading ψυχῇ, which was replaced by Kepler with ῥοπῇ; by Pohlenz with τύχῃ; and simply deleted by Purser.[57] These modifications are not only unnecessary, but they also create a poorer text: the concept of ψυχή is clearly fundamental throughout the treatise and to replace an occurrence of the word instead of integrating its appearance into the greater picture is, in my view, a mistake. In this case, Lamprias defends that the universe's order must be ruled by something superior to natural positions: each body occupies a specific place due to a specific type of soul and nature (ψυχῇ καὶ φύσει). The two nouns transmitted by our manuscripts are pregnant with meaning—soul and nature are inherent to every cosmological body. The corrections 'inclination' and 'fortune,' on the contrary, present outer dispositions and are consequently inferior to EB's reading.

Finally, there is a lacuna between μᾶλλον and διαφοραί. It would seem that μᾶλλον requires ἤ, so thought Wyttenbach, who reorganized the whole sentence in the apparatus: ὡς ἑτέρᾳ τινὶ, (*sic*) ψυχικῇ μᾶλλον ἢ φυσικῇ καὶ τοπικῇ; Bernardakis, who added ἢ τόπου; and Cherniss, who simplified Wyttenbach's proposal into ἢ τοπικῇ. All of them must, then, correct the case of διαφοραί into διαφορᾷ in order to connect it with the other nouns in dative (τινὶ ψυχῇ καὶ φύσει). Other scholars, however, maintained διαφοραί: Amyot simply supplied the article αἱ in the lacuna; and Raingeard (in the apparatus) supplied the verb γίνονται.[58] Raingeard's conjecture fits the syntax better, providing a verb for the subject διαφοραί, which in turn does not need to be modified.

---

56  Wyttenbach did not mention that E and B differ; and Raingeard, oddly enough, stated that εὑράμενος αἰτίαν is the reading of both E and B, and that the transposition was due to the Aldine edition.
57  Kepler, *Ioh. Keppleri Mathematici*, 112; Purser, "Mr. Prickard's Translation," 313.
58  Raingeard's translation, however, suggests that he was indeed accepting Bernardakis' ἢ τόπου: "c'est à une hétérogénéité de vie et de nature plutôt qu'à une raison de place que nous devons de voir cette différence."

926CD 1–4   Διὰ τοῦτο οὖν σώματι ψυχὴν μὴ λέγωμεν εἶναι μηδὲ νοῦν, χρῆμα θεῖον, ὑπὸ βρίθους καὶ πάχους, οὐρανόν τε πάντα καὶ γῆν καὶ θάλασσαν ἐν ταὐτῷ περιπολοῦντα καὶ διιπτάμενον εἰς σάρκας ἥκειν καὶ νεῦρα καὶ μυελοὺς καὶ παθέων μυρίων μεστὰς ὑγρότητας;

EB   διατοῦτο οὖν σώματι ψυχὴν μὴ λέγωμεν E/ λέγομεν B εἶναι μηδὲν οὐ χρῆμα θεῖον ὑπὸ βρίθους καὶ πάχους. οὐρανόν τε πάντα καὶ γῆν καὶ θάλασσαν ἐν ταυτῶ περιπολοῦντα καὶ διιστάμενον εἰς σάρκας ἥκειν καὶ νεῦρα καὶ μυελούς. καὶ παθέων μυρίων μετὰ ὑγρότητος.

Here we find a passage that poses quite a few textual problems. Not only has the text been corrected in several places by different scholars—see, for instance εἶναι, μηδὲν οὐ, διιστάμενον, and μετὰ ὑγρότητος—but also parts of it have been transposed—ὑπὸ βρίθους καὶ πάχους. Let us see the modifications more in detail.

The first change concerns the infinitive εἶναι, which was turned into ἐνεῖναι by Van Herwerden, a modification accepted by later scholars.[59] Although the meaning of the verb ἔνειμι, 'to be in,' or 'to be among,' fits in smoothly, the syntagma σώματι ψυχὴν μὴ λέγωμεν εἶναι, with the complement of the infinitive in dative, can be maintained.

Then follows the modification of the strange reading μηδὲν οὐ: the first emendations to this text are from an annotation in the Aldine RJ94 that reads μηδενί, and Kepler's correction μηδεμίαν.[60] Both interpreted that everything that follows relates to the soul, as the component opposed to the body. More interesting, from the point of view of contents, are the corrections that introduce a third component into the text: the intellect. Dübner was the first scholar to introduce it, with a rather smart switch: he attributed the nu of μηδέν to the following word οὐ (μηδὲ νοῦ); a few decades later, Madvig proposed the variant μηδὲ νοῦν, which provides the correct case.[61]

Given the central role that the intellect has in the development of the treatise, the inclusion of νοῦς is necessary in a passage that opposes a divine immaterial component to a material one (the body). Besides, Madvig's conjecture has the convenience of fitting the syntax better.

---

59   Van Herwerden is the conjecturer according to Cherniss. I have not been able to check Van Herwerden's study of 1882, and there is no trace of this correction in "Novae curae criticae." If the attribution happens to be a mistake, the author of ἐνεῖναι should then be Raingeard.
60   Kepler, *Ioh. Keppleri Mathematici*, 114.
61   Madvig, *Adversaria critica*, 665.

This intervention, however, introduces a new complication, since the syntagma ὑπὸ βρίθους καὶ πάχους cannot allude to the immaterial intellect.[62] Emperius solved this issue in two different ways: by modifying the text into ὑπὸ τοῦ ἀβριθοῦς καὶ ἀπαχοῦς, or by changing the preposition into ἀπὸ βρίθους καὶ πάχους. Adler stated that ὑπὸ βρίθους ἢ πάχους must have been a text added in the margin and later integrated in the text by the copyist of our manuscripts, but in the wrong place; he solved the issue by transposing the whole syntagma almost to the end of the passage, between μεστάς and ὑγρότητας. Pohlenz added ἀήττητον in front of ὑπὸ βρίθους καὶ πάχους; and Cherniss and Donini followed Adler's idea of transposing the syntagma.[63] The former transposed it after καὶ μυελούς, which, in turn, allows him to maintain the otherwise problematic μετὰ ὑγρότητος (below); the latter transposed it to the very end of the passage, as the explanation for μεστὰς ὑγρότητας.[64] When understood as a parenthetical remark there is no need to move the syntagma.[65]

The following modification was Wyttenbach's suggestion (in the apparatus) to transform the participle διιστάμενον, whose meaning 'to separate,' or 'to turn away' hardly fits the context. Its subject is the intellect, its complement is οὐρανόν τε πάντα καὶ γῆν καὶ θάλασσαν ἐν ταὐτῷ, and it is coordinated with περιπολοῦντα ('to round about,' or 'wander about').[66] Wyttenbach's correction into διιπτάμενον merely modifies the verb by one letter—lowercase sigma and pi can easily be misinterpreted by a scribe—and offers a better meaning: 'to fly through.'

Finally, μετὰ ὑγρότητος, in genitive, is coordinated through καί with the accusative εἰς σάρκας ἥκειν καὶ νεῦρα καὶ μυελούς. This is probably due to a scribal mistake influenced by the syntagma that immediately precedes it in genitive (παθέων μυρίων). Cherniss was able to maintain it because he previously transposed ὑπὸ βρίθους καὶ πάχους after καὶ μυελούς, thus turning καὶ παθέων μυρίων μετὰ ὑγρότητος into a coordination, not with the syntagma in accusative but

---

62   The Aldine edition transformed the conjunction into a disjunctive (ὑπὸ βρίθους ἢ πάχους), a modification accepted by many scholars, among which is Wyttenbach who did not mention in the apparatus that it is not EB's reading, Adler, and, surprisingly, Cherniss, who put the syntagma between brackets to transpose it—[ὑπὸ βρίθους ἢ πάχους]—and then offered the correct reading of the manuscripts a few lines below where he interpreted it should be placed—(ὑπὸ βρίθους καὶ πάχους).
63   Emperius, *Opuscula*, 289; Adler, *Dissertationes philologae Vindobonenses*, 98.
64   Donini commented on his choice in *Plutarco. Il volto della luna*, 277 n. 121.
65   In this, I concur with Pérez Jiménez, "Plutarch and Transgressions of Nature," 223 n. 17. Notice that all the modifications I accepted find backup in stylistic and rhythmic principles that Pérez Jiménez defended in his study.
66   Bernardakis added the breathing in EB's ταυτῶ.

with the genitives βρίθους and πάχους. However, his transposition, as noted above, is unnecessary. The problem with μετὰ ὑγρότητος was solved by Dübner: μεστὰς ὑγρότητας corrects the wrong case and also modifies the preposition that does not have the right meaning with the new accusative. He also transformed the punctuation of the manuscripts into a question mark.

926D 4–6  Ὁ δὲ Ζεὺς ὑμῖν οὗτος, οὐ τῇ μὲν αὐτοῦ φύσει χρώμενος ἕν ἐστι, μέγα πῦρ καὶ συνεχές; Νυνὶ δὲ ὑφεῖται καὶ κέκαμπται καὶ διεσχημάτισται, πᾶν χρῶμα γεγονὼς καὶ γινόμενος ἐν ταῖς μεταβολαῖς;[67]

EB  ὁ δὲ ζεὺς ἡμῖν οὗτος, οὐ τῇ μὲν αὐτοῦ E B s.l. / αὐτοῦ B φύσει χρώμενος ἕν ἐστι E / ἔνεστι B μέγα πῦρ καὶ συνεχές; νυνίδε E/ νυνὶ δὲ B ὑφεῖται καὶ κέκαμπται καὶ διεσχημάτισται. πᾶν χρῶμα γεγονὼς καὶ γινόμενος ἐν ταῖς μεταβολαῖς· E/ μεταβολαῖς; B

The two manuscripts report several different readings. Most of them, however, are of minor relevance and can be easily solved: see that E provides the correct form in αὐτοῦ against αὐτοῦ—although Stephanus, Xylander and Wyttenbach follow B, the latter without any mention of E's reading in the apparatus—and in ἕν ἐστι against ἔνεστι. B, however, provides the correct accentuation and punctuation in νυνὶ δέ against νυνίδε and μεταβολαῖς against μεταβολαῖς·. The interventions in this passage affect the pronoun at the beginning (ἡμῖν), the noun (χρῶμα), and the punctuation.

Concerning the pronoun, it is transmitted by both manuscripts as ἡμῖν, but is soon modified by Xylander into ὑμῖν. This correction has been accepted by most scholars, whom I join, because Lamprias refers to Zeus from the specific point of view of Stoicism, namely pure fire (μέγα πῦρ καὶ συνεχές). As a Platonist, he would hardly have accepted such a Zeus as his supreme god, and therefore must have used the 2nd person plural instead of the 1st. Raingeard, who does not accept the emendation, sees in Lamprias' definition of Zeus a dative of interest, and he believes that Empedocles' influence can be appreciated.[68] This theory seems to me excessively complex, especially if we take into account that the confusion between 1st and 2nd person is a rather common mistake in textual transmission.[69]

The following problem seems to be created by scholarship, rather than by real textual difficulties: ever since the annotation χρῆμα appeared in the Aldine

---

67  The participle γινόμενος appeared in accusative in Xylander's edition, although it was probably an erratum and not an intended modification of EB's reading.
68  Raingeard, Le peri toy prosopoy, 87.
69  See above, footnote 34.

copy that belonged to Leonicus, most scholars accepted the correction against the manuscripts' reading χρῶμα. Thus, Zeus no longer becomes every 'color' (πᾶν χρῶμα γεγονώς), but rather becomes 'everything' (πᾶν χρῆμα γεγονώς). As Pérez Jiménez has pointed out, the manuscripts' reading can be accepted on the grounds of both style and philosophy.[70]

A final, minor issue concerns the punctuation. Here, Lamprias poses the last in a series of rhetorical questions. While I accept B's question mark at the end of the passage—as opposed to the point above the line of E—I do not accept the elimination of the manuscripts' question mark after καὶ συνεχές proposed by the Aldine edition. Despite the general tendency to accept this correction, Lamprias may be dividing his question into two parts, and therefore both question marks may be maintained.

| | |
|---|---|
| 927B 4–7 | οὐδὲ κηπουρῶν οὐδὲ οἰκοδόμων, εἰ πῇ μὲν αὐτὸ τὸ ὕδωρ ἀφ' αὑτοῦ πέφυκεν ἐπεῖναι τοῖς δεομένοις καὶ κατάρδειν ἐπιρρέον, πῇ δὲ πλίνθοι καὶ ξύλα καὶ λίθοι ταῖς κατὰ φύσιν χρώμενα τροπαῖς καὶ νεύσεσιν ἐξ ἑαυτῶν καταλαμβάνειν τὴν προσήκουσαν ἁρμονίαν καὶ χώραν. |
| EB | οὐδὲ κηπουρῶν οὐδὲ οἰκοδόμων, εἰ πῇ μὲν αὐτὸ τὸ ὕδωρ ἀπ' αὐτοῦ E / ἀφ' αὑτοῦ B πέφυκεν ἐπεῖναι τοῖς δεομένοις καὶ κατάρδειν ἐπιρρέον· πῇ δὲ πλίνθοι καὶ ξύλα καὶ λίθοι ταῖς κατὰ φύσιν χρώμενα τροπαῖς καὶ νεύσεσιν ἐξ ἑαυτῶν καταλαμβάνειν τὴν προσήκουσαν ἁρμονίαν καὶ χώραν. |

Manuscripts differ in the transmission of a pronoun: B provides the correct reflexive pronoun ἀφ' αὑτοῦ, against the form ἀπ' αὐτοῦ transmitted by E. The main difficulties of this passage, however, concern the infinitive ἐπεῖναι and the noun τροπαῖς; both of them are changed by scholarship.

The infinitive present ἐπεῖναι (of ἔπειμι, composite of εἰμί) was replaced by an annotation of the Aldine RJ94 with ἐπιρρεῖν (infinitive of ἐπιρρέω) and by Amyot with the infinitive ἐπιέναι (of ἔπειμι, composite of εἶμι). While the verb of movement suggested by Amyot fits smoothly, the subject of the sentence (water), the form transmitted by the manuscripts, can be maintained on the grounds that the sense of the sentence remains intact: whether water "runs" towards the places that need it or "remains" in the places that need it, the point is that gardeners are then useless.

Regarding the noun, τροπαῖς, meaning 'turning,' or 'direction,' it was soon corrected by an annotation in Turnebus' Aldine copy to ῥοπαῖς. This correction was

---

70  Pérez Jiménez, "Plutarch and Transgressions of Nature," 224.

accepted by most scholars, on the grounds that the replacement fits the context and finds support in the following passage (927C, Ὡς εἴ γε πάντα δεῖ ταῖς κατὰ φύσιν ῥοπαῖς χρῆσθαι καὶ φέρεσθαι καθὸ πέφυκε). The meaning of ῥοπαῖς, 'inclination' or 'impulse,' however, excessively resembles the noun with which it is coordinated (καὶ νεύσεσιν, 'inclination towards earth'). Furthermore, the noun transmitted by both manuscripts does not suppose an unsurmountable difficulty and can be maintained in coordination with καὶ νεύσεσιν.

927D 22–24   Οὐ μὴν ἀλλ' εἴ γε δεῖ τὰς καταδεδουλωμένας ἕξεις ⟨καὶ⟩ δόξας ἀφέντας ἤδη τὸ φαινόμενον ἀδεῶς λέγειν, οὐδὲν ἔοικεν ὅλου μέρος αὐτὸ καθ' ἑαυτὸ τάξιν ἢ θέσιν ἢ κίνησιν ἰδίαν ἔχειν, ᾗ ἄν τις ἁπλῶς κατὰ φύσιν προσαγορεύσειεν·

EB   οὐ μὴν ἀλλ' εἴ γε δεῖ τὰς καταδεδουλωμένας ἕξεις ... δόξας ἀφέντας ἤδη τὸ φαινόμενον ἀδεῶς λέγειν, οὐδὲν ἔοικεν ὅλου μέρος αὐτὸ καθ' ἑαυτὸ τάξιν ἢ θέσιν ἢ κίνησιν ἰδίαν ἔχειν, ᾗ ἄν τις ἁπλῶς κατὰ φύσιν προσαγορεύσειεν·

Two issues have to be dealt with in the passage. Firstly, there is a lacuna in both manuscripts between ἕξεις and δόξας: E reports a gap of only three letters, while B reports one of six; secondly, the form ᾗ, transmitted by the manuscripts, was changed into ἥν in the 16th century, a correction accepted by later scholarship almost unanimously.

Concerning the lacuna, the first attempts to supply the missing text were those of Amyot and Xylander (in the commentary to his translation). While the former supplied the missing conjunction and the article in accusative plural (καὶ τάς), the latter only supplied the conjunction.[71] Emperius suggested the correction of ἕξεις into ἕξει and the elimination of the blank that follows; Madvig proposed ἔθει instead of ἕξεις; and Bernandakis merged his predecessors' corrections and supplied the gap with ἕξει καὶ ἔθει; Pohlenz also accepted Emperius' emendation and used the final sigma of the manuscripts' ἕξεις as the beginning of the word that would have been lost in the lacuna: ἕξει σαθρᾷ.[72]

The only necessary element in the sentence is the coordination between the two nouns ἕξεις and δόξας, which is the reason why I integrate Xylander's conjecture in the body of text. While this fills the lacuna in E, the conjecture of Amyot (καὶ τάς), close in sense and also correct, would fill B's gap.

---

71   Xylander, *Plutarchi Chaeronensis*, 718. Raingeard would present this conjecture as his own more than three centuries later.
72   Emperius, *Opuscula*, 290; Madvig, *Adversaria critica*, 665.

Concerning the replacement of ᾗ, scholars, in general, accepted the accusative ἥν suggested by an annotation in the Aldine RJ94 and the *Basiliensis* edition. Consequently, the verb προσαγορεύσειεν would count with two accusatives: the relative pronoun that refers to τάξιν ἢ θέσιν ἢ κίνησιν ἰδίαν and the syntagma κατὰ φύσιν.[73] I believe, however, that the manuscripts' reading can be maintained with a consecutive value.

928D 2-4   Ἀλλ' ὅμως ὁρᾶν πάρεστιν οὐκ ἀποκεκριμένην τοῦ αἰθέρος τὴν σελή-
νην, ἀλλ' ἔτι πολλῷ ἐν τῷ περὶ αὐτὴν ἐμφερομένην, πολλὴν δὲ ὑφ'
ἑαυτὴν ἔχουσαν ἀνέμων ⟨δίνην⟩ δινεῖσθαι καὶ κομήτας·

EB   ἀλλ' ὅμως ὁρᾶν πάρεστιν οὐκ ἀποκεκριμένου E/ ἀποκεκρυμμένου B
τοῦ αἰθέρος τὴν σελήνην· ἀλλ' ἔτι πολλῷ ἐν τῷ περὶ αὐτὴν ἐμφερομέ-
νην. πολλὴν δὲ ὑφ' ἑαυτὴν ἔχουσαν ἀνέμων ... δινεῖσθαι καὶ κομήτας·

Here we find a complex passage that has been intervened many times in the attempt to provide a more distinct syntax. First, the manuscripts differ in one verb; second, minor modifications affect the construction πολλῷ ἐν τῷ, the pronoun αὐτήν, and the adjective πολλήν; and finally, near the end of the passage there is a lacuna of approximately 25 letters.

Concerning the divergence between E and B, while E reads ἀποκεκριμένου (of ἀποκρίνω, 'to separate'), B reads ἀποκεκρυμμένου (of ἀποκρύπτω, 'to hide'). The context points to E's verb, although the case seems to be mistaken. An annotation in both the Aldine RJ94 and the *Basiliensis* edition suggested to transform the genitive into an accusative (ἀποκεκριμένην); Raingeard, however, maintained E's reading. While Raingeard's choice is interesting, implying that there is a genitive absolute (οὐκ ἀποκεκριμένου τοῦ αἰθέρος), it can hardly be accepted given the development of the sentence. Not only do the other participles in the passage (ἐμφερομένην, ἔχουσαν) modify the moon in accusative, but more importantly, just after the supposedly genitive absolute is the adversative ἀλλ' ἔτι, which causes the rest of the passage to oppose this first part, something that Raingeard's construction cannot admit—in point of fact, he suggests (in the apparatus) the modification of ἀλλ' into ἅμ' and does not translate the opposition: "Ce n'est pas cela, mais on peut voir sans mettre l'éther de côté, la lune emportée à travers celui qui l'environne."

Regarding the construction πολλῷ ἐν τῷ, it has been modified in different fashions. An annotation in the Aldine RJ94 corrected πολλῷ into the feminine

---

[73] Among the followers of the correction, we have Wyttenbach, who did not clarify in the apparatus that it is an emendation of EB's text; Bernardakis, who did not attribute the correction to anyone; and Cherniss, who only mentioned the *Basiliensis* edition.

accusative (πολλήν); Amyot transposed the preposition before πολλῷ (ἐν πολλῷ τῷ); Dübner deleted the preposition; Benseler replaced it with the particle μέν.[74] While the construction transmitted by EB is not the most common, it does not require a change.

Concerning the pronoun αὐτήν, it is corrected by Bernadakis into αὑτήν. An emendation that is not required by the text.

In what regards πολλήν, because the moon is the subject of both the following participle and its complement (ὑφ' ἑαυτὴν ἔχουσαν), it cannot also be the object modified by this adjective in accusative. Amyot corrected it into πολλύν (sic), obviously meaning to write πολύν, namely the aether. While it is a reasonable option, given that the previous part of the passage deals precisely with aether (τοῦ αἰθέρος and πολλῷ), I believe the reading of the manuscripts can be maintained if the lacuna is also taken into account (below).

As for the lacuna, its length has allowed for many conjectures over time, which, in turn, tend to further modify the surrounding text. An annotation in RJ94 conjectured αἰθεροειδῆ οὐσίαν τῷ καὶ αὐτοῖς; Amyot proposed a simple noun, χώραν; Wyttenbach proposed (in the apparatus) βίαν, ὑφ' ἧς ἄλλα τε εἰκός ἐστι; Emperius transformed the nouns ἀνέμων and κομήτας and the verb following the lacuna into ἀνέμῳ ἐνδινεῖσθαι καὶ κομήταις; Bernardakis conjectured (in the apparatus) τε ῥιπάς ὑφ' ὧν (aut αἷς) ἄλλα τε εἰκός; Pohlenz (also in the apparatus), βίαν ὑφ' ὧν ἐκθλιβέντας φασὶν ἐν τῷ αἰθέρι; and Cherniss who had previously accepted Madvig's transformation of ἀνέμων into ἐν ᾧ, conjectured λέγουσιν αὐτοὶ τοὺς πωγωνίας.[75] Cherniss justified his suggestion by saying that ἀνέμων must have been a false doubling of the two last letters of ἔχουσαν and the following syntagma ἐν ᾧ and that the lacuna must have included a noun parallel to κομήτας, but he did not explain the reason of the noun he chose or the reason to add λέγουσιν αὐτοί.[76]

In my view, there is a simpler solution that solves both the issue with the adjective πολλήν and the content of the lacuna. If a feminine noun is added in the blank space, the adjective can then modify it instead of modifying the aether, and therefore would not need to be corrected. I conjecture δίνην, which functions as an object of the participle ἔχουσαν, modifies the preceding ἀνέμων, and is linked through καί with the accusative κομήτας. Furthermore, its loss might be explained by the repetition of δίνη(ν) δινεῖ(σθαι).

---

74   Benseler, *De hiatu in oratoribus Atticis*, 518.
75   Emperius, *Opuscula*, 290; Madvig, *Adversaria critica*, 71.
76   Cherniss, "Notes on Plutarch's *De facie*," 141.

928E 13–14   "... ὥστε ἐμέ τε πραγμάτων ἀπηλλάχθαι." Καὶ ⟨ὁ⟩ Λεύκιος ... "ὠγαθὲ" εἶπεν[77]

EB           ὥστε ἐμέ τε πραγμάτων ἀπηλλάχθαι καὶ ... λεύκιος ... ὦ γαθὲ E / ὦ' γαθὲ B εἶπεν.

In the transition from the last words of Aristotle to the reply of Lucius, both manuscripts transmit two lacunae, only separated by a word, Λεύκιος: the first one has a gap of approximately eight letters in E, and 10 in B; the second one amounts to around 10 letters in both manuscripts.

Everything that precedes the first lacuna might belong to Aristotle's words. In this case, the conjunction καί should link either ἐμέ with another subject of the subordinate clause, πραγμάτων with another noun, or ἀπηλλάχθαι with another infinitive. So thought Amyot who suggested to complete the lacuna with τὸν κλέαρχον ἀλλά; also Wyttenbach who proposed (in his apparatus) ⟨σὲ, (sic) ὦ Λεύκιε.⟩ καὶ ⟨ὁ⟩ Λεύκιος; and Pohlenz who proposed (in the apparatus) σὲ τό γε καθ' ἡμᾶς· ὁ δέ. Aristotle's sentence, however, makes complete sense as it has been transmitted, therefore καί might initiate a new sentence, functioning then as adverb, rather than as conjunction. I am inclined to this solution, as are other schorlars, such as Emperius, who added only the article ὁ before Λεύκιος—following part of Wyttenbach's suggestion—; and Cherniss with ὑπολαβὼν ὁ.[78] Both of them, in any case, supply the missing article preceding Lucius' name, the only thing required by the text.

Various conjectures were proposed for the second lacuna: Wyttenbach supplied (in the apparatus) the negation οὐκ; Bernardakis suggested ἥκιστα; and Raingeard οὐδ' ἐλάχιστον. None of these conjectures seems either necessary or based on firm grounds. The sentence, furthermore, makes sense as it is, which is the reason why I simply signal the lacuna in the text.

928EF 14–17   "ἀλλὰ τὰ ἄλλα μὲν ἴσως ἄστρα καὶ τὸν ὅλον οὐρανὸν εἴς τινα φύσιν καθαρὰν καὶ εἰλικρινῆ καὶ τῆς κατὰ πάθος ἀπηλλαγμένην μεταβολῆς τιθεμένοις ὑμῖν καὶ κύκλον ἄγουσι, δι' οὗ καὶ ἀτελευτήτου περιφορᾶς ... οὐκ ἄν τις ἕν γε τῷ νῦν διαμάχοιτο,"

EB            ἀλλὰ τὰ ἄλλα μὲν ἴσως ἄστρα καὶ τὸν ὅλον οὐρανὸν εἴς τινα φύσιν καθαρὰν καὶ εἰλικρινῆ· καὶ τῆς κατὰ πάθος ἀπηλλαγμένην μεταβολῆς τιθεμένοις ἡμῖν καὶ κύκλον ἄγουσι· δι' οὗ καὶ ἀτελευτήτου περιφορᾶς ... οὐκ ἄν τις ἕν γε τῷ νῦν διαμάχοιτο·

---

77   This is Stephanus' correction of the nonexistent forms of EB (E, ὦ γαθέ, B, ὦ' γαθέ).
78   Emperius, Opuscula, 291.

The reply of Lucius to Aristotle, besides being interrupted by a lacuna at the end, has been modified by scholarship in four places: a) at the beginning (ἀλλὰ τὰ ἄλλα); b) the pronoun ἡμῖν; c) the participle ἄγουσι; and d) the syntagma δι' οὗ.

Let us first examine the interventions of scholars in the text. At the beginning (ἀλλὰ τὰ ἄλλα), the article was transformed by the Aldine and *Basiliensis* editions into τε, while Emperius eliminated the adversative.[79] Neither of these modifications are necessary. The beginning of Lucius' intervention makes perfect sense within his argument: he is willing to disregard, for the moment, some of the beliefs of Aristotle and his companions in order to focus on one point only—the moon's nature.

The pronoun ἡμῖν was corrected by an annotation in RJ94 into the 2nd person ὑμῖν. Given that Lucius is replying to Aristotle and, by extension, to those who think both that stars move in circle and that there is a substance superior to the four elements found in the sublunary realm, it seems obvious that he cannot include himself in this group.

The participle ἄγουσι is coordinated with τιθεμένοις and has the pronoun ὑμῖν as a subject. Pohlenz (in the apparatus) and Cherniss seemed to have thought that its subject is τινα φύσιν, given that they corrected it to ἄγουσαν. Instead of taking "a nature" as the object of the participle and Aristotle and his companions (ὑμῖν) as the subject, they assumed this was the subject ('a nature which moves in circles'). Cherniss' interpretation, which in my view is incorrect, might result from the parallelism he established with Aristotle's speech a few lines above (κύκλῳ τε κινεῖσθαι κατὰ φύσιν), which may have forced him to modify the transmitted text in order to make τινα φύσιν the subject of the participle.[80]

The form δι' οὗ, appearing right after the participle, was corrected by Kepler into δίου θείου; and by Dübner into ἀϊδίου—a correction accepted by Emperius, Bernardakis and Pohlenz.[81] While Kepler's suggestion seems rather difficult to explain, Dübner's proposal coordinates the adjective with the following καὶ ἀτελευτήτου: both of them are linked by their meaning given that the former means 'forever' and the latter, 'without ending.' Once again, there is no need for such an intervention, since the transmitted text is reasonably coherent.

Returning to the lacuna in this passage, it has 16 letters in E and 14 in B. Amyot supplied the blank with the participle μετέχουσι; Wyttenbach (in the apparatus) with the infinitive κινεῖσθαι; Adler, explaining that there is no need for a new verb in the sentence, proposed τῶν οὐρανίων; Pohlenz (also in the apparatus),

---

79 Emperius, *Opuscula*, 291.
80 Cherniss, "Notes on Plutarch's *De facie*," 142.
81 Kepler, *Ioh. Keppleri Mathematici*, 119; Emperius, *Opuscula*, 291.

ὁμαλῶς περαινόμενον; and Cherniss, οἷόν τε φύσιν ἔχειν—again, making φύσιν the explicit subject of the subordinate clauses.[82] Donini followed Cherniss, but suggested that the repetition of φύσιν so soon after the previous occurrence of this noun would hardly fit in Plutarch's style, so he proposed the alternative κίνησιν.[83]

Taking the passage's structure into consideration, I believe that the best option is a participle in dative that is coordinated with the other two participles, whose subject is ὑμῖν. Amyot's proposal, in this sense, is the most suitable, but it seems preferable to simply note the lacuna in the apparatus.

| | |
|---|---|
| 929A 22–2 | Αὐτῆς δὲ νώθειαν καὶ τάχους ἀμβλύτητα καὶ τὸ θερμὸν ἀδρανὲς καὶ ἀμαυρόν, ⟨ᾧ⟩ κατὰ τὸν Ἴωνα<br>μέλας οὐ πεπαίνεται βότρυς,<br>εἰς τί θησόμεθα πλὴν ἀσθένειαν αὐτῆς καὶ πάθος, ⟨εἰ πάθους⟩ ἀιδίῳ σώματι καὶ ὀλυμπίῳ μέτεστιν;[84] |
| EB | αὐτῆς δὲ νώθειαν E/ νωθείαν B καὶ τάχους ἀμβλύτητα. καὶ τὸ θερμὸν ἀδρανὲς καὶ ἀμαυρόν, κατὰ E/ καὶ κατὰ B τὸν Ἴωνα μέλας οὐ πεπαίνεται βότρυς, εἰς τί θησόμεθα· πλὴν ἀσθένειαν αὐτῆς· καὶ πάθος ἀιδίῳ σώματι καὶ ὀλυμπίῳ μέτεστιν. |

Three issues appear in this passage: a) the manuscripts disagree in one reading; b) the introduction of an incomplete verse from Ion; and c) the lack of a complement required by the verb μέτεστιν in the last sentence.

Regarding the manuscripts' disagreement, while E transmits only the preposition κατά, B adds in front of it the conjunction καί, which is not necessary in the passage.

Concerning the quote of Ion's verse, the agent seems to be lost.[85] Plutarch quotes the same verse, complete, in *Quaest. conv.* 3.10: μέλας γὰρ αὐταῖς οὐ πεπαίνεται βότρυς. The dative αὐταῖς, which refers to the previously mentioned τὰς αὐγάς, functions in the verse as agent—a complement that has not been transmitted in *De facie*'s quote.[86] In this passage, the logical cause for the ripening

---

82 Adler, *Dissertationes philologae Vindobonenses*, 102.
83 Donini, *Plutarco. Il volto della luna*, 290 n. 158.
84 Even though νώθειαν is the reading of E, Bernardakis strikingly presented it as his own, and Raingeard attributed it to his predecessor. Furthermore, according to Raingeard, ὀλυμπίῳ is the reading of B only, while E would transmit the form ὀλυμπίοο, which is only a misreading of the admittedly strange form of the omega in that manuscript.
85 *TGF* 57 Snell.
86 The presence of αὐγάς in *Quaest. conv.* might explain the correction suggested by Sandbach in "Second Meeting," 15, which was accepted by Pohlenz, reading αὐτῆς into αὐγῆς.

of grapes is τὸ θερμὸν ἀδρανὲς καὶ ἀμαυρόν. The Aldine SR67 corrected οὐ into οὗ, which only complicates the matter further, given that it eliminates the negation necessary for the correct meaning of Ion's verse. The Aldine RJ94 and the *Basiliensis* edition proposed the addition of the relative pronoun ᾧ before κατά, and, for that matter, they also deleted the conjunction καί that the Aldine edition maintained, following B's reading. In my view, ᾧ is preferable because it fits the syntax better and, being a monosyllable, it may have easily dropped out by the scribe's lack of attention.

Concerning the grammatical issue at the end of the passage, the problem arises through the lack of a complement required by μέτεστιν. In the Aldine SR67 we find the annotation εἰ πάθους to be added after καὶ πάθος.[87] The corruption can be explained by the simplification of the polyptoton (ἀσθένειαν αὐτῆς καὶ πάθος εἰ πάθους). In the margin of RJ94 there is the addition of ὧν οὐδετέρου also to be inserted after ἀσθένειαν αὐτῆς καὶ πάθος; Xylander suggested (in the commentary of 1570) the modification of the text into καὶ ὁ Ἀριστοτέλης· πάθος ἄρα ἀιδίῳ, which not only is unnecessary but also unjustified; Stephanus proposed εἰ πάθος; and Pohlenz suggested the addition of πόθεν οὖν πάθους.[88] Differently, Raingeard solved the problem by modifying EB's punctuation: if Xylander's question mark after αὐτῆς and the Aldine and *Basiliensis* editions' question mark after μέτεστιν are accepted, then two different questions are created. While I appreciate the simplicity of Raingerad's solution, Leonicus' proposal seems to be more suitable from both a stylistic and a palaeographic point of view.

929BC 14–15   εἰ μὴ στέγει μηδὲ ἀντιφράττει τὸν ἥλιον, ἀλλὰ δίεισιν ὑπὸ μανότητος
              ἢ κατὰ σύγκρασιν εἰσλάμπει καὶ συνεξάπτει περὶ αὐτὴν τὸ φῶς·
EB            εἰ μὴ στέγει μὴ δὲ ἀντιφράττει τὸν ἥλιον, ἀλλὰ δίεισιν ὑπὸ μανότητος.
              ἢ κατὰ σύγκρασιν εἰσλάμπει καὶ συνεξάπτει περὶ αὐτὴν τὸ φῶς·

---

This is a mistake: both νώθειαν and ἀμβλύτητα refer specifically to the moon (αὐτῆς), not to its rays. Sandbach, furthermore, modified the order of most elements in the sentence: αὐγῆς δὲ ἀμβλύτητα καὶ τάχους νώθειαν.

87   This suggestion was copied in all the Aldines exemplars that transmitted Leonicus' corrections and was accepted by most editors, although Bernardakis, Pohlenz and Cherniss erroneously attributed it to Dübner. It is interesting to note that the contributor to RJ94 who systematically copied Leonicus' corrections presented, in this case, the reading εἰ παθῇ instead of εἰ πάθους. For the explanation of such a mistake, see my analysis in Lesage Gárriga, "Aldinas anotadas," 258 and 262.

88   Xylander, *Plutarchi Chaeronensis*, 718. Wyttenbach incorporated Stephanus' conjecture in the text of his edition without specifying that it is not the manuscripts' reading.

Three main modifications have been made to this sentence: the verb δίεισιν, the verb εἰσλάμπει, and its complement περὶ αὐτήν. All of them are, in my view, motivated by a misunderstanding of the passage's syntax. A few scholars assumed that the whole passage has the same subject: the moon. Consequently, they are compelled to modify the text transmitted by EB, because it presents semantic difficulties.

Concerning δίεισιν, the verb was switched by Madvig into the same tense of διίημι (διίησιν) because of its meaning.[89] While EB's reading means 'to go through,' or 'to pass,' Madvig's proposal means 'to send,' or 'to let go.' Madvig—and with him Bernardakis and Cherniss—was compelled to replace the verb with a more suitable one because the moon, indeed, cannot 'go through' itself, but rather 'lets something go.' Therefore, the object according to Madvig is τὸ φῶς.

Concerning the modification of εἰσλάμπει, it was motivated by the supposedly unfitting meaning of the preverb. Sandbach changed the verb into ἐκλάμπει, which means 'to shine suddenly,' or 'to enlighten,' whose transitive value can have τὸ φῶς as object, and thus fits the structure of the sentence, in his view, better that εἰσλάμπω, 'to shine in.'[90]

Regarding περὶ αὐτήν, it was corrected by an annotation in RJ94 to περὶ αὑτήν, so that it would reinforce the idea of the moon being the recipient of light ('in itself').

While it is true that the moon is the subject of the first part of the passage (929B, Οὕτω γὰρ οὐδὲν ἧττον ἐν νουμηνίαις ἢ διχομηνίαις ἔσται πανσέληνος ἡμῖν, εἰ μὴ στέγει μηδὲ ἀντιφράττει τὸν ἥλιον), there is a switch of subject in the second part of the sentence: τὸ φῶς is not the object—as these scholars supposed—but the new subject. In this sense, the first verb that both manuscripts report (δίεισιν) can be maintained, because light can 'go through' the moon. Also the forms εἰσλάμπει and περὶ αὐτήν are valid if the moon no longer is the subject: light, in point of fact, can 'shine in' the moon when going through it, and can also join in kindling the moon when 'around it.'

929D 6–7   ὅθεν οὐδὲ θερμὸν οὐδὲ λαμπρὸν ἀφικνεῖται πρὸς ἡμᾶς, ὥσπερ ἦν εἰκὸς ἐξάψεως καὶ μίξεως ⟨τῶν⟩ φώτων γεγενημένης,[91]

---

89   Madvig, *Adversaria critica*, 665.
90   I have not been able to trace where he proposed such a change; I, therefore, rely on Cherniss' attribution.
91   The participle γεγενημένης was transmitted by a mistake of iotacism as γεγενημένοις in the Aldine and the *Basiliensis* editions. A mistake soon corrected into the genitive by annotations in the copies of Leonicus, Turnebus and Amyot.

EB             ὅθεν οὐδὲ θερμὸν οὐδὲ λαμπρὸν ἀφικνεῖται πρὸς ἡμᾶς ὥσπερ ἦν εἰκὸς
               ἐξάψεως καὶ μίξεως ... φώτων γεγενημένης·

A lacuna is reported by the manuscripts between μίξεως and φώτων: E presents a gap of five letters, and B a gap of only three. The first conjecture is found in the Aldine SR67 with τῶν, which is the article that should accompany the following φώτων. Xylander simply deleted the lacuna, interpreting that no text is missing. Wyttenbach stunningly stated (in the apparatus) that there is no lacuna in B, and proposed τινός, thus relating the missing part to the preceding syntagma ἐξάψεως καὶ μίξεως; Raingeard conjectured δύο; and Pohlenz, the variation δυοῖν. Curiously, Raingeard affirmed in the commentary that τῶν cannot be the right conjecture, because "nous ne savons pas expressément de quelles lumières il s'agit," but he then suggested δύο, which implies that he had indeed two particular lights in mind—I suppose the lights of the sun and the moon, as the passage itself suggests and most scholars infer.[92]

The two nouns in genitive singular preceding the lacuna can be understood as an indefinite without the need of adding the pronoun, but φώτων does need a determinative. The addition of the article in genitive plural seems to me the most appropriate option: while the options of numeral and dual are both correct, they simply make explicit information already contained in the article.

930B 28–3      διαβάλλεται δὲ τοῖς διπτύχοις κατόπτροις, ὡς ἐπικλιθέντων πρὸς
               ἄλληλα καὶ γωνίας ἐντὸς γενομένης, ἑκάτερον τῶν ἐπιπέδων διττὴν
               ἔμφασιν ἀποδίδωσι καὶ ποιεῖ τέτταρας εἰκόνας ἀφ' ἑνὸς προσώπου,
               δύο μὲν ἀντιστρόφους τοῖς ἔξωθεν ἐναργεστέρας μέρεσι, δύο δὲ δεξι-
               οφανεῖς ἀμαυρὰς ἐν βάθει τῶν κατόπτρων,[93]
EB             διαβάλλεται δὲ τοῖς διπτύχοις κατόπτροις ὡς ἐπικριθέντων πρὸς
               ἄλληλα· καὶ γωνίας ἐντὸς γενομένης ἑκάτερον τῶν ἐπιπέδων διττῆς
               ἔμφασιν ἀποδίδωσι· καὶ ποιεῖ τέτταρας εἰκόνας ἀφ' ἑνὸς προσώπου·
               δύο μὲν ἀντιστρόφους τοῖς ἔξωθεν ἀριστεροῖς μέρεσι· δύο δὲ δεξιοφα-
               νεῖς ἀμαυρὰς ἐν βάθει τῶν κατόπτρων,

---

92  Raingeard, *Le peri toy prosopoy*, 99.
93  There is a dittography in both manuscripts, from ὅταν ἐμφάσεις ποιῇ to διαβάλλεται δέ, after that they present a lacuna—14 letters E, 11 letters B. This repetition is also transmitted in the Aldine and the *Basiliensis* editions. Many scholars of the 16th century either underlined or crossed out the repetition, among which are Leonicus and Turnebus; although, only the latter is credited for the elimination of the doubled sentence. Furthermore, the Aldine edition reads γενομένοις instead of γενομένης, a mistake probably due to iotacism and soon corrected by Forteguerri, Leonicus and Turnebus in their copies.

The whole passage deals with the law of reflexion, which it refutes on the grounds of two examples: firstly, of convex mirrors (930AB, διαβάλλεται μὲν ἐπὶ τῶν κυρτῶν κατόπτρων, ὅταν ἐμφάσεις ποιῇ μείζονας ἑαυτῶν πρὸς ἓν τὸ τῆς ὄψεως σημεῖον); secondly, of folding mirrors.[94] The explanation of the type of images created by these mirrors includes some problems.

The first one is the manuscripts' reading ὡς ἐπικριθέντων: the meaning of the verb, 'to decide about or against,' or 'to choose,' does not seem to fit the context, and the adverb seems somehow out of place, which is a reason why both were modified by an annotation in RJ94 to read ὧν ἐπικλιθέντων. The relative pronoun refers to the antecedent τοῖς διπτύχοις κατόπτροις and the verb's meaning, 'to lean on,' or 'to bend toward,' which is a simple but effective emendation.

While I agree with the replacement of a verb that made no sense in the present passage, I have reservations about the modification of the adverb. It is true that ὧν improves the syntax of the sentence, but ὡς is not *per se* a bad reading, which is the reason why I maintain EB's text.

The second issue is the form διττῆς, transmitted by EB: given that it modifies the noun ἔμφασιν, it must be corrected into an accusative. The correction was first suggested by Forteguerri. Raingeard, however, maintained EB's reading and pointed (in his commentary) that it modifies γωνίας.[95] In that case, the subject of the main clause (ἑκάτερον τῶν ἐπιπέδων) breaks the genitive absolute in two pieces, which is doubtful. Furthermore, it is more plausible that the numeral modifies the noun that immediately follows it, rather than a noun mentioned significantly earlier.

Then comes the problematic nature of the images created by the folding mirrors. These, being inclined towards each other and having formed an inner angle, are said to give a double image of a single object and to create four likenesses: two of a kind, and the other two of another. The first two images are ἀντιστρόφους, 'reversed,' and are located τοῖς ἔξωθεν ἀριστεροῖς μέρεσι in 'the parts that are outer left.' The first issue at stake is that the two left parts of two folding mirrors cannot both be at the same time "outer." The other two images are ἀμαυράς, 'dim,' or 'faint,' located ἐν βάθει τῶν κατόπτρων, 'in the depth of the mirrors.' But they are also said to be δεξιοφανεῖς, an adjective that has two different meanings: 'shown straight,' namely not reversed (thus opposed to ἀντιστρόφους, above), and 'shown on the right side' (thus opposed to ἀριστεροῖς, above). Amyot, Wyttenbach and Prickard interpreted its second meaning,

---

94   This entry represents a shorter version of the analysis of the passage developed in L. Lesage Gárriga, "Plutarch and the Law of Reflection: Critical and Literary Commentary to *De facie* 930A–C," *Ploutarchos* 15 (2018) 29–42.

95   Raingeard, *Le peri toy prosopoy*, 101.

which, in turn, poses the same problem as ἀριστεροῖς: the two right parts of two folding mirrors cannot be both in depth, namely in the inner angle.[96] This allows for the exclusion of δεξιοφανεῖς' second meaning, but the problem with ἀριστεροῖς still remains.

Other scholars tried to solve it differently. First, Wyttenbach reorganized most of the sentence into δύο μὲν ἀριστεράς, δύο δὲ δεξιοφανεῖς, τὰς μὲν ἀντιστρόφους τοῖς ἔξωθεν μέρεσι, τὰς δὲ ἀμαυρὰς ἐν βάθει τῶν κατόπτρων. While his conjecture provides the passage with sense, it is difficult to explain how the text could have been so corrupted from the reading transmitted by the manuscripts. Dübner added the preposition ἐν before the syntagma τοῖς [...] μέρεσι and secluded the problematic ἀριστεροῖς, which should be seen as a gloss integrated in the text following a misinterpretation of the meaning of δεξιοφανεῖς. Most scholars adopted this solution. However, while the seclusion of the problematic term appears to be the easiest solution, it actually presumes two different mistakes: the misinterpretation of δεξιοφανεῖς, and the wrong inclusion of a gloss meant to parallel that term. A few scholars solve the problem differently. Emperius accepted Dübner's interventions and turned the preposition ἐν before βάθει into the article τῷ.[97] Schmidt suggested to modify ἀριστεροῖς into σαφεστέρας, meaning 'clearer,' or 'more distinctive;' and Raingeard, in the same line, wrote ἐναργεστέρας, meaning 'clearer,' or 'more visible.'[98] And Pohlenz, while accepting only the seclusion by Emperius, added ἀλλ' after δεξιοφανεῖς, which is superfluous.

The meaning of Schmidt's and Raingeard's corrections fits the context, but the solution of the latter is the most suitable from a palaeographic perspective: ἐναργεστέρας would have been corrupted into ἀριστεροῖς by the loss of the first syllable (ἐν) due to haplography with the ending of the previous word (ἔξωθεν), and by the attraction to the case of the surrounding words, all in dative (τοῖς [...] μέρεσι). I thus accept Raingeard's ἐναργεστέρας.

930EF 24–27    εἰ γὰρ αἰθέριον ὄγκον ἢ πύρινον ὄντα τὸν τῆς σελήνης ἐφώτιζεν ὁ ἥλιος, οὐκ ἂν ἀπέλειπεν αὐτῇ σκιερὸν ἀεὶ καὶ ἀλαμπὲς ἡμισφαίριον πρὸς αἴσθησιν, ἀλλ' εἰ καὶ κατὰ μικρὸν ἔψαυε περιιὼν πολλὴν ἀναπίμπλασθαι καὶ δι' ὅλης τρέφεσθαι τῷ φωτὶ πανταχόσε χωροῦντι δι' εὐπετείας ἦν προσῆκον·[99]

---

96   Amyot, *Les Œuvres Morales*, 619; Prickard, *Plutarch on The Face*, 29.
97   Emperius, *Opuscula*, 291.
98   L. Nix, & W. Schmidt, *Heronis Alexandrini opera quae supersunt omnia*, vol. 2. Mechanica et Catoptrica (Berlin: De Gruyter, 2010 [1900]) 313 n. 2.
99   Stephanus, and Wyttenbach, without any mention in the apparatus—therefore, I cannot

EB  εἰ γὰρ αἰθέριον ὄγκον ἢ πύρινον ὄντα τὸν τῆς σελήνης ἐφώτιζεν ὁ ἥλιος, οὐκ ἂν ἀπέλειπεν αὐτῇ σκιερὸν ἀεὶ καὶ ἀλαμπὲς ἡμισφαίριον πρὸς αἴσθησιν· ἀλλ' εἰ καὶ κατὰ μικρὸν ἔψαυε περὶ ὧν πολλὴν ἀναπίμπλασθαι καὶ δι' ὅλης τρέφεσθαι τῷ φωτὶ πανταχόσε χωροῦντι δι' εὐπετείας ἦν προσῆκον·

This passage presents an uncommon syntax (the construction ἀπέλειπεν with dative, αὐτῇ), along with presenting some problems in the substantive clause depending on ἦν προσῆκον.

Concerning the dative, it was transformed by Wyttenbach (in the apparatus) into genitive; Raingeard (also in the apparatus) suggested the addition of the preposition ἐν in front of the pronoun. Admittedly, the construction of ἀπολείπω with dative is unusual, but Cherniss provided a few valid examples of occurrences within Plutarch's works, which is the reason why I maintain the text of EB.[100]

Concerning the problems in the subordinate clause, the first issue regards the syntagma περὶ ὧν, for there is no plural noun that could act as its antecedent. In the Aldine copy of Forteguerri, there is the correction περὶ ἥν; Kepler, for his part, suggested the substitution of the syntagma for περίοδον.[101] More interesting are the emendations found in Leonicus' and Turnebus' Aldine copies. The former transformed the syntagma into περιιών; the latter read περιιών, in which a second iota has probably been forcibly introduced by a different hand.[102] Leonicus' proposal, περιιών, seems to be preferable, both from a palaeographic and a semantic point of view, to περὶ ἥν and περίοδον; also, being a verb of movement, it applies better to the present context than περιών. The nominative singular relates to the sun, which was the subject of the preceding sentence: his revolution around the moon and the subtle touch

---

tell if it was a conscious modification of EB's text or simply the acceptance of the text he used as basis for his own edition—transmitted the aorist ἀπέλιπεν, instead of the imperfect ἀπέλειπεν.

100  Cherniss, "Concerning the Face," 112 n. a.
101  Kepler, *Ioh. Keppleri Mathematici*, 131.
102  See Lesage Gárriga, "Aldinas anotadas," 259–260, for a detailed study on the contributor who copied Leonicus' corrections into the Aldine RJ94. In this case, he seems to have added the second iota to a conjecture previously made by another of the contributors. The wrong attribution of authorship concerning this particular case astounds me: Raingeard and Cherniss attributed περιιών to RJ94, and Cherniss, together with Wyttenbach, stated that περιιών comes from Stephanus, who, in turn, copied it from Leonicus. Bernardakis, in a much simpler mistake, attributed περιιών to Wyttenbach.

(κατὰ μικρὸν ἔψαυε) is a somewhat sexual allusion that can be found elsewhere in the treatise.[103]

The second problem derives from the adjective transmitted by both manuscripts, πολλήν. Lucius is making an argument that the minimum touch of light should illuminate the whole moon, if, indeed, it is of a fire-like nature. The idea of completeness in the verb τρέφεσθαι is reinforced by the appearance of δι' ὅλης, but the adjective πολλήν was not thought to be strong enough to highlight this idea with regards to the verb ἀναπίμπλασθαι. For this reason, the correction proposed by Forteguerri, ὅλην, was accepted by most scholars.[104] EB's reading, however, is coherent from the stylistic perspective: there is, in the passage, a gradation from little (κατὰ μικρόν), to a lot (πολλήν), to completeness (δι' ὅλης). Consequently, the manuscripts need no intervention.

The third and last issue concerns the infinitive τρέφεσθαι, whose meaning seems slightly off in the present context. While, according to EB, the moon is completely 'condensed,' or 'cherished,' or 'nourished' by the sun's light, an annotation in RJ94 transformed the verb into τρέπεσθαι, 'to turn,' or 'to alter.' Despite the general tendency to accept this correction, EB's verb might be maintained: either with the meaning 'to cherish,' which would fit the allusion to the relationship between the sun and the moon mentioned above, or with the general meaning 'to nourish,' if the light coming from the sun is taken as the nourishment needed by the moon.

931E 3–7    Εἰ δὲ μή, Θέων ἡμῖν οὗτος τὸν Μίμνερμον ἐπάξει καὶ τὸν Κυδίαν καὶ τὸν Ἀρχίλοχον, πρὸς δὲ τούτοις τὸν Στησίχορον καὶ τὸν Πίνδαρον ἐν ταῖς ἐκλείψεσιν ὀλοφυρομένους τὸν φανερώτατον κλεπτόμενον καὶ μέσῳ ἄματι τὴν νύκτα γινομένην καὶ τὴν ἀκτῖνα τοῦ ἡλίου σκότους ἀτραπὸν ⟨ἐσσυμέναν⟩ φάσκοντας,[105]

EB    εἰ δὲ μὴ θεῶν ἡμῖν οὗτος ἐργομίμναμον ἐπάξει καὶ τὸν κυδίαν καὶ τὸν ἀρχίλοχον· πρὸς δὲ τούτοις τὸν στησίχορον καὶ τὸν πίνδαρον ἐν ταῖς ἐκλείψεσιν ὀλοφυρομένους τὸν φανερώτατον κλεπτόμενον. καὶ μέσω

---

103   See, for instance, 933A and 944E.
104   With misattributions, once again: Wyttenbach did not explain, in the apparatus, that ὅλην is a correction of the manuscripts' text; Bernardakis did not specify the provenance; and both Pohlenz and Cherniss attributed the correction to Stephanus.
105   According to Bernardakis, Bergk read σκότου—from the masculine noun σκότος, -ου—but this is an unnecessary correction, given that B reports the correct case from the less common neuter noun σκότος, -ους. This unusual form is used in at least two occasions (929D, καθάπερ εἰς νύκτα καὶ **σκότος** and 932A, εἰ δὲ οὐχ οὕτω τὸ περὶ τὰς ἐκλείψεις **σκότος** βύθιόν ἐστιν), which proves B correct.

ἅμα τὴν νύκτα γινομένην· καὶ τὴν ἀκτῖνα τοῦ ἡλίου σκότος E / σκότους B ἀτραπὸν ... φάσκοντας·

This passage presents a number of textual corruptions (θεῶν, ἐργομίμναμον, ἅμα τὴν νύκτα) and a lacuna. None of these issues, fortunately, obscures the general meaning. It has also been intervened to improve its readability.

Concerning the textual corruptions, the first problem derives from the manuscripts' obviously incorrect reading θεῶν. Lucius is naming his colleague, specialist in literature, Theon: Theon will be in charge to recall various authors who wrote about eclipses, if need be. Consequently, the genitive plural θεῶν was soon changed by the Aldine SR67 into Θέων.

The second corruption concerns the otherwise non-existent form ἐργομίμναμον, transmitted by both manuscripts. The context, full of references to well-known authors (καὶ τὸν Κυδίαν καὶ τὸν Ἀρχίλοχον, [...] τὸν Στησίχορον καὶ τὸν Πίνδαρον), helps to correctly interpret the text: a reference to yet another author must have been included here. Forteguerri and Leonicus were the first scholars to provide a correct reading, τὸν Μίμνερμον—the latter added ἢ Μίμερμνον, a form that does not exist—; in Turnebus' Aldine copy, we can find a correction as well, ἔργῳ Μίμνερμον, which, perhaps, is closer to the manuscripts' reading yet the sense of which is not suitable in the present context; the *Basiliensis* edition included Μίμνερμον without the article.[106]

The third corruption affects the text καὶ μέσῳ ἅμα τὴν νύκτα γινομένην where a complement of time in dative seems to be lacking.[107] The first modifications are located in the Aldine edition, which (most probably involuntary) transmitted the participle in masculine, and the *Basiliensis*, which maintained this mistake and also deleted the article τήν. More interesting, however, is Leonicus' suggestion to correct ἅμα into ἅματι (sic) (ἅματι τὴν νύκτα γινομένην), for this improves the sentence by including the missing complement. Wyttenbach transmitted ἅματι (sic) νύκτα γινομένην—transforming the article into the ending of the noun (-την = -τι)—and Bernardakis, Raingeard, Pohlenz, and Cherniss read

---

106   See Lesage Gárriga, "Aldinas anotadas," 256–257, on the different versions of Leonicus' correction found in compilations and how this helped to sort the relationships between those compilations. Again, some issues with the authorship appeared with later scholars. Wyttenbach integrated τὸν Μίμνερμον in the text with no reference in the apparatus; Bernardakis did not explicitly refer to any provenance; Raingeard attributed the correction to Turnebus' Aldine copy; Pohlenz, to the rather unsatisfactory "ς;" and Cherniss, to Stephanus. It is true that Turnebus' Aldine copy presents the correction τὸν Μίμνερμον beside the aforementioned ἔργῳ Μίμνερμον, but it belongs to the contributor that I have proved provided a copy of Leonicus' corrections.

107   This seems to be a verse from Stesichorus: fr. 94 Page.

ἄματι νύκτα γινομένην—again, deleting the article, but with the correct breathing for ἄματι in this case.[108]

The correction from ἅμα into ἄματι is necessary, and Leonicus' suggestion is preferable given that the corruption, namely the loss of the last syllable (τι), is explainable by haplography with the following article (τήν).

Regarding the lacuna, it occupies a space of 16 letters in both manuscripts. It is preceded by an allusion to the behaviour of the sun during the eclipses (καὶ τὴν ἀκτῖνα τοῦ ἡλίου σκότους ἀτραπόν) and followed by the participle (φάσκοντας) that modifies all the preceding subordinate clauses in which different writings about eclipses by various authors are listed. It seems, thus, that the subject of this clause (τὴν ἀκτῖνα) lacks its verb.

Amyot conjectured ἱεμέμην; Xylander conjectured (in the commentary to his translation) ὑποδῦναι; Wyttenbach suggested (in the apparatus) that perhaps nothing is missing—thus, interpreting the sentence as non-verbal: "the sun's ray, a path of shadow"—; and Adler proposed ἐσσυμέναν.[109] Given that the remaining subordinate clauses depending on φάσκοντας are both constructed with participles (κλεπτόμενον and γινομένην), one may assume a parallel structure. Furthermore, Adler's conjecture is based in a fragment of Pindar's *Paean*, 9.5 that transmits the verse ἐπίσκοτον ἀτραπὸν ἐσσυμένα. Indeed, Pindar is the last author quoted in the passage of *De facie* before the citation, which makes reasonable to accept ἐσσυμέναν.

We now come to the intervention in the text. In the sentence about the disappearance of the sun during eclipses (ἐν ταῖς ἐκλείψεσιν ὀλοφυρομένους τὸν φανερώτατον κλεπτόμενον), Wyttenbach suggested (in the apparatus) to add θεόν after τὸν φανερώτατον; Theodor Bergk, according to Bernardakis, added ἄστρον between the article and the adjective, but, according to Cherniss, he transformed the article into ἄστρον. The poetic language of the section, however, seems to make these corrections unnecessary.

---

108  All of them, with no exceptions, wrongly attributed the correction to Leonicus. Here we have a very fine example of how modern editors worked with 16th century scholars: many times Leonicus is not acknowledged for his contributions, but, in a few cases, even worse, he is mentioned as conjecturer of an emendation he did not make! Other examples are found in the headings to 930EF and 944BC. See Lesage Gárriga, "Aldinas anotadas," on this problem.

109  Xylander, *Plutarchi Chaeronensis*, 719; Adler, *Dissertationes philologae Vindobonenses*, 105. Adler, in fact, suggested that the uncommonness of the word may have urged the copyist to leave a blank. See W.H. Race, *Pindar*, vol. 2 (Cambridge-Massachusetts: Loeb Classical Library, 1997) for Pindar's edition.

931EF 7–10   ἐπὶ πᾶσι δὲ τὸν Ὅμηρον νυκτὶ καὶ ζόφῳ τὰ πρόσωπα κατέχεσθαι τῶν ἀνθρώπων λέγοντα καὶ τὸν ἥλιον ἐξαπολωλέναι τοῦ οὐρανοῦ περὶ τὴν σελήνην καὶ … τοῦτο γίνεσθαι πεφυκέναι, τοῦ μὲν φθίνοντος μηνός, τοῦ δὲ ἱσταμένου.[110]

EB   ἐπὶ πᾶσι δὲ τὸν ὅμηρον νυκτὶ καὶ ζόφῳ τὰ πρῶτα κατέχεσθαι τῶν ἀνθρώπων λέγοντα. καὶ τὸν ἥλιον ἐξαπολωλέναι τοῦ οὐρανοῦ περὶ τὴν σελήνην καὶ … τοῦτο γίνεσθαι πέφυκε. τοῦ μὲν, φθίνοντος μηνὸς τοῦ δὲ, ἱσταμένου.

Two textual problems occur in this passage. Firstly, the words attributed to Homer; then, a lacuna of around 12 letters after περὶ τὴν σελήνην καί.

Regarding the first issue, the text νυκτὶ καὶ ζόφῳ τὰ πρῶτα κατέχεσθαι τῶν ἀνθρώπων seems to be taken from *Odyssey* 20.351–352: νυκτὶ μὲν ὑμέων/ εἰλύαται κεφαλαί τε πρόσωπά τε νέρθε τε γοῦνα. In Homer's text, the parts of men that are shrouded in night are the heads, faces, and knees; in *De facie*, however, there is no subject. An annotation in RJ94 suggested the correction of τῶν ἀνθρώπων into an accusative singular (τὸν ἄνθρωπον), thus making this noun the subject of the quote; Xylander suggested (in the commentary to his translation) to correct τὰ πρῶτα into τὰ πρόσωπα, providing the sentence not only with a subject but also bringing it closer to Homer's words.[111] This emendation has been unanimously accepted by scholars, and I agree with them.

In what concerns the lacuna, it seems to leave the syntagma περὶ τὴν σελήνην unconnected with the rest of the passage, given that what precedes it corresponds to another quotation of Homer (καὶ τὸν ἥλιον ἐξαπολωλέναι τοῦ οὐρανοῦ) and what follows is a proper, complete sentence (τοῦτο γίνεσθαι πέφυκε).[112]

Xylander wrote (in the commentary to his translation): "*nihil (ut videtur) praeterea inter καὶ τοῦτο frustra est asteriscus.*"[113] In this sense, the problem can be solved by correcting the punctuation: to finish a sentence after Homer's words and to delete the lacuna. This option is appealing were it not for what follows, which is, again, a quote of Homer (τοῦ μὲν φθίνοντος μηνός, τοῦ δὲ ἱσταμένου).[114] Of course, it could be that this second quote is not grammatically attached to the first one, but it seems more reasonable to think that both depend on ἐπὶ πᾶσι δὲ τὸν Ὅμηρον […] λέγοντα.

---

110   Raingeard strangely presented λέγονται instead of λέγοντα, which absolutely cannot fit the grammar. The fact that he did not explain this in the apparatus points to an erratum.
111   Xylander, *Plutarchi Chaeronensis*, 719.
112   *Od.* 20.356–357.
113   Xylander, *Plutarchi Chaeronensis*, 719.
114   *Od.* 19.307.

This is the reason why most editors opted to complete the lacuna and even modify the surrounding text. An annotation in RJ94 corrected πέφυκε into πεφυκέναι because it fits the syntax better: it coordinates this verb with κατέχεσθαι and ἐξαπολωλέναι, since both verbs of the subordinate clauses depend on λέγοντα. Wyttenbach (in the apparatus) incorporated this modification into his larger correction, although he did not mention the Aldine copy: καὶ περὶ τὴν σελήνης σύνοδον τοῦτο γίνεσθαι πεφυκέναι; Bernardakis proposed (in the apparatus) the combination of a correction and a conjecture παρὰ τὴν σελήνην καὶ ὡς ἐν συνόδῳ; Adler supplied ἡλίου σύνοδον and also corrected the verb into πεφυκέναι; Pohlenz modified the transmitted text and proposed a conjecture for the lacuna as well, περὶ τὴν σύνοδον καὶ ἐπιστάμενον ὅτι τοῦτο; Cherniss supplied αἰνιττόμενον ὡς; Herwig Görgemanns, προσδηλοῦντα ὡς.[115]

The correction from πέφυκε into πεφυκέναι is required for proper syntax. On the basis that what follows the lacuna is *Odyssey* 19.307, I suggest that the text lost in the lacuna could have been τελεῖσθαι, a verb included in *Odyssey* 19.305 (τάδε πάντα τελεῖεται), which fits the context. The lack of certainty, however, makes preferable to note the lacuna.

| | |
|---|---|
| 932BC 1–3 | Ἀριστοτέλης δὲ ὁ παλαιὸς αἰτίαν τοῦ πλεονάκις τὴν σελήνην ἐκλείπουσαν ἢ τὸν ἥλιον καθορᾶσθαι, πρὸς ἄλλαις τισὶ καὶ ταύτην ἀποδίδωσιν· ἥλιον γὰρ ἐκλείπειν σελήνης ἀντιφράξει, σελήνην δὲ ⟨γῆς⟩. |
| EB | ἀριστοτέλης δὲ ὁ παλαιὸς αἰτίαν τοῦ πλεονάκις τὴν σελήνην ἐκλείπουσαν ἢ τὸν ἥλιον καθορᾶσθαι· πρὸς ἄλλαις τισί, καὶ ταύτην ἀποδίδωσιν· ἥλιον γὰρ ἐκλείπειν σελήνης ἀντιφράξει. σελήνην δὲ … |

Both manuscripts present a lacuna after σελήνην δέ: E has a gap of 30 letters and B has a gap of 23. The missing text was most certainly part of the previous sentence, given that σελήνην δέ is the counterpart to ἥλιον γάρ and that what comes after the lacuna is clearly the beginning of a new sentence (Ὁ δὲ Ποσειδώνιος …). The passage deals with Aristotle's account of types and frequency of eclipses: that of the sun occurs when the moon intercepts it, the lacuna, however, interrupts the part concerning that of the moon. It can safely be assumed that at least one thing has been lost, which is most likely the element that intercepts the moon in order to cause an eclipse—the earth.

This conclusion is what we find as an annotation in the Aldine RJ94 (γῆς), and all other conjectures included this element as well, but as a part of larger

---

115    Adler, *Dissertationes philologae Vindobonenses*, 106; H. Görgemanns, *Untersuchungen zu Plutarchs Dialog De facie in orbe lunae* (Heidelberg: Heidelberg University Press, 1970) 128.

proposals: Amyot suggested γῆς πολλῷ (sic) μείζονος; Wyttenbach (in the apparatus), γῆς, ἣν πολὺ μείζονα οὖσαν πλεονάκις ἀποκρύπτειν τὴν σελήνην—a sentence whose disappearance could be explained by haplography from σελήνην δέ to the repetition of the same noun—; Bernardakis (in the apparatus) proposed γῆς πλεονάκις μείζονος οὔσης; and Adler proposed γῆς, πολλῷ μείζονος οὔσης, which merely adds the participle to Amyot's proposal.[116]

All these larger conjectures point to the size of the earth as the reason for the moon being eclipsed more frequently than the sun, but the context only requires a mention of the element causing eclipses of the moon (γῆς).

932C 3–6   Ὁ δὲ Ποσειδώνιος ὁρισάμενος οὕτως· τόδε τὸ πάθος ἔκλειψίς ἐστιν ἡλίου, σύνοδος σκιᾶς σελήνης οἷς τὴν ἔκλειψιν ⟨πάθουσιν·⟩ ἐκείνοις γὰρ μόνοις ἔκλειψίς ἐστιν ὧν ἂν ἡ σκιὰ τῆς σελήνης καταλαβοῦσα τὴν ὄψιν ἀντιφράξῃ πρὸς τὸν ἥλιον·[117]

EB   ὁ δὲ ποσειδώνιος ὁρισάμενος οὕτως. τὸ δὲ πάθος· E/ τόδε τὸ πάθος, B et E s.l. ἔκλειψις ἐστὶν ἡλίου, σύνοδος σκιᾶς σελήνης, ἧς EB/ οἷς E i.t. τὴν ἔκλειψιν· ... ἐκείνοις γὰρ μόνοις ἔκλειψις ἐστιν· ὧν ἂν ἡ σκιὰ τῆς σελήνης καταλαβοῦσα τὴν ὄψιν ἀντιφράξαι πρὸς τὸν ἥλιον·

The passage seems to transmit the idea that a solar eclipse does not obscure everything, but only the part that is affected by the cone of umbra, namely that there is an eclipse only for those that are in the spot covered by the shadow. Unfortunately, the combination of several divergences between the manuscripts (τὸ δὲ πάθος· against τόδε τὸ πάθος, and ἧς against οἷς), an extensive lacuna—22 letters in E and 11 letters in B—, together with the problematic infinitive at the end of the passage complicates a proper understanding, which gives raise to a rather problematic definition of the phaenomenon of the eclipse by Posidonius.

Let us start with the lacuna, given that conjectures affect the syntax of the rest of the passage. Wyttenbach (in the apparatus) not only supplied the lacuna, but also deeply modified the transmitted text: ὁρισάμενος, ὅτι τόδε τὸ πάθος τῆς ὄψεως ἔστιν οὐχ ἡλίου, καὶ σύνοδος σκιᾷ σελήνης ἣν δὴ ἔκλειψιν ⟨ἡλίου καλοῦμεν· ὁμολογῶν γε⟩; Bernardakis (also in the apparatus) modified the text and sup-

---

116   Adler, *Dissertationes philologae Vindobonenses*, 107.
117   The Aldine and the *Basiliensis* editions transmitted the pronoun ἐκείνης, a mistake probably caused by iotacism, reason why ἐκείνης was replaced with EB's reading ἐκείνοις by Leonicus, Turnebus and Amyot in their personal copies. Oddly, none of the modern editors signaled that manuscripts differ in one reading: B and E *supra lineam* present τόδε τὸ πάθος, while E presents τὸ δὲ πάθος. See Appendix 2 on this emendation by E.

plied the lacuna: ⟨ἡ σελήνης σκιᾷ γ⟩ῆς τὴν ἔκλειψιν ⟨οὐκ ὀρθῶς ὡρίσατο⟩ ἐκείνοις κέ; Adler corrected σύνοδος σκιᾶς σελήνης, ἧς τὴν ἔκλειψιν into σύνοδος σελήνῃ, ἧς σκιὰ τὴν ἔκλειψιν and supplied the lacuna with τοῖς ἀφωτίστοις τῆς γῆς μέρεσι ποιεῖ ὀρθῶς μὲν μείζονα τὴν γῆν εἶναι τῆς ὑπέθετο; Purser reversed the order of the syntagmata τόδε τὸ πάθος and τὴν ἔκλειψιν and supplied the lacuna with ἂν ᾖ ταὐτό πως λέγει; Prickard deleted τὴν ἔκλειψιν; this option was accepted by Cherniss who also accepted the pronoun οἷς provided by E and supplied the lacuna with ἂν γῆς μέρεσι κατασκιάζῃ; Görgemanns deleted σύνοδος, turned σκιά into σκιᾶς and supplied the lacuna with ποιεῖ, τούτοις ἐπισκοτοῦσα.[118]

Differently, I suggest a conjecture that does not imply the modification of the transmitted text, however complex it might look at first: with the addition of a verb of affection followed by a point above the line (πάθουσιν·) and the selection of the more suitable readings among the divergences in the manuscripts (τόδε τὸ πάθος and οἷς), the text provides the required reasoning, namely that a solar eclipse is the concurrence of the shadow of the moon with the people that are affected by the shadow.

Concerning the issue with the infinitive transmitted by EB, ἀντιφράξαι, it is unfitting for the sentence's grammar, which needs a main verb in optative or subjunctive, because of the presence of ἄν.[119] It was soon changed by an annotation in Turnebus' Aldine copy into ἀντιφράξῃ, a correction accepted by modern scholars.

| | |
|---|---|
| 933A 9–10 | Ἐπιβάλλει δέ, ἐκείνῳ μὲν ἀφ' ἑσπέρας, ἡ σελήνη πρὸς αὐτὸν ἁμιλλωμένη, ταύτῃ δὲ ἀπὸ τῶν ἀνατολῶν, ὡς πρὸς τοὐναντίον ὑποφερομένη. |
| EB | ἐπιβάλλει δὲ ἐκείνῳ μὲν ἀφ' ἑσπέρας ἡ σελήνη πρὸς αὐτὸν ἁμιλλωμένη· ταύτῃ δὲ ἀπὸ τῶν ἀνατολῶν, ὡς πρὸς τοὐναντίον ὑποφερομένη· |

Several modern scholars believe that the passage needs emendation, since, while the subject is expressed in the first sentence (ἡ σελήνη), it is lacking in the second one. In order to solve this, Madvig suggested the addition of ἡ γῆ after ταύτῃ δέ. More complexly, Adler stated that what covers the moon in 932F is the earth's shadow, not the earth itself, which is the reason why he added ἡ σκιὰ τῆς γῆς after ἀπὸ τῶν ἀνατολῶν, thus paralleling the order of elements in

---

[118] Adler, *Dissertationes philologae Vindobonenses*, 109; Purser, "Mr. Prickard's Translation," 315—he noted that a definition of an eclipse would hardly include the noun ἔκλειψιν—; Prickard, *Plutarch on The Face*, 58; and Görgemanns, *Untersuchungen zu Plutarchs Dialog*, 144.

[119] See LSJ II and *DGE* B II for the use of ἄν with subjunctive to indicate limitation or condition.

COMMENTARY TO THE CRITICAL EDITION                                                159

the first sentence: ἐκείνῳ μὲν ἀφ᾽ ἑσπέρας ἡ σελήνη—ταύτῃ δὲ ἀπὸ τῶν ἀνατολῶν ἡ σκιὰ τῆς γῆς.[120]

Perhaps, the text needs no intervention, if the syntax is interpreted differently. In the first part of the passage, ἡ σελήνη πρὸς αὐτὸν ἁμιλλωμένη does not function as a subject, but as an apposition to the subject, which is expressed in the previous sentence: τὸ ἐπιπροσθοῦν. This is also the subject in the second part of the passage, which is the reason why there is no need to introduce any modifications.

It should be noted that the manuscripts' participle ὑποφερομένη must be interpreted as a dative: it modifies the moon, whose last occurrence is the pronoun ταύτῃ, which parallels the structure of the previous sentence: ἐκείνῳ μέν—ταύτῃ δέ.[121] Because the Aldine edition transmitted the participle as a nominative, most scholars—with the exception of the RJ94 copy and the *Basiliensis* edition, which read, indeed, the dative—have assumed that the manuscripts meant ὑποφερομένη, and that it modifies the subject that they themselves introduced in the text—ἡ γῆ, or ἡ σκιὰ τῆς γῆς.[122] The participle, however, modifies the moon, which is undertaken by the shadow.

| | |
|---|---|
| 933EF 5–10 | Ἔδει τοίνυν διὰ τοσούτων χρόνων φαίνεσθαι τὴν σελήνην ἐν τῇ σκιᾷ λαμπρυνομένην, ἡ δέ, ἐν ⟨αὐτῇ⟩ μὲν ἐκλείπει καὶ ἀπόλλυσι τὸ φῶς, ἀναλαμβάνει δὲ αὖθις ὅταν ἐκφύγῃ τὴν σκιάν [...] Εἰπόντος δὲ τοῦτο τοῦ Λευκίου, συνεξέδραμον ἅμα πως τῷ ⟨λέγειν⟩ ὅ τε Φαρνάκης καὶ ὁ Ἀπολλωνίδης· |
| EB | ἔδει τοίνυν διὰ τοσούτων χρόνων φαίνεσθαι τὴν σελήνην ἐν τῇ σκιᾷ λαμπρυνομένην· ἡ δέ, ἐν ... μὲν ἐκλείπει καὶ ἀπόλλυσι τὸ φῶς· ἀναλαμβάνει δὲ αὖθις ὅταν ἐκφύγῃ τὴν σκιάν· [...] εἰπόντος δὲ τοῦτο τοῦ λευκίου, συνεξέδραμον ἅμα πως τῷ ... ὅ τε φαρνάκης καὶ ὁ ἀπολλωνίδης· |

A series of short lacunae have been transmitted at the end of 933 and at the beginning of 934. In order to simplify the commentary, I will discuss them in separate headings.

The first lacuna occupies five letters in both manuscripts; it appears after ἡ δέ, ἐν and is followed by the particle μέν that correlates with ἀναλαμβάνει δέ later

---

120  Madvig, *Adversaria critica*, 665; Adler, *Dissertationes philologae Vindobonenses*, 109.
121  The manuscripts do not write down the subscribed iota. See footnote 4 in "Editorial Criteria" for another example in which this issue has given rise to different interpretations of a passage.
122  The Aldine edition, in fact, also claimed the nominative for the pronoun (ταύτη).

on in the same sentence. The context clearly points to the disappearance of the moon's light, as opposed to its reappearance when escaping the shadow (ἀναλαμβάνει δὲ αὖθις ὅταν ἐκφύγῃ τὴν σκιάν), and the preposition ἐν further points to the place where the moon is eclipsed: a dative is needed.

An annotation in RJ94 suggests the addition of σκιᾷ; Wyttenbach proposed (in the apparatus) τῇ σκιᾷ; Cherniss followed the latter in the text, but added (in the apparatus) αὐτῇ as another possibility—the pronoun obviously refers to the syntagma ἐν τῇ σκιᾷ in the preceding sentence.[123] Cherniss' suggestion is appealing, insofar as it avoids the repetition of the same substantive three times in the same passage (ἐν τῇ σκιᾷ, τῇ σκιᾷ, and τὴν σκιάν), which is the reason why I integrate it in the body of the text.

The second lacuna, a blank after τῷ that has approximately six letters, does not seem to compromise the general sense of the sentence but needs to be completed in order to provide all the required syntactical elements. An annotation in the Aldine RJ94 suggested αὐτῳ; Amyot suggested λόγῳ ἐπιβαλλόμενοι, which, despite being too long for the space of the manuscripts, seems to point in the right direction by including the noun λόγος; Wyttenbach (in the apparatus) supplied the lacuna only with this noun (λόγῳ); later scholars played with this term in its verbal form: Raingeard suggested (in the apparatus) λήγοντι; Pohlenz (also in the apparatus) and Cherniss both proposed as their own λέγειν.

The infinitive better conveys the notion of finality required by the context.[124] Given the high number of occurrences of τῷ followed by λέγειν in Plutarch's work, I opt to include Pohlenz's and Cherniss' conjecture in the text.[125]

| | |
|---|---|
| 933F 13–15 | Ὁ δὲ Ἀπολλωνίδης ἐνέστη περὶ τῆς σκιᾶς· ἀεὶ γὰρ οὕτως ... ὀνομάζειν τοὺς μαθηματικοὺς τὸν ἀλαμπῆ τόπον ... σκιάν τε μὴ δέχεσθαι τὸν οὐρανόν. |
| EB | ὁ δὲ ἀπολλωνίδης ἐνέστη περὶ τῆς σκιᾶς· ἀεὶ γὰρ οὕτως ... ὀνομάζειν E / οὕτως ὀνομάζειν ... B τοὺς μαθηματικοὺς τὸν ἀλαμπῆ τόπον ... σκιάν τε μὴ δέχεσθαι τὸν οὐρανόν· |

According to both manuscripts, the current text includes two lacunae, but, at first glance, the section does not seem to lack anything. Besides, the first lacuna is registered in different places by both manuscripts: while E has a gap of three letters before the infinitive ὀνομάζειν, B has a gap of six letters after it. Filling

---

[123] Wyttenbach mistakenly attributed the whole syntagma to RJ94.
[124] E. Crespo, L. Conti, & H. Maquieira, (eds.), *Sintaxis del griego clásico* (Madrid: Gredos, 2003) 419.
[125] According to the *TLG*, τῷ λέγειν has 25 occurrences.

B's lacuna was first initiated by an annotation in the Aldine RJ94 that proposed to supply πάντα; Amyot suggested ὄντως. Kepler was the first scholar to delete the lacuna (he commented "*videtur nihil deesse*"). Raingeard followed E and suggested a preverb for the infinitive to fill the gap (ἐξονομάζειν). And, lastly, Pohlenz (in the apparatus) provided two options: the first, to fill E's blank, was μόνον; and the second, for B's blank, supplied κατά in the lacuna after transforming ἀεί into δεῖν.[126]

The second lacuna, of approximately four letters in E and seven letters in B, comes after τὸν ἀλαμπῆ τόπον. In the wake of the Aldine and the *Basiliensis* editions, most modern scholars deleted it; Pohlenz, however, suggested (in the apparatus) two options, each of them in correlation with each of the conjectures for the previous lacuna: the first was ἐπὶ γῆς and the second, μόνον.

Given that the sentence stands on its own and does not need any grammatical or syntactical element to be understood, I tend to agree with the scholars that deleted the lacunae.

934A 16–20  "τὸν γὰρ ἀντιφραττόμενον ὑπὸ τῆς γῆς τόπον εἰ μὴ σκιάν τις ἐθέλοι καλεῖν ἀλλ' ἀφεγγὲς χωρίον, ὅμως ἀναγκαῖον ἐν αὐτῷ τὴν σελήνην γενομένην ... Καὶ ὅλως" ἔφη "εὔηθές ἐστιν ἐκεῖ μὴ φάναι τῆς γῆς ἐξικνεῖσθαι τὴν σκιάν ⟨ὅθεν⟩ ἡ σκιὰ τῆς σελήνης ἐπιπίπτουσα τῇ ὄψει καὶ ... πρὸς τὴν γῆν ἔκλειψιν ἡλίου ποιεῖ."[127]

EB  τὸν γὰρ ἀντιφραττόμενον ὑπὸ τῆς γῆς τόπον. εἰ μὴ σκιάν τις ἐθέλοι καλεῖν ἀλλ' ἀφεγγὲς χωρίον, ὅμως ἀναγκαῖον ἐν αὐτῷ τὴν σελήνην γενομένην ... καὶ ὅλως ἔφην εὐηθές ἐστιν ἐκεῖ μὴ φᾶναι τῆς γῆς ἐξικνεῖσθαι τὴν σκιάν ... ἡ σκιὰ τῆς σελήνης ἐπιπίπτουσα τῇ ὄψει καὶ ... πρὸς τὴν γῆν, ἔκλειψιν ἡλίου ποιεῖν·

Lamprias' answer to Apollonides' remark, concerning the lack of shadow in the universe, has been transmitted with three lacunae and a minor textual issue regarding the last verb, ποιεῖν. Nevertheless, from the beginning of the passage, it is clear that Lamprias refutes the problem raised by Apollonides: whether we call the space "shadow" or "lightless" does not change the fact that the moon moves to that place and is eclipsed.

The first lacuna appears after the participle γενομένην: E has a gap of 30 letters, and B has a gap of 34 letters. The grammar requires, at least, an infinitive that modifies the subject of the subordinate clause, τὴν σελήνην. Futhermore,

---

126  Kepler, *Ioh. Keppleri Mathematici*, 144.
127  The infinitive φάναι is correctly accentuated by the Aldine and the *Basiliensis* editions, while both manuscripts read φᾶναι.

the context demands that the lacking verb specifies how the moon reacts when caught in the lightless spot. If the moon is an earthy body—as Lamprias and Lucius defend—it should disappear out of sight; if it is a star—as the Stoics defend—it should shine even more. Among the conjectures proposed over the centuries, it is possible to distinguish two trends.

In the consideration that the moon is earthy, Amyot conjectured two possibilities, either ἐξαμαυροῦσθαι or ἐκκλείψαι; Wyttenbach proposed (in the apparatus) σκοτοῦσθαι; Bernardakis (also in the apparatus) accepted Wyttenbach's conjecture and added another infinitive, σκοτοῦσθαι καὶ ἀμαυροῦσθαι; Adler supplied the lacuna with ἐπιπροσθεῖσθαι ὑπὸ τῆς γῆς καὶ ἐκλείπειν; Purser, with εἴ γε γῆ τίς ἐστι, ἀφεγγῆ καὶ ἀλαμπῆ γενέσθαι; Pohlenz conjectured (in the critical apparatus) two options, the first agreeing with the earthy nature, καὶ ἐπισκοτουμένην ἄστρον μὴ εἶναι; and Cherniss suggested ἐπισκοτεῖσθαι τοῦ ἡλιακοῦ φωτὸς στερομένην.[128] Siding with the second trend, the star-like nature of the moon, an annotation in RJ94 suggested μᾶλλον λάμπειν καὶ διαφαίνεσθαι, and Pohlenz, as second option, suggested εἴ γ' ἄστρον ἐστίν, καὶ μᾶλλον ἐκλάμπειν.

Lucius had already distinctly refuted the Stoic theory of the moon as a star-like body, because, as he says, it should be concealed when it shines (933E, Ἔδει τοίνυν διὰ τοσούτων χρόνων φαίνεσθαι τὴν σελήνην ἐν τῇ σκιᾷ λαμπρυνομένην, ἡ δέ, ἐν ⟨αὐτῇ⟩ μὲν ἐκλείπει καὶ ἀπόλλυσι τὸ φῶς, ἀναλαμβάνει δὲ αὖθις ὅταν ἐκφύγῃ τὴν σκιάν). Furthermore, here, Lamprias is specifically answering Apollonides' concern, so he is not yet speaking to Pharnaces. Consequently, Lamprias would not again be refuting the Stoic view on the moon, which means that we can disprove the conjectures by RJ94 and Pohlenz. Given the large dimension of the lacuna in both manuscripts, however, I prefer to maintain the lacuna in the body of text.

The second lacuna affects Lamprias' new thought on the shadows of both the earth and the moon and breaks the sentence in the middle: between τῆς γῆς ἐξικνεῖσθαι τὴν σκιάν and ἡ σκιὰ τῆς σελήνης there is a void of eleven letters in E and a void of eight letters in B. The text lacks a correlative adverb that connects both parts: an annotation in RJ94 proposed ὅπου; Amyot, ὅθεν; Bernardakis (in the apparatus), ἔνθαπερ; Purser, ὁπόθεν καί; Pohlenz (in the apparatus), ὅθεν ἔοικεν; and Raingeard accepted ὅπου and suggested (in his commentary) the further addition of δύναται.[129]

---

128   Adler, *Dissertationes philologae Vindobonenses*, 109; and Purser, "Mr. Prickard's Translation," 315.

129   Purser, "Mr. Prickard's Translation," 315; and Raingeard, *Le peri toy prosopoy*, 114. Cherniss accepted Purser's ὁπόθεν καί and interpreted that it is the sense implied by Amyot's translation.

COMMENTARY TO THE CRITICAL EDITION 163

Despite the effort of the editors to take the lacuna's length into account, statistically, the low chances for ἔνθαπερ, ὁπόθεν καί and ὅθεν ἔοικεν to be the correct conjecture compel me to dismiss them; between RJ94's and Amyot's proposals, I chose the latter because it is far more common in Plutarch's vocabulary.[130]

The third lacuna, of seven letters in both manuscripts, is placed after the conjunction καί, which suggests that a second participle was coordinated with ἐπιπίπτουσα, and its meaning must have been concerned with the moon's relation with the earth, given that its complement is πρὸς τὴν γῆν. There are only three conjectures so far suggested for this lacuna: an annotation in RJ94 proposed διήκουσα, which has been accepted by most modern scholars; and Amyot proposed either ἀντερείδουσα or φερομένη. Here again, the possibilities for the selection of the proper verb are vast, which is the reason why I do not include any in the body of text.

A final, minor problem in the passage concerns the verb ποιεῖν. While transmitted by both manuscripts as an infinitive, it necessarily must be changed into a personal form, given that the subject is ἡ σκιὰ τῆς σελήνης. I, along with all scholars, accept RJ94's correction into ποιεῖ.

935B 7–9   τό γε μὴν τίμιον οὐκ ἀπόλλυσι τῆς δόξης οὐδὲ τὸ θεῖον ἡ σελήνη· ἥτις ... ἱερὰ πρὸς ἀνθρώπων νομιζομένη, μᾶλλον ἢ πῦρ θολερόν, ὥσπερ οἱ Στωικοὶ λέγουσι, καὶ τρυγῶδες·

EB          τό γε μὴν τίμιον οὐκ ἀπόλλυσι τῆς δόξης οὐδὲ τὸ θεῖον ἡ σελήνη· ἥτις ... ἱερὰ πρὸς ἀνθρώπων νομιζομένη· ἢ μᾶλλον πῦρ θολερὸν ὥσπερ οἱ στωικοὶ λέγουσι καὶ τρυγῶδες·

Two issues should be discussed in this section: while the main one is the lacuna after ἥτις, there is also a minor difficulty that concerns the reading ἢ μᾶλλον.

As far as the lacuna is concerned, it is a blank space of 10 letters in E and 13 letters in B. The sense of the passage is clear, despite the lacuna: Lamprias praises the sacred nature of the moon and compares it with the highly esteemed earth. Most scholars, however, opt to make the comparison with the earth more explicit by introducing a noun referring to it. An annotation in RJ94 simply supplied the lacuna with γῆ; Amyot corrected ἥτις into γὴ τις (*sic*) and supplied the lacuna with ὀλύμπια καί; Wyttenbach, differently, suggested (in the apparatus)

---

130   According to the *TLG*, among the three first options, ὅθεν ἔοικεν appears in Plutarch's work only in one occurrence. Between ὅπου and ὅθεν, the latter counts with approximately 200 cases more than the former.

ἥ τις θεὸς διατελεῖ καί; Emperius offered γῆ τις instead of ἥτις and deleted the lacuna; Bernardakis stated that Emperius' correction was ἥτις γῆ τις and proposed as his own, γῆ τις, as well as ὀλύμπια καί.[131]

While Amyot's suggestion is interesting, it has been accepted on the grounds of the expression γῆν οὖσαν ὀλυμπίαν used a few lines below (935C) and ὀλυμπίαν γῆν in *De defectu* 416E. In neither of those passages does Plutarch connect ὀλύμπια with ἱερά. While *De defectu* highlights the moon's mixed nature, *De facie* highlights its sacredness. Lamprias distinctly refers to this trait, not only here by the use of ἱερά, but also in the previous sentence with τό γε μὴν τίμιον [...] τῆς δόξης οὐδὲ τὸ θεῖον ἡ σελήνη. The reasons adduced to supply the lacuna with ὀλύμπια are, consequently, not fully convincing.

Kepler, for his part, did not supply the lacuna, nor introduced the noun earth, but corrected ἱερά into ἀερία, interpreting the moon to be an "aerial earth," which is a beautiful image but an unnecessary modification of the text.[132]

In what regards the difficulty with the reading ἢ μᾶλλον, the presence of ἢ in first place supposes the construction of two options in which the second option is considered to be better than the first ('this or rather that'). Here, however, Lamprias presents the moon's earthy nature as the first option and the Stoic view of its fiery nature as the second option. It is hardly conceivable that Lamprias suggests the Stoic theory as the best option, especially taking into account that the following sentence connects fire with barbaric traditions (935B, πῦρ μέν γε παρὰ Μήδοις καὶ Ἀσσυρίοις βαρβαρικὰς ἔχει τιμάς). In fact, Lamprias defends the opposite point of view; therefore, the first alternative must be preferred to the second one. Thus, an annotation in the Aldine RJ94 inverted the order into μᾶλλον ἤ.

936EF 16–18   Καίτοι καὶ ταῦτα δήπουθεν, ἐὰν ἀμυχή τις ἢ ῥύπος ἢ τραχύτης καταλάβῃ τὸ σημεῖον [ἂν] ἀφ' οὗ πέφυκεν ἡ ὄψις ἀνακλᾶσθαι, τυποῦται, καὶ βλέπεται μὲν αὐτά, τὴν δὲ ἀνταύγειαν οὐκ ἀποδίδωσιν.[133]

---

131   Emperius, *Opuscula*, 292. Three scholars corrected the relative pronoun into a noun and an indefinite pronoun and claimed the authorship for it. Later scholars maintained the error of attribution. The whole correction, as a matter of fact, was already proposed by Amyot in the 16th century.

132   Kepler, *Ioh. Keppleri Mathematici*, 146.

133   The Aldine edition made the mistake of reading ταραχύτης in place of τραχύτης—and once again a bit below, in 937C, with ταραχύτητα instead of τραχύτητα. Annotations in the Aldine copies of Forteguerri, Leonicus and Turnebus corrected it into the manuscripts' reading; the *Basiliensis* edition and those of Stephanus and Xylander corrected it into ταραχή τις.

EB  καίτοι καὶ ταῦτα δήπουθεν ἐὰν ἀμυχή τις ἢ ῥύπος ἢ τραχύτης καταλάβῃ, τὸ σημεῖον ἂν ἀφ' οὗ πέφυκεν ἡ ὄψις ἀνακλασθὲν τυποῦται. καὶ βλέπεται μὲν αὐτὰ τὴν δὲ ἀνταύγειαν οὐκ ἀποδίδωσιν·

The passage presents a few difficulties: a) an erroneous modal particle (ἄν); b) a missing infinitive; c) the problematic participle ἀνακλασθέν; and d) a dubious pronoun (αὐτά).

Concerning the particle ἄν, not only there is no verb in subjunctive or optative that could legitimate it, but, in fact, the construction of the passage does not need one. Perhaps the transmission of ἄν was influenced by the preceding ἐάν, which has its own verb (καταλάβῃ). This sentence, however, is the main clause on which the previous conditional depends, and thus there is no need for verbal forms other than indicative. In line with Wyttenbach and most of the subsequent editors, I delete the particle.

Next is the issue of the missing infinitive, which is required by the presence of πέφυκεν. Some scholars sought it in the problematic participle (ἀνακλασθέν): Kepler suggested to transform it into ἀνακλᾶσθαι; Dübner, into ἀνακλασθῆναι.[134] Amyot, differently, looked for the missing infinitive in one of the main verbs, τυποῦται. This, however, compelled him to delete the following conjunction καί. Amyot also corrected the dubious participle neuter nominative singular (ἀνακλασθέν) into the equivalent in feminine (ἀνακλασθεῖσα) so that it modifies ἡ ὄψις. The participle in neuter is evidently an erratum, given that it is included in the relative clause and therefore must modify an element within that clause. Perhaps, the mistake was due to the close presence of τὸ σημεῖον, which, however, is part of the main clause, not of the relative clause.

Kepler's correction provides the most suitable solution. On the one hand, from the point of view of textual transmission, the similarity in sound between the final syllables of both the participle (ἀνακλασθέν) and the infinitive (ἀνακλᾶσθαι) sufficiently explains the corruption; on the other, the replacement of the participle, with no noun to modify, into the required infinitive avoids further modifications, such as that of the main verb.

Despite this, Dübner suggested to replace the verb τυπόω with τυφλόω (τυφλοῦται), a modification which is accepted by all following scholars except Raingeard. I follow the latter who thought that the meaning of τυπόω, 'to mark an imprint,' fits in the context, especially when related to mirrors receiving dirt and scratches.

---

134 Kepler, *Ioh. Keppleri Mathematici*, 151; Bernardakis accepted Kepler's emendation, but strangely attributed it to Wyttenbach, and so Cherniss, who attributed it to Bernardakis. Pohlenz transmitted Dübner's emendation, but claimed it as his own.

Concerning the pronoun αὐτά, it can be interpreted in two ways. Either the pronoun relates to ταῦτα, namely the mirrors, and can be maintained; or it refers to τὸ σημεῖον and needs to be corrected. The latter option is chosen by Leonicus, who wrote in the margin of his Aldine copy αὐτό. In this sense, ταῦτα functions as the subject of the first part of the sentence and τὸ σημεῖον as subject of the rest. This is not the case, however, since that leaves us with no verb for the first subject. As a matter of fact, the entire passage has the mirrors as its subject, with its three main verbs (τυποῦται, βλέπεται and ἀποδίδωσιν), while τὸ σημεῖον is the object within the conditional clause. The pronoun αὐτά, therefore, is a mere actualization of the subject.

937AB 1–3   τὰ δὲ κυρτὰ καὶ τὰ σφαιροειδῆ, τῷ μὴ πανταχόθεν ἀντερείδειν ἀσθενῆ
            καὶ ἀμαυράν· ... ὁρᾶται δήπουθεν, ὅταν ἴριδες δύο φανῶσι, νέφους
            νέφος ἐμπεριέχοντος, ἀμαυρὰν ποιοῦσαν καὶ ἀσαφῆ τὰ χρώματα τὴν
            περιέχουσαν.[135]

EB           τὰ δὲ κυρτὰ καὶ τὰ σφαιροειδῆ E/ καὶ σφαιροειδῆ B, τῷ μὴ παντα-
            χόθεν ἀντερείδειν ἀσθενῆ καὶ ἀμαυράν· ...· ὁρᾶται δήπουθεν· ὅταν
            ἴριδες δύο φανῶσι νέφους νέφος ἐμπεριέχοντος, ἀμαυρὰν ποιοῦσαν
            καὶ ἀσαφῆ τὰ χρώματα τὴν περιέχουσαν·

The passage includes a couple of difficulties: firstly, both manuscripts include a lacuna; and secondly, the words ὁρᾶται and ἀμαυράν, in the last part of the passage, have been modified.

In what concerns the lacuna, it appears after ἀσθενῆ καὶ ἀμαυράν: E presents a 13-letter-gap and B presents a 17-letter-gap. The preceding sentence has complete sense, and both manuscripts present a point above the line after ἀμαυράν, which suggests that no text is missing. The following sentence seems to be complete as well: Lamprias is about to provide a practical example of the way in which convex and spherical mirrors operate.

Different conjectures supply the lacuna with a verb in 3rd person to display a parallel structure between this section and the previous part of the passage,

---

135   The second occurrence of τά is omitted in B, and although it is gramatically correct, E offers a better syntax. All editions from the 16th century transmitted B's reading, and so did Wyttenbach without noting, in the apparatus, that E provides a different reading. The editions of Basel and Xylander read the particle μέν instead of the negative μή. The editions of the 16th century and Wyttenbach, without stating in the apparatus that this was not the manuscripts' reading, all transmitted περιτρέχουσαν instead of περιέχουσαν. This form, whether is due to a conscious modification of EB or an accident, does not offer a better meaning and should not be accepted.

starting with τὰ μέν (937A, τὰ μὲν κοῖλα τῶν ἐσόπτρων, εὐτονωτέραν ποιεῖ τῆς προ-ηγουμένης αὐγῆς τὴν ἀνακλωμένην). Amyot wrote ποιεῖ; Bernardakis conjectured (in the apparatus) ἀποδίδωσιν; Adler, αὐτὴν ἀναδίδωσιν; Raingeard (in the apparatus), αὐγὴν ἀποδίδωσιν; and Pohlenz proposed (also in the apparatus) μᾶλλον ἀποδίδωσιν.[136] All are small variations around the same idea, none of which is not mandatory. The verb ποιεῖ, of the previous section, can be applied here even if omitted.

Concerning the modifications in the last part of the passage, the first is the verbal form in 3rd person singular, ὁρᾶται. Ever since an annotation in RJ94 corrected the indicative into the imperative ὁρᾶτε, most scholars have accepted the emendation on the grounds that Lamprias is requiring the attention of his audience in order to introduce the practical example. The reading of EB, however, is not necessarily mistaken and can be maintained.

The second intervention concerns ἀμαυράν. The accusative singular was understood as a mistake probably due to the two occurrences of participles in accusative singular in this sentence (ποιοῦσαν and τὴν περιέχουσαν) and corrected in order to coordinate with ἀσαφῆ, both depending on τὰ χρώματα. The emendation into ἀμαυρά was suggested by Amyot under the erroneously accentuated form ἄμαυρα; Kepler (in the notes to his Latin translation of the treatise) also transmitted it with the correct accent.[137] In my view, the reading ἀμαυράν can function as a predicative complement of the verb ὁρᾶται, and consequently needs no intervention.

| | |
|---|---|
| 937E 28 | τοὺς δὲ οἰκοῦντας αὖ πάλιν ἐπ' αὐτῆς ὥσπερ Ἰξίονας ἐνδεδεμένους ῥύμῃ τόσῃ ... |
| EB | τοὺς δὲ οἰκοῦντας αὖ πάλιν ἐπ' αὐτῆς ὥσπερ ἰξίονας ἐνδεδεμένους ῥύμῃ τόσῃ ... |

Both manuscripts report an extensive lacuna: E leaves an entire line blank (approximately 42 letters), and B leaves two half lines blank (32 letters). The sentence that precedes this lacuna is correlated with the previous one, as indicated by the construction τοῖς μέν—τοὺς δέ. They are both subordinate clauses depending on an infinitive, which functions as the object of the verb in personal form (φασί). The sentence that concerns us now lacks the infinitive that should function as the verb.

---

136  Adler, *Dissertationes philologae Vindobonenses*, 110.
137  It was not uncommon for Amyot to confuse the accents of a word, see headings in 920EF, 932BC, and 935B, for other occurrences. Kepler, *Ioh. Keppleri Mathematici*, 152.

Amyot suggested περικινεῖσθαι ὥστε μὴ πεσεῖν; Wyttenbach, for once, provided (in the apparatus) a simple conjecture, τοσαύτῃ δινεῖσθαι—where τοσαύτῃ is a correction of the demonstrative adjective τόσῃ, which modifies the substantive in dative ῥύμῃ—; Bernardakis followed him in the main text, but added in his apparatus the possibility of τοσαύτῃ περιδινεῖσθαι, ὥστ' ἐκπεσεῖν μὴ δύνασθαι; Adler proposed τοσαύτῃ κινουμένης ἀεὶ περιδινεῖσθαι, Purser suggested τοσαύτῃ καὶ δίνῃ περιφερομένους μὴ ἐκπεσεῖν, Pohlenz conjectured τοσαύτῃ περιδινουμήνης οὐδέποτ' ἐν ἀσφαλεῖ βεβηκέναι, although he also suggested, for the last part of his conjecture, the option ἡσυχίαν ἄγειν; Cherniss proposed τοσαύτῃ, τῆς καταφορᾶς κωλύειν τὴν κύκλῳ περιδίνησιν; and Görgemanns conjectured τοσαύτῃ πληγαῖς τοῦ περιέχοντος ἀέρος ἀεὶ χειμάζεσθαι.[138]

With the exception of Amyot, all other editors correct, unnecessarily, the adjective τόσῃ into τοσαύτῃ, some probably motivated by their use of ὥστε afterwards or in an effort to add letters to complete the space of the lacuna. A number of conjectures seem to understand the speed of the moon's movement as something that would prevent its possible inhabitants from falling. I am not fully convinced by this interpretation, since Theon's following words argue that the moon's velocity seems to make life on it impossible: the fact that we do not see people falling from the moon is in fact the proof, according to him. Perhaps, the sense of this passage was that those who live under the moon have the constant fear that it might fall upon them (like Tantalus), and those who live on it, even though fixed like Ixions, would fear to be ejected by such a high velocity. The lacuna, however, is too long to entertain any hypothesis as probable.

938B 17–18   ἀλλ' ... ἤδη καὶ σάλον ἔχων ὑπὸ κουφότητος ὁ ἀὴρ ἐκφεύγει τὴν σύστασιν ταύτην καὶ πύκνωσιν·

EB   ἀλλ' ... ἤδη καὶ σάλον ἔχων ὑπὸ κουφότητος ὁ ἀὴρ, ἐκφεύγει τὴν σύστασιν ταύτην καὶ πύκνωσιν·

Both manuscripts report a lacuna of 10 letters. After that space, we encounter the conjunction καί, followed by the noun σάλον and the participle ἔχων. It seems rather probable, then, that either a noun, or a combination of participle and complement, were in place of the current lacuna, coordinated with what follows.

---

138   Adler, *Dissertationes philologae Vindobonenses*, 110; Purser, "Mr. Prickard's Translation," 318; Görgemanns, *Untersuchungen zu Plutarchs Dialog*, 83. Cherniss, "Notes on Plutarch's *De facie*," 146, believed that what is said in this passage refers to Lucius' speech in 923C (ὥσπερ ὅσα ταῖς σφενδόναις ἐντεθέντα τῆς καταφορᾶς κώλυσιν ἴσχει τὴν κύκλῳ περιδίνησιν), which is the reason why Lucius' words should somehow be included in the lacuna.

Some scholars chose the first option: Wyttenbach proposed (in his apparatus) λεπτότητα; Purser, μάνωσιν; and Pohlenz conjectured (in the apparatus) διάχυσιν.[139] Other editors included the second option in their conjectures: Amyot proposed εἰλικρινὴς ὤν and corrected the text following the lacuna into ἤδη καὶ σάλον οὐκ ἔχων; Emperius also corrected the passage in the same idea: ἀλλὰ γαλήνην ἀσάλευτον ἔχον; Bernardakis conjectured (in the apparatus) two options, λεπτός and ἀραιὸς ὤν; and Pohlenz suggested another option, beside the substantive, seen above, καθαρὸς ὤν.[140]

Perhaps, given that the adversative previous to the lacuna is preserved as ἀλλ' and not ἀλλά, a noun or a participle beginning with a vowel would be most probable. However, the lack of any certainty makes it preferable not to include these possibilities in the main body of the text.

938BC 22–24  Τὴν μὲν γὰρ Ἰνδικὴν ῥίζαν, ἥν φησι Μεγασθένης τοὺς μήτε πίνοντας, ἀλλ' ἀστόμους ὄντας ὑποτύφειν καὶ θυμιᾶν καὶ τρέφεσθαι τῇ ὀσμῇ, πόθεν ἄν τις ἐκεῖ φυομένην λάβοι μὴ βρεχομένης τῆς σελήνης;

EB  τὴν μὲν γὰρ ἰνδικὴν ῥίζαν ἥν φησὶ μεγασθένης τοὺς μήτε πίνοντας, ἀλλ' εὐστόμους ὄντας ὑποτύφειν καὶ θυμιᾶν καὶ τρέφεσθαι τῇ ὀσμῇ, πόθεν ἄν τις ἐκεῖ φυομένην λάβοι μὴ βρεχομένης τῆς σελήνης·

This passage poses two problems, both are related to the description of certain men, who do not drink and, as a result, only feed on vapors. The first problem arises from the presence of μήτε πίνοντας with no correlation; the second concerns the qualification εὐστόμους. Additionally, one minor issue concerns the passage's punctuation.

Regarding the first difficulty, some scholars thought that a section of the text is missing: to begin with there is the presence of μήτε πίνοντας with no correlation; then, the fact that "not drinking" does not provide a strong argument to explain the tradition of smoking vapors. Thus, Leonicus suggested the inclusion of μήτε ἐσθίοντας after the article (τοὺς μήτε ἐσθίοντας μήτε πίνοντας); Stephanus accepted Leonicus' conjecture, and, furthermore, eliminated the preceding article.

Perhaps, the sense of the text can be maintained without any intervention. The negation can be understood through the definition 'not even,' in which case, men who cannot even drink would also not be able to consume solid food,

---

139   Purser, "Mr. Prickard's Translation," 318.
140   Emperius, *Opuscula*, 293.

which is the reason why they have no option other than to feed through the smoke and vapours from a root.[141]

Concerning the second problem, the non-drinking men are described as εὐστόμους ὄντας. The meaning of the adjective, 'big-mouthed,' 'of a beautiful mouth,' or 'that which is pleasant to the palate,' certainly clashes with the rest of the passage. Forteguerri and Leonicus emended it by suggesting ἀστόμους; Dübner, Bernardakis and Raingerard, however, maintained the manuscripts' adjective, although neither LSJ nor Bailly provides the meaning they attribute to it: "sed ore prorsus casto puroque sint," "se gardent la bouche pure." Forteguerri's and Leonicus' suggestion is more suitable. I find reasonable justification for this emendation in other authors who also mention Megasthenes and these peculiar men together. Furthermore the confusion α/ευ is frequent in the manuscript transmission.[142]

Regarding the punctuation issue, it is necessary to correct the point above the line transmitted by both manuscripts. Theon is suggesting the improbability of a root growing on the moon's soil if it does not receive rainwater. The dubitative aspect of his statement is confirmed by the presence of the correlative adverb πόθεν. I follow Stephanus who was the first scholar to suggest the correction into a question mark.

938C 1–3   Ταῦτα τοῦ Θέωνος εἰπόντος, "⟨κάλλιστά⟩ γε" ἔφην "καὶ ἄριστα τῇ παιδιᾷ τοῦ λόγου τὰς ὀφρῦς ... ἃ καὶ θάρσος ἡμῖν ἐγγίνεται πρὸς τὴν ἀπόκρισιν, μὴ πάνυ πικρὰν μηδὲ αὐστηρὰν εὐθύνην προσδοκῶσι."[143]

---

141 According to the *TLG*, there are a few occurrences in Plutarch's work where μήτε appears with no correlation: see *Arist.* 3.4; *Flam.* 7.3; *Sept. sap. conv.* 153A; *De gar.* 514B.

142 See Pliny, *H.N.* 7.2, 25 and Strabo, *Geogr.* 2.1, 9 and 15.1, 57. For the confusion α/ευ, see West, *Textual Criticism and Editorial Technique*, 25, and, concerning specifically *De facie*, the comment in 945B with ἀπαθές (EB) and εὐπαθές (Leonicus' correction). The correction of Forteguerri and Leonicus was followed by many editors, although with misattributions again: Cherniss assigned it to the *Basiliensis* and the copy RJ94 and Raingeard indicated in his apparatus that ἀστόμους is a correction of the thin handwriting found in RJ94, while the thick one would suggest σύστομοι ἅ. Concerning Raingeard's strange note in the apparatus, I believe the second option actually refers to the correction proposed in 940B, which is a passage which comes back to the same creatures described here, and thus it is not a correction to the text itself. In fact, the case (nominative plural) corresponds to that later passage, not to the accusative plural we are dealing with here. See heading below for that passage.

143 It is rather striking that the Aldine edition, followed by those of Basel, Stephanus, Xylander and Wyttenbach all transmitted the verbal form περιδοκῶσι in place of προσδοκῶσι, for which there is no entry neither in LSJ nor in Bailly.

EB   ταῦτα τοῦ Θέωνος εἰπόντος, ... γε ἔφην καὶ ἄριστα τῇ παιδιᾷ τοῦ λόγου τὰς ὀφρῦς ... ἃ καὶ θάρσος ἡμῖν ἐγγίνεται πρὸς τὴν ἀπόκρισιν, μὴ πάνυ μικρὰν EB / πικρὰν B s.l. μὴ δὲ αὐστηρὰν εὐθύνην προσδοκῶσι.

There are two consecutive lacunae in this passage. After the genitive absolute ταῦτα τοῦ Θέωνος εἰπόντος, both manuscripts leave a gap of approximately eight letters; and after τὰς ὀφρῦς, another lacuna appears, of around 16 letters in the case of E and of 12 letters in the case of B.

The first lacuna appears after Theon just finishes his speech and Lamprias intervenes to congratulate him. Most probably, the lost section should include an adverb or an adjective in superlative degree with adverbial function coordinated with the following καὶ ἄριστα. We find several suggestions in this sense: Amyot proposed δεξιώτατα; Wyttenbach conjectured (in the critical apparatus) κάλλιστα; Raingeard suggested εὐκαίρως; and Cherniss, ὑπέρευ. Emperius, besides completing the lacuna, corrected the following text: he added καλῶς and substituted καὶ ἄριστα for καθαιρεῖς—thus providing the required verbal form that most scholars supply in the following lacuna (see below).[144] Wyttenbach's proposal is quite plausible: besides its simplicity, κάλλιστα frequently appears together with ἄριστος.[145]

Concerning the second lacuna, it effects the part in which Lamprias praises Theon's intervention. From the context, we know that the narrator applauds the participation of his colleague, that he underscores the ludic aspect that the meeting is acquiring—as opposed to the seriousness of the previous discussion—and that he is willing to reply to Theon's concerns without expecting a harsh or severe critique.

Immediately preceding the lacuna there is a reference to the eyebrows (τὰς ὀφρῦς)—it is a reference to facial expressions in general—which functions as the object of the sentence. Immediately following the lacuna there is the relative pronoun in adverbial function ἅ, which implies that the following καί must function as an adverb and not as a conjunction. The lacuna should then have included the main verb of the sentence, and given that Lamprias is directly addressing Theon in his reply, this verb must have been in 2nd person singular.

In fact, various conjectures affirm this direction: Amyot suggested ἀφήρηκας, and also corrected ἅ into ᾗ—this is an unnecessary modification since the relative has an adverbial function here. Wyttenbach, in turn, proposed ἡμῶν ἀνῆκας,

---

144 Emperius, *Opuscula*, 293.
145 According to the *TLG*, in Plutarch's work it specifically appears in superlative degree coordinated with ἄριστα four times, which makes it convincing enough to be integrated in the text.

δι' and erroneously corrected θάρσος into θάρσον; Bernardakis suggested ἡμῶν ἔλυσας· δι'; and Cherniss, ἡμῶν καθῆκας, δι'.

While I accept Wyttenbach's conjecture for the first lacuna, infinite possibilities could fit into the second one. If we add the fact that the general sense of the passage is clear from the context, adopting any of the conjectures is unnecessary.

938D 7–9   οὐδὲ γὰρ τήνδε τὴν γῆν δι' ὅλης ἐνεργὸν οὐδὲ προσοικουμένην ὁρῶμεν, ἀλλὰ μικρὸν αὐτῆς μέρος, ὥσπερ ἄκραις τισὶν ἢ χερρονήσοις ἀνεχούσης ἐκ βυθοῦ, γόνιμόν ἐστι ζῴων καὶ φυτῶν·[146]

EB   οὐδὲ γὰρ τήνδε τὴν γῆν δι' ὅλης ἐνεργὸν οὐδὲ προσοικουμένην ὁρῶμεν· ἀλλὰ μικρὸν αὐτῆς μέρος ὥσπερ ἄκροις τισὶν ἢ χερρονήσοις Ε / χεροννήσοις Β ἀνέχουσιν ἐκ βυθοῦ γόνιμόν ἐστι ζῴων καὶ φυτῶν·

This passage presents two textual complications related to one another: the adjective ἄκροις and the participle ἀνέχουσιν, both part of the comparison ὥσπερ ἄκροις τισὶν ἢ χερρονήσοις ἀνέχουσιν. They have been modified several times, because the construction ὥσπερ with dative is unusual.[147]

The Aldine edition changed the adjective into ἄκρως, noting a corruption that might be simply due to an erroneous reading. Forteguerri's annotation to his Aldine copy, however, changed it into ἄκραις. The fact is that this correction does not simplify the syntax, but makes it more complex: ἄκραις τισὶν and χερρονήσοις would, then, be two feminine words referring to a masculine or neuter participle (ἀνέχουσιν). This is the reason why an annotation in RJ94 changed the participle into neuter nominative singular (ἀνέχον), in order to match it with μέρος instead of with ἄκραις τισὶν ἢ χερρονήσοις. Emperius suggested another solution: he transformed the participle into feminine dative plural (ἀνεχούσαις); and Raingeard, who stressed (in his commentary) the syntactic problem, solved it by adding the preposition ἐν in front of the datives.[148] Pérez Jiménez accepted

---

146   The noun χερρονήσοις is correctly reported by E, while B transmits it with a single rho and two nu (χεροννήσοις). This form is maintained by the Aldine and Xylander's editions, and was corrected, erroneously, into χερονννήσοις by an annotation in RJ94—a correction that both Stephanus and Wyttenbach followed, the latter without commenting in the apparatus that it is not the manuscripts' reading.

147   On the construction, see the thoughts of A. Pérez Jiménez, "Las regiones fértiles de la tierra: nueva propuesta crítica a Plu., *De facie* 938D," in M. Sanz Morales, R. González Delgado, M. Librán Moreno & J. Ureña Bracero (eds.), *La (inter)textualidad en Plutarco. Actas del XII Simposio Internacional de la Sociedad Española de Plutarquistas* (Cáceres, 8–10 de Octubre de 2015) (Coimbra: Coimbra University Press, 2017) 44–46.

148   Emperius, *Opuscula*, 293; Raingeard, *Le peri toy prosopoy*, 127.

the correction ἄκραις and suggested to change the participle into a feminine genitive singular (ἀνεχούσης), thus, modifying the pronoun αὐτῆς, instead of μέρος.[149]

The emendation of RJ94 is hardly explainable: from a syntactical point of view, the corruption from a common neuter nominative singular into a problematic masculine or neuter dative plural is dubious, and, from a palaeographic point of view, there is no explanation. Emperius' correction does not solve the problem of the construction ὥσπερ with dative; and, in Raingeard's conjecture, it is difficult to explain the disappearance of ἐν. By inserting a genitive absolute, Pérez Jiménez's emendation solves both the problem posed by two feminine words referring to a particle neuter or masculine and that of the construction ὥσπερ with dative. Furthermore, the corruption from genitive singular (-ης) into dative plural (-ιν) could be explained as caused by an attraction to the surrounding datives; the corruption of the feminine adjective (-αις) into a masculine or neuter (-οις) would be motivated by the participle's previous corruption.

939A 1–4  εἰ δὲ μὴ δι' ἑαυτὴν καὶ τὸ ποικίλον τοῦτο τῆς φορᾶς καὶ πεπλανημένον οὐκ ἀνωμαλίας οὐδὲ ταραχῆς ἐστιν, ἀλλὰ θαυμαστὴν ἐπιδείκνυνται τάξιν ἐν τούτοις καὶ πορείαν οἱ ἀστρολόγοι κύκλοις τισὶ περὶ κύκλους ἑτέρους ἐξελιττομένοις συνάγοντες αὐτήν·

EB  εἰ δὲ μὴ δὲ αὐτὴ καὶ τὸ ποικίλον τοῦτο τῆς φορᾶς καὶ πεπλανημένον, οὐκ ἀνωμαλίας οὐδὲ ταραχῆς ἐστιν· ἀλλὰ θαυμαστὴν ἐπιδείκνυνται τάξιν ἐν τούτοις καὶ πορείαν οἱ ἀστρολόγοι κύκλοις τισι περὶ κύκλους ἑτέρους ἐξελιττομένοις συνάγοντες αὐτήν.

The main problem of the passage lies in its beginning—εἰ δὲ μὴ δὲ αὐτή in EB—but the verb ἐπιδείκνυται, in the second part of the passage, also poses some difficulties.

Concerning the beginning of the sentence, the pronoun αὐτή has caused some trouble for editors. Amyot suggested a very innovative correction, since he read εἰ μὴ καὶ αὐτή, where αὐτή refers to the moon, and attached this conditional to the previous sentence, thus stating: the only possibility for the inhabitants of the moon to fall is if the moon itself falls. Wyttenbach suggested (in the apparatus) ἔτι δὲ, νὴ Δι', αὐτό γε, which appears to overload the text with unnecessary interventions; Dübner proposed ἡ δὲ μεταλλαγή, a correction which was slightly modified by Bernardakis into ἡ τε μεταλλαγή. Raingeard was the only

---

149  Pérez Jiménez, "Las regiones fértiles," 46.

one to accept the manuscripts' text, pointing (in the commentary) to the reference δίνη and translating it as "la rotation à part."[150] Admittedly, αὐτή could refer to ἡ δίνη, mentioned a few lines above (938F), but, in that case, the syntax of the sentence needs to be adjusted. Pohlenz thought that the passage might be a *locus desperatus* but suggested (in the apparatus) ἤ τε μὴ διὰ μιᾶς κίνησις αὕτη; Cherniss corrected αὐτή into ἁπλῆ.

In my view, δίνη might be, indeed, the antecedent of the pronoun, not as the subject of the sentence, but as the cause for the moon's harmonious movement. Lamprias states that if the moon's harmonious movement is not convincingly explained by its rotation alone, then τὸ ποικίλον τοῦτο τῆς φορᾶς καὶ πεπλανημένον should also be added as cause. As a result, I propose to change δὲ αὐτή into δι' ἑαυτήν. The corruption is due to the transformation of the preposition into a particle by misplacing the epsilon; the disappearance of the preposition, in turn, explains the change of case.

Regarding the verb, ἐπιδείκνυται poses a problem, because it has been transmitted in singular and the subject of the sentence is οἱ ἀστρολόγοι. The mistake might have been caused by the presence of καὶ τὸ ποικίλον τοῦτο τῆς φορᾶς καὶ πεπλανημένον, which precedes the verb and could be interpreted as its subject—thus allowing a singular, since both are neuters. This interpretation, however, cannot be adopted, for οἱ ἀστρολόγοι would lack its verb. Additionally, the *Basiliensis* proposed the plural ἐπιδείκνυνται.[151]

939B 8–10    Τὴν δὲ πολλὴν θερμότητα καὶ συνεχῆ πύρωσιν ὑπὸ ἡλίου οὐ παύσῃ φοβούμενος ἂν πρῶτον μὲν ἀντιθεὶς ταῖς ⟨ἐνθάδε⟩ ἕνδεκα θερινὰς ⟨σὺν⟩ συνόδοις τὰς πανσελήνους,

EB           τὴν δὲ πολλὴν θερμότητα καὶ συνεχῆ πύρωσιν ὑπὸ ἡλίου E / ἡλίου οὐ B, E s.l. παύσῃ φοβούμενος ἂν πρῶτον μὲν ἀντιθῆς E / ἀντιθεὶς B ταῖς ἕνδεκα θερινᾶις συνόδοις τὰς πανσελήνους,

In this passage, Lamprias refutes Theon's theory (938A) according to which the excessive warmth due to 12 summer solstices—equivalent to the 12 full moons—would make any form of life impossible to subsist. The text, however, presents many dubious readings that must be dealt with separately.

Firstly, the beginning of the text reads, τὴν δὲ πολλὴν θερμότητα καὶ συνεχῆ πύρωσιν ὑπὸ ἡλίου οὐ παύσῃ φοβούμενος. The negation before παύσῃ φοβούμενος

---

150  Raingeard, *Le peri toy prosopoy*, 128.
151  This correction was accepted by most editors, although Wyttenbach and Bernardakis did not allude to the change—as if it were EB's reading—and Pohlenz, strangely enough, seems to have understood that the singular is E's reading only.

has often been regarded as an error, given that Lamprias seems to be making the opposite point: Theon can cease his fear of excessive warmth and continuous abrasions, because the situation is not as he described. All modern editors agreed on this point and eliminated the negation—although, Raingeard suggested (in his commentary) that the text could be maintained if a question mark is added to the sentence.[152]

This intervention, however, is actually motivated by additional modifications in the following text, which transformed it to say the opposite of its original form.[153] Lamprias, contrary to the general opinion, warns Theon that he will *not* cease to fear the excessive warmth if he insists on thinking the way he does. He then explains Theon's theory, in order to refute it.

Secondly, the numeral transmitted by EB, ἕνδεκα, has also been regarded as a mistake, for both Theon and Lamprias are dealing with the 12 full moons. Amyot changed it into the (too obvious) form δώδεκα. It is quite difficult to explain how a dubious ἕνδεκα would have found its way into the text, replacing a perfectly suitable δώδεκα. Purser suggested that perhaps the number 11 was given by accident on Plutarch's part, on the idea that the moon has 11 more summers than the earth.[154] I believe that Lamprias is indeed adding 11 to the one already mentioned by Theon in his speech, thus arriving, admittedly in a rather unorthodox way, to the expected 12. Thus, EB's reading can be maintained.

The third issue arises from the two syntagmata at the end of the passage, which are at the very least confusing: ταῖς—θεριναῖς συνόδοις τὰς πανσελήνους.[155] Given that editorial interventions have transformed the first part of the passage into an affirmative clause ('you will cease to fear'), they now try to introduce the reason for Theon not to fear the excessive warmth of the moon: while the 12 summery full moons (moon in opposition) might bring too much warmth, the 12 new moons in which the moon is occluded from the sun (in conjunction, as the text says) should, in turn, appease this warmth. Adler, followed by Raingeard and Cherniss, proposed the correction ταῖς—θεριναῖς πανσελήνοις τὰς συνόδους, and Bernardakis proposed τὰς—θερινὰς συνόδους ταῖς πανσελήνοις.[156]

---

152 Raingeard, *Le peri toy prosopoy*, 129.
153 Perhaps, the elimination of οὐ might not be conditioned only by following interventions in the sentence, but also by the odd way in which it is transmitted in E (see Appendix 2). It would seem as if the copyist transformed the ending of the preceding noun into a negative (ἡλίου), after which he added ου in abbreviated form above the line. Some editors might have interpreted this οὐ as a scribal mistake later maintained by the manuscripts copied from E and decided to eliminate it.
154 Purser, "Mr. Prickard's Translation," 319.
155 The symbol "-" stands for the number, either 11 as EB transmit, or 12, as all editors corrected.
156 Adler, *Dissertationes philologae Vindobonenses*, 112. He correctly indicated that "σύνοδοι

My suggestions, differently, are the following:
1) To transform, in the first place, the dative θεριναῖς into an accusative (θερινάς), which is then related to τὰς πανσελήνους;
2) To add ⟨ἐνθάδε⟩ before ἕνδεκα, which may have easily dropped off because of the similarity between both words; and,
3) To add (for the sake of clarity, although the text could do without it) the preposition σύν before the dative συνόδοις, the fall of which is easily explained by way of haplography.

With the resulting text, ταῖς ⟨ἐνθάδε⟩ ἕνδεκα θερινὰς ⟨σὺν⟩ συνόδοις τὰς πανσελήνους, Lamprias derisively affirms that Theon, after adding to our only yearly summer eleven other summers due to the full moons (thus reaching a yearly total of 12 summers), necessarily fears the excessive warmth.

Fourthly, there is a minor issue regarding the verbal choice between E's and B's different readings. I prefer B's reading, ἀντιθείς, because it allows us to keep the verb εἴσῃ—2nd person singular, future of εἴδω (εἴσομαι)—a bit below. Most scholars, however, choose E's ἀντιθῇς, which, in turn, imposes the modification of εἴσῃ, given that the sentence already presents a main verb. The edition of Basel changed it into εἶτα; Pohlenz (in the apparatus) into εἰκός; and Cherniss into ὑποθῇ.

By limiting the modifications of the transmitted text to a minimum—accepting EB's negative οὐ, ἕνδεκα, ταῖς—συνόδοις, τὰς πανσελήνους, and εἴσῃ—our text provides a reasonable and coherent answer to Theon's fear of an excessive temperature on the moon.

| | |
|---|---|
| 939E 6–8 | τί δὴ θαυμαστόν ἐστιν εἰ γίνονται περὶ τὴν σελήνην ῥίζαι καὶ σπέρματα καὶ ὗλαι μηθὲν ὑετῶν δεόμεναι μήτε χιόνων, ἀλλὰ πρόσφορον ἀέρα καὶ λεπτὸν εὐφυῶς ἔχουσαι;[157] |
| EB | τί δὲ θαυμαστόν ἐστιν εἰ γίνονται περὶ τὴν σελήνην ῥίζαι καὶ σπέρματα καὶ ὗλαι E / ὗλαι B μηθὲν ὑετῶν δεόμενα μήτε χιόνων· ἀλλὰ πρόσθερον ἀέρα καὶ λεπτὸν εὐφυῶς ἔχουσαι· |

---

non θεριναί esse possunt," a point unnoticed to Bernardakis, given his emendation to the text.

157 Bernardakis, followed by Pohlenz and Cherniss, changed μηθέν and μήτε into μηδέν and μηδέ, but the change is not mandatory. And χιόνων ('of snows') was changed into χειμώνων ('of storms') by the Aldine and the *Basiliensis* editions. This unnecessary alteration of the text was maintained by Stephanus, Xylander and Wyttenbach. The modification might have been motivated by the appearance of χειμῶσιν a few lines above (939C), which, incidentally, E unnecessarily corrected *supra lineam* into χιόσιν. On this emendation by E, see Appendix 2.

This sentence needed an intervention in three places: a) the particle δέ; b) the participle δεόμενα; and c) the adjective πρόσθερον.

Regarding the first particle, there is no opposition between this sentence and what was said in the previous, yet there is a correlation with the following conditional. It was changed, for the first time by an annotation in SR67, into δή.

Regarding the participle neuter plural, it must be an error of transmission, given that it refers to ῥίζαι καὶ σπέρματα καὶ ὗλαι, a plural formed by both feminine and neuter nouns. An annotation in the margin of RJ94 corrected it into δεόμεναι.

Concerning the adjective, both manuscripts transmit the inexistent form πρόσθερον. An annotation in SR67 changed it into πρὸς θερινόν; RJ94 also provided this correction and added καὶ ξηρόν; Bernardakis also opted for πρὸς θερινόν, but suggested (in the apparatus) πρὸς θέρειον; and Raingeard (also in the apparatus) suggested πρὸς θερμόν. Another option is possible: πρόσφορον, meaning 'useful,' or 'suitable.' The corruption into a false compound of θέρος may be explained by the influence of the reference to the summer season in the passage (939D, Σπείρεται δέ, τὰ μὲν πρὸς χειμῶνος, τὰ δὲ θέρους ἀκμάζοντος). This text, thus, refers to the propitious conditions of the air on the moon, which are adapted to its nature.

940A 18–21   λέγεις γὰρ ἡμῖν ἐξηγούμενος ταυτὶ τὰ Ἀλκμᾶνος·[158]
              ⟨Διὸς⟩ θυγάτηρ Ἔρσα τρέφει καὶ Σελάνας,
              ὅτι νῦν τὸν ἀέρα καλεῖ καὶ Δία, φησὶν αὐτὸν ὑπὸ τῆς σελήνης καθυγραινόμενον εἰς δρόσους τρέπεσθαι.

EB            λέγεις γὰρ ἡμῖν ἐξηγούμενος ταύτῃ τὰ ἀλκμᾶνος ... θυγάτηρ ἔργα τρέφει καὶ σελάνας· ὅτι νῦν τὸν ἀέρα καλεῖ· καὶ δία φησὶν αὐτὸν ὑπὸ τῆς σελήνης καθυγραινόμενον εἰς δρόσους τρέπεσθαι·

The difficulties of this passage concern Alcman's verse and the causal clause after the quotation.[159]

Alcman's verse underwent some alterations during textual transmission. Both manuscripts present a lacuna of seven letters at the beginning, and read θυγάτηρ ἔργα τρέφει καὶ σελάνας. Firstly, concerning the lacuna, the first conjectures date from the 16th century and all introduce the name of Zeus: Xylander

---

158   Ταυτί was Bernardakis' correction, instead of ταύτῃ, in both manuscripts. Before him, the *Basiliensis*' edition, which some scholars followed, proposed to correct the case into neuter accusative plural, ταῦτα. The attic equivalent later proposed by Bernardakis is better explained from a palaeographic point of view: the corruption would be due to iotacism.
159   Fr. 57 Page.

(in the commentary to his translation) proposed οἷα Δίος (sic); Stephanus conjectured Διός.¹⁶⁰ This inclusion seems supported by the fact that the god is mentioned in the following line.

Secondly, if the verse deals with a daughter of Zeus and the moon, it seems evident that the noun ἔργα should be modified. The mistake was noted by many 16th century scholars, first of all by Forteguerri, who turned the noun into ἔρσα.

This verse underwent a third and last alteration. Some scholars stressed the lack of the adjective "divine" modifying the moon: Stephanus—followed by Wyttenbach, Dübner and Cherniss—added δίας after σελάνας; Bernardakis and Pohlenz added it before the noun. Plutarch quotes this same verse in two other treatises. The suggestion of οἷα Δίος—instead of Zeus' name only—by Xylander and the addition of δίας by the above mentioned scholars were dependent on these texts. Notwithstanding this, they omitted to mention that the quotes found in *Quaest. conv.* 3.10 and *Quaestiones naturales* (*Quaest. nat.* from now on) 918A also show variations caused by textual corruption. In *Quaest. conv.* the text reads: οἷα φησὶ Διὸς θυγάτηρ μέγα τρέφει καὶ ἀσελάνας, with errata in μέγα and ἀσελάνας. In *Quaest. nat.* it appears as: Διὸς θύγατερ Ἔρσα τρέφει καὶ Σελάνας [δίας], with the erroneous form θύγατερ, instead of θυγάτηρ, and the adjective was secluded by editors because it was unmetrical.

Given that the other attestations by Plutarch do not provide a reliable version, I only keep the conjecture Διός and the correction to ἔρσα, since they are the only required emendations that assure meaning.

Regarding the causal clause, EB read: ὅτι νῦν τὸν ἀέρα καλεῖ· καὶ δία φησὶν αὐτὸν ὑπὸ τῆς σελήνης καθυγραινόμενον εἰς δρόσους τρέπεσθαι. Lamprias provides an explanation of the verse's meaning, but the strong pause after καλεῖ implies that the verb lacks a second substantive in accusative.

Xylander suggested (in the commentary to his translation) the conjecture ὅτι τὸν δία τὸν ἀέρα καλεῖ, καὶ φησίν (sic); Kepler suggested to delete the strong punctuation after καλεῖ and to invert the order of words from καὶ δία φησὶν into δία καί φησιν.¹⁶¹ In both cases, καλεῖ receives two accusatives (τὸν ἀέρα and δία) and the conjunction links this verb with φησίν. Raingeard opted to maintain the manuscripts' reading and stated that changing the text would create confusion, for the text reads: "le poète nomme l'air et raconte que Zeus lui-même humidifié par la lune se tourne en rosée."¹⁶²

Another plausible solution is to interpret καί as an adverb. In this sense, after the elimination of the strong punctuation, no other intervention is required:

---

160   Xylander, *Plutarchi Chaeronensis*, 719.
161   Xylander, *Plutarchi Chaeronensis*, 719; Kepler, *Ioh. Keppleri Mathematici*, 165.
162   Raingeard, *Le peri toy prosopoy*, 132.

τὸν ἀέρα and διά are associated through the adverb to the verb καλεῖ. This verb belongs to the causal clause and consequently does not need a link with the verb of the main sentence, φησίν.

| | |
|---|---|
| 940BC 1–3 | Καὶ σύστομοι μὲν ἄνθρωποι καὶ ὀσμαῖς τρεφόμενοι μὴ ἔστωσαν, εἰ μὴ ⟨Θέωνι ἄστο⟩μοι δοκοῦσι, τὴν δὲ ἀτμῶν οὓς ἡμῖν αὐτὸς ἐξηγεῖτο δύναμιν ἠνίξατο μὲν Ἡσίοδος εἰπών· |
| EB | καὶ σύστομοι μὲν ἄνθρωποι καὶ ὀσμαῖς τρεφόμενοι μὴ ἔστωσαν, εἰ μὴ ... μὴ δοκοῦσι· τὴν τε ἄμμονος ἡμῖν αὐτὸς ἐξηγεῖτο δύναμιν, ἠνίξατο μὲν ἡσίοδος εἰπών· |

This passage includes three problems. Firstly, the adjective σύστομοι; then, the lacuna of approximately eight letters transmitted in both manuscripts preceded and followed by μή; and finally, the reading ἄμμονος, otherwise not attested.

In what regards σύστομοι, the adjective is used in correlation with Theon's words explaining the men who feed on smoke and steam from an Indian root (938D). Despite the presence of a lacuna and textual corruption, the references to the utility of plants, such as mallow and daffodil (μαλάχῃ and ἀσφοδέλῳ), and to the sufficiency of small quantities of food points to the fact that Lamprias is indeed replying to Theon's words. He, however, used the term εὐστόμους ('of good mouth') when referring the vapor feeding men, which required a correction.[163]

The problem in this passage is that the meaning of σύστομοι, 'of a narrow mouth,' does not seem to fit in the context. As stated above, the aforementioned men should feed through their nostrils (smell), due to the fact that they do not have an aperture allowing the ingestion of solids or liquids. Forteguerri's and Leonicus' emendation to ἄστομος seems to suit the context better. Dübner—followed by Bernardakis and Raingeard—however, corrected the adjective to match the one in 938D (εὔστομος), as he had previously accepted it there.

The adjective σύστομοι can be maintained depending on what is conjectured for the following lacuna, since Lamprias might not be repeating Theon's thought word for word.

Regarding the lacuna, most scholars attempted to make the reference to the previous passage (938D) more explicit. Amyot was the first to propose a correction: ζῆν ἄσιτοι δυνάμενοι; Wyttenbach proposed (in the apparatus) μη⟨δὲ εἶναι⟩ μοι, and corrected the conditional conjunction that precedes the first

---

163 See heading in 938BC, above.

negation into the relative οἵ; Purser supplied ὑπάρχειν δή and eliminated the second occurrence of μή; Pohlenz, based on one of Adler's proposals, referred to Theon in his conjecture, εἶναι Θέωνι; Cherniss accepted the relative pronoun and, based on another of Adler's proposals, referred to Megasthenes, the character mentioned in the previous passage, Με⟨γασθένει γ᾽ εἶ⟩ναι.[164]

While Lamprias does not directly address Theon, but the audience in general, he is, however, referring to Theon's speech. Consequently, a new character should not be introduced in the lacuna, as some scholars have proposed. Lamprias might not be questioning whether Theon doubts the existence of people feeding through smoke and vapours, but only the fact that they are 'mouthless,' the word used by Theon in 938D. Lamprias, therefore, instead of using Theon's adjective, uses σύστομοι, 'narrow-mouthed,' to correct the idea of people having no mouth at all, even if doubting their existence. Consequently, I maintain EB's σύστομοι, and I suggest to supply the lacuna with Θέωνι ἄστο and to modify the following μή into μοι. While this perfectly fits the space provided by the manuscripts, the corruption into the negation is explained by iotacism.

Regarding the corruption of ἄμμωνος, many corrections have been suggested over time that not only corrected this word, but also changed the particle τε into γε or δέ, and included a pronoun, either replacing the article τήν or adding the pronoun after the article. The Aldine RJ94 included the annotation ἤν γε ἄμμωνος; Amyot wrote ἤν δ᾽ ἀμμώνιος, referring to Plutarch's teacher; Adler, firstly, proposed ἤν δὲ ἄμμεως, and then τὴν δ᾽ ἄλιμον along with ἤν after δύναμιν; Cherniss and Pohlenz both suggested τὴν δ᾽ ἄλιμον, ἧς.[165]

It is necessary to correct τε into δέ, for what follows is a restriction to what was said before. The changes ἄμμωνος and ἀμμώνιος imply the introduction of a new subject for the pronoun αὐτός and the verb ἐξηγεῖτο, which further complicates the comprehension of the sentence. As I suggested above, Lamprias is referring to Theon, who is, consequently, the subject (in 3rd person) of the sentence. Conjectures to solve the problem with ἄμμονος—as those previously to supply the lacuna—should not introduce a new subject.[166] The addition of

---

164 Purser, "Mr. Prickard's Translation," 320. Adler studied the passage in three occasions— 1910, 1921 and 1933—providing different solutions each time. Pohlenz used M. Adler, "Ein Zitat aus des Megasthenes Ἰνδικά bei Plutarch," in O. Stein & W. Gampert (eds.), *Festschrift Moriz Winternitz* (Leipzig, 1933) 301, where Adler proposed εἰ ⟨Θέωνι γ᾽ εἶναι⟩ μή; Cherniss differently used Adler, *Dissertationes philologae Vindobonenses*, 112, with the conjecture καὶ Μεγασθένει δοκοῦσι εἶναι.

165 Adler, *Dissertationes philologae Vindobonenses*, 114; Adler, "Ein Zitat aus des Megasthenes Ἰνδικά bei Plutarch," 301.

166 Cherniss, "Notes on Plutarch's *De facie*," 148, thought that Theon cannot be the subject of ἐξηγεῖτο, since Lamprias is addressing him directly in this passage (if he were the

a relative, however, seems necessary: τὴν δέ—δύναμιν is the object of the sentence ἠνίξατο μὲν Ἡσίοδος, but the sentence ἡμῖν αὐτὸς ἐξηγεῖτο lacks its own object. I propose τὴν δὲ ἀτμῶν οὕς in place of τὴν τε ἄμμονος. The noun ἀτμός refers to the vapour or steam obtained from the Indian root alluded to previously by Theon (938BC, Τὴν μὲν γὰρ Ἰνδικὴν ῥίζαν [...] ὑποτύφειν καὶ θυμιᾶν καὶ τρέφεσθαι τῇ ὀσμῇ). Lamprias, here, questions the authenticity of the existence of mouthless or narrow-mouthed men, but accepts the possibility of another way of being fed, by suggesting that even Hesiod made an allusion to this topic.

941A 6–8    Ἐγὼ μὲν οὖν ὑποκριτής εἰμι, πρότερον δὲ αὐτοῦ φράσω τὸν ποιητὴν
             ἡμῖν εἰ μή τι κωλύει καθ' Ὅμηρον ἀρξάμενον·
EB           ἐγὼ μὲν οὖν ὑποκριτής εἰμί· πρότερον δὲ αὐτοῦ φράσω τὸν ποιητὴν
             ἡμῖν εἰ μή τι κωλύει EB / κωλύοι B s.l. καθ' ὅμηρον ἀρξάμενον·

Scholarship has tended to modify the beginning of the myth: the participle in accusative singular (ἀρξάμενον) was transformed into a nominative; the pronoun in dative 1st person plural (ἡμῖν) was changed into a 2nd person plural. If we analyse these alterations carefully, I believe either of them is justified. Furthermore, the manuscripts present different readings for the verb of the conditional clause.

Regarding the participle, Amyot changed it into the nominative singular based on the understanding that Sulla is the author of the story that is told immediately afterwards. This intervention is unnecessary, if we understand that the subject is not ἐγώ (Sulla), but τὸν ποιητήν. This "creator" is no other than the Stranger, the character who had told the whole myth to Sulla in the first place when they met in Carthage. This is the reason why Sulla calls himself 'a mere actor' (ἐγὼ μὲν οὖν ὑποκριτὴς εἰμι); he is not the author but the narrator.

Turning to the pronoun, if τὸν ποιητήν ... ἀρξάμενον refers to the Stranger, we can conclude that the pronoun in dative plural refers to the audience present when the Stranger first narrated the tale, including Sulla himself, and not to the interlocutors of the dialogue in *De facie*. Therefore, Sulla uses the 1st person plural to refer to those present in Carthage. Thus, the change proposed by Stephanus into a 2nd person plural is dismissed as well.

---

subject, Lamprias should use the 2nd person singular). This is the reason why Cherniss accepted Adler's correction introducing Megasthenes, instead of Adler's very last intervention (Θέωνι γ' εἶναι): if he introduces a reference to Megasthenes, Lamprias can use the verb in 3rd person ἐξηγεῖτο.

Finally, in what concerns the verb of the conditional clause, while it appears in both manuscripts in indicative, it is corrected *supra lineam* by B into an optative (κωλύοι).[167] This was probably motivated by the presence of εἰ μή preceding the verb. The form εἰ μή, however, appears in Plutarch's work followed by indicative, subjunctive, and optative, thus, B's correction of κωλύει is not mandatory.[168]

941A 12–14 τὸν Κρόνον οἱ βάρβαροι καθεῖρχθαι μυθολογοῦσιν ὑπὸ τοῦ Διός, τόνδε ὡς υἱὸν ἔχοντα φρουρόν, τῶν τε νήσων ἐκείνων καὶ τῆς θαλάττης ἣν Κρόνιον πέλαγος ὀνομάζουσι παρακάτω κεῖσθαι.

EB  τὸν Κρόνον οἱ βάρβαροι καθεῖρχθαι μυθολογοῦσιν ὑπὸ τοῦ Διός· τὸν δὲ, ὡς υἱὸν ἔχοντα φρουρὸν τῶν τε νήσων ἐκείνων καὶ τῆς θαλάττης ἣν κρόνιον πέλαγος ὀνομάζουσι. παρακάτω κεῖσθαι.

The text transmitted by EB has suffered changes in three places, all closely related to each other: a) ὡς υἱόν appears to be out of place in this context; b) the intervention in ὡς υἱόν implied the change of φρουρόν, a word that should not be a problem in-itself; and c) παρακάτω and the infinitive κεῖσθαι have also been corrected into different proposals.

Regarding the form τὸν δὲ, ὡς υἱόν (*sic*), it was modified in order to introduce a subject for the following participle, ἔχοντα. Amyot was the first to change the text. He included a reference to Briareus, taking as basis *De defectu* 420A, a passage where this character is explicitly mentioned as Cronos' guardian: τὸν δὲ, ὤγυον. Most editors changed the text with the same idea, seeking to include, in one way or another, an allusion to Briareus: Apelt, τὸν δ᾽ Ὤγυγον; Adler, Βριάρεων δὲ τὸν υἱόν; Pohlenz (in the apparatus), τὸν δὲ Βριάρεων ὡς υἱόν; and Cherniss, τὸν δ᾽ ὠγύγιον Βριάρεων.[169] The only scholars who maintained Cronos as the subject were Wyttenbach, who changed the text (in the critical apparatus) into ὡς ὕπνον, and Purser, who turned it into τὸν δ᾽ ὑπνώδως.[170] Only one editor maintained the manuscripts' reading, Raingeard. According to Raingeard, Zeus is guardian of Cronos and of the islands in his role of son of the god; additionally, he claimed there is no contradiction with the passage of *De defectu*, because

---

167  See the emedation in Appendix 2.
168  See *Num.* 14.15, *Publ.* 2.1, and *Tim.* 30.5, for a few instances in which εἰ μή appears with present indicative. Furthermore, see LSJ I.1 for the use of εἰ with any tense of the indicative.
169  Apelt, "Zu Plutarch und Plato," 17; Adler, *Dissertationes philologae Vindobonenses*, 117.
170  Purser, "Mr. Prickard's Translation," 321.

Briareus is a minister of Zeus, which means that, ultimately, it is Zeus who holds Cronos prisoner.[171]

The problem with the introduction of a new character and with Raingeard's choice to maintain the manuscripts arises because scholars assumed that the rest of sentence referred to either Briareus or Zeus. On one side, either would be the subject of the participle ἔχοντα, which in turn cannot have as subject φρουρόν. Johann Friedrich Salomon Kaltwasser thus suggested to correct it into φρουράν. On the other, either would also have to be the subject of the infinitive at the end of the passage. This, in turn, locates either Briareus or Zeus on the island, despite the fact that it is explicitly stated further below that the only inhabitants of the island are Cronos and his servitors (941A and 941E).

The term παρακάτω preceding κεῖσθαι poses some issues: Bailly does not include it and some editors affirmed that it does not exist; in LSJ, however, it appears with the meaning 'just below' with genitive or as an adverb. Both of them, the infinitive mainly due to the difficulty raised by the adverb, have gone through various modifications: Amyot proposed παρακατακίσθαι; Dübner, πέραν κατῳκίσθαι; and Apelt, παρακατῳκίσθαι.[172]

Cronos has a guardian (ἔχοντα φρουρόν) and is located below the ground (παρακάτω κεῖσθαι). Thus, τὸν Κρόνον functions as the subject of both ἔχοντα and κεῖσθαι. This statement is supported by the context: firstly, Cronos is, in fact, also the subject of the infinitive in the previous sentence, καθεῖρχθαι; secondly, the description of Cronos' imprisonment in a later passage, when he is said to be held in a deep cave, corroborates the use of the problematic 'just below,' here (941F, αὐτὸν μὲν γὰρ τὸν Κρόνον ἐν ἄντρῳ βαθεῖ περιέχεσθαι πέτρας χρυσοειδοῦς καθεύδοντα). I, consequently, suggest to correct τὸν δέ, ὡς υἱόν into τόνδε ὡς υἱὸν and to eliminate the pause after ὀνομάζουσι. The first intervention, the replacement of the article with a demonstrative pronoun, allows for the maintenance of Cronos as the subject of ἔχοντα, while still conceding that Zeus, as son, is his guardian. With the second intervention, the syntagma with its relative clause τῶν τε νήσων ἐκείνων καὶ τῆς θαλάττης ἣν Κρόνιον πέλαγος ὀνομάζουσι no longer belongs to the domain of the guardian, but to the place where Cronos is located. In this sense, παρακάτω, while placed by the verb, actually rules the syntagma in genitive. The prolepsis of the syntagma regarding the islands and the sea can be explained as relevant to the tale explaining the geographical description were Cronos is imprisoned.

---

171  Raingeard, *Le peri toy prosopoy*, 135.
172  Apelt, "Zu Plutarch und Plato," 17.

941BC 21–23   καλεῖν δὲ καὶ νομίζειν ἐκείνους ἠπειρώτας μὲν αὐτοὺς ταύτην τὴν γῆν
              κατοικοῦντας, ὡς καὶ κύκλῳ περίρρυτον ⟨οὐκ⟩ οὖσαν ὑπὸ τῆς θαλάσ-
              σης.[173]
EB            καλεῖν δὲ καὶ νομίζειν ἐκείνους ἠπειρώτας μὲν αὐτοὺς ταύτην τὴν γῆν
              κατοικοῦντας ὡς καὶ κύκλῳ περίρρυτον οὖσαν ὑπὸ τῆς θαλάσσης·

This sentence caused a couple of problems for scholars: firstly, neither the pronouns ἐκείνους and αὐτούς nor the participle κατοικοῦντας seem to have a clear referent; and secondly, the presence of the particle μέν without the correlation δέ contributes to the feeling that the text lacks something.

Forteguerri was the first scholar to intervene in the text, by modifying αὐτούς into αὑτούς—a correction that I follow. Later on, most probably unaware of Forteguerri's modification, the *Basiliensis* edition added νησιώτας δέ after the counterpoint ἠπειρώτας μὲν αὐτούς: ἐκείνους are the Greeks of the Great Continent, self-referring as 'continentals' (ἠπειρώτας μέν), and αὐτούς are those who inhabit ταύτην τὴν γῆν, Ogygia, whom they call 'islanders' (νησιώτας δέ). Following the correction suggested by the *Basiliensis* but seeking to strengthen the nominalization of the participle κατοικοῦντας, Wyttenbach proposed (in the apparatus) the addition of the article τούς after νησιώτας δέ (νησιώτας δὲ τοὺς ταύτην τὴν γῆν κατοικοῦντας).

The main problem of these interventions lies in that they produce a text that has no informative value whatsoever: Greeks from the mainland call themselves "continentals" and regard the people living in the island of Ogygia as "islanders." Furthermore, the digression following this passage (ὡς καὶ κύκλῳ περίρρυτον οὖσαν ὑπὸ τῆς θαλάσσης) has no sense whatsoever, since it is obvious that they would think that an island is surrounded by the sea. Another possible interpretation would be that ταύτην τὴν γῆν κατοικοῦντας does not refer to the inhabitants of Ogygia, but to our continent, Europe, which will be called later in the narration 'the big island' (942B, τῆς μεγάλης νήσου). In this case, the different denominations and the digression, taken as the origin of those denominations, would make sense. This is the interpretation of most scholars, but a reference to our continent is improbable in this passage, because it is focused on the description of the Atlantic Ocean, the archipelago of Ogygia, and the Great Continent beyond the Ocean.

To solve the passage's difficulties, I suggest to modify only the explicative clause. Obviating the generally accepted addition of νησιώτας δέ, the text only

---

[173] Bernardakis presented, in his edition, the form λαλεῖν instead of καλεῖν, which is probably a mistake and not a purposeful intervention.

refers to ἠπειρώτας ('continentals'), employed by the Greeks of the Great Continent to qualify the inhabitants of elsewhere. Since I believe the core of the description is composed by the Great Continent and Ogygia's archipelago, the denomination "continentals" is being applied to the inhabitants of the island, thus the need of an explicative clause to explain the reason for such a denomination. I propose to add οὐκ before οὖσαν, in order to transform the sentence into a negative one and to understand ὡς as providing subjective value: ὡς καὶ κύκλῳ περίρρυτον ⟨οὐκ⟩ οὖσαν ὑπὸ τῆς θαλάσσης.

The corruption can be explained without trouble: because the negation and the participle begin with the same syllable, the copyist may have easily omitted οὐκ. The wrong belief that Ogygia was not an island would be provoked by what had been said above (941B): the sea is muddy and earthy, giving the impression of being frozen, solid. And so, the digression is justified: mainlanders call the islanders of Ogygia "continentals," on the grounds of a belief that does not fit reality—that Ogygia is not surrounded by sea.

941CD 30–3  παρασκευασαμένους ἐν χρόνῳ πολλῷ τὰ περὶ τὴν θυσίαν καὶ τὸν ἀ ... ἐκπέμπειν κλήρῳ λαχόντας ἐν πλοίοις τοσούτοις θεραπείαν τε πολλὴν καὶ παρασκευὴν ἀναγκαίαν μέλλουσι πλεῖν πέλαγος τοσοῦτον εἰρεσίᾳ καὶ χρόνον ἐπὶ ξένης βιοτεύειν πολὺν ἐμβαλλομένους.

EB  παρασκευασαμένους ἐν χρόνῳ πολλῷ τὰ περὶ τὴν θυσίαν καὶ τὸν ἀ ... ἐκπέμπειν κλήρῳ λαχόντας ἐν πλοίοις τοσούτοις· θεραπείαν τε πολλὴν καὶ ... σκευὴν E / παρασκευὴν B ἀναγκαίαν μέλλουσι πλεῖν πέλαγος τοσοῦτον εἰρεσίᾳ· καὶ χρόνον ἐπὶ ξένης βιοτεύειν πολὺν ἐμβάλλομεν· οὓς

Two issues must be solved in this passage: both manuscripts report a lacuna after τὸν ἀ: approximately 23 letters in E, and 17 letters in B; and a verb in 1st person plural clashes with the context.

Regarding the lacuna, it is preceded by a participle with its complement (παρασκευασαμένους—τὰ περὶ τὴν θυσίαν) and the conjunction καί, which makes rather probable the supposition that the missing text was a noun coordinated with τὰ περὶ τὴν θυσίαν, both complements of παρασκευασαμένους.

The first scholars to complete the lacuna were Amyot and Xylander (in the commentary of his translation): they both suggested ἀπόπλουν, which, despite being too short for the space available, perfectly adapts to the context.[174] This noun was accepted by most scholars, including Bernardakis and

---

174  Xylander, *Plutarchi Chaeronensis Moralia*, 719.

Pohlenz, who also proposed (in the apparatus) ἀπὸ τῆς οἰκείας πλοῦν, and ἀπόπλουν ἐπὶ τὴν Κρόνου νῆσον, both in an attempt to complete the whole space of the manuscripts. Also, Raingeard followed this option, but further observed (in the commentary) that in the lacuna should appear the sum of envoys, in order to justify τοσούτοις, which corresponds to a number mentioned before.[175] Cherniss might have been inspired by this comment for his conjecture, which not only provided the lacking complement for παρασκευασαμένους but also an object for ἐκπέμπειν: ἀπόστολον θεωροὺς ἱκανούς.

For the lost noun, one might suggest ἀνάπλουν, as an alternative to ἀπόπλουν. In fact, ἀνά provides a more specific meaning of departure, compared to that of 'return home' by ἀπό.[176] To mention one example of this, the verb used a few lines below (ἀποπλεῖν οἴκαδε) is precisely used in the sense of "return to the fatherland."

Regarding the verbal form in 1st person plural, ἐμβάλλομεν, it clashes with the context, given that the myth is being narrated by Sulla, who transmits the words of the Stranger. Amyot suggested to emend the text into ἐμβαίνοντας οὖν καί; and Kepler proposed ἐμβαλλομένους—a participle formed by fusioning the verb with pronoun οὕς transmitted after the verb by both manuscripts.[177] Kepler's proposal is more plausible from both the palaeographical perspective, and the syntactical, since the participle refers to the infinitive ἐκπέμπειν and has as complements ἐν πλοίοις τοσούτοις θεραπείαν τε πολλὴν καὶ παρασκευὴν ἀναγκαίαν.

| | |
|---|---|
| 942A 26–2 | εἶναι δὲ ἀνάστασιν τὰ τιτανικὰ πάθη καὶ κινήματα τῆς ψυχῆς (ἕως) ἂν αὐτῷ παντάπασιν ὁ ὕπνος ... καὶ γένηται τὸ βασιλικὸν καὶ θεῖον αὐτὸ καθ' ἑαυτὸ καθαρὸν καὶ ἀκήρατον. |
| EB | εἶναι δὲ ἀνάστασιν τὰ τιτανικὰ πάθη καὶ κινήματα τῆς ψυχῆς ἐν αὐτῷ παντάπασιν ὁ ὕπνος· ... καὶ γένηται τὸ βασιλικὸν καὶ θεῖον αὐτὸ καθ' ἑαυτὸ καθαρὸν καὶ ἀκήρατον· |

The manuscripts present some textual problems, the beginning εἶναι δὲ ἀνάστασιν, the subjunctive γένηται, and a lacuna of around 10 letters in E and 13 letters in B that complicates the correct interpretation of the passage.

Generally speaking, the passage seems to have two parts neatly differentiated, both related to Cronos: his titanic and rebellious nature on the one hand, and his divine and royal nature on the other. The only editor disagreeing with

---

175  Raingeard, *Le peri toy prosopoy*, 137.
176  See LSJ I and *DGE* I.2.
177  Kepler, *Ioh. Keppleri Mathematici*, 171.

this view was Raingeard, who, incomprehensibly in my opinion, interpreted that τὰ τιτανικὰ πάθη is the suffering caused by Zeus upon his enemies, which causes Cronos to stand up in distress when he foresees it.[178]

Many editors modified the first part of the passage (εἶναι δὲ ἀνάστασιν): Kepler replaced the verb, κατ' ἀνάστασιν; Wyttenbach (in the apparatus) added αὐτοῦ after ἀνάστασιν; Van Herwerden proposed the addition of ἐν and the correction of the noun into ἀναστάσει; Pohlenz replaced it with ἐπειδὰν στασιάσαντα, based in Madvig's text (ἐπειδὰν παύσῃ); Cherniss corrected it into εἶναι δ' ἀνάτασιν; and Donini presented here one of the few cases of personal interventions in the text, either ἔχειν δ' οὕτως ἵνα or εἶναι δὲ τοῦτο ἵνα.[179] Madvig, Pohlenz and Donini looked for a conjunction that, as we shall see below, is lacking in the text; Van Herwerden and Cherniss believed that the text could not be understood as it stands. All of them, in any case, took the chance to substitute ἀνάστασιν, which supposes a difficulty to them. Cherniss, for example, believed that it is a scribal mistake for ἀνάτασιν, a term that he defended as being common in Neoplatonic vocabulary.[180] However correct this opinion might be, it provides no reason to alter Plutarch's text in order for it to fit the vocabulary of later authors. Furthermore, in the present context, I believe that Cronos' titanic passions and commotions do imply a 'revolt,' a 'destabilization,' (ἀνάστασιν) which will be appeased through sleep. Therefore, I propose to maintain the manuscripts' text.

The following difficulty is posed by the lacuna. The text presents two subjects—ὁ ὕπνος, before the lacuna, and τὸ βασιλικὸν καὶ θεῖον, after the lacuna—and a single verb, γένηται, that clearly cannot refer to both subjects. Since this verb is preceded by the copulative conjunction καί, I believe the lacuna might have included another verb in subjunctive, the subject of which is ὁ ὕπνος. This is the position of Wyttenbach (in the apparatus), with συστέλλει, ἕως κοσμηθῇ; Bernardakis (in the apparatus), with καὶ κατακοσμήσῃ; Pohlenz, with κατακοιμήσῃ; or Cherniss, with καταστήσῃ. Van Herwerden, however, deleted the lacuna and secluded καί.[181]

Due to their introduction of a verb that requires an object, Bernardakis and Cherniss were forced to modify the adverb παντάπασιν to include one. Bernardakis corrected it into πάντα παύσῃ, which, in addition to an object, included a new verb to be coordinated with the one lost in the lacuna, κατακοσμήσῃ, and

---

178 Raingeard, *Le peri toy prosopoy*, 140.
179 Kepler, *Ioh. Keppleri Mathematici*, 172; Van Herwerden, "Novae curae criticae," 214; Madvig, *Adversaria critica*, 666; and Donini, *Plutarco. Il volto della luna*, 343–344 n. 365.
180 Cherniss, "Notes on Plutarch's *De facie*," 150.
181 Van Herwerden, "Novae curae criticae," 214.

with γένηται. Cherniss corrected παντάπασιν into πάλιν ἀνάπαυσιν. I see no reason to modify the text in this sense, since the adverb fits the context perfectly: sleep, the remedy designed by Zeus for the titanic nature of Cronos, completely soothes him—we do not know exactly what the effects are, as this is part of the lost text.

Concerning the subjunctive γένηται, it requires a subordinating conjunction that has not been preserved. This conjunction cannot have been part of the text lost in the lacuna, given that it must precede the subjects of the subordinate clause and the first of these subjects, ὁ ὕπνος, appears before the lacuna. Consequently, the conjunction should have been placed in the first part of the passage. As seen above, Pohlenz and Donini placed it at the very beginning—ἐπειδάν στασιάσαντα, and ἔχειν δ' οὕτως ἵνα or εἶναι δὲ τοῦτο ἵνα. It would be more plausible to place the conjunction near the circumstantial complement ἐν αὐτῷ, where the opposition between the titanic passions and the effect of sleep, liberating the god's divine and royal nature, begins. The first to have placed it there was Bernardakis, who added the temporal conjunction ἕως, followed by the modal particle ἄν before ἐν αὐτῷ; Cherniss proposed to substitute the preposition ἐν for ἄν (ἕως ἄν αὐτῷ). The corruption is better explained in this way: influenced by the dative that follows, the copyist would have transformed both words (ἕως ἄν) into the preposition ἐν in a sort of crasis.

This minimal modification is enough to maintain the sense of the passage. I, therefore, follow Cherniss' proposal regarding the subordinating conjunction and maintain the rest as transmitted. I do not include, in the body of text, any of the attempts to supply the lacuna: not only are the possibilities much too broad, but the context provides enough sense to the passage.

942C 12–14   Πλεῖστον γὰρ ἐν Καρχηδόνι χρόνον διέτριψεν, ἅτε δὴ παρ' ἡμῖν μεγάλας ἔχοντος ⟨τιμὰς⟩ καὶ τινὰς ὅτε ἡ προτέρα πόλις ἀπώλλυτο διφθέρας ἱεράς
EB            πλεῖστον γὰρ ἐν καρχηδόνι χρόνον διέτριψεν. ἅτε δὴ παρ' ἡμῖν μεγάλας ἔχοντος καὶ τινὰς ὅτε ἡ προτέρα πόλις ἀπώλλυτο διφθέρας ἱεράς

Even if neither of the manuscripts reports a lacuna, the text surely lacks something in the subordinate clause ἅτε δὴ παρ' ἡμῖν μεγάλας ἔχοντος καὶ τινάς: there is an adjective and a participle without a noun to modify and a conjunction without anything to link.

The first to correct the text was the *Basiliensis* edition, which proposed to substitute μεγάλας ἔχοντος καὶ τινάς with μεγάλης ἔχοντος καὶ τιμάς. Amyot wrote, in the margin of his copy, the emendation μεγάλης τυχὼν ἀξιώσεως καὶ τιμῆς. Wyttenbach proposed another correction: he suggested (in the apparatus) μεγάλας ἔχοντος τοῦ Κρόνου τιμάς· καί, introducing the figure of Cronos in the passage and laying the foundations for following conjectures. Emperius proposed μεγάλας ἔχοντος τοῦ Κρόνου τιμάς, καὶ τινάς—maintaining the pronoun τινάς transmitted by the manuscripts—; Bernardakis (in the apparatus) proposed μεγάλας τοῦ Κρόνου τιμάς ἔχοντος, placing the subject of the genitive absolute before its verb.[182]

These suggestions are not quite convincing. First, there is no indication in the text that would validate the inclusion of Cronos. Second, most of these editors do not even explain how Cronos' syntagma went lost. Only Raingeard suggested that it might have been due to the proximity of the noun χρόνον, which is not a very strong argument.[183]

A stronger argument for the Stranger's stay in Carthage would be the gratitude and appreciation on behalf of the city due to his discovery of sacred writings (as the text states below, 942C, διφθέρας ἱερὰς ὑπεκκομισθείσας κρύφα καὶ διαλαθούσας πολὺν χρόνον ἐν γῇ κειμένας ἐξεῦρεν). In the tradition of Amyot and Kepler, who both changed the participle in genitive into a nominative— the former into τυχών and the latter into ἔχων—I believe that the Stranger is the subject of the construction and that there is no need to introduce another character in the passage.[184] Differently, however, I maintain the genitive absolute (ἔχοντος), because it does not prevent the Stranger from being the (omitted) subject. I think τιμάς might have appeared before καὶ τινὰς ὅτε in the original text, which would have been omitted by haplography, since the two are seemingly similar words. The text, then, looks as follows: ἅτε δὴ παρ' ἡμῖν μεγάλας ἔχοντος τιμὰς καὶ τινάς.

943B 19–21   καὶ ὁ μέν ἐστιν ἐν τῇ τῆς Δήμητρος ⟨γῇ⟩ ... ἐν αὐτῇ τελεῖν καὶ τοὺς
             νεκροὺς Ἀθηναῖοι δημητρείους ὠνόμαζον τὸ παλαιόν, ⟨ὁ⟩ δὲ ἐν τῇ
             σελήνῃ τῆς Φερσεφόνης·[185]
EB           καὶ ὃ μέν ἐστιν ἐν τῇ τῆς δήμητρος ... ἐν αὐτῇ τελεῖν· καὶ τοὺς νεκροὺς
             ἀθηναῖοι δημητρείους ὠνόμαζον· τὸ παλαιὸν δὲ ἐν τῇ σελήνῃ τῆς φερ-
             σεφόνης EB/ περσεφόνης E s.l.

---

182   Emperius, *Opuscula*, 295.
183   Raingeard, *Le peri toy prosopoy*, 140.
184   Kepler, *Ioh. Keppleri Mathematici*, 173.
185   Note that both ὁ μέν and ὁ δέ refer to ὃν δὲ ἀποθνήσκομεν θάνατον, appearing a few lines above (943AB). Amyot suggested the correction into the plural, ὧν δὲ ἀποθνήσκομεν θανάτων, taking into account the development of the text, which evidently refers to more than one death. Although it is a clever correction, it unnecessarily modifies the manuscripts' text.

There are two lacunae in the passage; while the first one is a blank left by the manuscripts after the syntagma ἐν τῇ τῆς Δήμητρος—21 letters in E and 26 letters in B—the second is assumed from the context.

Regarding the first lacuna, the preceding syntagma points to its possible content. There is a sequence of two articles, one in genitive followed by Δήμητρος and another in dative with no noun attached: we miss, therefore, a substantive. More text could be lost however: both the length of the lacuna and the fact that the rest of the passage seems to be incomplete point in this direction.

Given that the first section of the passage deals with Demeter and the second deals with Persephone and the moon (ὁ δὲ ἐν τῇ σελήνῃ τῆς Φερσεφόνης), it seems rather probable that the lost noun accompanying τῇ is γῇ. Madvig was the first scholar to suggest this conjecture, with a proposal that replicates the structure of the second section of the passage (ἐν τῇ ⟨γῇ⟩ τῆς Δήμητρος—ἐν τῇ σελήνῃ τῆς Φερσεφόνης); Raingeard proposed to replace the article in dative with the noun (ἐν γῇ τῆς Δήμητρος).[186] However, the noun might have been placed in the lacuna, since the genitive is frequently introduced in the middle of the syntagma on which it depends. Therefore, I propose not to alter the text preceding the lacuna and to supply part of it with γῇ (ἐν τῇ τῆς Δήμητρος γῇ).

The conjectures proposed for the lacuna rely on the incompleteness of the following part of the sentence (ἐν αὐτῇ τελεῖν). Wyttenbach conjectured (in the apparatus) μοίρᾳ· ὅθεν τὸ μυεῖσθαι, παρωνύμως τῷ τελευτᾶν; Bernardakis (also in the apparatus), διὸ προσέοικε τῷ τελευτᾶν; Adler proposed ὅθεν τὸ τελευτᾶν ὁμωνύμως and replaced ἐν αὐτῇ with λέγεται τῷ; Pohlenz suggested (in the apparatus) ὅθεν αὐτὴ τελεῖσθαί φαμεν καὶ τὸν βίον ἐν; Cherniss, διὸ τελευτᾶν λέγεται τὸν βίον, where the last syllable of βίον is the emendation of the preposition ἐν transmitted by EB; Alain Lernould followed Cherniss' conjecture and further replaced the active voice infinitive τελεῖν with a passive form (τελεῖσθαι).[187]

The reason why all these scholars proposed the inclusion of the terms τελευτᾶν and τελεῖσθαι is that the following reference to the denomination given by Athenians to their dead is an allusion to the mystery cults of Eleusis (καὶ τοὺς νεκροὺς Ἀθηναῖοι δημητρείους ὠνόμαζον τὸ παλαιόν). Lernould's correction of the infinitive following the lacuna is motivated by the fact that the verb τελέω in its

---

186 Madvig, *Adversaria critica*, 666.
187 Adler, *Dissertationes philologae Vindobonenses*, 119. A. Lernould's τελεῖσθαι in *Plutarque. Le visage qui apparaît dans le disque de la lune* (Villeneuve d'Ascq: Presses Universitaires du Septentrion, 2013) 80, was clearly inspired by Cherniss' suggestion in "Notes on Plutarch's *De facie*," 151; although, he did not mention his predecessor. On this, see L. Lesage Gárriga, "Review of A. Lernould, *Plutarque. Le visage qui apparaît dans le disque de la lune* (Villeneuve d'Ascq: Presses Universitaires du Septentrion, 2013)," *Ploutarchos* 11 (2014) 140–141.

meaning 'initiate in mystery rites' normally appears in passive. Notwithstanding the statistics, the passive form is not mandatory, thus the modification is not necessary.[188]

While I do not include any of the conjectures into the body of text because there are too many possibilities and it is difficult to determine which one is correct, I do agree with previous editors in the general sense of the passage: there seems to be a connection between the role that the goddess plays in the death on earth and the mystery rites associated to her, which means that there is a play on words between "to die" and "to be initiated."

Regarding the second lacuna, as stated above, the correspondence between the first and the second sections is evident. While the former reads, at the beginning, ὁ μέν, the latter includes no article in nominative masculine that could refer to the previously mentioned 'death' (943A, ὃν δὲ ἀποθνήσκομεν θάνατον). Amyot corrected this problem by adding the article ὁ at the beginning of the second section. In this sense, the parallel structure is complete: καὶ ὁ μὲν ἐστιν ἐν τῇ τῆς Δήμητρος γῇ—ὁ δὲ ἐν τῇ σελήνῃ τῆς Φερσεφόνης.

| | |
|---|---|
| 943C 6–8 | ⟨ἐν ᾧ⟩ οἷον ἐξ ἀποδημίας ἀνακομιζόμεναι φυγαδικῆς εἰς πατρίδα γεύονται χαρᾶς οἷον οἱ τελούμενοι μάλιστα θορύβῳ καὶ πτοήσει συγκεκραμένῃ μετ' ἐλπίδος ἰδίας ἔχουσι. |
| EB | οἷον ἐξ ἀποδημίας ἀνακομιζόμεναι φυγαδικῆς εἰς πατρίδα γεῦνται χαρᾶς, οἷον οἱ τελούμενοι μάλιστα θορύβῳ καὶ πτοήσει συγκεκραμένῃ, μετ' ἐλπίδος ἰδίας ἔχουσι· |

This passage lacks a connector to link it with the previous passage. Beside this, scholars have further modified several parts—οἷον, συγκεκραμένῃ and ἰδίας—which need no intervention.

The text describes the feelings that souls have when they are waiting to be completely purified in the air between the earth and the moon, during the process of returning to the moon after the first death. While there is a thematic switch regarding the preceding passage, which focuses on the purification process itself, some editors also saw a temporal switch. They interpreted, wrongly in my view, that the variety of feelings experienced by the souls (joy, fear, exaltation, hope) happens when they are finally back on the moon. In this sense, the *Basiliensis* edition proposed to add εἶτα before οἷον ἐξ ἀποδημίας ἀνακομιζόμεναι, and Bernardakis suggested (in the apparatus) μεθ' ὄν. Pohlenz, who did

---

188 See Bailly IV. Within Plutarch's work, the active voice appears in *Agis et Cleomenes* 54.2 and *Non posse* 1105B.

not suppose the aforementioned temporal switch, nevertheless, proposed the addition of ἔνθ'.

I agree with previous scholars in that we need a link between this passage and the preceding one. However, I agree only with Pohlenz's claim that the varied range of feelings experienced by souls occurs during their sojourn in the air between the earth and the moon, while being purified, and not after reaching the astral body. Consequently, there is no temporary split between both scenes. I propose to amend the lack of connection between the two scenes with ἐν ᾧ, whose antecedent is χρόνον τινὰ τεταγμένον, and which implies the simultaneity of both scenes. The corruption can be explained by the resemblance between the last two syllables of the preceding participle, τεταγμένον, and the preposition with the relative pronoun.

Regarding the interventions in the rest of the passage, the first one concerns οἶον. The *Basiliensis* edition changed it into οἵαν—οἶαν (*sic*)—in order to connect it with the feminine χαρᾶς. This correction was accepted by several scholars, but EB's reading appears in adverbial function and needs no emendation.[189]

The same conclusion can be applied to the modification of the participle συγκεκραμένη. It appears in nominative (συγκεκραμένη) in the Aldine and the *Basiliensis* editions. Amyot corrected this error by turning it into an accusative (συγκεκραμένην), thus referring to the previous correction οἵαν. The participle's subject, however, is πτοήσει ('exaltation'). It is this noun, in dative, that is mixed with hope: the participle in dative singular of the manuscripts is then correct.

This leads us to the adjective ἰδίας, also corrected by most editors into ἡδείας, an adaption of Xylander's translation "*suavi spe.*" I do not consider the emendation appropriate, given that the text makes sense and is superior to the correction. The hope felt by these souls is compared to the similar feeling experienced by initiates: it is not a usual hope, but a special hope belonging to a very limited group. Thus, in the same way that not all people are initiated, not all souls reach the moon—as the text explicits in 943D—and so, their feelings are 'peculiar,' or 'particular.'

943D 10–12   Αἱ δὲ ἄνω γενόμεναι καὶ βεβαίως ἱδρυθεῖσαι πρῶτον μέν, ὥσπερ οἱ νικηφόροι, περιίασιν ἀναδούμεναι στεφάνοις πτερῶν εὐσταθείας λεγομένοις,

---

189   Pohlenz held that οἶον was given by E, from which it should be deducted that οἵαν is the reading of B—which is not the case—; and Raingeard, who maintained the reading of EB, believed that οἵαν was Reiske's correction.

EB    αἱ δὲ ἄνω γενόμεναι καὶ βεβαίως ἱδρύθησαν· πρῶτον μὲν, ὥσπερ οἱ
νικηφόροι περιίστασιν E / περιιστᾶσιν B ἀναδούμενοι στεφάνοις πτε-
ρῶν εὐσταθείας λεγομένοις·

Here, we are faced with a complex passage that needs to be emended in several places. The whole passage moves from αἱ δὲ ἄνω γενόμεναι to οἷον τὰ στομούμενα βαφὴν ἴσχουσι, all of which has the subject αἱ δὲ ἄνω γενόμεναι καὶ βεβαίως ἱδρύθησαν, according to EB's text, namely referring to the souls that finally arrived to the moon and firmly settled in. Within the passage, there is a division into two sections: the first (πρῶτον μέν) explains the behavior of these souls; the second (δεύτερον ⟨δέ⟩) focuses on their appearance and nature. To simplify the analysis of such a long passage, I have created an entry for each of its sections (πρῶτον μέν and δεύτερον δέ).

All the difficulties concerning this first section are related to the verbal forms: ἱδρύθησαν, περιίστασιν, ἀναδούμενοι, and λεγομένοις.

Regarding ἱδρύθησαν, EB transmit a 3rd person plural, aorist passive, but this must be a mistake given that it is linked to the participle of aorist γενόμεναι by means of the conjunction καί. A more plausible text, from a syntactic point of view, is the one proposed by Wyttenbach (in the apparatus): ἱδρυθεῖσαι, a participle in nominative plural, aorist passive, matching the participle γενόμεναι. Despite orthographic differences, both forms sounded similar due to iotacism (θη = θεῖ).

In what concerns the main verb, both manuscripts present the 3rd person plural of περιίστημι differently accentuated: E περιίστασιν and B περιιστᾶσιν. The problem with this verb is its transitive value: 'to place around.' This was corrected, already in the 16th century, by one of the contributors in the Aldine RJ94, using, as a replacement, a verb of movement, περίασιν (περίειμι, 'to surround,' or 'go around').

Concerning the participle ἀναδούμενοι, it is a mistake probably resulting from the influence of the closest nominative plural, a masculine (οἱ νικηφόροι).[190] Hutten corrected it with a feminine, ἀναδούμεναι. As mentioned above, the subject of the participle is the same as that of the rest of the passage, the souls. The closest nominative in masculine only concerns the comparison, ὥσπερ οἱ νικηφόροι. The reason why those girded with crowns cannot be the winning athletes is provided in the following lines: the crowns are called 'crowns of righteous-

---

190 Wyttenbach in his text wrote νικηφόροις, and explained in the apparatus "*lego* νικηφόροι," from what it can be deducted that, according to him, νικηφόροις is the reading transmitted by the manuscripts, which is a mistake.

ness' due to the proper behavior of the souls during life (943D, στεφάνοις πτερῶν εὐσταθείας λεγομένοις, ὅτι τῆς ψυχῆς τὸ ἄλογον καὶ τὸ παθητικὸν εὐήνιον ἐπιεικῶς τῷ λόγῳ καὶ κεκοσμημένον ἐν τῷ βίῳ παρέσχοντο).

Regarding the last participle (λεγομένοις), several editors modified it, needlessly. The Aldine and the *Basiliensis* editions presented the form λεγομένας. The use of an accusative can only be explained if εὐσταθείας is understood as an accusative plural instead of a genitive singular and, consequently, taken as its subject. Perhaps, this is why the Aldine RJ94 has an annotation correcting the participle into a genitive singular (λεγομένης), which maintains εὐσταθείας as subject, but turns the participle into the case in which the noun actually appears in the sentence. However, the participle in dative plural modifies στεφάνοις πτερῶν. It is the crowns of feathers which are called "of righteousness."

943D 13–16   Δεύτερον ⟨δὲ⟩ ἀκτῖνι τὴν ὄψιν ἐοικυῖαι, περὶ δὲ τὴν φύσιν ἄνω κουφιζομένην ὥσπερ ἐνταῦθα τῷ περὶ τὴν σελήνην αἰθέρι, καὶ τόνον ἀπ' αὐτοῦ καὶ δύναμιν οἷον τὰ στομούμενα βαφὴν ἴσχουσι·

EB   δεύτερον, ἀκτῖνι τὴν ὄψιν ἐοικέναι περὶ δὲ τὴν ψυχὴν ἄνω κουφιζομένην ὥσπερ ἐνταῦθα τῷ περὶ τὴν σελήνην αἰθέρι, καὶ τόνον ἀφ' αὐτοῦ καὶ δύναμιν, οἷον τὰ στομούμενα βαφὴν ἴσχουσι·

The second part of the passage has also gone through many interventions, due to its complexity.[191] The difficulties concern the beginning of the sentence, the infinitive ἐοικέναι, the syntagma περὶ δὲ τὴν ψυχήν, the comparison ὥσπερ ἐνταῦθα, the pronoun in ἀφ' αὐτοῦ, and the term βαφήν.

Concerning the very beginning, as stated above, the whole passage deals with souls settling on the moon and is divided into two sections: while the first one starts with πρῶτον μέν, the second lacks the correlative particle after δεύτερον. Leonicus added δέ.[192]

Concerning the infinitive transmitted by both manuscripts (ἐοικέναι), it is clearly wrong, since the syntax requires a participle. Wyttenbach suggested correcting it with ἐοικυῖαι. His conjecture seems to be corroborated by the chiastic construction of both parts of the passage: the first one with γενόμεναι and ἱδρυθεῖσαι πρῶτον μέν; the second with δεύτερον ⟨δὲ⟩ [...] ἐοικυῖαι.

This verb is followed by the syntagma περὶ δὲ τὴν ψυχήν, which clearly does not fit into the context. Given that the subject of the sentence are the souls that

---

191   On the first part of the passage, see the preceding heading.
192   Oddly, Pohlenz attributed the authorship to the Aldine edition, and Raingeard stated that the Aldine edition transposed δέ after περί, as if the manuscripts actually do read δέ, which is incorrect as well.

settled on the moon, the text, as preserved, poses a problem both of content and grammar, by stating that souls are "regarding their soul." Wyttenbach suggested (in the apparatus) to correct περί into πυρί, so the soul would be similar to fire; Sandbach considered the possibility of περὶ δὲ τὴν ψυχὴν ἄνω being a marginal note altogether; but, in case it were not, he accepted Wyttenbach's intervention and further suggested to replace ψυχήν for φύσιν; Cherniss proposed the maintenance of the preposition περί and accepted Sandbach's replacement of ψυχήν.[193]

While Wyttenbach's suggestion solves the grammatical issue by including the missing complement, it does not solve the problem of content, for the text now states that the souls are, regarding their soul, similar to fire. Sandbach's correction, however, replaces the problematic occurrence of τὴν ψυχήν with a more suitable noun, so the text reads: the souls are, regarding their nature, similar to fire. The mistaken noun could be due to the remoteness of the subject, which is present at the very beginning of this long passage. Although I agree with the intervention concerning ψυχήν, the replacement of περί with πυρί is difficult to maintain. It is primarily based on the assumption that most of the passage presents Stoic notions, which is not important enough to modify the text accordingly. Cherniss' proposal is consequently the most plausible and suitable for the context. The structure of this part of the sentence becomes clearer with his intervention: the participle ἐοικυῖαι has two groups of complements, each formed by an accusative of specification and an indirect complement: on the one side, τὴν ὄψιν and ἀκτῖνι, and, on the other side, περὶ δὲ τὴν φύσιν and τῷ [...] αἰθέρι.

Interpretations and modifications of the text also motivated other interventions in what follows, ἄνω κουφιζομένην ὥσπερ ἐνταῦθα τῷ περὶ τὴν σελήνην αἰθέρι. Amyot was the first to suggest a correction: ὥσπερ ἐντετᾶσθαι; Wyttenbach proposed (in his apparatus) to place the comparison before ἄνω κουφιζομένην and to add the preposition ἐν before τῷ αἰθέρι (ὥσπερ ἐνταῦθα, ἄνω κουφιζομένην, ἐν τῷ περὶ τὴν σελήνην αἰθέρι); Sandbach added τῷ ἀέρι after ὥσπερ ἐνταῦθα; and Lernould secluded the comparison altogether.[194]

Once we accept the correction περὶ δὲ τὴν φύσιν, the comparison presents no problems: since τῷ περὶ τὴν σελήνην αἰθέρι is ἐοικυῖαι's indirect complement—and not πυρί, rejected as emendation—it no longer needs the addition of a

---

193 Sandbach, "Second Meeting," 15.
194 Sandbach, "Second Meeting," 15. On Lernould's textual choices, see Lesage Gárriga, "Review of A. Lernould," 140; and H. Görgemanns, "Review of A. Lernould, *Plutarque. Le visage qui apparaît dans le disque de la lune* (Villeneuve d'Ascq: Presses Universitaires du Septentrion, 2013)," *Gnomon* 88 (2016) 20–23.

preposition for it to function as complement of location (as Wyttenbach suggested). But, it does not need the addition of a second element to be contrasted with either (as Sandbach proposed); nor to be agent of the participle κουφιζομένην (as Lernould interpreted). The text states that the soul preserves the light nature that characterizes it both during its stay in a material body, here on earth, and after the first death, on the moon.

Concerning the pronoun, the manuscripts' reading cannot be maintained on the grounds that the noun to which the syntagma refers, aether, should have been the subject of the sentence. This not the case, since it appears in dative (τῷ περὶ τὴν σελήνην αἰθέρι). Wyttenbach correctly solved the issue by replacing ἀφ' αὐτοῦ with ἀπ' αὐτοῦ.

Regarding the difficulty with βαφήν, the form transmitted by EB was modified by a few scholars in the attempt to improve the quality of the comparison in which it appears. Bernardakis proposed (in the apparatus) to change the accusative into a dative (βαφῇ), and Lernould replaced it with the syntagma ἀπὸ βαφῆς. Both editors interpreted that there is only one object for ἴσχουσι (καὶ τόνον [...] καὶ δύναμιν), which affects both subjects, the souls and weapons. In the latter case, weapons obtain "strength and vigour" through the temper, hence the dative or the preposition ἀπό with genitive, according to each editor. The verb ἴσχουσι, however, has a different object for each subject: souls obtain strength and vigour (καὶ τόνον [...] καὶ δύναμιν) and weapons obtain their temper (βαφήν). As a matter of fact, in the syntagma (καὶ τόνον ἀπ' αὐτοῦ καὶ δύναμιν), ἀπ' αὐτοῦ refers to aether, a substance that in no case can cause the strength and vigour of weapons—it can only invigorate the souls. This eliminates the possibility of both subjects sharing the same object. Both scholars were conditioned by the main meaning of βαφή, 'inmersion of red-hot iron in water in order to strengthen it,' but, as LSJ and Bailly prove, it can also point to the result of such inmersion, thus meaning 'strength.'

| | |
|---|---|
| 943F 1–3 | Πλάτων γάρ ἐστιν ὁ καὶ τῶν ἀστέρων ἕκαστον ἐκ γῆς καὶ πυρὸς συνηρμόσθαι διὰ τῶν ⟨δυοῖν⟩ μεταξὺ φύσεων ἀναλογίᾳ δοθεισῶν ἀποφηνάμενος· |
| EB | πλάτων γάρ ἐστιν ὁ καὶ τῶν ἀστέρων ἕκαστον ἐκ γῆς καὶ πυρὸς συνηρμόσθαι διὰ τῶν ... μεταξὺ φύσεων ἀναλογίᾳ δοθεισῶν ἀποφηνάμενος· |

This passage presents a gap of approximately five letters, and editors have modified the participle δοθεισῶν, unnecessarily.

Regarding the lacuna, it most probably included a determinative for τῶν—μεταξὺ φύσεων, since it is placed in the middle of the syntagma. Given that the whole passage is inspired by *Timaeus* 31–32, it is useful to turn to Plato's vocabulary, in order to sort out which type of information can be applied here: Plato speaks about the combination of fire and earth with the other two elements. With this in mind, Adler supplied the lacuna with τούτων; Purser proposed two conjectures, either δυεῖν or διττῶν; Pohlenz, probably based on Purser's conjecture, although he did not mention his predecessor, proposed the variant δυοῖν.[195]

These conjectures fit into the context perfectly, and have the right length for the space provided by the manuscripts. Purser's and Pohlenz's proposals are more specific than that of Adler, given that we know from *Timaeus* that the quoted passage specifically deals with two intermediate natures, beside fire and earth. The conjecture suggested by Pohlenz is more plausible, based on the grounds that there are other two occurrences in *De facie* (943A and 943B) wherein the manuscripts read δυοῖν, not the attic δυεῖν.

The participle aorist passive (δοθεισῶν) was modified in the attempt to provide the text with a more accurate meaning. Leonicus corrected the verb transmitted by EB, δίδωμι, into δέω, 'to tie together' (δεθεισῶν). His emendation has been followed by most editors ever since, with the exception of Raingeard. Cherniss, for instance, supported this intervention on *Timaeus* and *De animae procreatione* 1017A. This is questionable, given that the verb used in both texts is τίθημι, 'to put,' or 'to position' (θείς). These two texts provide support to maintain EB's verb rather than to replace it. In both, the divinity "disposes" the intermediate natures; in *De facie*, with a change into the passive voice, intermediate natures 'have been given' (δοθεισῶν). None of the three passages include an allusion to "tying" or "uniting," as Leonicus' intervention would imply.

| 944A 9–10 | καταμετρεῖ δὲ τὴν σκιὰν τῆς γῆς ὀλιγάκις τοῖς ἑαυτῆς μεγέθεσιν οὐχ ὑπὸ σμικρότητος, ἀλλὰ θερμότητι ἐπείγει τὴν κίνησιν, |
|---|---|
| EB | καταμετρεῖ δὲ τὴν σκιὰν τῆς γῆς ὀλιγάκις τοῖς ἑαυτῆς E / ἑαυτοῦ B μεγέθεσιν, οὐχ ὑπὸ σμικρότητος, ἀλλὰ θερμ ... ἐπείγει E / θερμότητι ἐπείγει B τὴν κίνησιν· |

The manuscripts present two different readings in this sentence: a pronoun and a noun. While the first issue poses no trouble, the later has led to many corrections.

---

[195] Adler, *Dissertationes philologae Vindobonenses*, 119; Purser, "Mr. Prickard's Translation," 323.

Concerning the pronoun, while E reads ἑαυτῆς, B reads ἑαυτοῦ. The election is easily solved, because the subject of the sentence is the moon, the feminine must be maintained.

Concerning the second disagreement, while E reports a lacuna of seven letters after θερμ, it has traditionally been accepted that B reads θερμότητος. I say "traditionally been accepted" because B actually ends the last two syllables of the noun with the abbreviation τ<sup>τ</sup>. I have checked the appearances of this abbreviation throughout the treatise: 15 times in total, of which 12 represent an accusative singular, one is a dative singular (936A, βαθύτητι), another is a genitive singular (it is the word σμικρότητος appearing in this sentence), and the last appearance is the word concerning us here. Consequently, nothing compels θερμότης to be in genitive, in this case.

The Aldine edition, the first to modify the passage, transmitted ἀναθερμότητα ἐπάγει. The preverb (ἀνα) replaces the adversative conjunction, the noun is corrected into an accusative, and the verb of the manuscripts ἐπείγει ('to press,' or 'to push vividly') is unnecessarily corrected into ἐπάγω, which has almost the same meaning ('to take toward,' or 'to push against'). We cannot be sure if the accusative is due to the assumption that the abbreviation was meant only for accusatives, or if it is an intended emendation of what was thought to be a genitive. The modification of the verb implies that many scholars took the new reading for their corrections. Leonicus proposed ἀλλὰ θερμοτάτην ἐπάγει—he returned to the original adversative and suggested the superlative of θερμός, instead of the noun θερμότης. His replacement from noun to adjective is, in turn, followed by some editors: the *Basiliensis* edition read ἀλλὰ θερμότατα ἐπάγει; and Von Arnim corrected it into ἀλλὰ θερμότερον ἐπείγει.[196] Wyttenbach adopted, in the main body of the text, Leonicus' correction, and, while he did not mention (in the apparatus) the source of such a correction, he did say that B's reading is θερμότητος, in genitive. He further proposed the emendation ἀλλὰ θερμότητος, ᾗ ἐπείγει; this, Pohlenz would take as the basis for his proposal, ἀλλὰ θερμότητος, ᾗ κατεπείγει—here, however, the modification of the verb into κατεπείγω ('to press,' or 'to hasten') not only makes the correction too long for the space provided by E, but also adds no substantial value to the verb's meaning.

Wyttenbach's claim about θερμότης being in genitive, which is incidentally accepted by following scholars, is conditioned by the proximity of the noun, σμικρότητος, in genitive. This genitive, however, is imposed by the preposition preceding it (ὑπό), which does not apply to θερμότης. The abbreviation in B can

---

196   H. von Arnim, *Plutarch über Dämonen und Mantik* (Amsterdam: Johannes Müller, 1921) 56–57.

be interpreted as a dative: this option, as far as I know, has not been contemplated by any scholar, and is backed up by the occurrence in 936A, where βαθύτ⁻ undubitably stands for βαθύτητι. If interpreted in this way, there is no need to modify the sentence at all: ἀλλὰ θερμότητι επείγει τὴν κίνησιν.

| | |
|---|---|
| 944A 10–11 | ὅπως ταχὺ διεκπερᾷ τὸν σκοτώδη τόπον ὑπεκφέρουσα ⟨τὰς⟩ τῶν ἀγαθῶν σπευδούσας καὶ βοώσας·[197] |
| EB | ὅπως ταχὺ διεκπερᾷ τὸν σκοτώδη τόπον ὑπεκφέρουσα τῶν ἀγαθῶν σπευδούσας καὶ βοώσας· |

Neither of the manuscripts signal a lacuna, but it is evident that a noun is missing: it should funtion as the object of ὑπεκφέρουσα, be the reference of τῶν ἀγαθῶν, and the subject of the two participles at the end, σπευδούσας καὶ βοώσας.

This problem was noticed by Leonicus, who conjectured ⟨τὰς⟩ τῶν ἀγαθῶν ⟨ψυχάς⟩; the *Basiliensis* edition conjectured ⟨ψυχὰς⟩ τῶν ἀγαθῶν; Bernardakis suggested (in the apparatus) that τὰς ψυχάς should be placed after βοώσας; and Pohlenz proposed τῶν ἀγαθῶν ⟨τὰς ψυχάς⟩, but strangely assigned it to Bernardakis.

Based on Leonicus' proposal, I suggest to insert only the article into the text, which would nominalize the following participles: τὰς τῶν ἀγαθῶν σπευδούσας καὶ βοώσας. Syntactically, this is the only addition required by the text, but obviously the presence of the article τάς implies that there is a noun underlying. In this case, the noun is easily deducted from the context: the souls. While they have been left aside for a moment in the previous passage, they are the focus of the whole myth and always in the readers' minds.

| | |
|---|---|
| 944BC 20–22 | Καλοῦσι δὲ αὐτῶν τὸ μὲν μέγιστον Ἑκάτης μυχόν, ὅπου καὶ δίκας διδόασιν αἱ ψυχαὶ καὶ λαμβάνουσιν ὧν ἂν ἤδη γεγενημέναι δαίμονες ἢ πάθωσιν ἢ δράσωσι, τὰ δὲ δύο Μακάρων· |
| EB | καλοῦσι δὲ αὐτῶν τὸ μὲν μέγιστον, ἑκάτης μυχόν. ὅπου καὶ δίκας διδόασιν αἱ ψυχαὶ καὶ λαμβάνουσιν, ὧν ἂν ἤδη γεγενημέναι δαίμονες, ἢ πάθωσιν ἢ δράσωσι. τὰς δὲ δύο μακράς· |

---

[197] The Aldine and the *Basiliensis* editions read the verb διαπερᾷ—I cannot tell whether intentionally or not, given that it has the same meaning as the verb transmitted by EB. Wyttenbach also included διαπερᾷ, without specifying in the apparatus that it is not the manuscripts' reading.

The passage deals with the moon's geographical accidents and the name they receive. EB state that the largest one is called 'recess of Hecate' (τὸ μὲν μέγιστον ἑκάτης μυχόν) and the other two, 'the long ones' (τὰς δὲ δύο μακράς).[198] Two difficulties need to be solved. The first is that these geographical accidents refer to the two neuter nouns given the previous sentence (944B), βάθη καὶ κοιλώματα. While the gender is maintained in the first part of our passage (τὸ μὲν μέγιστον), it is not in the second (τὰς δὲ δύο μακράς). The second difficulty regards the semantics of the name: the use of length for the second designation seems to clash with the the first one, since it alludes to magnitude.

Leonicus transformed the syntagma τὰς δὲ δύο μακράς into a neuter and switched the adjective into μικρός (τὰ δὲ δυο μικρά). This emendation was followed by all scholars of the 16th century and Wyttenbach. The latter, however, affirmed (in the apparatus) that μικρά was the correction of Stephanus, Turnebus, and Amyot, and added that Leonicus' correction was μακρά. This statement actually makes Wyttenbach the involuntary author of τὰ δὲ δύο μακρά—an emendation that appears nowhere before his edition, least of all in Leonicus' Aldine copy.[199] Raingeard suggested (in the commentary) the addition of ὁδούς after τὰς δὲ δύο μακράς—the feminine transmitted by EB can then be maintained and explained by the attraction to the following feminine noun—; Cherniss conjectured τὰ δὲ δύο μακρὰ ⟨τὰς Πύλας⟩; Pérez Jiménez conjectured τὰ δὲ δύο Μακάρων.[200]

While I agree with Raingeard and Cherniss in that part of the text seems to be missing—perhaps, as they suggest, a noun modified by the adjective transmitted by EB—I do not follow their proposals because the corruption does not seem to be explainable, from a palaeographic point of view. Pérez Jiménez's conjecture is more adequate: given the evident similarity between μακράς and μακάρων, the copyist may have written the adjective influenced by the presence of μέγιστον lines above.[201]

---

198   On this passage, see, also, Cherniss, "Notes on Plutarch's *De facie*," 153 and A. Pérez Jiménez, "Selenographic Description: Critical Annotation to Plutarch, De facie 944C," in J. Opsomer, G. Roskam & F.B. Titchener (eds.), *A Versatile Gentleman. Consistency in Plutarch's Writing* (Leuven: Leuven University Press, 2016) 255–265.

199   Wyttenbach's misattribution was maintained by later scholars: Dübner and Bernardakis accepted μακρά, the latter attributing it to Leonicus; Raingeard maintained the mistaken text of EB in his edition, but offered Leonicus' suggestion in the apparatus with Turnebus as author; Cherniss stated that he based the first part of his proposal in Leonicus' correction.

200   Raingeard, *Le peri toy prosopoy*, 151; Pérez Jiménez, "Selenographic Description," 260–261.

201   From the point of view of content, the allusion to the Isles of the Blessed is relevant in the first part of the myth. On the connection between both parts, see L. Lesage Gárriga, "Ima-

944D 6–9    Ἐκ δὲ τῶν βελτιόνων ἐκείνων οἵ τε περὶ τὸν Κρόνον ὄντες ἔφασαν
αὐτοὺς εἶναι, καὶ πρότερον ἐν τῇ Κρήτῃ τοὺς Ἰδαίους Δακτύλους ἔν τε
Φρυγίᾳ τοὺς Κορύβαντας γενέσθαι, καὶ τοὺς περὶ Βοιωτίαν ἐν αὐλῶνι
Τροφωνιάδας, καὶ μυρίους ἄλλους πολλαχόθι τῆς οἰκουμένης·

EB    ἐκ δὲ τῶν βελτιόνων ἐκείνων οἵ τε περὶ τὸν κρόνον ὄντες, ἔφασαν
αὐτοὺς εἶναι καὶ πρότερον ἐν τῇ κρήτῃ τοὺς ἰδίους δακτύλους ἔν τε
φρυγία τοὺς κορύβαντας γενέσθαι· καὶ τοὺς πε E / περὶ Β βοιωτίαν ἐν
οὐδώρα τροφωνιάδας· καὶ μυρίους ἄλλους πολλαχόθι τῆς οἰκουμένης·

This passage, dealing with first order daemons, presents a couple of corruptions in the text: ἰδίους and ἐν οὐδώρα.

The adjective ἰδίους, transmitted by EB in the syntagma τοὺς ἰδίους Δακτύλους, seems to be an erratum. The correction of the Aldine edition into Ἰδαίους is an efficient intervention, given that it includes an epithet often associated to the dactyls. It has been maintained by all editors with no exception, whom I join.

Concerning the second issue, not only is ἐν οὐδώρα a hapax, so it is also the community of daemons associated to this place, τροφωνιάδας. While the nonexistent place must be corrected, the group of daemons might be a reference to Trophonius—in the sense of 'followers of Trophonius'—and does not need emendation. The Aldine edition replaced ἐν οὐδώρᾳ with the form ἐνουδώσα, which seems to be an erratum due to the misunderstanding of the text; Leonicus proposed ἐν λεβαδείᾳ, so did the *Basiliensis* edition, under the form ἐν λεβαδίᾳ. Pohlenz, differently, suggested to correct the text ἐν οὐδ' ὥρας and added μιᾶς πολὺ πλέον ἐντεῦθεν ἀπέχοντι χωρίῳ; Luigi Lehnus proposed three variants of the same verb: ἐνιδρυμένους, ἐνιδρυθέντας, or ἐνιδρύοντας; and Pérez Jiménez conjectured ἐν αὐλῶνι.[202]

I agree with Bernardakis in that it seems unlikely that the original text would have read "Lebadea," because each group of daemons is associated to a location where they develop their activities and, in this case, two places are provided for only one community of daemons (περὶ βοιωτίαν and ἐν οὐδώρα). Also, Cherniss agreed in that is a small likelihood of Lebadea being part of the original text,

---

gen y función de Ogigia en el mito de *De facie in orbe lunae*," in S. Amendola, G. Pace & P. Volpe Cacciatore (eds.), *Immagini letterarie e iconografia nelle opere di Plutarco* (Madrid: Ediciones Clásicas, 2017) 179–188.

202  Lehnus, *Plutarco. Il volto della luna*, 174–175 n. 309; A. Pérez Jiménez, "Los habitantes de la Luna (Plut., *De fac.* 944C–945B). Notas críticas sobre las propuestas textuales y traducciones del XVI," in F. Frazier & O. Guerrier (eds.), *Plutarque. Éditions, Traductions, Paratextes* (Coimbra: Coimbra University Press, 2016) 129–130.

but not for the same reasons. He adduced that the passage only refers to inactive oracles; and, because *De defectu* 411EF states that the oracle of Lebadea was the only one still active during Plutarch's time, he concluded that it could not be the oracle mentioned in *De facie*.[203] His statement relies on an understanding of the passage to a certain extent mistaken. The passage is constructed as a series of dependent substantive clauses, coordinated through three καί where the several groups of daemons, in accusative, are the subject of the infinitives εἶναι and γενέσθαι. Because, after the mention of Cronos' caretakers, there is καὶ πρότερον, Cherniss interpreted that all the remaining groups are older than this one and already disappeared. However, within this first coordinated group where πρότερον is included, there are two communities of daemons (dactyls and coribants) coordinated through τε and with their own verb, the infinitive aorist γενέσθαι. The text, thus, presents the following structure within the subordinate clauses: subject + verb εἶναι, καί (subject τε subject + verb γενέσθαι), καί subject, καί subject. While πρότερον only applies for the part of the subordinate clause in which it is included, the rest is coordinated through καί with the main sentence, and, thus, it has as main verb the infinitive present εἶναι. Consequently, there are groups of daemons still alive and functioning, just as Cronos' caretakers.

Pérez Jiménez's correction is the most interesting: the noun αὐλών ('hollow,' or 'channel') suggests a reference to Trophonius' cave, and, from a palaeographic point of view, given that capital delta and lambda are quite similar, the two intermediate syllables of his correction could be easily interchangeable with (ἐν) οὐδώ(ρα).[204]

| | |
|---|---|
| 945B 8–10 | ἐπεὶ δ' αὐτὰς τὸ ἄστατον καὶ τὸ ἀπειθὲς ἐξίστησι καὶ ἀφέλκει τῆς σελήνης πρὸς ἄλλην γένεσιν, οὐκ ἐᾷ ... ἀλλ' ἀνακαλεῖται καὶ καταθέλγει. |
| EB | ἐπεὶ δ' αὐτὰς τὸ ἄστατον καὶ τὸ ἀπαθὲς ἐξίστησι. καὶ ἀφέλκει τῆς σελήνης πρὸς ἄλλην γένεσιν, οὐκ ἐᾷ ... ἀλλ' ἀνακαλεῖται καὶ καταθέλγει E, B *i.l.* / ἀναθέλγει B.[205] |

---

203  Cherniss, "Concerning the Face," 213 n. e.
204  Pérez Jiménez, "Los habitantes de la Luna," 129–130.
205  The verbal form in B, ἀναθέλγει, does not exist. Its presence is probably influenced by the preverb of the previous verb (ἀνακαλεῖται). The copyist must have noticed the mistake right away, given that the correct preverb is written below the line, next to a cross. See this emendation in Appendix 2.

This sentence presents two textual problems: a nominalized adjective whose meaning does not fit the context, and a lacuna—E presents a gap of around 13 letters, and B presents a gap of 11 letters. The temporal conjunction ἐπεί, at the beginning, has also been modified, unnecessarily.

Let us examine the replacement of the conjunction ἐπεί first. The sentence, as it has been transmitted, states that at some point the troubled souls will attempt to go back to earth to resume the disordered life that they lived there. Pohlenz transformed the temporal clause into a conditional clause by replacing ἐπεί with εἰ. According to him, it is uncertain whether these souls will have such a temptation or not.

Concerning the problematic adjective, the meaning of ἀπαθές, 'that which does not suffer,' or 'impassible,' clashes with the context. Not only does it mean almost the opposite of the adjective with which it is coordinated (τὸ ἄστατον, 'that which is unstable,' or 'uncertain'), but also seems to be opposite to the type of souls treated in the passage—souls which are impelled to be ruled by their visceral part, hence their desire to go back to earth, where they could give free expression to their passions.

Leonicus proposed the emendation εὐπαθές, whose meaning 'sensible,' or 'easily affected' still poses an issue because of its positive nuance; Kepler corrected it into ἀειπαθές, meaning 'perpetually passive;' Wyttenbach suggested (in the apparatus) ἐμπαθές—he stated that this was the word suggested by Amyot in his translation, but he is the real author of such proposal.[206] These corrections improve the general sense of the passage, but, in my opinion, what drives these souls away from the moon is not what is affected in them, but rather that which allows them to be affected, their unruly nature. Pérez Jiménez's correction seemed to go in this direction: ἀπαγές, which means 'inconsistent,' or 'what is not fixed or established.'[207] However, I believe that this adjective has a meaning too close to the one with which it is coordinated, ἄστατον.

I suggest ἀπειθές, meaning 'desobedient,' or 'that which cannot be dominated.' From a palaeographic perspective, it is easy to confound alpha with the symbol used in EB for the diphthong ει—an inclined bar with a semicircle on the left side—and, from a semantic perspective, the word expresses exactly the unruly part of the souls' nature, which cannot adapt to the established process towards their dissolution. It is because of that undisciplined and rebellious character that the moon is obliged to invoke and seduce the souls

---

206  Kepler, *Ioh. Keppleri Mathematici*, 180. Amyot, in fact, wrote in the margin of his *Basiliensis* copy the same correction of Leonicus, εὐπαθές.
207  Pérez Jiménez, "Los habitantes de la Luna," 134.

(ἀνακαλεῖται καὶ καταθέλγει). This adjective is used in seven occurrences throughout Plutarch's work—four of them nominalized, as in this passage.[208]

Regarding the lacuna, it is placed between a negative sentence (οὐκ ἐᾷ) and an adversative (ἀλλ' ἀνακαλεῖται καὶ καταθέλγει), of which the moon is subject. The first scholar to propose a conjecture was Wyttenbach, with a proposal too extense and not very justifiable: οὐδ' ἐᾷ πρὸς τοὺς σώφρονας βίους τρέπεσθαι, ἀλλὰ πρὸς τοὺς ἀκολάστους; Bernardakis suggested καταμένειν, probably influenced by Amyot's and Kepler's translations; Pohlenz proposed καθησυχάζειν; and Cherniss completed the lacuna with νεύειν ἐπὶ γῆν—a calembour between the syntagmata γένεσις and γῆν νεῦσις based in *De sera* 566A.

Here, as in other places where a lacuna is marked by the manuscripts, there is nothing missing in the text. While all the conjectures include an infinitive to be the object of ἐᾷ, the text does not require it, and, in fact, the sentence can be understood as it has been preserved.

945BC 11–14  Τιτυοὶ δὲ καὶ Τυφῶνες, ὅ τε Δελφοὺς κατασχὼν καὶ συνταράξας τὸ χρηστήριον ὕβρει καὶ βίᾳ τύφων, ἐξ ἐκείνων ἄρα τῶν ψυχῶν ἦσαν, ἐρήμων λόγου καὶ τύφῳ πλανηθέντι τῷ παθητικῷ χρησαμένων·

EB  τιτυοὶ δὲ καὶ τυφῶνες, ὅ τε δελφοὺς κατασχὼν καὶ συνταράξας τὸ χρηστήριον ὕβρει καὶ βία τυφών, ἐξ ἐκείνων ἄρα τῶν ψυχῶν ἦσαν ἔρημοι λόγω καὶ τύφω πλανηθέντι τῷ παθητικῷ χρησαμένων·

This text presents three problems: the word τυφών, the adjective ἔρημοι, and the noun λόγῳ.

Firstly, τυφών has been interpreted by editors to be the name of the monster Typhon, but this can certainly not be the original word for two reasons: there is already a reference in the first part of the sentence to this creature, in plural (τυφῶνες), in the sense of 'beings such as Typhon;' and Typhon had nothing to do with the episode of the attack perpetrated against Delphi, as the text reads (ὅ τε δελφοὺς κατασχὼν καὶ συνταράξας τὸ χρηστήριον ὕβρει καὶ βία τυφών).

In order to solve this issue, Kaltwasser conjectured to replace τυφών with Πύθων, the monstrous being that, in fact, attacked the oracle at Delphi. For Günther Zuntz, who agreed with Kaltwasser, the corruption from Πύθων to τυφών must have been due to the proximity both of the name in plural (Τυφῶνες), lines above, and of the noun τύφῳ, lines below.[209] Pérez Jiménez, differently, suggested to maintain EB's form with a different accent, obtaining the present

---

208   On this, see L. Lesage Gárriga, "Las almas indisciplinadas: comentario crítico y estilístico de Plut., *De facie* 945B," *Humanitas* 68 (2016) 185.

209   G. Zuntz, "Notes on Plutarch's *Moralia*," *RhM* 96, 3 (1953) 234.

participle in nominative singular of the verb τύφω (τύφων).²¹⁰ He proved that the polyptoton of the root shared by both the verb and the noun is part of the stylistic play that Plutarch is developing in the passage. The anecdote still alludes to Python, obviously, but there is no need to explicitly express the name, given that Plutarch's readership would easily recognize the creature involved in Delphi's episode.

Secondly, the adjective ἐρήμοι presents a problem, because EB transmit it in nominative plural; therefore, it modifies the subject—the three monstrous beings: Tityus, Typhon and Python. The problem occurs right before ἐρήμοι, thus, the text refers once again to the souls, not to the monsters (ἐξ ἐκείνων ἄρα τῶν ψυχῶν ἦσαν) and, right after it, continues referring to the souls: it seems improbable for the adjective to modify the subject, rather far from it now, instead of modifying the word, souls, which precede and follow it. Kepler proposed to correct the case into genitive plural, so that it concerts with the souls' case (ἐρήμων); Wyttenbach corrected it into ἐρημίᾳ, in order to connect it with the following λόγῳ καὶ τύφῳ (see below).²¹¹

Concerning the noun in dative singular λόγῳ, it appears coordinated with τύφῳ, despite their meaning not being relatable to each other, especially if associated to passionate souls: 'reasoning' and 'slumber.' Wyttenbach connected his previous correction ἐρημίᾳ with τύφῳ and corrected λόγῳ into a genitive (λόγου), because, while the main meaning of ἔρημος is 'desert,' or 'empty,' when followed by a genitive, it acquires the sense of 'to be devoid of.'²¹² While Wyttenbach's correction into λόγου solves the problem concerning the two nouns, Kepler's correction of ἐρήμοι into ἐρήμων is more plausible for the problem concerning the adjective. Consequently, I accept the combination of both scholars' corrections: ἐρήμων λόγου καὶ τύφῳ.

| | |
|---|---|
| 945C 16–19 | Οὐδὲν γὰρ αὕτη δίδωσι μετὰ θάνατον ὅσα λαμβάνει πρὸς γένεσιν· ἥλιος δὲ λαμβάνει μὲν οὐδέν, ἀπολαμβάνει δὲ τὸν νοῦν διδούς, σελήνη δὲ καὶ λαμβάνει καὶ δίδωσι καὶ συντίθησι καὶ διαιρεῖ καὶ κατ' ἄλλην καὶ ἄλλην δύναμιν, ὧν Εἰλείθυια μὲν ἡ συντίθησιν, Ἄρτεμις δὲ ἡ διαιρεῖ, καλεῖται. |
| EB | οὐδὲν γὰρ αὕτη δίδωσι μετὰ θάνατον ὅσα λαμβάνει πρὸς γένεσιν· ἥλιος δὲ λαμβάνει μὲν οὐδέν· ἀπολαμβάνει δὲ τὸν νοῦν διδούς. σελήνη |

---

210   A. Pérez Jiménez, "De Titios y Tifones. Anotaciones estilísticas a Plu., *De facie in orbe lunae* 945B," in A. Setaioli (ed.), *Apis Matina. Studi in onore di Carlo Santini* (Trieste: Trieste University Press, 2016) (POLYMNIA *Studi di filologia classica* 20, special issue) 525–523.
211   Kepler, *Ioh. Keppleri Mathematici*, 180.
212   See LSJ II, Bailly II.1.

> δὲ καὶ λαμβάνει καὶ δίδωσι καὶ συντίθησι καὶ διαιρεῖ καὶ κατ' ἄλλην καὶ ἄλλην δύναμιν ὧν εἰλείθυια E / εἰλήθυια B μέν, ἡ συντίθησιν· ἄρτεμις δέ, ἡ διαιρεῖ καλεῖται·

This passage, which deals with the contribution of each of the cosmological bodies (earth, moon, sun) to the creation of the human being, poses two syntactic issues: the first concerns the verbs dealing with the earth; the second concerns the moon's duties and powers, at the end of the sentence.

To fully comprehend the changes applied to the part concerning the earth, an overview of the whole structure and its verbs will be useful. The sentences concerning the sun and the moon pose no problem: the sun does not take anything (new), it recovers the intellect previously given (ἥλιος δὲ λαμβάνει μὲν οὐδέν, ἀπολαμβάνει δὲ τὸν νοῦν διδούς), and the moon takes the intellect (new to it) and gives it together with the souls it creates to the earth (σελήνη δὲ καὶ λαμβάνει καὶ δίδωσι), and also joins and separates—joins the intellect to the soul first, for the birth, and then separates them, in the second death—(καὶ συντίθησι καὶ διαιρεῖ). The part concerning the earth (οὐδὲν γὰρ αὕτη δίδωσι μετὰ θάνατον ὅσα λαμβάνει πρὸς γένεσιν), however, has been modified by some editors, all of them with proposals that introduce the verb ἀποδίδωμι, for they interpret that, as it stands, the text states that the earth does not return anything of what it takes at the beginning, which is not the case.

The first scholar to establish that part of the text might be missing was Wyttenbach, who conjectured (in his apparatus) τοῖς ἄλλοις δυσί, ἀλλ' ἀποδίδωσι after δίδωσι; Dübner simplified the proposal of his predecessor into ἀλλ' ἀποδίδωσι, although he signaled with two asterisks that more text could be missing between δίδωσι and the conjecture; and Cherniss entered ἀποδιδοῦσα after γένεσιν, at the end of the sentence.

While Wyttenbach's emendation offers a very elaborate structure, proper to his style, he never was concerned with finding a conjecture that could be explained on the grounds of textual corruption, Dübner's ἀλλ' ἀποδίδωσιν, however, is explainable by haplography, with the preceding verb (δίδωσι). Cherniss' conjecture seems to be mediocre, given that, on the one hand, it is difficult to explain why the copyist would have omitted the participle and, on the other, it does not present a syntax as polished as Wyttenbach's.

There is no need to modify EB's text. The adverb ὅσα can have as secondary meaning 'only up to,' or 'so far as.'[213] Thus, it can be interpreted that the earth does not give anything after death—where δίδωσι means 'to give something

---

213   See LSJ IV.2, Bailly B I.3.

new,' because the body it created remains there (οὐδὲν γὰρ αὕτη δίδωσι μετὰ θάνατον)—'only up to' what it takes for the generation, namely the soul and the intellect, which is precisely what it returns after the first death (ὅσα λαμβάνει πρὸς γένεσιν).

Concerning the second issue, after the four coordinated verbs, whose subject is the moon, there is a fifth καί which is not followed by a verb. This last conjunction is followed by κατ' ἄλλην καὶ ἄλλην δύναμιν, a syntagma that depends upon the two last verbs of the preceding relation (συντίθησι καὶ διαιρεῖ), and then by a relative clause (ὧν Εἰλείθυια μὲν ἡ συντίθησιν, Ἄρτεμις δὲ ἡ διαιρεῖ καλεῖται). The problem was easily solved with the suggestion of the *Basiliensis* edition's to delete the conjunction interposed between the two verbs and their complement. This solution has been adopted by every editor since Wyttenbach.

The fifth καί, however, can be maintained if understood as coordinating the previous verbs with καλεῖται, at the end of the passage. The relative clause, in turn, would not have this as its main verb, as it has been generally assumed, but only an omitted εἰμί. Consequently, the subject of καλεῖται remains the moon, as for the other four verbs, and not the goddesses Eileithyia and Artemis, as generally assumed. These two, in turn, are the appellations of the moon's powers.

# Appendix 1: Discrepancies between the Manuscripts

| | | |
|---|---|---|
| 920B | Ὀαυνοσυλλας E: Ὁ μὲν οὖν σύλλας B |
| 920D | οπου E: ὅπου B |
| 920E | μέσση E: μέση B |
| 921A | κατ' εὐθυωρίαν E: κατευθυωρίαν B |
| 921A | ἶ *vac.* E: *vac.* B |
| 921C | νη E: νὴ B |
| 921E | τοῦτο E: τούτων B |
| 922B | ἀεὶ τοῖς αὐτοῖς μέρεσι E: τοῖς αὐτοῖς ἀεὶ μέρεσι B |
| 922D | ἀμαυροῦσθαι E: ἀμαυροῦσθαι B |
| 923B | ἐλάττω E: ἐλάττων B |
| 923C | ῥοιζῶδες E: ῥιζῶδες B |
| 924C | τις E: τίς B |
| 924C | παραδοξολογιῶν E: παραδόξων λογιῶν B |
| 924D | ἐστί E: ἐστίν B |
| 924D | προσήκοντα E: προσήκονται B |
| 925A | καταδεδυκυῖαν. E: καταδεδυκυῖαν; B |
| 925B | νυκτέριον E: νυκτερινὸν B |
| 925C | αὐτὴ E: αὕτη B |
| 926A | εὑράμενος αἰτίαν E: αἰτίαν εὑράμενος B |
| 926B | αὑτὸ E: αὐτὸ B |
| 926C | εἶπον E: εἶπεν B |
| 926D | λέγωμεν E: λέγομεν B |
| 926D | ἕν ἐστι E: ἔνεστι B |
| 926D | νυνίδε E: νυνὶ δὲ B |
| 926D | μεταβολαῖς· E: μεταβολαῖς; B |
| 927A | μηδεμιᾶς E: μὴ δὲ μιᾶς B |
| 927B | υ E: οὐ B |
| 927B | ἀπ' αὐτοῦ E: ἀφ' αὐτοῦ B |
| 927C | μὲν *om.* E |
| 927C | φαίνεσθαι E: φέρεσθαι B |
| 927E | τὰ E: τὸν B |
| 928B | ζυγῶ σταθμοῦ E: ζυγω σταθμοὺς B |
| 928B | ῥέψαντος E: ῥέψαντας B |
| 928C | σπλάγχνον E: σπλάχνον B |
| 928D | ἀποκεκριμένου E: ἀποκεκρυμμένου B |

| | |
|---|---|
| 928E | ὦ γαθὲ E: ὤ' γαθὲ B |
| 929A | νώθειαν E: νωθείαν B |
| 929A | καὶ om. E |
| 929B | παρυμῶν E: παρ' ὑμῶν B |
| 929B | τοῦτο om. B |
| 929C | αὐτὴ E: αὕτη B |
| 929C | γλαυκώπιδος ἔπλετο μήνης E: ἔπλετο γλαυκώπιδος μήνης B |
| 929D | διαυτῆς E: δι' αὐτῆς B |
| 929D | ὅλος E: ὅλως B |
| 929E | ἀμαυροτέραν E: ἀμαυρωτέραν B |
| 929E | εὐρὺν E: εὑρὺν B |
| 930C | ῥήμασι E: ῥεύμασι B |
| 930D | ἀνακλᾶσθαι τὲ E: ἀνακλᾶσθαί τε B |
| 930D | ἑαυτῇ E: ἑαυτὴ B |
| 930F | ατὰ E: κατὰ B |
| 930F | κατὰ νύξιν E: κατάνυξιν B |
| 930F | ἐξηλιοῦσθαι E: ἐξηλλοιοῦσθαι B |
| 930F | κεράννυσθαι E: κεράννισθαι B |
| 930F | δι' ὅλου E: διόλου B |
| 931A | περὶ E: πρὸς B |
| 931A | νοειδεῖς E: μηνοειδεῖς B |
| 931A | εὖρο E: δεῦρο B |
| 931B | ἀπὸ φωτὸς E: ἀποφωτὸς B |
| 931C | τοσοῦτον E: τοσοῦτο B |
| 931D | τῆς om. E |
| 931E | σκότος E: σκότους B |
| 932AB | πελοπόνησος E: πελοπόννησος B |
| 932D | ποιεῖ E: ποιεῖν B |
| 932D | δὴ τί E: τί δὴ B |
| 932D | ὑπομνήσας E: ὑπέμνησας B |
| 932D | πεπεισμένων E: πεποιημένων B |
| 933A | τι E: τοι B |
| 933A | λάβε om. B |
| 933B | εὐρυτάτη E: εὐρυτάτη B |
| 933C | ἰδία E: ἰδίους B |
| 933C | ἀπορρεύσεις E: ἀπορεύσεις B |
| 933F | vac. ante ὀνομάζειν E: lac. post ὀνομάζειν B |
| 934C | τοῦ om. B |
| 934C | ἤδη E: ἢδη B |
| 934E | περιελαυνομένου E: ἐλαυνομένου B |

# APPENDIX 1: DISCREPANCIES BETWEEN THE MANUSCRIPTS 211

| 934F | κύμα E: κῦμα B |
|---|---|
| 934F | ὥσπερ *om.* B |
| 935A | ἁλουργοὺς E: ἁλουργὰς B |
| 935B | τινὶ E: τινι B |
| 935B | θεῶν E: θεὸν B |
| 935B | δεῖ ὅϊ μὲν E: δεῖ οἱ μὲν B |
| 935D | ἀκούοιτε δὲ καίπερ οὐκ ἀγνοοῦντες E: καίπερ οὐκ ἀγνοοῦντες ἀκούοιτε δὲ B |
| 935E | ἀλλωάδων E: ἀλωάδων B |
| 935E | ἐκεῖν E: ἐκείνων B |
| 935E | εἶναι μείζονας E: μείζονας εἶναι B |
| 935F | τεθρυλλημένον E: θρυλλούμενον B |
| 936A | ὁρῶν E: ὀρῶν B |
| 936C | ἐπιδεικνύναι E: ἐπιδεικνῦναι B |
| 936C | μεθ' ἡμέραν E: μεθημέραν B |
| 936D | οὐ E: οὐδὲ B |
| 936E | ἐσόπρων E: ἐσόπτρων B |
| 937A | ἄλλεσθαι E: ἅλλεσθαι B |
| 937A | τὰ *om.* B |
| 937B | ἤ που E: ἦ που B |
| 937E | φερομένη E: ἐπιφερομένη B |
| 937F | δεὸν E: δὲ B |
| 937F | ἔχούσαις E: ἔχουσαν B |
| 937F | πελοπόνησον E: πελοπόννησον B |
| 937F | υἵων E: βίων B |
| 938A | γὰρ *om.* E |
| 938A | δυναται E: δύναται B |
| 938D | χερρονήσοις E: χεροννήσοις B |
| 938D | ἀναγινώσκοντος E: ἀναγινώσκων B |
| 938E | τε *om.* B |
| 938E | τε *om.* E |
| 938EF | αὐτ *lac.* E: αὐτὴν B |
| 939B | ἀντιθὴς E: ἀντιθεὶς B |
| 939B | ἐχούσαις E: ἐχούσας B |
| 939C | λιβύη E: λιβύι B |
| 939C | γε δροσίας E: γεδρωσίας B |
| 939C | τρωγλοδύτιδος E: τρωγλοδίτιδος B |
| 939D | τὸ E: τὸν B |
| 939E | ὕλαι E: ὗλαι B |
| 940B | τὴν *om.* B |
| 940B | πλέονας E: πλείονας B |

940C  ἐπὶ E: ἔτι B
940D  παντοδαπὰ E: πανταδοπὰ B
940D  τούτοις ἀσκεῖν E: τούτους ἀσκεῖν B
940E  ὅσον E: ὅσσον B
940E  ἐνταῦθα *dupl.* B
940F  ἀπωκίσθαι E: ἀποκεισθαι B
941B  κεῖσθαι E: κινεῖσθαι B
941C  οὖν E: δὲ B
941D  *vac.* σκευὴν E: παρασκευὴν B
941D  καὶ *om.* E
942A  ἐξαγγέλλειν E: ἐξαγγέλειν B
942A  προδιανοεῖται E: προσδιανοεῖται B
942B  ἀσπασάμενος E: ἀσπασαμένους B
942B  ἐν *om.* B
942B  τε *om.* B
942D  τὴν *om.* E
942D  φωσφόρος E: φοσφόρος B
942E  ἔνεστιν E: ἔνεστι B
943A  μόνων E: μόνον B
943A  αὖ E: οὖν B
943D  καταδυομένας E: καταγινομένας B
943D  περιίστασιν E: περιιστᾶσιν B
944A  ἀέρος E: πυρὸς B
944A  εὐρος E: εὖρος B
944A  ἑαυτῆς E: ἑαυτοῦ B
944A  θερμ *lac.* E: θερμότητι B
944C  παιδίον E: πεδίον B
944C  ἀνωτάταις E: ἀνωτάτω B
944D  πε E: περὶ B
944E  περιπεριπολεῖν E: περιπολεῖν B
945A  περιπτύσσουσα E: περιπτύσσου B
945A  κἂν χωρὶς ἑκατέρου γένηται, πολὺν χρόνον E: κἂν πολὺν χρόνον χωρὶς ἑκατέρου γένηται B
945C  εἰλείθυια E: εἰληθυια B
945D  μέτεστι E: μετέστι B

# Appendix 2: Emmendations by the Manuscripts

921D, ἐπεχούσης B et E *supra lineam*: ἐχούσης E

921F, ἀναπιμπλάντας E et B *supra lineam*: ἀναπιπλάντας B

922C, μήτι EB: μή τοι B *supra lineam*

923C, βάρος EB: βορὸς B *supra lineam*.

924B, περὶ πόλιν E: περὶ πόλλων B: περὶ πόλον B *supra lineam*

924D, αὐτῆς EB: αὐτοῖς B *in textu*

925B, ὅσον—μέτρον E et B *supra lineam*: ὅσω—μέτρῳ B

214   APPENDIX 2: EMMENDATIONS BY THE MANUSCRIPTS

925C, ἐν τοῖς γῆς ὅροις EB: ἐν τῆς γῆς ὅροις E *supra lineam*

925C, ἀπέχει EB: ἀπέχειν B *supra lineam*

926A, τινὶ B *et* E *supra lineam*

926D, αὑτοῦ E *et* B *in textu*: αὐτοῦ B

927C, παραγένηται B *et* E *supra lineam*: γένηται E

927E, ἐκφύονται E *et* B *supra lineam*: ἐμφύονται B

929A, περίεισι E *et* B *supra lineam*: περίεστι B

929B, ὕελλον E *et* B *supra lineam*: ὕελον B

APPENDIX 2: EMMENDATIONS BY THE MANUSCRIPTS        215

929C, αὐτὴν B et E *in textu*: αὐτὴν E

929C, τόσσον E et B *supra lineam*: τόσον B

930F, οἴονται B et E *in textu*: οἴονται E

931A, τε B et E *supra lineam*

932C, τόδε τὸ πάθος B et E *supra lineam*: τὸ δὲ πάθος E

932C, ἧς EB: οἷς E *in textu*

932D, ποιήσωμαι EB: ποιήσωμεν B *supra lineam*

932E, μέν τι E: μέν B et τοι *supra lineam*

216    APPENDIX 2: EMMENDATIONS BY THE MANUSCRIPTS

933B, ἀποκρύπτεται E et B *supra lineam*: απολεί-
πεται B

933C, ταχύτητι EB: ταχυτῆτι B *supra lineam*

933D, βληχροῦ E et B *in textu*: βαηχροῦ B

934B, στορέσας EB: στορέσασα B *supra lineam*

934C, ἴησι EB: ἴησι B *in textu*

934C, καὶ E et B *supra lineam*

935F, πλευρὰς EB: πλευρὰς B *in textu*

936B, τὴν B et E *supra lineam*

APPENDIX 2: EMMENDATIONS BY THE MANUSCRIPTS 217

936D, καὶ E et B supra lineam

936D, τῇ γῇ τὴν κορυφὴν E et B supra lineam:
τὴν κορυφὴν τῇ γῇ B

937B, τὴν ἴσην EB: τὸν ἴσον B supra lineam

938C, μικρὰν EB: πικρὰν B supra lineam

939B, ἡλίου οὐ B et E supra lineam: ἡλίού E

939C, χειμῶσιν EB: χιόσιν E supra lineam

941A, κωλύει EB: κωλύοι B supra lineam

943B, Φερσεφόνης EB: Περσεφόνης E supra lineam

943C, ὃν B et E supra lineam

944A, τοῦ E et B *supra lineam*

945B, καταθέλγει E et B *infra lineam*: ἀναθέλ-
γει B

945C, αὐτὴν EB: αὐτὴν B *in textu*

945D, σύμμιγμα E et B *supra lineam*: σύμιγμα B

# Bibliography

## Editions, Translations, Commentaries to *De facie*

Adler, M., *Dissertationes philologae Vindobonenses. Quibus ex fontibus Plutarchus libellum "De facie in orbe lunae" hauserit* (Vienna-Leipzig: Bibliopola Acad. Lit. Caes. Vind., 1910).

Amyot, J., *Les Œuvres Morales, meslees de Plutarque translatees du Grec en François par Messire Iacques Amyot* (Paris: Michel de Vascosan, 1572).

Bernardakis, G.N., *Plutarchi Chaeronensis Moralia recognovit Gregorius N. Bernardakis*, 7 vols. (Leipzig: Teubner, 1888–1896).

Boulogne, J., "Introduction," in A. Lernould (ed.), *Plutarque. Le visage qui apparaît dans le disque de la lune* (Villeneuve d'Ascq: Presses Universitaires du Septentrion, 2013) 11–17.

Cherniss, H., "Notes on Plutarch's *De facie quae in orbe lunae*," *CPh*, 46, 3 (1951) 137–158.

Cherniss, H., "Concerning the Face which Appears in the Orb of the Moon," in H. Cherniss & W.C. Helmbold (eds.), *Plutarch's Moralia*, vol. 12 (Cambridge-Massachusetts: Loeb Classical Library, 1957).

Del Corno, D., "Introduction," in *Plutarco. Il volto della luna* (Milan: Piccola Biblioteca Adelphi, 1991) 9–41.

Donini, P.L., *Plutarco. Il volto della luna* (Naples: M. D'Auria, 2011).

Dübner, J.F., *Plutarchi Scripta Moralia. Ex codicibus quos possidet regia bibliotheca omnibus ab Konto cum reiskiana editione collatis emendavit Fredericus Dübner*, 2 vols. (Paris: Firmin Didot, 1841).

Ducas, D. (ed.), *Plutarchi Opuscula LXXXII, index Moralium omnium & eorum quae in ipsis tractantur* (Venice: Aldus Manuzius, 1509).

Frobenius, J. & Episcopius, N. (eds.), *Plutarchi Chaeronei Moralia Opuscula, multis mendarum milibus expurgata* (Basel: Frobenium & Episcopium, 1542).

Görgemanns, H., *Untersuchungen zu Plutarchs Dialog De facie in orbe lunae* (Heidelberg: Heidelberg University Press, 1970).

Hutten, J.G., *Plutarchi Chaeronensis quae supersunt omnia. Cum adnotationibus variorum adjectaque lectionis diversitate. Opera Joannis Georgii Hutten*, 14 vols. (Tübingen: Impensis Joannis Georgii Cottae, 1791–1804).

Kaltwasser, J.F.S., *Plutarchs moralische Abhandlungen*, 9 vols. (Frankfurt: Johann Christian Hermann, 1783–1800).

Kepler, J., *Ioh. Keppleri Mathematici olim Imperatorii Somnium, seu opus posthumum de astronomia lunari. Divulgatum a M. Ludovico Kepplero filio, Medicinae Candidato* (Frankfurt: Impressum partim Sagani Silesiorum, 1634).

Lehnus, L., *Plutarco. Il volto della luna* (Milan: Piccola Biblioteca Adelphi, 1991).

Lernould, A., *Plutarque. Le visage qui apparaît dans le disque de la lune* (Villeneuve d'Ascq: Presses Universitaires du Septentrion, 2013).
Mota, B., *Plutarco. Obras Morais. Sobre a Face Visível no Orbe da Lua* (Coimbra: Coimbra University Press, 2010).
Pohlenz, M., "De facie in orbe lunae," in C. Hubert & M. Pohlenz (eds.), *Plutarchus. Moralia*, vol. 5, fasc. 3 (Leipzig: Teubner, $^2$1960 [1955]).
Prickard, A.O., *Plutarch on The Face Which Appears on the Orb of the Moon* (Winchester: Warren & Son / London: Simpkin, 1911).
Raingeard, P., *Le peri toy prosopoy de Plutarque* (Paris: Belles Lettres, 1934).
Ramón Palerm, V., "Sobre la cara visible de la luna," in V. Ramón Palerm & J. Bergua Cavero (eds.), *Obras Morales y Costumbres*, vol. 9 (Madrid: Gredos, 2001).
Reiske, J.J., *Plutarchi Chaeronensis quae supersunt omnia opera graece et latini principibus ex editionibus castigavit, virorumque doctorum suisque annotationibus instruxit Ioa. Iac. Reiske*, 12 vols. (Leipzig: Impensis Gotth. Theoph. Georgi., 1774–1782).
Stephanus, H., *Plutarchi Chaeronensis quae extant opera, cum Latina interpretatione. Ex vetustis codicibus plurima nunc primum emendata sunt, ut ex Henr. Stephanii*, vol. 2 (Geneva: apud Henr. Stephanum, 1572).
Wecheli's Heirs (eds.), *Plutarchi Chaeronensis Omnium quae exstant operum tomus secundus, continens Moralia, Gulielmo Xylandro interprete*, vol. 2 (Franckfurt: Andreæ Wecheli heredes, 1599).
Wyttenbach, D., *Plutarchi Chaeronensis Moralia, id est opera, exceptis vitis, reliqua graeca emendavit, notationem emendationum et latina Xylandri interpretationem castigatam subiunxit, animadversiones explicandis rebus ac verbis, item indices copiosos adiecit Dan. Wyttenbach*, 8 vols. (Oxford: Typogr. Clarendoniano, 1795–1830).
Xylander, G., *Plutarchi Chaeronensis philosophorum et historicorum principis varia scripta, quae Moralia vulgo dicuntur, vere autem Bibliotheca et Penus omnis doctrinae appellari possunt* (Basel: apud Eusebium Episcopium, 1574).
Xylander, G., *Plutarchi Ethicorum sive Moralium, quae usurpantur, sunt autem omnis elegantis doctrinae Penus: id est, varii libri: morales, historici, physici, mathematici, denique, ad politiorem literaturam pertinentes et humanitatem. Guilielmo Xylandro augustano interprete*, 3 vols. (Basel: Thomas Guarinus, $^2$1619 [1570]).

## Articles, Monographies

Adler, M., "Ein Zitat aus des Megasthenes Ἰνδικά bei Plutarch," in O. Stein & W. Gampert (eds.), *Festschrift Moriz Winternitz* (Leipzig: O. Harrassowitz, 1933) 298–302.
Adler, M., "Zwei Beitrage zum Plutarchischen Dialog *De facie in orbe lunae*," *Jahresbericht des K.K. Staatsgymnasiums in Nikolsburg*, 1909–1910 (Nikolsburg: Verlag des K.K. Staats-Gymnasium, 1910).

Alarcón Navío, A., "La traducción en Francia durante el siglo XVI: Jacques Amyot," in J.L. Chamosa, J.C. Santoyo, T. Guzmán González, R. Rabadán (eds.), *Fidus Interpres. Actas de las Primeras Jornadas Nacionales de Historia de la Traducción*, vol. 1 (León: León University Press, 1987) 54–58.

Aldobrandini, Th., *Laertii Diogenis De vitis dogmatis et apophthegmatis eorum qui in philosophia claruerunt; libri X. Thoma Aldobrandino interprete, cum annotationibus eiusdem. Quibus accesserunt Annotationes H. Stephani, & Utriusque Casauboni; cum uberrimis Aegidii Menagii observationibus* (London: Typis Tho. Radcliffe, 1664).

Apelt, O., "Zu Plutarch und Plato," in *Jahresbericht über das Gymnasium Carolo-Alexandrinum zu Jena* (Jena: Universitäts-Buchdruckerei G. Neuenhahn, 1905) 10–22

Astruc, Ch., & Concasty, M.L., *Catalogue des manuscrits grecs*, vol. 3. *Le supplément grec* (Paris: Bibliothèque Nationale, 1960).

Aulotte, R., "Jacques Amyot et l'humanisme français du XVI$^e$ siècle," in M. Balard (ed.), *Fortunes de Jacques Amyot. Actes du colloque international (Melun, 18–20 avril 1985)* (Paris: A.G. Nizet, 1986) 181–190.

Aulotte, R., *Amyot et Plutarque. La tradition des Moralia au XVI$^e$ siècle* (Geneva: Librairie Droz, 1965).

Aulotte, R., "Plutarque et l'Humanisme en France et en Italie," in M. Ishigami Iagoninitzer (ed.), *Les humanistes et l'Antiquité grecque (Recueil de communications au Séminaire de l'IRHT, présenté par Mitchiko Ishigami Iagoninitzer)* (Paris: CNRS, 1989) 99–104.

Babbit, F.C., "Introduction," in *Plutarch's Moralia*, vol. 1 (Cambridge-Massachusetts: Loeb Classical Library, 1927) IX–XXXVII.

Bailly, A., *Dictionnaire Grec-Français* (Paris: Librairie Hachette, $^{16}$1950 [1895]).

Beck, M. (ed.), *A Companion to Plutarch* (Chichester: Blackwell, 2014).

Benseler, G.E., *De hiatu in oratoribus Atticis et historicis Graecis, libri duo* (Freiberg: J.G. Engelhardt, 1841).

Benseler, G.E., *Manual de crítica textual y edición de textos griegos* (Madrid: Ediciones Clásicas, 1992).

Boulogne, J., "Le visage des citations dans le cercle du dialogue," in A. Lernould (ed.), *Plutarque. Le visage qui apparaît dans le disque de la lune* (Villeneuve d'Ascq: Presses Universitaires du Septentrion, 2013) 91–101.

Caballero, R., "La tradición manuscrita del *De exilio* de Plutarco," *ASNP* 5 (2000) 159–185.

Carena, C., "I *Moralia* di Plutarco nel Rinascimento europeo. Erasmo, Amyot, Montaigne," in G. Zanetto & S. Martinelli Tempesta (eds.), *Plutarco: Lingua e Testo* (Milan: Cisalpino, 2010) 71–84.

Carratta, A. & D'Alberti, M. (eds.), *Dizionario Biografico Trecani*: http://www.treccani .it/enciclopedia/ [07/2016].

Costa, V., "Sulle prime traduzioni italiane a stampa delle opere di Plutarco (sec. XV–XVI)," in M. Accame (ed.), *Volgarizzare e Tradurre. Dall'Umanesimo all'Età contemporanea* (Roma: Tored, 2013) 83–107.

Crespo, E., Conti, L., & Maquieira, H. (eds.), *Sintaxis del griego clásico* (Madrid: Gredos, 2003).

Cuvigny, M., "Giannotti, Turnèbe, Amyot: Résultats d'une enquête sur quelques éditions annotées des *Moralia* de Plutarque," *RHT* 3 (1973) 57–77.

Decorps-Foulquier, M., "À propos des différentes écritures marginales dans l'exemplaire aldin des *Moralia* d'Adrien Turnèbe," *RHT* 8 (1978) 281–287.

Denniston, J.D., *The Greek Particles* (Oxford: Clarendon Press, $^2$1981 [1934]).

Diels, H., & Kranz, W., *Die Fragmente der Vorsokratiker. Griechisch und Deutsch* (Hildesheim: Weidmann, $^{17}$1974 [1903]).

Diels, H., "Studia Empedoclea," *Hermes* 15 (1880) 161–179.

Diels, H., *Doxographi Graeci* (Berlin: De Gruyter, $^4$1965 [1879]).

Emperius, A., *Opuscula Philologica et Historica* (Göttingen: F.G. Schneidewin, 1874).

Engels, M.H.H., "Erasmus' handexemplaren: vijf Griekse Aldijnen in de Franeker collectie van de Provinciale Bibliotheek van Friesland [Tresoar] te Leeuwarden" (2006). Retrieved from http://www.mpaginae.nl/UitbiblE/vijfaldijnen.htm [26/01/2021].

Engels, M.H.H., "Erasmiana in Leeuwarden" (2002). Retrieved from http://www.mpaginae.nl/Aldijnen/Erascoll.htm [26/01/2021].

Fernández García, A.J., "Ediciones y manuscritos del tratado *De musica* de Ps.-Plutarco," *Fortunatae* 15 (2004) 53–60.

Flacelière, R., *Plutarque. Dialogue sur les oracles de la Pythie* (Paris: PUF, 1962).

Flacelière, R., "La tradition manuscrite des traités 70–77 de Plutarque," *REG* 65 (1952) 351–362.

Frazier, F., "De la physique à la métaphysique. Une lecture du *De facie*," in E. Amato (ed.), *ΚΑΛΟΙΣ ΚΟΙΝΟΠΡΑΓΙΑ. Hommages à la mémoire de P.L. Malosse et J. Bouffartigue* (Paul-Valéry Montpellier University / Nantes University, 2014), 243–264 (*RET* suppl. 3, special issue).

Frazier, F., "The Reception of Plutarch in France after the Renaissance," in Beck, *A Companion to Plutarch*, 549–555.

Frazier, F., "Le corpus des 'Œuvres Morales' de Byzance à Amyot. Essai de synthèse," *Pallas* 67 (2005) 77–93.

Frazier, F., "Prolégomènes à une édition critique des *Œuvres morales et meslées*. Les annotations d'Amyot au *De Pythiae oraculis*," *ExClass* 8 (2004) 171–193.

Geanakoplos, D.J., "The Career of the Little-known Renaissance Greek Scholar Nicholas Leonicus Tomaeus and the Ascendancy of Greco-Byzantine Aristotelianism at Padua University (1497)," *Byzantina* 13 (1985) 357–372.

Ginzel, F.K., *Spezieller Kanon der Sonnen- und Mondfinsternisse für das Ländergebiet der klassischen Altertumswissenschaft und den Zeitraum von 900 vor Chr. bis 600 n. Chr.* (Berlin: Mayer & Müller, 1899).

Görgemanns, H., "Review of A. Lernould, *Plutarque. Le visage qui apparaît dans le disque de la lune* (Villeneuve d' Ascq: Presses Universitaires du Septentrion, 2013)," *Gnomon* 88 (2016) 20–23.

Guerrier, O., "The Renaissance in France. Amyot and Montaigne," in Beck, *A Companion to Plutarch*, 544–548.

Hagen, H., *Catalogus codicum Bernensium, Bibliotheca Bongarsiana* (Bern: Typis B.F. Haller, 1875).

Hansen, P.A., *Carmina Epigraphica Graeca saeculi IV a. Chr. n.* (Berlin: De Gruyter, 1989).

Hansen, P.A., *Carmina Epigraphica Graeca saeculorum VII–V a. Chr. n.* (Berlin: De Gruyter, 1983).

Hansen, P.A., "The Manuscript Tradition of Plutarch's *De Malignitate Herodoti*," *CIMAGL* 2 (1969) 23–38.

Hartman, J.J., *De Plutarcho scriptore et philosopho* (Leiden: Brill, 1916).

Heinze, R., *Xenokrates. Darstellung der Lehre und Sammlung der Fragmente* (Hildesheim: Georg Olms, 1965 [Leipzig: Teubner, 1892]).

Hubert, K., "Die Handschriftliche Überlieferung für Plutarchs *Moralia* 70–77," *RHM* 93 (1950) 330–336.

Huguet, V., "Les procédés d' adaptation chez Amyot," *Revue du Seizième Siècle* 12 (1929) 47–77.

Humbert, J., *Syntaxe Grecque* (Paris: C. Klincksiek, ³1970 [1945]).

Hutten, J.G., "Introduction," in *Plutarchi Chaeronensis quae supersunt omnia. Cum adnotationibus variorum adjectaque lectionis diversitate. Opera Joannis Georgii Hutten*, vol. 1 (Tübingen: Impensis Joannis Georgii Cottae, 1791) V–XI.

Irigoin, J., "Histoire du texte des 'Œuvres Morales' de Plutarque," in *Plutarque. Œuvres Morales*, vol. 1 (Paris: Belles Lettres, 1987) CCXXVII–CCCII.

Irigoin, J., "Le Catalogue de Lamprias. Tradition manuscrite et éditions imprimées," *REG* 99 (1986) 318–331.

Isnardi Parente, M., *Senocrate, Ermodoro. Frammenti* (Naples: Bibliopolis, 1981).

Jones, C.P., "Towards a Chronology of Plutarch's Works," *JRS* 56 (1966) 61–74.

Kannicht, R., *Tragicorum Graecorum Fragmenta*, vol. 5 Euripides (Göttingen: Vandenhoeck & Ruprecht, 2004).

Karsten, S., *Philosophorum graecorum veterum praesentim qui ante Platonem floruerunt operum reliquiae*, vol. 2 (Amsterdam: Johannis Müller, 1838).

Kronenberg, A.J., "Ad Plutarchi *Moralia* (Continued)," *Mnemosyne* 10 (1941) 33–47.

Kronenberg, A.J., "Ad Plutarchi *Moralia* (Continued)," *Mnemosyne* 52 (1924) 61–112.

Leroy, J., *Les types de réglure des manuscrits grecs* (Paris: CNRS, 1976).

Lesage Gárriga, L., "L'étranger (*De facie*) et Diotyme (*Symp.*): récits de sages absents," in D. Leâo & O. Guerrier (eds.), *Figures de sages, figures de philosophes dans l'oeuvre de Plutarque* (Coimbra: Coimbra University Press, 2019) 169–181.

Lesage Gárriga, L., "Aldinas Anotadas: una puesta al día de la contribución de los humanistas a través del estudio de *De facie*," *CFC(G)* 28 (2018) 243–265.

Lesage Gárriga, L., "Imagen y función de Ogigia en el mito de *De facie in orbe lunae*," in S. Amendola, G. Pace & P. Volpe Cacciatore (eds.), *Immagini letterarie e iconografia nelle opere di Plutarco* (Madrid: Ediciones Clásicas, 2017) 179–188.

Lesage Gárriga, L., *Plutarch's Moon: A New Approach to* De facie quae in orbe lunae apparet, in preparation.

Lesage Gárriga, L., "Las almas indisciplinadas: comentario crítico y estilístico de Plut., *De facie* 945B," *Humanitas* 68 (2016) 181–189.

Lesage Gárriga, L., "Le mythe du *De facie* de Plutarque traduit par Amyot," in F. Frazier & O. Guerrier (eds.), *Plutarque. Éditions, Traductions, Paratextes* (Coimbra: Coimbra University Press, 2016) 87–97.

Lesage Gárriga, L., "Algunas consideraciones sobre la tradición textual del tratado *De facie* de Plutarco," in C. Macías Villalobos, J.Mª. Maestre Maestre & J.F. Martos Montiel (eds.), *Europa Renascens. La cultura clásica en Andalucía y su proyección europea* (Zaragoza: Pórtico, 2015) 201–209.

Lesage Gárriga, L., "Review of A. Lernould, *Plutarque. Le visage qui apparaît dans le disque de la lune* (Villeneuve d'Ascq: Presses Universitaires du Septentrion, 2013)," *Ploutarchos* 11 (2014) 139–142.

Lesage Gárriga, L., "Plutarch and the Law of Reflection: Critical and Literary Commentary to *De facie* 930A–C," *Ploutarchos* 15 (2018) 29–42.

Liddell, H.G., Scott, R., & Jones, H.S., *A Greek-English Lexicon* (Oxford: Clarendon Press, ⁹1996 [1843]).

Madvig, J.N., *Adversaria critica ad scriptores graecos*, vol. 1 (Copenhagen: J.H. Schultz, 1871).

Manfredini, M., "Un famoso codice di Plutarco: il Paris. gr. 1672," *SCO* 39 (1990) 127–131.

Manfredini, M., "Su alcune Aldine di Plutarco," *ASNP* 14 (1984) 1–12.

Manfredini, M., "La tradizione manoscritta dei *Moralia* 70–77 di Plutarco," *ASNP* 6 (1976) 453–485.

Manfredini, M., "Giorgio Gemisto Pletone e la tradizione manoscritta di Plutarco," *ASNP* 2 (1972) 569–581.

Manton, G.R., "The Manuscript Tradition of Plutarch *Moralia* 70–7," *CQ* 43 (1949) 97–104.

Martin, H.Jr., "Plutarch's *De facie*: the Recapitulations and the Lost Beginning," *GRBS* 15, 1 (1974) 73–88.

Martinelli Tempesta, S., "La tradizione manoscritta dei *Moralia* di Plutarco. Riflessioni per una messa a punto," in G. Pace & P. Volpe Cacciatore (eds.), *Gli scritti di Plutarco: Tradizione, traduzione, ricezione, commento* (Naples: M. D'Auria, 2013) 273–288.

Martinelli Tempesta, S., "Pubblicare Plutarco: L'eredità di Daniel Wyttenbach e l'ecdotica plutarchea moderna," in G. Zanetto & S. Martinelli Tempesta (eds.), *Plutarco: Lingua e Testo* (Milan: Cisalpino, 2010) 5–68.

Martinelli Tempesta, S., "Un postillato di Nicolò Leonico Tomeo perduto e ritrovato," *SMU* 2 (2004) 347–353.

Meineke, A., "Kritische Blätter," *Philologus* 14 (1859) 1–44.

Mioni, E., *Introduzione alla paleografia greca* (Padua: Liviana, 1973).

Morwood, J., *Oxford Grammar of Classical Greek* (Oxford: Oxford University Press, 2001).

Nix, L., & Schmidt, W. (eds.), *Heronis Alexandrini opera quae supersunt omnia*, vol. 2. Mechanica et Catoptrica (Berlin: De Gruyter, 2010 [1900]).

Omont, H., *Catalogue des manuscrits grecs de Fontainebleau sous François I$^{er}$ et Henri II* (Paris: Imprimerie Nationale, 1889).

Omont, H., *Inventaire sommaire des manuscrits grecs de la Bibliothèque Nationale*, vol. 2 (Paris: Alphonse Picard, 1888).

Pade, M., "The Reception of Plutarch from Antiquity to the Italian Renaissance," in Beck, *A Companion to Plutarch*, 531–543.

Page, D.L., *Poetae Melici Graeci* (Oxford: Clarendon Press, 1962).

Paton, W.R., "Review of Prickard, Plutarch on the Face in the Moon (Winchester, 1911)," *CR* 26 (1912) 269.

Pearson, L., "Notes on the Text of Plutarch *De malignitate Herodoti*," *AJPh* 80, 3 (1959) 255–275.

Pérez Jiménez, A., "Las regiones fértiles de la tierra: nueva propuesta crítica a Plu., *De facie* 938D," in M. Sanz Morales, R. González Delgado, M. Librán Moreno & J. Ureña Bracero (eds.), *La (inter)textualidad en Plutarco. Actas del XII Simposio Internacional de la Sociedad Española de Plutarquistas (Cáceres, 8–10 de octubre de 2015)* (Coimbra: Coimbra University Press, 2017) 43–51.

Pérez Jiménez, A., "De Titios y Tifones. Anotaciones estilísticas a Plu., *De facie in orbe lunae* 945B," in A. Setaioli (ed.), *Apis Matina. Studi in onore di Carlo Santini* (Trieste: Trieste University Press, 2016) 520–531 (POLYMNIA *Studi di filologia classica* 20, special issue).

Pérez Jiménez, A., "Los habitantes de la Luna (Plut., *De fac.* 944C–945B). Notas críticas sobre las propuestas textuales y traducciones del XVI," in F. Frazier & O. Guerrier (eds.), *Plutarque. Éditions, Traductions, Paratextes* (Coimbra: Coimbra University Press, 2016) 123–138.

Pérez Jiménez, A., "Selenographic Description: Critical Annotations to Plutarch, *De facie* 944C," in J. Opsomer, G. Roskam & F.B. Titchener (eds.), *A Versatile Gentleman. Consistency in Plutarch's Writing* (Leuven: Leuven University Press, 2016) 255–265.

Pérez Jiménez, A., "Plutarch and Transgressions of Nature: Stylistic Analysis of *De facie in orbe lunae* 926CD," in M. Meeusen & L. van der Stockt (eds.), *Natural Spectac-*

ulars. Aspects of Plutarch's Philosophy of Nature (Leuven: Leuven University Press, 2015) 215–226.

Pérez Jiménez, A., "En el reino de las Moiras: comentario estilístico de Plu., De facie in orbe lunae 945C–945D," GIF 67 (2015) 181–213.

Pérez Jiménez, A., "The reception of Plutarch in Spain," in Beck, A Companion to Plutarch, 556–576.

Pérez Jiménez, A., "En las praderas de Hades. Imágenes, metáforas y experiencias escatológicas de las almas buenas en Plu., De facie 943C–E," in L. van der Stockt, F.B. Titchener, H.G. Ingenkamp & A. Pérez Jiménez (eds.), Gods, Daimones, Rituals, Myths and History of Religions in Plutarch's works (Málaga: Málaga University Press / Logan: Utah State University Press, 2010) 333–344.

Pérez Jiménez, A., "Gestos, palabras y actitudes en el De facie in orbe lunae de Plutarco," Ploutarchos 1 (2003/2004) 63–78.

Pérez Jiménez, A., "Valores literarios del mito de Sila: anotaciones estilísticas a la antropología de Plu., De facie 943a–943b," in L. Torraca (ed.), Scritti in onore di Italo Gallo (Naples: Ed. Scientifiche Italiane, 2002) 463–478.

Pérez Jiménez, A., "Ciencia, religión y literatura en el mito de Sila de Plutarco," in M. Brioso & F.J. González (eds.), Actitudes literarias en la Grecia romana (Seville: Pórtico, 1998) 283–294.

Pérez Martín, I., "El estilo 'Hodegos' y su proyección en las escrituras constantinopolitanas," Segno e testo 6 (2008) 389–458.

Perrin, B., Plutarch's Parallel Lives, vol. 8 (Cambridge-Massachusetts: Loeb Classical Library, 1919).

Pohlenz, M., "Praefatio," in Plutarchus. Moralia recensuerunt et emendaverunt W.R. Paton et J. Wegehaupt, praefationem M. Pohlenz, vol. 1 (Leipzig: Teubner, 1925) V–XLIII.

Puech, B., "Prosopographie des amis de Plutarque," ANRW II, 33, 6 (1992) 4831–4893.

Purser, L.C., "Mr. Prickard's Translation of Plutarch's De facie," Hermathena 16 (1911) 309–324.

Race, W.H., Pindar, vol. 2 (Cambridge-Massachusetts: Loeb Classical Library, 1997).

Radt, S.L., Tragicorum Graecorum Fragmenta, vol. 4. Sophocles (Göttingen: Vandenhoeck & Ruprecht, 1977).

Reiske, J.J., "Introduction," in Plutarchi Chaeronensis quae supersunt omnia opera graece et latini principibus ex editionibus castigavit, virorumque doctorum suisque annotationibus instruxit Ioa. Iac. Reiske, vol. 1 (Leipzig: Impensis Gotth. Theoph. Georgi., 1774) X–XXXIX.

Rodríguez Adrados, F. (ed.), Diccionario Griego-Español (Madrid: CSIC, 1980).

Rose, V., Aristoteles Pseudepigraphus (Hildesheim: Georg Olms, 1971).

Ruiz, E., Manual de codicología (Madrid: Fundación Germán Sánchez Ruipérez, 1988).

Russo, L., & Medaglia, S.M., "Sulla presunta accusa di impietà ad Aristarco di Samo," *QUCC* 53 (1996) 113–121

Sandbach, F.H., "Plutarch and Aristotle," *ICS* 7, 2 (1982) 207–232.

Sandbach, F.H., "Fragments," in idem (ed.), *Plutarch's Moralia*, vol. 15 (Cambridge-Massachusetts: Loeb Classical Library, 1969).

Sandbach, F.H., "Second Meeting," *Proceedings of the Cambridge Philological Society*, 1943.

Sandbach, F.H., "The Date of the Eclipse in Plutarch's *De facie*," *CQ* 23, 1 (1929) 15–16.

Sandys, J., *The Odes of Pindar: Including the Principal Fragments* (Cambridge-Massachusetts: Loeb Classical Library, 1978).

Sieveking, W., *Plutarchus. Moralia ediderunt recensuerunt et emendaverunt W.R. Paton, M. Pohlenz et W. Sieveking*, vol. 3 (Leipzig: Teubner, 1929).

Smyth, H.W., *Greek Grammar* (Cambridge: Harvard University Press, $^4$1966 [1920]).

Snell, B., *Tragicorum Graecorum Fragmenta*, vol. 1 (Göttingen: Vandenhoeck & Ruprecht, 1971).

Socas, F., *Kepler. El sueño o la astronomía de la Luna* (Huelva: Seville University Press / Huelva University Press, 2001).

Stephenson, F.R., & Fatoohi, L.J., "The Total Solar Eclipse Described by Plutarch," *Histos* 2 (1998) 72–82.

Sturel, R., *Jacques Amyot traducteur des Vies Parallèles de Plutarque* (Paris: Honoré Champion, 1908).

Tanga, F., *Plutarco. La vertù delle donne (Mulierum virtutes). Introduzione, testo critico, traduzione italiana e note di commento* (Leiden: Brill, 2019).

Teodorson, S.T., *A Commentary on Plutarch's Table Talks*, vol. 3 (Gothenburg: Acta Universitatis Gothoburgensis, 1996).

Teodorson, S.T., "The Psychology of *De facie* and *De virtute morali*," in M. García Valdés (ed.), *Estudios sobre Plutarco: Ideas Religiosas* (Madrid: Ediciones Clásicas, 1994) 115–122.

Teodorson, S.T., *A Commentary on Plutarch's Table Talks*, vol. 1 (Gothenburg: Acta Universitatis Gothoburgensis, 1989).

*Thesaurus Linguae Graecae* (Irvine: University of California, 1972).

Tod, M.N., *A Selection of Greek Historical Inscriptions*, vol. 1 (Oxford: Clarendon Press, 1946).

Trenard, L., "Du nouveau sur Plutarque et Amyot," *Information Historique* 30, 5 (1968) 222–224.

Treu, M., *Zur Geschichte der Überlieferung von Plutarchs Moralia*, vol. 2 (Oława: Dr. v. A. Bial, 1881).

Van Groningen, B.A., *Short Manual of Greek Palaeography* (Leiden: Sijthoff, 1940).

Van Herwerden, H., "Novae curae criticae Moralium Plutarchi (Ed. Bern.)," *Mnemosyne* 37 (1909) 202–223.

Von Arnim, H., *Plutarch über Dämonen und Mantik* (Amsterdam: Johannes Müller, 1921).
Von Arnim, H., *Stoicorum Veterum Fragmenta*, vol. 2 & 3 (Stuttgart: Teubner, ²1964 [1903]).
West, L., *Textual Criticism and Editorial Technique Applicable to Greek and Latin Texts* (Stuttgart: Teubner, 1973).
Wilson, N., "Some Notable Manuscripts Misattributed or Imaginary, I. Maximus Planudes and a Famous Codex of Plutarch," *GRBS* 16 (1975) 95–97.
Wyttenbach, D., "Praefatio," in *Plutarchi Chaeronensis Moralia, id est opera, exceptis vitis, reliqua graeca emendavit, notationem emendationum et latina Xylandri interpretationem castigatam subiunxit, animadversiones explicandis rebus ac verbis, item indices copiosos adiecit Dan. Wyttenbach*, vol. 1 (Oxford: Typogr. Clarendoniano, 1795) VII–CXLV.
Ziegler, K., *Plutarco* (trans. by M.R. Zancan Rinaldini) (Brescia: Paideia, 1965 [*RE* 21, I 1951]).
Zuntz, G., "Notes on Plutarch's *Moralia*," *RhM* 96, 3 (1953) 232–235.

# Index Nominum et Locorum

Academy 922EF
Achilles 938B
Aeschylus 923B
Aetna 926C
Agesianax 920E, 921B
Alcman 940A
Aloades 935E
Anaxagoras 929B, 932A
Aphrodite 926F
Apollonides 920F, 921C, 925A, 933F, 935C, 935E, 936C
Arabian 939E
Archilocus 931E
Aristarchus 923A, 925C, 932A, 938D
Aristotle (ancient) 920F, 932B
Aristotle 920E, 928D, 929A
Artemis 922A, 938F, 945C
Assyrian 935B
Astronomer 925B, 930A, 933F, 934A, 934C, 937F, 939A
Athena 922A, 938B
Athenian 943B
Athos 935F
Atlas 923B
Atropos 945C

Boeotia 944D
Britain 941A
Builder 927B

Carthage 942C
Caspian 941B, 944B
Cleanthes 923A
Clearchus 920E, 920F, 921D
Clotho 945D
Comrade 921F, 929B, 929E
Cora 942D, 942E
Corybant 944D
Crates 938D
Crete 944D
Cronian 941A
Cronus 941A, 941C, 941F, 942A, 944D, 945D
Cydias 931E

Delphi 945B
Demeter 942D, 943B

Demetrian 943B
Democritus 929C
Doctor 923F

Egypt 939C
Egyptian 932A, 938A
Eileithyia 945C
Elysian 942F, 944C
Empedocles 920C, 922C, 925B, 926E, 926F, 927F, 929C, 929D, 934D
Endymion 945B
Epicurus 921D
Epimenides 940C
Eros 926F
Ethiopia 939C
Ethiopian 923C

Gardener 927B
Gedrosia 939C
Giant 926E
God(s) 926F, 927B, 935B, 938B, 938D, 940E, 941E, 942A, 942C, 942D, 944F, 945D
Greek 935B, 941B, 941C, 941D, 942D

Hades 940E, 940F, 942E, 943C, 943E, 944F
Hecate 944B
Hephaestus 922B
Heracles 941C, 944B, 944F
Heraclitus 943E
Hermes 943B
Hesiod 926F, 940B
Hipparchus 921D
Homer 931E, 934B, 934F, 941A, 942F, 944F
Homeric 940E

Idaean Dactyl 944D
Indian 938B
Ion 929A
Ixion 937E

Lachesis 945D
Lamprias 937D, 940F, 945E
Lemnos 935F
Libya 939C
Lucius 921E, 921F, 922F, 923E, 928D, 928E, 929E, 930A, 931D, 932E, 933F

230                                   INDEX NOMINUM ET LOCORUM

Maeotis   941B
Mede   935B
Megasthenes   938B
Menelaus   930A
Metrodorus   928B
Mimnermus   931E
Moira   945C

Nycturus   941C

Ogygia   941A, 941B

Parmenides   926F, 929AB
Peloponnesus   932A, 937F
Peripatos   920F
Persephone   942D, 943B, 944C
Phaenon   941C
Pharnaces   921E, 922E, 923C, 923E, 933F, 934A, 934C, 939F
Pherecydes   938B
Philosopher   922B, 923F, 934A, 942B
Phosphorus   925A, 927C
Phrygia   944D
Pindar   923C, 931E
Plato   926F, 930B, 937E, 938E, 943F
Poet(s)   922A, 923F, 934D
Posidonius   929D, 932C

Red sea   944B

Socrates   934F
Soldier   927B
Sophocles   923F
Stesichorus   931E
Stilbon   925A
Stoic   921E, 922F, 935B
Stranger   942A, 945D
Sulla   920B, 929E, 937C, 940F, 942D, 942F, 945D
Syene   939C

Tactician   927B
Tantalus   937E
Taprobanian   923C
Tartarus   940F
Taurus   941C
Thebes   939C
Theon   923F, 932D, 937D, 938C, 938F, 940A, 940B
Titan   926E
Tityus   945B
Trogoldyte   938A
Trophoniad   944D
Typhon   945B

Xenocrates   943F

Zeus   921D, 926c, 926d, 927A, 930A, 932D, 938B, 940A, 941A, 941F, 942A